The Jews of the United States, 1790-1840

The Jews of the United States
1790-1840
A Documentary History

Edited by
JOSEPH L. BLAU AND
SALO W. BARON

In Three Volumes

VOLUME TWO

Columbia University Press
New York and London 1963
The Jewish Publication Society of America
Philadelphia 5724

Joseph L. Blau is Professor of Religion, Columbia University.
Salo W. Baron is Professor Emeritus of Jewish History, Literature,
and Institutions on the Miller Foundation, Columbia University.

The edition of this work for The Jewish Publication Society of
America is Number 17-19 in the Jacob R. Schiff Series of Jewish
Contributions to American Democracy. A contribution from the
American Jewish Tercentenary Committee helped make publication
possible.

Contents

Contents

Contents

The Jews of the United States, 1790-1840

Part Four

The First Jews in
American Politics

It was the first, and unrealizable, dream of the founders of the American nation that it should be a land in which, because politics was everybody's business, there would be no politicians. The hope was that, just as there was to be little or no professional military group, but national reliance in emergencies was to be placed on the civilian temporarily turned soldier, so there would be no professional governing group, but national administration was to depend upon the civilian temporarily turned governor. Just as the citizen-soldiers were to be kept in trim for emergency duties by occasional muster and drill on the village green, the citizen-rulers were to be trained for their tour of duty in government by occasional town meetings and election rallies. Furthermore, it was the hope, even of those most realistic three who wrote the Federalist Papers, Hamilton, Madison and Jay, that political parties—"factions," Madison called them in Federalist, no. 10—would not develop in the United States, but that each man would consider every issue and every candidate on its or his own merits, and reach a decision independently of his friends and neighbors. A government of citizens temporarily turned to politics, chosen by an electorate guided only by the merits of the case was the ideal and dream; and, as Hamilton was among the first to realize, it was the dream of those who had no experience in governing, and, we might add, a deep-seated resentment of the governors who had been set over them.

Once things had passed the blueprint stage, it became apparent that the ideal of a politician-free government could never be achieved. Running a country was something other than running a general store. Not just common sense, but certain large expertness was essential to success. The first recognition of the need of expertness came with regard to foreign affairs; it was no accident that the presidents from John Adams to John Quincy Adams had served their apprenticeship either in diplomacy or in the Department of State or both. But the recognition was more general than this, and soon government service became a career.

At the same time, the United States was relearning the age-old lesson that parties are inevitable; that even if all men were in complete agreement on any one issue, they would divide into parties over the question of expressing their agreement, or even of celebrating it. Not that the disagreements in American life were as trivial as this; there was a rather sharp line drawn between those who regarded government as the protector of the people and those who regarded government as the unpaid promoter of the interests of property. Party names and programs have switched from time to time in American political history, but the basic division between Jeffersonians and the Hamiltonians remains constant. Within these fundamental divisions, there have been many factional splits over issues or over men. Divisions have been perpetuated as organizations, and party organizations have bred party leaders and partisans.

Whatever, then, may have been the dream of the Founding Fathers, the American experience produced both politics and political parties, both politicians and political partisans. Indeed, from the dream only one point carried over into the realization; for many years, through the entire early national period, the American government remained very close to the people. Its officers, up to the President himself, were hedged by no divinity. Men like other men, they had to remain approachable for reasons of personal ambition or retention of party control. Some with more grace, some with less, all submitted themselves to the yoke of popular favor and official familiarity.

Into the arena of politics as public service, the Jews of America came at the very beginning of national existence. Where certain limited types of expertness were required, there were Jews who found it worth their while to acquire the necessary skills to do necessary jobs. Frequently, these skills were extensions of skills they already had; young men whose early lives had been spent in families whose livelihood was gained in foreign trade became officers of the port, sometimes in their home towns. Those who had gone to sea in merchant vessels during the Napoleonic Wars where every merchant vessel went armed transferred to the United States Navy. Men who had been Indian traders became Indian agents. Jewish merchants who traded much with foreign ports became American consular agents in those ports. Considering the small size of the Jewish population in America, its proportion among government employees was high.

The entrance of Jews into partisan politics, while it did not come about as early as their entry into government service, was not long delayed. In a sense, it was inevitable, for local party organization tended to center in government employees in any community. They had the ear of the higher-ups; they were in a position to learn the views of the people and to transmit these views to party leaders, to be translated into legislative programs. They were better able to learn what was in the wind because of the absence of a gap between the public and the public official. The greatest contribution of the partisan placed in government offices has been the retention of a "grass-roots" character in the public policy of the United States. Jewish officeholders or would-be officeholders submitted not only official reports reflecting the activities for which they received government salaries, but also unofficial reports to their party-chiefs, keeping those leaders abreast of the thoughts and feelings of local communities. They took part, too, in election campaigns, for reasons of self-interest as well as principle. For the "spoils system" was an early development in American government, and continuation in a political appointment often depended upon keeping one's own party in power.

Jews were to be found in every party and in every faction. Isaac Harby of South Carolina was a leader among the Jeffersonians. If Mordecai Noah, in New York, belonged to an anti-Van Buren faction of the Democratic Party, Benjamin Hart of the same place was a strong Van Buren partisan. The Jews of America did not constitute a "Jewish bloc." When it was suggested in 1832 in South Carolina (during a presidential campaign year, when the States rights question was sharply agitated in the controversy over Nullification) that there was a Jewish vote, a communication signed by 84 Jews appeared in *The Courier* (Oct. 1, 1832) denying any such allegation, and asserting the complete freedom of every Jew to vote

as an individual. Indeed, the absurdity of the charge is evident
from the presence of Jews of South Carolina in both contesting
parties, the States Rights Party and the Union Party.

In the years with which we are concerned, there was a close
affiliation between political factions and newspapers. There was no
pretense of objectivity or concealment of partisan distortion behind
a facade of independence. Each newspaper gave the point of view
of a party or a fragment of a party; it was to the interest of each
party to see that a partisan newspaper appeared in as many locali-
ties as possible. A word about Jewish owners and editors of newspapers is, therefore, appropriate to a discussion of the first Jews in
American politics. The omnipresent Mordecai M. Noah deserves to
be mentioned here; among his other services to the Tammany Democrats of New York, he edited *The National Advocate* (whose
owner, Naphtali Phillips, was a Jew). When he was removed from
the editorial chair, it was as a result of political maneuvering, and
he later edited other papers with a Tammany bias. Isaac Harby,
too, should be named as one who served his party by editing a
newspaper, *The Southern Patriot*, in Charleston.

Thus, as we have seen, and as the documents below show in more
detail, the Jews of America took part in every phase of political
activity. They served in government jobs; they took part in partisan
politics and intra-party struggles; they played a role in political
journalism. It would be tempting to find some "Jewish" character
to their public service, even to find that they were more often on
the side of the party of the people. Honest reporting dictates no
such conclusion. In the early national period, the Jews in American
politics were there as American citizens, realizing their equal status
with other citizens, not as Jews or representatives of a Jewish interest or a Jewish ideology.

LX

The Quasi-Naval War
with France, 1798-1799

The problem of Franco-American relations in the early years of government under the Constitution was complicated by two large factors. First, the Treaty of Paris, 1783, ending the Revolutionary War, was viewed by France as setting up an alliance between Britain and the United States, and was resented especially for its treatment of neutral rights.[1] Inasmuch as the Federalist administrations of Washington and John Adams were not disposed to be pro-French, little was done to overcome this French view of the Treaty. Second, the XYZ Affair, in which a French agent openly "conspired" with opponents of the Federalist administration, and the impact on America's merchant class of the French Revolution led not only to American resentment of France but also to a major split between the Federalist and Jeffersonian parties in American domestic politics.[2]

It was in this atmosphere of mutual suspicion and distrust that, in 1798, an undeclared naval war broke out between the United States and France.[3] Fourteen American men-of-war and over two hundred merchant vessels were armed with letters of marque and reprisal. In this situation, Benjamin S. Judah,[4] on a visit to London, offered to serve his country in the purchase of munitions.

117. BENJAMIN JUDAH TO
ALEXANDER HAMILTON, 1798 [5]

London Septembr. 5th, 1798

Dear Sir

I find by private & public Intelligence that my Country has been roused to a just sense of dignity, and is determined to defend her claims against an insidious Foe, I am sorry to think she is likely to sustain the depression of War, but in a cause on which depends her Independent Existance, every American must feel the ardour of aiding his Country to justify her rights, and if I can in the least contribute (as an Individual) I shall feel myself happy in my Endeavour to do my duty.

I have been in Europe about two years, and probably may continue a year or two longer; from the connections I have both here, and on the Continent, I trust that I could procure on the lowest terms, any quantity of Arms etc. that our Government may want, at foot I note the prices at the Foundry at Berlin, transmitted to me by my agent there, I presume I may procure them somewhat lower. What has led me to this, are applications that have been made to me by my Friends, & acquaintances, even the Money Contractors to this Government. I am in the habits of Friendship, & intimacy with, several of the principal Negotiators, they have Informed me, that they are ready to aid our Government with a loan, which I sincerely hope she may not stand in need off. not haveing the honor of Personal acquaintance with our President, I have not presumed to address him on the subject, but as you do not let the smallest incident escape you, that may terminate in the service of your Country, If you judge my feeble aid may benefit Her, you may if you think proper, transmit this, with what comments or Recommendation to him you please, as a Citizen I have the advantage of being known to you, and if his Excellency requires any further references, at the session of Congress in Philadelphia, he will find that opportunity, as I am Personally known to Genl. Jonathan Dayton [6][,] Speaker, Doctr. Wm Henderson [7] of New Jersey. Genl. Philip Van Cortlandt [8] the Member for the City of New York, & several Representatives in Congress. I am with every sentiment of respect & Esteem.

Dear Sir   Your Most Obd &   Vy Hble Servt.   BenjJudah
My address in London to the care of Doctr. Joseph H[art] Myers,[9] No 8 John Street America Square. or a letter left at my House in New York will be forwarded.

LXI

Democratic Simplicity
in Government, 1804-1827

Whatever tendencies toward the formation of a "court" may have marked the Federalist administrations of Washington and John Adams, there was a return to a democratic simplicity with the coming of the Jeffersonians to power in 1800. This simplicity and the sense of personal relationship to officials of the government that is indicated in the letters printed below is a charming reminder that, in the times with which we are here concerned, including the Washington and Adams administrations, the United States was a new and small nation founded in the democratic ideal of equality. Whether the question was one relating to the issuance of a passport or the appointment of a consul, the government was thought of and treated as the servant of the people, not its master.

118. PASSPORT APPLICATION, 1815 [10]

New York January 1 1815

Dr Sir

It is in your power to render me a service for which I shall hold myself obliged to you, My daughter Mrs Harriet J. Hart [11] wife of Benjamin Hart [12] Merchant of Three Rivers in the Province of Lower Canada, has for some time past been in delicate health, Having been advised by her Physician to remove to a more southern climate She is anxiously solicitous to come on to this city as soon as permission from our government can be had and before the winter setts in with severity.

Now my good Sir you will materially serve me by procuring from the Secretary of State the necessary passport for my daughter and children together with a female servant, and forward the same to me as soon as you conveniently can. An early attention to this request will be gratefully acknowledged by Your friend and Servant   Ephm. Hart [13]

119. SAMUEL MYERS [14] TO JOHN QUINCY ADAMS, 1820 [15]

Norfolk Jan. 17 1820

Sir

Mr. John Higginson arrived at this port some days since, from Valparaiso with certain despatches for Government, which I deposited in the Port Office. Mr. H. has suffered so severely by illness during the passage as to be wholly unable to write to the department as he seems to wish, & therefore requests me to transmit the enclosed documents. I infer that he intends to proceed to Washington when his strength will admit, but I am apprehensive that such will not speedily be the case.

I have the honor to be With perfect respect Your mo obt sert
                                                          Saml Myers

The Honble J. Q. Adams &c &c &c

120. SAMUEL MYERS TO JOHN QUINCY ADAMS, 1820 [16]

Norfolk Feb. 2. 1820

Sir

I have the honor to inform you that Mr. John Higginson who lately arrived here from Chili, has breathed his last. I know not that it is necessary to give you the information, but in doing so I conclude to err on the safer side. I have taken charge of the effects of the deceased, & shall hold them unexamined, untill the wishes are known of those interested.

I have the honor to be very respectfully Sir Yr mo obt St
                                                          Saml Myers

Honble J. Q. Adams

121. MORDECAI(?) MYERS [17] TO JAMES MADISON, 1808 [18]

New York June 3rd. 1808

Sir.

I take the liberty to enquire of you as the proper source of such Information if there is a vacant Consulship either in India on the coast of Barbary, or in the West Indias, and if so if you will have the Condecention to Inform me I may be induc'd to make a formal application and produce a suitable recommendation from such persons in this State as are in the Confidence of the Government, being well acquainted with all the Public Characters in this State your answer Pr. Post will confer a lasting Obligation on Sir

Your most Obdt and Very Humble Servt.   M Myers

N.B. if you favour me with an Answer Please address to M Myers Auctioneer
New York

122. MOSES MYERS [19] TO RICHARD FORREST, [20] 1817 [21]

Norfolk Decr. 23. 1817

My Dear Sir

It is very long since I have had this Pleasure or that of hearing from you. Do me the favor to say If Robert Montgomery [22] continues to be the U States Consul at Alicant. It is of importance for me to know & Particularly If he has any claims on our Government. At your leisure please inform Yr.Self & advise me

There must soon be an appointment of a Consul for Amsterdam, can you tell who will get the place? no doubt the applicants are many.

All goes on very Smooth at head Quarters & I make no doubt Mr. Monroe will give general Satisfaction.

I shall be glad to hear from you & am with best regards to all your good family   Dear Sir   Yr friend & Obt. S   Moses Myers

Richd. Forrest Esqr.

123. HAYM M. SALOMON [23] TO HENRY CLAY, [24] 1827 [25]

New York 26th Jany 1827

Hon. Henry Clay
Washington
Dear Sir

I would thank you to inform me, if the appointment of Consul to Curacao has yet been made it is an office of so little emolument that no one would consent to go from America for that object alone; the one who died there last year (Mr Parker) [26] was a subject of the island, though a native of the U.S., and had been a merchant there sometime

My object in asking this information is that many of us merchants interested in the trade of that island from New York, would like a Gentleman to have the appointment who is now here from that island, and whose house does the principal business for our Merchants there

I am very respectfully   Yours sincerely   Haym M Salomon

LXII

Political Patronage for a Newspaper, 1815

The interests of the merchant class in Charleston bound its members to opposition to the administrations of Thomas Jefferson, James Madison, and James Monroe—Democratic-Republicans all. In addition, the War of 1812 and the events leading up to it were unpopular, especially among the merchants of the southern port cities. When Isaac Harby, a stalwart Jeffersonian, undertook to edit a newspaper, *The Southern Patriot,* to serve as the voice of the Republican party in Charleston, he faced great difficulties. The following letter shows how Harby applied for patronage printing on a strictly partisan basis. There persists in this letter (which was not the only one of its type that Harby wrote) something of the directness of approach to officers of the government that has been noted [27] as characteristic of its age.

124. ISAAC HARBY [28] TO LANGDON CHEVES, [29] 1815 [30]

[Feb. 8 1815]

To the Honble Langdon Cheves
Dr Sir

I take the liberty of intruding on your valuable time by addressing You on a Subject of importance to myself & I believe of some interest to the public. The "Southern Patriot" which paper I am the Editor Of, has drawn forth the patronage of the most respectable Republicans in the State, together with that of Governor Williams,[31] & all the other departments both civil & military. I cannot attribute this patronage wholly to my politics. A Public Journal that with independence advocates the present Administration has to contend against a great deal. It brings upon itself the enmity of a major part of the mercantile community together with a horde of disaffected characters, who infest our Seaport towns for the Object of gain, & who think a sacrifice of *National Character* unimportant when interfering with their individual interests. While on the one hand therefore, the "Patriot" is highly honourd with the most respectable patronage, it had withheld from it that Mercantile support which attached to the Federal party, & which is of Serious Consequence to a Printing establishment. To enable me therefore, properly to conduct my paper, I apply to those different Sources from which I think I should draw support.

My application to You, (as a Member of Congress) is that you will interest Yourself in procuring for me a participation of the benefit, arising from publishing the Laws &ca appertaining to the General Government. In most of the States *Two papers* are employed for that purpose, but in this State almost of equal importance to any in the Union but one paper is employed. It is well known in So Carolina that the Southern Patriot circulates in parts of the State where no other paper does & it is generally acknowledged as the leading Republican paper being Cherished under the Wing of the most influential members of the Republican family. My application therefore, is not to divest another of what he may be considered entitled to, but to *circulate* in a paper friendly to the *Union,* the laws *Which preserve the Union.* With deference to Your better judgement, you will Consider, whether it is right that one paper, Should for years monopolise the printing, alluded to, when there is another that has claims *at least* equally Strong

I am Sir with profound Respect   Yr friend & fellow Citizen

Isaac Harby

Charleston Febry 8th 1815

LXIII

Protest of Noah's Recall
from Tunis, 1815-1816

The appointment of Mordecai Manual Noah as United States Consul at Tunis in 1813 was the first major diplomatic award to a Jew.[32] Tunis, at that time, was a semi-independent country with which the new United States had had difficulties because of piracy. How valuable Noah's services were depends upon whose account of the service is read. It seems likely, from all accounts, that Noah's management of the financial affairs of his office was something less than satisfactory, although this, too, may have been a calumny circulated as a means of forcing Noah out of the consulship.[33] Whatever the reason or combination of reasons may have been, after two years in office Noah received a letter of recall, signed by James Monroe as Secretary of State, giving Noah's religion as the ostensible reason for terminating his appointment, and mentioning in passing the need for further explanation of his financial dealings. Noah devoted himself to his own vindication.

As a result of Noah's campaign to publicize the letter of recall, Isaac Harby of Charleston and Naphtali Phillips [34] of New York entered the lists in protest against the suggestion that religion could be any disqualification to government service. Harby's letter was particularly forceful and cogent in arguing the Jeffersonian view; but it is also clear that Harby wrote as a party man, concerned not only with principles but also with party success. The Department of State was able to enlist the support of A. A. Massias [35] to influence Harby. For Massias himself had a claim against the government, and the department suggested that his claim would be soonest taken care of in return for his help with Harby. If nothing else, the letter of Massias to Stephen Pleasanton [36] that is printed below reflects the importance of Harby in the party councils in South Carolina.

125. JAMES MONROE TO
MORDECAI M. NOAH, 1815 [37]

April 25, 1815

Sir

At the time of your appointment, as Consul at Tunis, it was not known that the Religion which you profess would form any obstacle to the exercise of your Consular functions. Recent information, however, on which entire reliance may be placed, proves that it would produce a very unfavourable effect. In consequence of which, the President [38] has deemed it expedient to revoke your commission. On the receipt of this letter, therefore, you will consider yourself no longer in the public service. There are some circumstances, too, connected with your accounts, which require a more particular explanation, which, with that already given, are not approved by the President.

I am, very respectfully, Sir,   Your obedient servant,

James Monroe

Mordecai M. Noah, esquire, &c. &c.

126. ISAAC HARBY TO JAMES MONROE, 1816 [39]

Office of the Southern Patriot
Charleston May 13th 1816

Honble James Monroe
Dr Sir

I have just finished the perusal of a pamphlet,[40] submitted to my inspection and *impartial Judgment,* by Mr. Noah, our late consul at Tunis. To say that the explanation & documents exhibited in this pamphlet, were Satisfactory, *to my mind,* of the zeal & ability with which Mr. Noah discharged his official duties, might possibly be attributed to the friendship contracted between us, during a long acquaintance. But You, Sir, who can look upon him from higher and more impartial ground; you, whose *candour* as a man blends so happily with that strict *justice* which should guide your public actions, can judge of Mr Noah's conduct with cooler and steadier calculation, than myself. On this impartiallity, this purity of mind that has ever distinguished your official life, Mr Noah must rely for a full justification. His friends are also willing to rely upon it.

When this gentleman was first recommended to the regard of government, he was supported by many worthy & influencial men. These men must think it due to themselves, to know how he has realized the expectations of his friends. May I add, Sir, that I think it due to *yourself,* to the *Country,* to the *Constitution,* to enquire into the nature of the *cause* why he has been so abruptly recalled?

I, certainly, am by no means authorized, to engage your valuable time with the discussion of particulars. I shall not enquire into the policy or honour resulting from the employment of such a man as Keane.[41] It should be considered, however, that throughout the transactions the Governt. of the U.S. *were not known*—that the selection of this man as an agent, was an act of *necessity*—and that the objects for which he was employed succeeded as far as practicable. Nor would I undertake to justify Mr Noah, or any other consul, in construing with too wide a latitude the discretionary power given him of drawing bills upon government. The exercise of this power should be carefully limited. But, I do think, that the successful termination of Mr. Noah's negociation, generally; his zeal and industry for the interests of his countrymen; his *manners* so well adapted to win his way among strangers; these, taken together, should at least have entitled him to a full and impartial hearing, before your sudden fiat had issued, to his injury & to the astonishment of his friends.[42]

Now, Sir, the sole and vital principle which prompts me to hazard a letter to Mr Monroe (to whom I am personally unknown, but from whose *public,* I cannot but draw the most favourable image of his *private* character), the ground, on which alone I am authorised to write to a gentleman, high in the estimation of his country, and soon to become the first citizen of the Republic, is the ground of Right. The first sentence in your letter of recal to Mr. Noah, contains these words: "It was not known at the time of your appointment as consul for Tunis, that the *religion* which you professed would form any *obstacle* to the exercise of your functions:"!! It was this sentiment, Sir, which immediately fixed and rivetted my attention, my astonishment. I would ask, since it was not *then* known, whether it has been *since* discovered, that *Religion* disqualifies a man from the exercise of his political functions? Or has this doctrine *ever* been known, since the first hour of the establishment of our invaluable Constitution? Had such a sentiment proceeded from an *intollerant* mind, had it been uttered by the minister of any other cabinet than that of America, we should not have wondered. But, proceeding from *You*, from a component part of the Executive of the United States, from you, one of the soundest constitutional lawyers in the country, surely we *might* wonder; and in respect for you, attribute the expression to haste and inconsiderateness rather than to principle. To *principle!* God forbid. When, in the convention of Virginia (a theatre filled with talents) You and other true and liberal statesmen, guarranty'd *perfect freedom of Religion,* then it was you acted upon *principle.* When the constitution of the United States declares that Liberty shall be *secured to every citizen,* this is *principle.* The principle of *equality of rights,* is inherent in every letter, and breathes its spirit throughout the whole mass of our laws. This salutary principle, which for ever destroys the union of Church & State, that bane of political happiness, that insult to Heaven, mingles with the feelings, and morals, and education of the American people. An objection, on the score of Religion, would sound to them "most monstrous and unnatural." They Know no Religious distinctions. One great character of *Citizenship* alone prevails.

> "Spiritus intus alit, totamque infusa per artus,
> Mens agitat molem, et magno se corpore miscet." [43]

It is upon the principle, not of *toleration* (for man has no *power* to tolerate Religion, that is a concern between Man and his maker) but upon the principle of equal inalienable, *constitutional Rights,* that we see Jews appointed to offices, that we see them elected in our State Representation, & that, in proportion as their talents and their influence can bear them through, we see their mingling in the honours of their country. They are by no means to be considered as a *Religious sect,* tolerated by the government; they constitute a portion of *the People.* They are, in every respect, woven in and compacted with the citizens of the Republic. Quakers and Catholics; Episcopalians and Presbyterians, Baptists and Jews, all constitute one great political family. "Simplex, duntaxat, et unum." [44] In this light, every wise Statesman must regard them. I do therefore appeal to you, not only as a Philanthropist, but as a politician; not only as a *just man,* but as the Secretary of State to this free government, to erase the sentence in your letter above alluded to, strike it from the records of your office. It can only remain to your own injury, and to the reproach of the liberal character of our institutions.

In taking the liberty, Sir, of addressing you on this Subject, I trust I have made no infringement on propriety. Your own sense of *Justice* will admit that, in the cause of Religious freedom every man in *this* country may raise his voice. I am not only Mr Noah's *co-religionaire;* I am his *fellow-citizen.* The latter relation is, in my mind, infinitely stronger than the former. I shall, certainly, while I have life and thought, contend for those rights which God and Nature and our free constitution have guarranty'd to me and my posterity. Should the *dictum* by which Mr Noah was recalled stand among the archives of the Government, the *opinion* will, in a short time, amount to *precedent,* and *precedent* become *Law!* What innumerable evils would spring from *one hasty sentence!* Let but *Religious distinctions* once prevail, and the Jews of the United States, however powerful by members, by wealth, or by talent, will prove too weak for the numerous disciples of other doctrines. They must, if they retain those proud feelings which an education in America implants, abandon their Country for ever and seek an asylum on some foreign shore, among rocks, and deserts, if *Liberty there* holds her residence.

Be assured, Sir, that Mr Noah's pamphlet has been seen by no one in Charleston, except myself. I have your public character and the interest of the Republican party too much at heart to suffer a syllable of its contents to transpire, if you desire its suppression. Mr Noah informed me, that when last at Washington some of his friends had read the work. I think he was wrong in showing it to any person but yourself. I was satisfied, and am so still, that upon cool reflection you will be induced to strike from your files the document I speak of. [45] Your political enemies shall never say, that Mr. Noah's *religion* was very well known *before* his appointment and that in the midst of his consular pursuits, the Secretary of State recalled him, because it was afterwards discovered that his religion constituted "an obstacle" to his appointment, "an obstacle to the discharge of his functions"!

With respect to any *reparation* (not on account of Mr Noah, he is only *secondary* in the affair) for the sake of a large portion of the American people, from whom such a transaction should be for ever buried, for the sake of Justice, of the constitution, of your own cause, I certainly must leave every thing remedial, to your well known candour and your better Judgement: suggesting, however, at the same time, that an appointment to an equal rank, or at least some public and honourable mention of Mr Noah, would be highly satisfactory to his feelings, to the feelings of all his co-religionaires and, I doubt not, to the feelings of your bosom.

What I have written, I trust you will regard (as I sincerely assure you it is meant to be) moderate, friendly and respectful. No Government, no officer of government, however highly endowed, but in the course of a long political carreer *may* commit an error. To remedy it, is in this case, left to *your* liberallity and justice.

Believe me Sir, to be with the highest   respect, Your obt. Servant

Isaac Harby

127. NAPHTALI PHILLIPS TO JAMES MONROE, 1816 [46]

Office of the National Advocate
New York Octr. 20th 1816

Sir

Entertaining for you an unfeigned Respect, I am induced to make one effort more, to obtain a reply to the letters I did myself the honour to address to you on the 22nd of August last, as President of the Jewish Congregation in this City,[47] in Relation to the Recall of Mr Noah from Tunis on account of his Religion: It would be a Source of Much gratification to me to be enabled to assure his friends that no charges of Malversation or improper Conduct in office have been preferred by the government against Mr Noah.[48] Your Silence on this head may operate against an innocent man: which, I am convinced your Goodness of character Will prevent.

I am With Respect   Sir   Your H. Servt   Naphtali Phillips

Hon James Monroe.

128. A. A. MASSIAS TO
STEPHEN PLEASANTON, 1816 [49]

Savannah Decemr 15th 1816

Saml Pleasanton Esqr
Dept of State
Dear Sir

I have this day addressed a long letter (rather a Narative) to the Secry on the Subject of my claim,[50] I took the liberty to mention the conversation I had with you & Mr Greham on the subject of *the Governors letter*,[51] I am persuaded you will do your best to close this affair for me,[52]

In compliance with my promise, I have been busy on the subject of Noah's Recall which at the time I last saw you appeared to have made some disagreeable impressions *in the South*. I am Now happy to State, upon showing the letter (or the copy) which you show me, I have [now(?)] perfectly Removed, and it appears those impressions were made in consequence of the Representations Mr N made when this way last Spring. I have also had a conversation with Mr Harby the Editor of the *Southern Patriot*, he is perfectly Satisfied with the interpretation given to the first *Sentence* in Mr Munroes letter of Recall, & which appears to be all that had excited this feeling in him or others. Mr H is astonished that N could have given it any other, he further says his wish to have the Matter explained, was not for the sake of Mr N but for the principal [sic] of the thing only, I am glad of this as Mr H not only exercises an influence with his Co-Religionists, But in No inconsiderable degree in the State where he Resides. I am happy therefore that the conviction in his mind is fixed, I Requested him to give me a Line expressive of his sentiments to that effect, he has, I *shall keep it,* to those of any *Consequence* among the *Israelites* I have spoken also, they are perfectly satisfied, & what I have left undone, Mr Harby has promised to finish, in his explanation *which is in writing,* he expresses his most exalted opinion of Mr Munroe and says altho he has been disappointed in Not Receiving an answer to a letter he wrote on the subject he feels a gratification even at the verbal explanation I have given, and further states, & wishes me to say, that under his *first* impressions, he wrote an angry letter to N concerning the affair, but as his opinion is Now fairly formed, should Mr N. ever mention or produce that letter, Mr Munroe will be aware that it expresses *feelings* which arose, on the first *hasty* view of the letter containing Mr N Recall, he has no anxiety about Mr N– only so far as he is concerned with the expression of a Sentiment on the part of the *Secry of State,* which on the first perusal had an equivocal appearance, and he candidly acknowledges that he Now sees Nothing in that Sentence but what is justifiable, let me hear from you & Believe me with Esteem   Yours   A A Massias [53]

LXIV

Nathan Levy's Difficulties in St. Thomas, 1820-1830

The career of Nathan Levy [54] in the service of the United States was a long one. He began as a Commercial Agent, whose duties were the procurement of naval supplies in the West Indies. Later, he became and remained the United States Consul in St. Thomas, Danish West Indies. The record shows Levy to have been zealous in the defense of American rights and in the protection of American seamen. It may well have been that his very zeal bred protests from those whose interests he had to overcome. Whatever the reason, from time to time, the State Department received letters of protest directed against Levy, on all grounds from the most trivial and ridiculous to the most fundamental and important. Two of these letters follow; one clearly motivated by personal animus; the other, by patriotic concern. The officials of the State Department must have appreciated the value of Levy's services in St. Thomas, however, for in spite of these letters and others like them, Levy was kept on at his post. For, in the third letter below, we find Levy, in 1830, presenting a defense against other charges that had been brought against him. In this case, too, Levy's defense was accepted, and he remained in office until 1832, when he retired voluntarily.

129. JOSEPH O'REILLY TO JOHN QUINCY ADAMS, 1820(?) [55]

To His Excellency John Quincy Adams
Sir
    Ever since your venerable and good Father was at the helm of our Government I have been floating on the Ocean, Master of a Vessel during which time I never was so basely treated as I have been this last Voyage to St. Thomas's by a Man of the name of

Nathan Levy, a Jew, who acts as vice Consul against the peace and dignity of all good Citizens of that Island, and the only reason I can assign for such unwarrantable conduct is because I would not submit to paying him illegal fees, which he is in the habit of charging to Masters of Vessels, when he can find an opportunity. I called on him on Saturday the 1st. day of April 1820 to sign a Certificate in order to obtain a Drawback; he told me he did no business on that day, but if I would call on the following day (Sunday) his Office would be open. I called and obtained the Certificate for which he wanted to charge me $4. I told him it was more than I had been in the habit of paying, and it was an illegal fee he told me if I did pay that I should have the Certificate. I repeated that I would not have it on his terms, and left him. A few days after, he sent for me, and gave it me by paying $2 he then observed that he must detain my Vessel, as my Register was not [   ] owing as he stated to an erasure being in it, (marked) I then went and represented his treatment to some respectable Merchants, they observed that he was at his old tricks again, and advised me to abandon the Vessel to him altogether, for on his hearing it was my determination to do so he sent for me, and said he had made up his mind to detain the Register only, and give me a Certificate, for which he should charge me a Joe ($8) this I also refused to do, stating to him, that if any error was in the Register, and I believed there was not as it could not have passed through so many Custom Houses without being noticed, that he ought to look to the Custom House from whence it came which I knew to be as correct as any in the Union, therefore if I was obliged to go to sea without my Register, especially when the Islands are surrounded with all sorts of Privateers that seldom let Vessels pass with regular Papers, letting alone a Vessel and Captain Without Papers that I should on my arrival at home appeal to you for redress. & thank Kind Providence that I have it in my power of informing you of my safe arrival on my native shore, and submitting my case for your consideration. having no hesitation in Saying it will meet with that Justice which the merits of the case will admit off. In compliance, you will confer an Obligation upon one who has and shall ever feel happy to have the honour to be   Sir   Your   Very Resp   & Obedt Servt.   Jos[ep]h O'Reilly

PS This N Levy is a Jew and lives with a Black Woman and frequently Walks the Streets with her arm in arm to the mortification of all the Americans who are under the painfull necessity of witnessing the Same for the correctness of this statement, I beg leave to refer your Excellency to the following most Respectable Houses on the Island Vizt

John M Souffrand & Co.

Mess   Ballister Bayly & Clark

John Kettle & Co

and in fact to any one who knows him

130. ROBERT M. HARRISON [56] TO JAMES H. MC CULLOCH, [57] 1820 [58]

Saint Thomas 10th March 1820

Dear Sir

As I before predicted to you Mr. Levy will not be permitted to hold the 2. Registers of American vessels, nor will he be allowed to note or extend Protests or any other document which falls within the province of the Danish Notary public's duties, this information I have from the Commandant who called and mentioned it to me and at the same time said he had received a letter from Mr. Levy ten days since which he supposed some person had written for him, insinuating that your humble servant was that person, as this suggestion was entirely incorrect I lost no time in undeceiving him, assured him that Mr. Levy never consulted me, and that he was fully competent to write for himself, the Commandant then farther informed me that it was not his intention to return any answer to the letter.

Our Government will naturally be astonished to learn that Mr. Levy has been so much restricted in the exercise of his Consular functions, more particularly as the appointment has been recognized by his Majesty the King of Denmark. The object of an agent to this place, is in part to prevent the Shameful abuse of our papers in being employed to protect foreign property and to cover the most fraudulent practices, injurious to our interests and derogatory to our honor. To carry the views of our Government completely into effect on that head the deposit of the Register with the Consul is necessary otherwise, how is he to detect spurious papers &c. It is also requisite in order to enable him to ascertain what vessels are in port to convey home destitute American Seamen, for it cannot be expected that a Consul should board every vessel in the harbor to ascertain those particulars and depend upon whatever answer the officers may think proper to give him. For my own part I conceive the deposit of the Register so necessary that without it the Consulate is a perfect nullity, it is true it does not prevent the agent from collecting the numerous vagabonds who resort to this colony assuming the character of American seamen, and supporting them at the expence of the United States; Mr. Levy is extremely zealous in this way and so far this Government will assist him as they thereby remove a burthen from their own shoulders: Indeed the Commandant in the conversation already mentioned observed that he would send every man calling himself an American to the Consul, should this be done I have no doubt that Mr. Levy will be weak enough to receive them, this he would do under the idea of its giving pleasure to the Commandant which in the end might induce the acknowledgement of those powers which had been already guaranteed to him by his recognition as vice Consul, such indeed is his weakness on this head that he goes to every person who he imagines has the least influence with the Commandant and states his case under the impression that they may assist him in gaining favor, unfortunately however such conduct has a contrary effect and draws on himself the contempt of all parties. You may imagine I am stepping out of my way in noticing those things, but having once held the appointment myself, and as an American Citizen I cannot tamely look on and see the representative of our country not only disgrace himself but disgrace that country also, the truth is he is universally laughed at and I am clearly of opinion that instead of his being of service to the United States, his demeanor only tends to lower our national character in the estimation of foreigners; a foreign agent never can nor ever will be respected unless he maintains that dignity of deportment which should correspond with the importance of the office he has been appointed to fill, which in the present case I am sorry to say is not the fact. It is very true that the Government of this colony has always been inimical to the residence of foreign agents as they are always considered as spies on their transactions, I also find that Mr. L has been making some enquiries, or rather, asking silly questions of and before persons whom he should rather avoid respecting a brig which arrived here a few days since from Africa with 500 slaves, many of whom have been landed here and the remainder no doubt will be if an encouraging market offers, it was owing to those enquiries that I was *honored* by the visit from the Commandant who in very unequivocal terms stated his displeasure. You will no doubt be astonished that this inhuman traffic is permitted to be carried on from this island since Denmark was amongst the first powers to promote its abolition, it is however carried on to a very large extent, principally by foreigners who avail themselves of the facilities this port affords for the purpose, facilities which may always be purchased by a well timed douceur [59] to the officers of Government. In my humble opinion it will ever be found impracticable to abolish the traffic without a conventional agreement between all maritime powers to admit the public armed vessels of each to visit and search every vessel, without respect to flag, suspected of being engaged in it.

I am much gratified to learn from the public papers that the Columbus is destined for Constantinople with a minister on board to negociate a treaty with that power, I am somewhat acquainted with that country and know the advantage our country will derive from such a treaty, those unacquainted will be astonished at the number of shipping to which this trade will give employment, I am however aware that Great Britain and France will throw every obstacle in our way to prevent us from a participation in a trade which they have heretofore almost exclusively enjoyed.

If the appointment I solicited for the Consulate at Buenos Ayres cannot be obtained I should be glad of a Similar one in the Ottoman dominions should a treaty be finally concluded. I have already extended this letter to a greater length than I had contemplated & shall now close by assuring you that I am Dear Sir Very Sincerely Yours   Robt. monroe Harrison

James H McCulloch Esq

131. NATHAN LEVY TO
MARTIN VAN BUREN, 1830 [60]

Consulate of the United States
St. Thomas 29th November 1830

To the Honble. Martin Van Buren   Secretary of State
Sir

I have the Honor to acknowledge the receipt of a despatch from the department of State, dated the 17th September, 1830, with your Honble Signature thereto annexed, which got to hand the 20th Inst also a Copy of a Letter addressed to the department by Mr Wm Hood a merchant residing at St. Thomas dated St. Thomas 23rd. July 1830. Flattering myself that a Statement of facts, unsophisticated will promptly remove the unfavorable impressions that Letter was intended to produce, and that the unmerited application of *unauthorised Cupidity* as applied to me, will loose its poignancy, however harsh is its expression. That I labour under the infirmity of being hard of hearing, I am constrained to acknowledge, and for the last Eight or Ten Years, it has given me much anxiety, But the great inconvenience is to myself in mixed and general Society, not to those with whom I come in contact in the performance of my Official duties; a tone or note higher than the usual mode of Speaking, obviates all inconveniences arising therefrom, and, although my Physical complaint is bad enough, yet it is not such I think, as to disable me to perform the duties of the Consulate as to my mental disabilities or incapacities, I can say nothing in behalf of Self. I have not as yet been conscious of their being lessened materially for the last Five or Six Years, and the delicacy of my Situation must apologize for my silence by not replying. and must leave the question to others to decide on. My Character is not that of Yesterday many Years I lived at Georgetown, D.C. where I am well Known as well as at Washington & Baltimore, and I once thought the Department of State, was well acquainted with my pretensions unaided by the recommendatory Letters, which are deposited in its Archives. Sir, The Official duties of a Consul I have [led] myself to believe I was fully Competent to execute, and continue still,

under that impression My General Consular transactions must however be referred to, and from the number of documents of a variety
of Character that has emanated from this Consulate to almost every
Atlantic Port in the Union, Satisfactory information, *I hope*, might
be obtained. There are few marine Insurance Companies in the
United States without some documents from this Consulate, and I
have never learnt a Complaint, either of insufficiency of those
Papers, or their want of accuracy. As to the *Obstinacy* of age which
among my Physical & mental disqualifications is introduced as an
appendage, I must premise when based on honesty, supported by
my best capabilities I have been, and [hope] I shall ever remain
an advocate for persevering and not acceding to demands which
I conceive to be unjust. Mr Hoods Letter no doubt was predicated on
my refusal to annull the Protest—This Person I have a very slight
Knowledge of, He is a Transient (non resident) Englishman, here
to day, and off tomorrow, at present in the United States. One or
two Cargoes of Rice or Parts thereof, I believe came to his address
from Charleston, S C which he placed under the direction of Resident merchants for Sale, and here Sir Permit me to introduce the
Circumstances attending the extension of the Protest complained
of, of the Schooner Samuel, Captn. Martin Stone belonging to Bel-
fast, Ste. Me. which Vessel arrived here the 24th June 1830. it
appears that on the same day the Captain Noted a Protest for which
he paid $2. On the 7th. July a Warrant of Survey was granted at
his request & issued to Captains Ozias Budington and E M. Don-
naldson, two respectable American Shipmasters, as Surveyors, this
document was recorded under signature and official Seal. & the
usual Charge of Four Dollars he was debited with The Report from
Surveyors being made in due form under Oath &c Recorded with
Official Seal & signature, the Captain was charged therefor the
usual fee of Four Dollars. The Surveyors Received their usual fee
of Eight Dollars each, which Sixteen Dollars paid them, Mr Hood
comprises in the amount $4. Some days previous to the 20th July,
the Captain delivered his Log Book to enable me to extend his
Protest, it exhibited a very imperfect Statement & it was so very
defective that it was impossible to extract from it more than was
bona fide done. all which appears in the Body of the Protest, when
a rought draft was first taken from the Log Book, the Captain read

& particularly examined it, and after some observation from me to him at the time, of the imperfections which his Log Book displayed, I enquired if this extract was in conformity to what was noted in his Log Book, to which he replied in the Affirmative. The Protest was then accordingly extended pro forma and on the 20th He with his mate & two Seamen appeared at the Consulate, and after the Protest was particularly read to them, It was signed by the parties & Sworn to accordingly & Signed & Sealed by your Consul and recorded. The Captain was charged Sixteen Dollars therefor, the usual fee for Extending Protests. Two Days thereafter the Consul was called on by the Consignee who wished to annull the Protest so made, and executed and to afford another, which might be expressed differently in language to suit better their purposes. I here used decission unequivocally and refused altering a record in any way whatever, after it had gone through all the Solemn Official forms. But observed if the parties had omitted any thing in the Body of that document, they might make an endorsement thereof under similar Official formalities, this being assented to, the said Captain, mate and the same two Seamen reappeared and further swore to that appendant article, which appears endorsed [on] said Protest, and it was Sealed, Signed & Recorded accordingly, for which Four Dollars was further Charged, these several Items making the aggregate of $44. As to the said appendant article so sworn to, I never observed, nor do I believe there was any thing thereof, on the Log Book of the Said Schooner Samuel either before or whilst it was in my possession, and when the article was brought to me to copy therefrom & indorse on the Protest, it was in the handwriting of some other Person than Captain Stone on a piece of Paper, formed no doubt so as to suit the Interest of those whom it concerned. This said Log Book had been returned to the Captain with the Protest and other documents, prior to the execution of the endorsed article and never afterwards was in my possession, As to the Consignees having Called on the Consul to annull the Protest it is admitted But that they ever "Shewed passages in the Log Book which fully explained how the damage arose," I solemnly deny. As to the general observations or Scu[ril]ity of Mr. Hoods letter with the malignant intentions therein displayed, I shall not condescent to notice. The allusion made however "That all Public Offices here are held by Patent" is a fact But that does not preclude any who may choose applying to the Public Notary of the Place, to have their Notarial documents made out through him, it is left optional, the Notarial or Scrivner Charges for Services rendered by me, have ever been uniformly the same, since I was honored with the Office, say for Twelve Years, and my predecessor charged the same. Consular fees are regulated by the Laws of the United States and Strictly adhered to But those of a Scrivner vary in accordance to the services required to be rendered. I pray Sir, to refer you to a letter, addressed to the Honble Clay, whilst Secretary of State, dated at Baltimore February 4th 1826, which lays in the archives of State. It will I hope elucidate the general subject more fully and satisfactory, it had that tendency heretofore. If Sir such a tissue of Complaints as Mr Hs Epistle Exhibited, could possibly have issued from the Pen of any *respectable Resident merchant of St Thomas,* it would have carried with it a corresponding force. But from an Alien Stranger, and not being founded on truth, it must be left to its own evaporation. Before this reaches its destination you will have received a Solicitation from me, dated the 4th Inst, requesting leave of absence, which indulgence I presume you will grant and after my return home, I shall early endeavour Personally to obviate all disagreeable impressions.

With Sentiments of High Respect I have the Honor to be The Honble. Secretary's Very Obt Servt Nathan Levy [61]

PS I cannot forbear offering & contrasting the Following Statement, viz

Charges of the Public Notary of this Port

For Noting Protest	$5.40
" Extending do	32.40
" Swearing Surveyors	23.16
" 3 Surveyors fees @ 8 $ ea	24.
	$84.96

Notarial Charges for the same emanating from this
Consulate .... 50.

Difference $34.96

LXV

Morris Goldsmith, Deputy Marshal, 1820-1834

Another American Jew who was a devoted government servant was Morris Goldsmith,[62] Deputy Marshal of South Carolina. At this time, piracy was one of the chief dangers to American merchant shipping. Goldsmith was untiring in tracking down and capturing the pirates and their vessels. He busied himself also in the prevention of smuggling at Charleston. Fortunately, Goldsmith's petition for the repayment of expenses he had incurred in the pursuit of the pirates was forwarded to Washington by politically prominent citizens and thus brought to the attention of the President of the United States, James Monroe. Certainly, the words of praise written on Goldsmith's behalf by Judge John Drayton [63] in the first letter printed below could scarcely be warmer.

132. JOHN DRAYTON TO CHARLES PINCKNEY,[64] 1820 [65]

Charleston Jany 28th: 1820

Dear Sir.

I beg leave to present you with the enclosed Petition of Morris Goldsmith,[66] to Judge Johnson [67] & Myself, which will sufficiently explain the Nature of the Case. It is certified & recommended by Judge Johnson & myself, With the hope & intention *that it may be presented to the President,* from whose Bounty through the Contingent fund, the petitioner may receive some assistance in his present necessities I take pleasure, in forwarding it to you. And do not doubt, that you will present the same to his notice; and aid the application, as much as may be in your power.

I assure you, Mr. Goldsmith is a very deserving officer: He is

the Cryer, of the District & Circuit Courts here: and acts as Deputy
for the Marshal. And I know, it was much through his exertions
both *night* & *day,* that the pirates were taken, who have been tried
here. And in performing this duty he much hazarded his life. They
were all taken up, by Bench Warrants from myself and I therefore
have much knowledge of the justness of Mr Goldsmith's hopes of
some relief, As an encouragement to future exertions. Judge Johnson who will be at Washington, & sets out for it today: will aid you
in every proper Support of this petition of Goldsmiths. Mr. Goldsmith, is an *Hebrew;* and a deserving one of that profession: but
in low & indigent circumstances; very active & Zealous, in the
Service of the US.

So soon as you are able to write me finally on this business, &
to transmit to me for Mr Goldsmith, any money which may be due
for him, I will be obliged to you.

With best regards & [   ]   I am Dear Sir Yr [   ]

John Drayton

Honble Charles Pinckney.

133. CHARLES PINCKNEY TO
JAMES MONROE, 1820 [68]

Dear Sir

I had intended for sometime to have had the pleasure to call
on you & congratulate you on the marriage of Miss Monroe which
I sincerely do & lament that the late inclement Weather & my
indisposition have alone prevented. The inclosed application has
been made & transmitted me by our Judges Johnson & Drayton
they are of opinion that the uncommonly meritorious Exertions of
Mr Goldsmith the Deputy Marshal in apprehending so many of
the Pirates as he has done & who through his exertions as I understand solely were taken & brought to Justice entitle him to the
particular attention of the Government & not knowing how he can
be remunerated in any way but from the Contingent Fund have
requested me to submit his application to you. I will thank you
therefore to peruse it & when I have the pleasure to call on you
which I intend shortly to do, you can then favour me with your
Opinion. I request you to present my best respects & congratula-

tions to Mrs Monroe & Mr & Mrs Gouverneur on the late happy occasion & hoping you are all well I remain with great regard & Esteem Dear Sir Yours Truly   Charles Pinckney

March 16 1820

The President of the United States

134. PETITION OF MORRIS GOLDSMITH, 1834 [69]

The State of South Carolina, ⎱
City of Charleston.   ⎰

To the Honorable W. B. Taney, Secretary of the Treasury of The United States of America.

The Humble Petetion of Morris Goldsmith and William Neve, of the City and State aforesaid.

Respectfully Shewith That Your petetioners conceiving they can only obtain redress of what they consider a deprivation of their rights, through an Appeal to the Honorable The Secretary of the Treasury, are induced respectfully to offer to his notice, a Statement of such facts as they hope will entitle them to releif [sic] Your first named Petetioner is now in the Capacity of Deputy Marshal for the South Carolina District, which situation he held under the former Marshal (Morton A. Waring) [70] for a period of nearly Twenty Years; for the manner in which he has performed its respective duties, he very respectfully begs leave to refer the Honorable Secretary, to various communications recommendatory of his services, which, he presumes, are of File in the Treasury Department and the Department of the Secretary of State, from the then Circuit and District Judges of this District; also from the former District Attornies, the late Thomas Parker [71] and John Gadsden; [72] and of T. P. Devereaux [73] Esquire, District Attorney of North Carolina District.

Soon after Your Petetioner's appointment, under the present Marshal, T. D. Condy [74] Esq, he referred, in familiar conversation, to the many infringements of the Revenue Law, which almost daily occurred, and expressed the Opinion, that some effecient means should be employed, to guard against, & detect the violators of these Laws. Upon which the Marshal suggested, that a night watch should be kept, as the Inspectors of the Customs were seldom found on board the Vessels of which they had charge, after sun down. It at once occurred, that it would be impractible [sic] to carry into effect this plan, without aid, and the Marshal, accordingly, appointed Your Petetioner William Neve, a Deputy, Solely with a view to assist in detecting Smuggling. He, with M. Goldsmith, then proceeded to a commencement of their duty, under the above arrangement. They occasionly [sic] procured other Assistance, for which they paid themselves, and soon made one or Two Small Seizures of Segars; and at the last District Court, Convicted a most notorious Smuggler whom they detected. It is true, his circumstances are such, that the Penalty cannot be recoverd of him, but it will be the means of preventing his again engaging in such business, and deter others of his Gang. Early in August last Your Petetioners ascertained that there was a Quantity of ready made Clothing on board the British Ship "Lady Rowena" in the Charge of the Steward intended to be smuggled ashore. That they accordingly informed Marshal Condy of the same, beleiving at the time, from the information they had obtained, that the Clothing were to come through the hands of a Mr. Lane a resident Taylor of this City, Immediately on the arrival of this Ship, Your Petetioners, called on the Marshal, and requested him to lodge the necessary information with the Collector, which he promised to do; Fearful lest he might have forgotten to do so, Your first named Petetioner went to the Custom House for the purpose of himself lodging such information, when he was told that the Marshal had already been there, and had done so. In consequence of which said information, a Guard was placed by order of the Collector on the Wharf, and between 8 & 9 O Clock at night, two persons, one the Steward of the Vessel, the other a resident of the City, were Stopped with three packages of Clothing. Information of said Seizure was then sent to the Surveyor, who ordered the Vessel to be searched, and Ten more packages, Nine of Clothing, and One containing a choudrometer, were found, which goods were Libelled, Condemned, and Sold; and the proceeds paid over to the Collector.[75] A few days after the Seizure above named, Your Petetioner, Morris Goldsmith, met the Collector, in the Street, and informed him that on board the British Ship "Nimrod," which was Shortly expected from New York, (at which Port she had arrived from Liverpool) there were concealed, for the purpose of being Smuggled into this Port, some packages of ready made clothing, and pieces of Broad Cloth. To which the Collector replied, "the Vessel was not yet arrived". Your Petetioner then informed him, she would be in port in a day or two; He then went to the Custom House and gave the Surveyor, Capt Jervey,[76] the same information; and shew him an affidavit (a Copy of which is herewith transmitted). The Surveyor Answerd, "it should be attended to." On the arrival of said Ship, a search was made on board of her. Three packages of Clothing, and two pieces of Broad Cloth were found, Seized, libelled, Condemned, and Sold.

Your Petetioners would respectfully Submit, that these Seizures were made Solely in consequence of the Information lodged by them, and that under the 91st Sect. of the Act of 2d March 1799, entitld "An Act to Regulate the Collection of Duties on Imports & Tonnage," they are entitled to One fourth of the same; But instead of receiving what the Act allows, they are informed, that because they *suspected the Goods were for Mr. Lane,* and they were directed to other persons, they are not entitled as Informers. The fact cannot be denied, that the goods were found and Seized *in consequence* of the Information lodged by Your Petetioners, and that they come not only within the Spirit, but actually the letter of the Law: Viz, *"in pursuance of such information."*

Your Petetioners would most respectfully State, that in addition to the Funds paid over to the Collector, there is Two prosecutions pending to be paid in the District Court (December Term) arising *in pursuance* of said Information.

Smuggling has been carried on in this Port to a much greater extent than is supposed. no Night Watch was ever thought of being kept by the Collector, until began by Your Petetioners, who have, night after night, exerted their Vigilence, and employed, at their own expence, when necessary, persons to assist them, *and under the Collectors Construction of the Law* all they are to gain by it, is the degrading name of Informers, while *their rights,* are divided between the Collector, Naval Officer, & Surveyor; This unjust division the Law certainly never contemplated. Had your petetioners been aware prior to the money being paid out of court that there was any dispute with regard to their rights (as informers) they would have applied to the Court, to decide the Question; but they were led to beleive, that there was no doubt about their right to that portion the law allowed, until after it was too late; And their only redress now lies in this appeal to Your Justice.[77]

LXVI

A Request for Naval Service, 1821

We have already seen [78] how persistently some Jewish young men sought careers in the United States Army. To others, it was service in the Navy of the United States that was appealing. In the letter printed below, from Henry H. Myers [79] to the Secretary of the Navy, we find the case of a young man who had fallen in love with the sea, on a voyage to China, and had, therefore, decided on a career in the Naval service. In addition to the urgency which is a clear sign of young Myers's commitment, it is again worthy of note that this letter reveals the personal directness, the sense of relatedness to the government that we have observed in other cases.

135. HENRY H. MYERS TO SMITH THOMPSON, [80] 1821 [81]

Norfolk 20th August 1821

Sir,

Some weeks having elapsed, since I had the honour to wait on you, I hope you will not think me troublesome, about my Warrant. After a Cruize of Two years, in which I have labored hard to deserve it, both my mind and habits, have become bent upon pursuing arms, in the service of my Country, as my future profession. An anxiety not easily to be imagined, causes me to venture again to address you, on that subject. It is not on account of any doubt I entertain, as I feel confident it will be granted. But I expect to advance by my own conduct in the service, and therefore wish to progress with perfect confidence in my studies ashore, with an undivided mind, and to have a right to ask for active service again, as soon as possible.

My Shipmates ask me questions too, which I do not like to evade. Indeed sir, my feelings, my interest, and my hopes, are in your hands. I beg leave to refer you to the approbations of the Commander and other officers of the Congress on her late Cruize to the China seas.

I have the Honour to be Sir, Yr: Mo: Obt. Svt

Henry H. Myers

The Honble Smith Thompson
Secretary of the Navy
Washington

LXVII

Consular Reports from Maracaibo, 1825-1827

The first of these consular reports of Abraham B. Nones [82] from the port of Maracaibo gives a good picture of the routine duties of the consular office in the South American port cities which were so important to the commercial life of the United States. Both from the interest taken by Jewish merchants in the naming of consuls to the various posts in the West Indies and in South America and from the number of Jews appointed to these posts, there is a clear inference that this aspect of American commerce was one in which Jewish business houses had a large part. Nones was occupied in Maracaibo, even as Nathan Levy in St. Thomas,[83] with the protection of American shipping, caring for the welfare of American seamen, and trying to defend the prestige of the United States.

While the primary function of the consulship is thus seen to have been commercial, the office also served as a political listening post. Under the great liberator, Simon Bolivar,[84] the South American countries we now know as Panama, Colombia, and Venezuela were joined into a single country, Greater Colombia. By 1827, however, Venezuelans had begun to resent their secondary position in this confederacy. What Nones reported to the State Department in the second letter printed below was the prelude to the establishment of an independent Venezuela two years later, in 1829.

136. ABRAHAM B. NONES TO
HENRY CLAY, 1825 [85]

Consulate of the U.S.A.
Maracaibo June 24th. 1825

Sir

I have the honour to acknowledge receipt of Yours of 16th. April covering the commission issued in Virtue of the appointment with which I was honored being ratified by the Senate of the United States, the bond you inclosed I have forwarded to my friends in the U.S. who will submit it, 'though previously to my departure I executed a Similar one which I had the honour of forwarding

Since my arrival here, every aid and facility requisite to the faithful discharge of my duties was extended towards me, until within a few days ago, a desertion of one of the crew of the Schooner Sophia of Philadelphia occured and on my applications, first to the Commander of Marines and afterwards to the Intendant, I was refused that aid and assistance requisite for the arrest of the Said Seaman, So that he might be returned to the United States by the Same Vessel. In the correspondence which I had with the Intendant he says "that the authorities here have received instructions, not to render any assistance to the Consul of the U.S. in arresting deserters in consequence of Colombia not enjoying equal rights in the United States." finding I could obtain no assistance here, I immediately forwarded to our Charge d'affaires at Bogota, a full Statement of this transaction with the copies of the correspondence; Such a System if continued would be highly injurious to our Commerce here. the port being remote and no opportunity of obtaining New Crews, might result not only in the loss of the Vessel but the property of the Citizens of the United States, at Same time precludes me from the exercise of one of the most important parts of my duty.

The American Schooner Perry Captn Wiggin Merrit arrived here from the Island of St. Thomas, a short time ago, and was Sold to an American Citizen, the Captain without my Knowledge or consent discharged and paid off his crew, on learning the fact (the purchase money being in my hands) I retained under the Act of Congress of 28th February 18[   ], Three months wages, to be applied as the Said act directs, being perfectly satisfied that her crew were all Americans, the articles under which they were shipped declaring their places of birth, and the enclosed affidavit being Sufficient to Satisfy me of the fact. I have and do consider myself justified in So doing, 'though the Captain has attempted to avoid the payment by applying to the Magistrates; by whom I was notified to attend before their Court, to answer the claim of Said Captain. I did not for a moment hesitate in refusing to obey the Summons, being as I conceive only responsible and accountable to my Government for acts in the discharge of my official duties.

The amount thus retained will be applied as the act directs, and Shall appear in the Acct Current which in Virtue of the Consular Instructions Shall have the honor of forwarding on the First of July next.

With Sentiments of the highest consideration and respect, remain, Your mo Obt Hble St   Ab B. Nones

The Honble Henry Clay Secretary of State of the U.S. Washington

137. ABRAHAM B. NONES TO HENRY CLAY, 1827 [86]

> *Consulate of the U.S.A.*
> *Maracaibo Decr 31st 1827*

To Honble. Henry Clay
Washington
   Sir
   I had last this honour under date of 24th inst. p Schr Economy to which most respectfully Crave reference. I now beg leave to wait on you with the Inclosed return of our Commerce to this port, for the entire year, ending this day; the Return of the first Six Months, I had the honour to remit under date of 6th August p Schr. Fame, which Vessel is presumed to have founder'd at Sea, in consequence of which, the present return embraces the whole period. It Shews a lamentable decrease of trade, as will appear by

reference to former Statements, and it is very much to be feared, that it will Still Continue to grow worse. under the System of the Decrees of the Libertador [87] of the 8th & 9th March last, the effect has been Sensibly felt by our Commerce, and as they are Still persisted in, & harshly enforced, I am induced to think, that all foreign Commerce will desert the ports where the decrees are in force; the Consequences to the Country truly distressing. a large and daily increasing Military force to Maintain, whom as well as the Civil officers of all Classes are without pay Since October last and the Government Scarce able to raise Ways & Means to procure daily rations, an impoverished Country, an exhausted and disorganised Treasury, distrust & jealousy in the Cabinet, treason and Civil War in the heart of the Country, presents a Most disastrous State of Affairs, but nevertheless too true. Such is the State of the Country and Not pretended to be denied by Men of the highest respectability and Known and tried patriotism who all appear to be almost in a State of dispair.

Yesterday was the day appointed by the Act of Congress for the Meeting of the Electors for the purpose of proceeding to the choice of Deputies for the Grand Convention, out of the twenty composing the Electoral College of this Department, only Eleven have made their appearance, therefore No Election took place ⅔s at least being required by Law. They Still expect Sufficient Number to arrive from day to day, & will then proceed with the election, many pretend to think there will be No Election and various reasons given as party feeling dictates. People are every day becoming more Suspicious of their Rulers, and considerable Sensation has been excited within the last few days, on account of a Rumor of a treaty with Spain, said to be negociating through the Mediation of England, for the purpose of obtaining a Recognition of the Independence of the S.A. States, on the payment of an Annual Sum of money for a certain Number of Years, and a perpetual tribute. Should this report be well founded, I do Not think the Government of Colombia possesses Sufficient confidence, or force even to propose it to the acceptance of the people, Should they, however, attempt to do So, nothing can avert a dreadful Storm of Strife, and Civil War on an extended Scale, the Country at large is under Strong excitement of feelings, and the credit of the Government was never, even in the Most Gloomy periods of the Revolution at So low an ebb as at present. Most Sincerely do I wish it were in power to Communicate a more favorable picture of the Country, but in truth, I scarce See, a ray of hope, of any good in Store; the policy of England doubtless has been, and Still is active and Sensibly felt in all the concerns of Colombia. As opportys offer will Keep you advised.

I have the honor, to be, Sir, with respect Your Mo Ob. Hb Servt.   A. B. Nones

LXVIII

Benjamin Sheftall in
Local Politics, 1833

In the same way as Noah [88] was involved in the local politics of
New York and Harby [89] in the local politics of Charleston, the
members of the Sheftall family were for a number of years active
participants in local politics in Savannah and its environs. At various times, they held minor patronage or elective positions as rewards for their partisan services. The letter below deals with a
protest lodged against Benjamin Sheftall's election as Justice of
the Peace for a district in which he did not reside. The suggestion
made by Sheftall in this letter is that the protest was motivated
by political vindictiveness rather than by concern for the letter of
Georgia's election law.

138. BENJAMIN SHEFTALL TO
WILSON LUMPKIN,[90] 1833 [91]

To His Excellency Wilson Lumpkin   Govr. of the State of Ga.
Sir:

I had the honor of receiving your Excellency's Communication
wherein I am informed you have received information from James
B. Lewis [92] and Elisha Wylly [93] Esquires "that I did not reside in
Cherokee Hill District of Chatham County in which I have recently
been elected Justice of the Peace". Mr. Lewis one of the Informers
and who was recently elected Justice of the Peace resided at the
period of his Election out of District No. 2 and Mr. Wylly the
other informer is known to his colleague Henry McDonnell to
reside out of his District and the same may be said of H. T. Valleau
& W. W. Oates [94] Equrs. These facts were well known to Messrs.
Wylly and Lewis and were the motives of these persons pure, and
not vindictive, they would have given to Your Excellency general

information and not have selected me as their anticipated victim for executive animadversion. I do reside Sir in District No 2 and have here been living many years while I represented District No. 1 as Justice of the Peace.

The place of my present Residence is on a Street which Divides District No. 2 from District No. 8 called Cherokee Hill District and, Sir, by a reference to the Constitution 3 Art. 5 Sect. Di 556 and the Law founded on said Constitution Dig 123 & 124 Your Excellency will readily perceive that there is nothing express or implied that prohibits persons from eligibility to the office of Justice of the peace though they live out of the District for which they may be elected. Both the Constitution and the Law speak only of the qualifications of *voters in their respective districts*. In the lifetime of Judge Davis [95] the subject was submitted to him for his opinion and his opinion was that neither the Constitution or Law required that the Justice of the peace elected should have resided in the District at the time of his election.

I take leave respectfully to observe that the Law only makes it imperative that acting Justices of the Peace shall hold their Courts in the District in which they are elected, and in the most central part. Convinced that your Excellency will give this subject its appropriate consideration, I tender assurances that I shall be perfectly satisfied with such direction as your Excellency shall think proper to give this matter.

Yr. Excellency's Obt. Svt.   Benja. Sheftall

Feb'y 1833

LXIX

Stormy Petrel of
New York Politics, 1821-1824

For many years during the journalistic phase of his career, Mordecai Manuel Noah stood at the storm center of New York City and State politics. The strongly entrenched Clintonian faction within the Democratic party was opposed by the more radical Tammany faction, in which Noah was a leader. This conflict went beyond the state borders in its implications; De Witt Clinton,[96] who was elected to the Governorship in 1816 and re-elected in 1820, in both instances with the assistance of the Federalists, envisioned himself as a candidate for the presidency in 1824. The Tammany Democrats did all they could to forestall this candidacy, having their eyes on William H. Crawford.[97] As the election of 1824 drew closer, a group within New York's Democratic Party gave its support to the candidacy of Andrew Jackson.

In the meantime, Noah decided to seek public office in 1821. Out of this arose charges that he had offered to "sell himself" to the Clintonians in exchange for preferment. This led to the airing of charges and countercharges and finally to a libel suit in which Noah was the defendant in an action brought by Silvanus Miller.[98] In another maneuver, Noah was driven from his post as editor of *The National Advocate* by one of the men who had put up money to continue the paper, Henry Eckford.[99] In 1826, the leaders of the opposition to Noah were charged with swindles aggregating millions of dollars. At least one of them was convicted.[100] Noah, in presenting the public with a prospectus for a "new" *National Advocate*, indicated that the whole affair was tied to the struggle for control of the Democratic Party of New York.

139. MORDECAI M. NOAH'S (LIBELLOUS?) SELF-DEFENSE, 1823 [101]

To the Editors of the Albany Argus:

Mr. Coleman,[102] editor of the New-York Evening Post, some days ago insinuated that I had offered myself for sale to Governor Clinton for $7000; he took the opportunity of making this insinuation while I was absent from the city. I lost no time, however, in demanding his proofs, and after some delay he has published a letter, signed Silvanus Miller!! in Monday's Post, in which Miller has endeavoured to make out a statement of something from his *recollections*, which he thinks will answer the present objects in view. *I will not avail myself of the advantages which I possess over this profligate old man, in consequences of his well-known habits of uttering what he knows to be false, but will suppose him worthy of belief in this instance, and proceed to explain a most simple and innocent event, which this* honourable *gentleman has attempted to turn into something criminal.*

Two years and seven months ago, (mark this time) Mr. Gilfert,[103] of the Charleston Theatre, wrote me a letter, acquainting me that the leases of the Charleston, Savannah, Augusta, Norfolk and Richmond theatres, were his property, and that he contemplated to establish a great and profitable concern, in which he invited me to become joint proprietor, setting forth the advantages, and requiring the sum of $20,000, 10,000 of which he demanded in cash. This pursuit, with which I considered myself familiar, and which I knew could be made profitable, I of course could not embrace, not having funds. I spoke of it generally, and regretted that I had not $10,000 to join the concern. Being one day in the store of Dr. Secor, an old acquaintance, I casually mentioned the circumstance, and he immediately said that it was an excellent opening, and would relieve me from my editorial pursuits, which were irksome and by no means profitable, and that being a director of the Franklin Bank, he would endeavour to obtain the $10,000. I gave him my full consent to obtain the sum, for which I offered to give ample security. In a day or two he informed me that no more than $2500 could be procured, which would have been of no service, and the project was dropped. Mr. Graham of New-York, furnished the money, and became Mr. Gilfert's partner. From that period until the present moment, the circumstance being of no consequence was never mentioned. Whether Dr. Secor invited Mr. Miller and his coadjutors to a meeting on the subject, I know not; it was never mentioned to me—never requested by me—*I never wrote a word on the subject, and the whole colouring given by Miller to the transaction, is false and scandalous.* But let me ask, if this was an attempt to "sell myself to Governor Clinton," why has not this important fact been previously published? *I have given Miller sufficient provocation, I have been for three years almost in the daily habit of representing him to the world as an unprincipled intriguer, a corrupt and profligate old man;* and Coleman himself, not a year ago, published him for having uttered a wilful and deliberate falsehood in the case of Mr. King, in some "facts that could be substantiated." Why, I say, when the Clintonian presses have teemed with profligate charges against me, has Miller concealed this fact from the world? Why, on the eve of his being *dismissed disgracefully from office*, on his retirement forever from public life, and when the current is setting rapidly and powerfully against him and his patron, does he coalesce with Coleman, *par nobile fratrum*,[104] to publish this ridiculous charge? The motives are obvious, he hopes to do me an injury with my friends; and if any thing from Miller, or Coleman, or the Clintonians, could injure me with those friends, I should feel, indeed, that I had mistaken their characters. Miller says, "a written paper was presented," which he "believes truly" was in my hand writing. Produce it, produce any document, and 'tis the fashion now to exhibit documents, of my handwriting in proof of this "offer to sell myself," and I shall say no more on the subject. Let it, however, be remembered that this offer, according to Miller's statement, was made, "some months after the election of Governor Clinton"—a very early attempt, indeed. But if I was to be purchased, why was not the purchase made? Because, says Silvanus Miller, it was "revolting to my sense of *duty*, and repugnant to my views and ideas of *morality and honour!!*" O dear, O dear, Silvanus Miller, talk of "*morality and honour!*" why, even Coleman would hesitate saying much on such a subject.

Finally, the whole is a false and discoloured statement, charac-
teristic of the man and his present object. Had there been truth in
it, the world would have known it long since. There has been
nothing concealed in my political course; it has been open, frank
and honourable, severe and decisive, if you please. I have studied
to obtain my own approbation; not fawningly stooped to obtain
the approbation of others. If I were for sale, Governor Clinton
would have found means to have purchased me. He *has purchased
several already;* and Silvanus Miller himself, with all his morality,
is known *and accredited as his political broker.*

M. M. Noah.

140. MORDECAI M. NOAH TO
AN UNKNOWN CORRESPONDENT, 1823 [105]

You will herewith receive the Argus, containing a reply to the
ridiculous and malicious charge of Silvanus Miller. When Coleman
ventured to declare that I "had offered myself for sale to Dewitt
Clinton," curiosity was excited here to learn the facts of the case,
but when the name of *Silvanus Miller* appeared to the communication, it defeated the hopes of political opponents, and created
much mirth among friends; and even admitting every thing that
he has said to be true, so far from having "offered myself for sale
to Dewitt Clinton for $7,000," he has been only able to state from
"*recollections,*" that I asked a friend to loan me $10,000, at "*legal*
interest, the *principal* to be paid by instalments, and the *whole*
secured by *property.*" (these are Miller's words) in order not to
sell myself to Clinton, but to purchase shares in the Charleston
and other theatres, and this was done *two years and seven months
ago.* Preposterous and absurd. Every body knows that I am on good
personal terms with my political opponents, and when I want a loan
of money I frequently give them the preference; but is this to be
construed into a political connexion? However, I do not blame
Miller for this attack, *his character for falsehood is proverbial:
even* truth *would be received with great caution from him; I blame
Coleman, knowing how frequently he has detected and disgraced
Miller for this habitual vice, for having taken advantage of my
absence, and formed a plot with this old hack, whom he himself*

despises, to make up a story, *which they hoped, together, would have* effect *at this peculiar juncture of affairs.* It was mean and pitiful. I have been mistaken in the character of Coleman. His moral and political depravity are generally acknowledged, yet I have considered him as being influenced by others, and having occasionally a spark of honour and feeling left, which might, by nourishing, preserve him in the decline of life. I have also been of opinion that the injuries received in the personal chastisements which have been inflicted upon him, have created temporary derangements; it is very certain that such a belief prevails in New-York; and very frequently, when I have written a paragraph which might have wounded his feelings, I have struck my pen through it and spared the merited lash. I did wrong. "He is more knave than fool," and "the dull ass will only mend his pace with beating."

Since he has made this attack upon my reputation, and in company with Silvanus Miller, has gone back two years and a half to search for materials against me, I am at liberty, after having exhibited the falsehood of the charge, to go back some years in looking for facts connected with the private and political character of Coleman, who sets up for a corrector of morals, and which, I promise him, shall live in the page of history. "I have a rod in pickle for him," which he must prepare for. In the mean time, I set him at defiance, in every thing which he may attempt to injure me: I ask him no favors; I shall accept of none; I shall do him full justice, and shall take care that he does not obtain $1100 out of my pocket as he has from Mr. Hegerman, for he may remotely hope that such a speculation will grow out of this affair. This being the last dying speech of Silvanus Miller, it has occasioned much mirth at the seat of government: that he should stand upon his "honour and morality," must have amused even Coleman. Instead of my taking $7000 from the poor Clintonians, I should have felt pity for their tailors, bakers, and butchers, and would have advised the payment of their honest debts before they purchased political partisans.

[February 1, 1823]

141. SILVANUS MILLER TO
THE NEW YORK "EVENING POST," 1821 [106]

We now present the narrative of facts and circumstances on which it may be remembered we were lately authorized to advance the charge that Mr. Noah had once offered to sell himself to the friends of Governor Clinton, and abandon his party, and to which he boldly replied by demanding even the *semblance* of proof. We submit it to the reader without a word of comment or illustration.

To the Editor of the *Evening Post*

Sir, In compliance with your request, I shall now proceed to state the facts and circumstances connected with the propositions made by M. M. Noah, to the friends of Gov. Clinton.

Some months after the election of the present Executive of this state, it was frequently mentioned to me by different persons intimate with the editor of the National Advocate, "that he was very anxious to abandon the editorial management of that paper, and apply himself to other pursuits: that there was no obstacle presenting itself, to carry into effect his desires, but the want of funds; and that if these could be obtained, his determination to leave his present business was certain.

These intimations were disregarded by me, although I was frequently spoken to, until I was ultimately requested to meet some political friends, in the year 1818, to consult and determine on the propositions. I accordingly met by appointment a select number of persons, to consider the proposals and requests to be submitted.

There was then a written paper presented, said (and I believe truly,) to be in the hand-writing of the editor of the Advocate, in which he required a loan of *ten thousand dollars,* at legal interest; the principal to be paid by instalments, and the whole secured by property which he contemplated purchasing in several theatres in the southern states, and of which he was to be the sole or joint manager with the representative of the late Mr. Holman.[107]

The arrangement proposed being merely a monied operation, it was natural for the persons present to ask why, and for what reason, *we* should enter in to the wishes of the borrower?

It was then stated, that, as a political measure it would be highly advantageous; that the editor of the Advocate was greatly dissatisfied in his then situation; that he spoke in terms of great disrespect of the party, whose objects he was obliged to maintain and support; and that he had expressed himself very freely and fully on those subjects; declaring that *his political supporters were grossly ignorant, and proverbially illiberal and parsimonious;* that from the political situation in which he was placed, he was *compelled* to oppose Mr. Clinton's administration, and friends, against which he felt no real hostility; and that a terrible battle was to be fought in this state, from which he was extremely anxious to retire; that he had also ulterior objects of a political character, which would be advantageous in their consequences. Many other, and similar observations, were made on the occasion above alluded to, and it was further observed, that although *ten thousand dollars* were asked, that *seven* thousand dollars, and probably a smaller sum, would accomplish the object contemplated.

The whole was considered a mere *political operation,* in its character and consequences; the *friends of Governor Clinton were only consulted,* and his opponents were studiously excluded from any knowledge or participation in the transaction.

The whole plan met with my unqualified disapprobation, and it failed in consequence of the unwillingness on the part of the persons applied to, to consummate the arrangement.

Efforts were subsequently made to effect the objects desired by the Editor of the National Advocate, in a form varying from that first proposed; and some one or two of the persons applied to, had agreed to contribute a certain amount, but there was a general hostility to the scheme, and the projector was left in his occupation.

This representation contains, substantially, what I understood at the time to be the nature and character of the propositions. There are other facts and circumstances which it cannot be necessary at this time to develope.

In closing these remarks I have further to observe, that the whole of this affair presented features revolting to my sense of duty, and repugnant to my views and ideas of morality and honour; and that I have felt myself at liberty so to say, on different occasions, without restraint or reserve. The subject has been spoken of frequently for a long time, and cannot have escaped the knowledge of the person inculpated; but with me he has never had a personal explanation on the subject: probably he had learned my opposition to his wishes and deemed it useless to approach me on that account.

In making this communication I have not consulted any of the persons to whom this transaction was known, but from my own recollections and impressions at the time and during its progress, as well as the general understanding of the import, intent, and meaning of all concerned, I have no doubt but that the narrative now given is substantially true. There are others who can confirm this representation in all its essential points.

I am, sir, with considerations of respect,   Your obedient servant,

Silvanus Miller.

142. MORDECAI M. NOAH'S
CANDID STATEMENT, 1824 [108]

I inform Mr. Eckford that I am ready to make the necessary advances, and repay his principle and interest. How does he act in this case? Why, says he, "rumours having come to me, that the political course of the National Advocate would be changed" I have determined to go on advancing. Mere subterfuge and evasion, no rumours ever reached Mr. Eckford that the political course of the Advocate would be changed, no such rumours existed, no cause existed for such rumours, Mr. Eckford never heard them. The gentleman who proposed joining me in business, was a democrat, and a supporter of Mr. Crawford. How did these rumours arise? I will answer that question. Mr. Eckford caused it to be insinuated in the American and Patriot, that the Advocate was about becoming a *Clay* paper [109] he did it to give himself grounds for raising these rumours—he never believed what he wrote, and no one else. But suppose, for the sake of argument, that cause existed for these rumours, has Henry Eckford become the guardian and conservator of the Democratic party and its press? Why, it is scarcely two years since we have admitted him into our ranks, it is very little more than that time since the columns of the National Advocate were effectually used to prevent his going to Congress, in opposition to Mr. Cambreleng,[110] the regularly nominated Democratic candidate.

He is at this moment in no farther communion with the old democratic party, than merely in supporting Mr. Crawford. He is at this
day attached to the friends and party of Mr. Clinton, and secretly
aiding his cause; and is it from such a quarter, that I am to receive
lessons of political fidelity? Mr. Eckford pays a sorry compliment
to the democratic party, and the general committee, when he represents himself as the only person capable of keeping the National
Advocate in the right path, supposing it to be capable of going
wrong under my charge. But Mr. Eckford, desirous of putting all
doubts of his political fidelity at rest, offers to give a bond of 50,000
dollars, that he will keep the Advocate on the democratic side, until
after the election. This is a novel proposition indeed. Men of
honour never offer a bond as a guarantee for principle, their *word*
is sufficient; but Mr. Eckford considers this as a moneyed transaction altogether, and the bond may therefore be in character. He
is willing to redeliver the paper to myself and Mr. Phillips [111]
only, when he made it originally a condition for his advances that
Mr. Phillips was to retire altogether from the establishment. He
charges him with gross neglect and indifference to the interest of
the paper by giving away 400 papers, and yet now, most liberally
offers to restore it to him and myself *only*, when he knows that
Mr. Phillips enjoys an eligible situation in the Custom-House,
and has no desire to have the paper.

But to be brief, Mr. Eckford never intended, AT ANY TIME, nor
does he now intend to surrender the paper, or put me in possession
of that which is mine of right, and which certainly has never been
his. His conduct throughout warrants this conclusion. In proof, I
may cite the violation of his written and personal obligation, his
attempt to purchase the paper of Mr. Thompson,[112] for his son-in-
law, his refusal to allow me to enter into co-partnership with a
person of property and character, the control and direction of the
Press, assumed without any authority, express or implied, his
tampering with the foreman of the office, and bringing him over
to his interest by promises that he should have the paper, a paper
which is no more his property than the Evening Post, his giving
orders to the carriers not to allow me to know the names and residence of the subscribers, in case I should find it necessary to establish another paper, his braving and defying the honourable gentle-

men I associated with him, the real, the Legal proprietors of the paper, Jonathan Thompson and John Targee; [113] and if these proofs are not conclusive, I have one more unanswerable one to cite. He went to the asignees of Mr. Phillips, and purchased from them all their right and title to the good will and future earnings of the National Advocate for $250, Mr. Davis,[114] who made the negotiations, giving them to understand that it was for my benefit. If all these facts do not warrant the belief that the public are deceived in character of Mr. Eckford, and that it may be well not to place themselves in his power, I know not what constitutes fair dealing.

I am therefore constrained to abandoned my post. I am driven from it. Since I made the transfer, I have been merely the nominal Editor, and I submit to those who know me; I submit to every liberal, independent, honourable man, whether I can remain in an office where my editorial labours, the concerns of the county, and of the republican family, are to undergo the inspection and approval of my foreman and a young fellow sent down from Eckford's ship yards.

I should have made this expose some time ago, but the delicacy of our political situation restrained me. I suppressed my f[e]elings until I saw the Legislature adjourn, and this state was safe. I need not say that the support of Messrs. Eckford, Davis, Barker [115] & Co. to the cause of Mr. Crawford has been ruinous, without being able to influence a solitary electoral vote, they have debarred him of a support which would have been nearly unanimous. In all my efforts to serve him among true and honourable democrats, the reply has been invariably, "I think highly of Mr. Crawford, but I cannot support him if his confidential advisers are to be Mr. Davis, Mr. Eckford, Mr. Barker, and some others." In vain I assured them that Mr. Crawford was not to be improperly influenced, the reply was still the same, and after fighting this battle under so many grievous disadvantages, and now, when success is dawning upon us, these drawbacks, these persons, who with good wishes can do him no possible service, undertake to deprive me of my rights, of my character, and even the means of subsistence.

Confiding, however, in the justice and liberality of my fellow-citizens, I shall attempt the establishment, or the continuance, of a newspaper, to be called The National Advocate, to be published under the protection of the Republican General Committee. and to take the rank which the National Advocate now holds, to support the same principles, and the same men. I shall, in this new paper, attempt to heal the unhappy divisions now existing in the republican party, and support all who declare themselves free from the influence of this speculating Junta. I have a list of the subscribers to the National Advocate, and shall have the honor to call on each in person, and solicit their patronage for my paper. Subscription lists will be issued shortly, and I have no doubts of success. Indeed a new, independent, and decided paper is necessary at this time.

There is a small select party in this city, who having peculiar views of their own, not only attempt to control the political affairs of the city, the state, and union, but are industriously employed in managing the whole moneyed operations of the city. They keep employed a gang of lobby members who hang on the skirts of the legislature, and attempt to overawe and control that body. They are continually devising new incorporations, in order to speculate upon a rise of stock, or rather by fictitious means to run up the stock, allowing themselves time to sell out to immense profits, leaving the unwary to be their dupes. They mingle in the affairs of the Banks and Insurance Companies, elevate or depress the stock at pleasure, interfere in the election of Directors, vamp up old and broken charters, and inundate the country with their bills. To carry their objects into view, they are anxious to control the delegates from this city to Albany and Washington, and wish to place themselves in an attitude which will enable them to say to the next administration of the general government, "we are the influential men of the democratic party, on all questions relating to city and state affairs, to contracts, appointments, and national measures, we are the persons to whom application must be made." It is needless to add, that the administration may never expect to hear the true state of the case, or of the fair claims of any man not devoted to their views. They are an intriguing, managing, overreaching, shaving junta, whose support is ruinous, and whose opposition is empty and unavailing. To protect the community against such men, a press is indispensibly necessary, and no man understands them better than I do, or can be more disposed to protect the public against them. I know the ulterior views of their leader, although professing to be wholly disinterested.

I have to apologise for the length of this statement, which, though it may appear to be a private transaction, is nevertheless one in which the public has an interest, and a deep interest, which is to keep the press of the country free from sinister motives, and speculating and deceptive objects.

I cannot stand the combined attacks of friends and opponents. I am to be led, not driven, subdued by acts of liberality and confidence, not trampled upon by wealth and power. If this expose brings into public disrepute some of Mr. Crawford's zealous friends, let it be remembered, that Mr. Crawford, a truly honourable and high-minded man himself, cannot be made accountable for the bad conduct of some, calling themselves his friends and supporters, and neither can it be required of me, that I should submit to insult and oppression from any quarter, or for any cause.

I respectfully solicit from Editors throughout the Union, a publication of this statement in their papers, or such part as they may have room for in their columns. I have been faithful in every trust reposed in me, and the wrongs of an individual become the wrongs of the community. The rights of every editor are in my case jeopardized. If men of property can lay their hands upon the presses of the country, and bend them to their sinister views, our freedom rests upon a frail basis indeed; and if a friend, called upon in the hour of distress, can discharge his obligations in the manner Mr. Eckford has done, mankind had better "dwell in their necessity," than place themselves in the power of such a friend.

M. M. Noah

New-York, August 23, 1824.

LXX
The Election of 1824

There were five pre-electoral candidates for the presidency in the election of 1824, all technically of the same party but representative of different factions within that party. In a close election that was ultimately decided by the House of Representatives, John Quincy Adams was the victor. Other candidates were Henry Clay, a spokesman for the new states of the Midwest and for a Hamiltonian program for a balanced economy; John C. Calhoun, outstanding political thinker and apostle of southern interests; William H. Crawford, an able southern Jeffersonian, opposed to Clay's expansionist program; and Andrew Jackson, whose military exploits provided his chief claim to consideration, and who appeared as spokesman for states rights and rampant individualism and as the champion of the newer southern states. Adams was regarded as the representative of the northeastern section of the country and as tarred with the brush of Federalism and aristocracy.

In a series of eleven articles, originally written for the *City Gazette* of Charleston in 1824, Isaac Harby discussed the issues and the candidates in this election with acute understanding, at times approaching brilliance. The standpoint from which he wrote was that of the Jeffersonian Democrats of South Carolina. He was opposed to high tariffs and in favor of moderate states rights. The major attacks, in his pieces on "The Presidency," were directed against Adams and Clay; yet partisan though he was, Harby's attacks were on matters of principle, not personality. The selection below, the concluding article of the series, sums up Harby's position and gives his reason for supporting General Andrew Jackson.

143. THE PRESIDENCY, 1824 [116]

I doubt not the reader will agree with me, that it is time to draw to a conclusion these observations upon the qualifications of the candidates for the Presidency, and the probable and ultimate tendency of their politics. I shall hasten towards this end with a few reflections, which I offer in that spirit of candour from which trust I have never departed.

The remark has already been made, that if Gen. Jackson have *fair play,* his chance is the best for fulfilling the wishes of the people. It is in vain to conceal the truth; bury it in the centre, it will still spring forth to the light. It is but a year ago, that attempts were made to win upon Gen. Jackson in Pennsylvania, to withdraw in favour of Mr. Calhoun! The tenor of the letter addressed to him, enquiring into the subject, may be gathered from his answer. It is said the writer is "a very intelligent and respectable inhabitant of Edgefield." But the report of the General's intention to withdraw in favour of Mr. Calhoun, was, at least, as insolent a trick, as the assertion in the Washington paper, of his intention to withdraw in favour of Mr. Adams. General Jackson writes thus, in rebuke of the impertinence of such a story; a story which would make Pennsylvania, or Carolina, a mere *Feodary;* [117] "holding her estate under the tenure of suit and service to a superior lord."

"The letter in answer to the Pennsylvania committee (says General Jackson,) was a just exposition of my feelings and my views. My name, unsolicited by me, has been brought before the American people, and although I have the highest esteem and regard for Mr. Calhoun, and some others whose names are before the people, I shall not interfere in any way. It is a question with the people whether or not they choose to drop me; but should they do so, I have no power to transfer political influence; and notwithstanding the high opinion I entertain of Mr. Calhoun, my political creed would prevent any attempt to exercise a power which does not legitimately belong to me." [118]

How noble is this simplicity, this elevation of feeling, the surest attribute of Genius! How easily and irresistibly does it put to flight all the sophistry of the schools, all the intrigue and circumvention that have been employed against this great man. He declares he has "no power to transfer his political influence." He has a "high opinion" of Mr. Calhoun; but as "his name unsolicited by him, has been brought before the American people he will leave to the people" whether they will "drop him" for Mr. Calhoun. The people have decided. They prefer him to all the candidates put together: and they will have him, if their wishes are correctly represented, if the maxim "Divide et impera," [119] which Macchiavelli [120] says is the policy of tyrants, is not to become also the policy of demagogues. Even in Massachusetts, Mr. Adams is regarded by the editors of the leading journals, with very different feelings. One [121] desires his election because the other candidates are all duellists and slave holders, and consequently, if so, ought to be considered anti-pacific, anti-republican, and anti-christian. "How far (it continues) Mr. Adams, if chosen, would venture to risk his popularity in the South, by endeavouring to effect the abolition of slavery, in a nation that boasts of holding equal liberty as the inalienable right of every man, will depend much on the reality of his moral and religious principles."

This is tolerably fair; we know now on what particular grounds *some* at least of his supporters stand. But that Mr. Adams should become President, under any circumstances, is by no means a general desideratum in Massachusetts. One of the best conducted presses in that State [122] after denouncing, in the strongest terms, the idea that he is supported by the genuine old Federal party, observes "Mr. Adams has verified in a remarkable manner, the truth of a maxim of Tacitus," "Proprium humani ingenii est, odisse quem læeris." [123]

It continues: "It is now settled, beyond all dispute, that if Mr. Adams is chosen President, this country, which ought to be the happiest than sun shines upon, must be torn by factions. Instead of using his talents to promote the peace, and prosperity of *interior*, and to maintain honour, and independence in all *exterior* relations, he must busy himself in satisfying the demands of his rapacious adherents, he must use his public trust, to compensate individual partizans. If he refuses to do this, he must quarrel with his own supporters, and having brought this to pass, his disturbed and comfortless distinction, will end with his first four years."

With Mr. Crawford the case is somewhat different. Though no "pious Eneas," he has lately escaped from the dense cloud which the "Goddess Mother" (of intrigue) threw around him, and he stands forth as a fair democratic candidate. He cannot, however, so easily escape from the extent and effect which his ultra admirers have given to his sentiments about the Navy and Army; and from the over-eager support of partizans, who watch and wait for the reward of their toils.

We are told by the Adams party that when Mr. Crawford becomes President, the Navy and Army will perish; we are to intermarry with the Indians, run about in the woods, and realize Rousseau's unsophisticated nature.[124]

We are told by the Crawford party when Mr. Adams shall be king, we shall have a standing army of 50,000 men, with all the contractors and plagues attendant; an union of church and state, &c. because Mr. Adams considers democracy, in the language of the wrong-headed Fisher Ames,[125] *"an illuminated hell!"* [126]

Now, for myself, I have no very material fear that any of these extravaganza will come to pass, let who will reign "lord of the ascendant." Were either of these factions to attempt such things, the good sense and majesty of the people would dash them to pieces. But it is very obvious, that the partizans of both gentlemen look out for "something handsome," as the saying is; they expect, and imagine they have a right to expect some office, some embassy, some *"moveables,"* which Buckingham [127] lost his head for in endeavouring to obtain. And they accordingly labour *per fas aut nefas,*[128] and have more or less their own particular interests to subserve. Both parties strive and have striven, with might and main, by every art, secretly as well as openly, to strike at the steady poise, the elevated flight, the beamy reputation of General Jackson. The Adams party divide themselves into two portions: one urges the superior claims of the civilian, in opposition to the military chief, the quiet of the closet, in preference to the dangers of the field, "and such conceits and vanities." The other portion takes a contrary course, and confounds the General's spiritual and political identity; they would argue him into a mere *abstraction* of Mr. Adams, who is, they contend, in all, but in *the* person,

> "The general's self, his council's consistory,
> His oracle, his prophet: his dear cousin"

As Hotspur says, "the Devil take such cozeners." [129] Now, the Crawford party go quite another way to work, and by the violence of their efforts completely overleap themselves. With them, the

General is a distinct, perceptible and hostile object. They acknowledge that to "frame of iron" he unites "a soul of fire." But then, like that devil Percy,[130] he generally kills some six or seven Scots at breakfast, washes his hands and cries "fie upon this quiet life!" General Jackson is, alternately a Nero and a Caesar; a Caligula and a Napoleon. According to Jesse Benton,[131] the civil and political career of the General has been one of accumulated horrors; and he concludes what, by the figure of *Ironia* may be called his *elegant phillipic,* with these portentous words: "It will be well for us, should we not, by the appearance of another *Caesar* in the history of republics, require yet another *Brutus* to wind up the scene!"[132] The said Jesse Benton being, I presume, especially reserved as the representative of this modern Brutus, this shadow of a philosophical regicide!

But I must leave these Parthians shooting at the sun their ineffectual arrows. When the *alternative* arrives, I should not hesitate to take the democratic candidate, Mr. Crawford, with his sober good sense and republican habits, in preference to his rival, Mr. Adams, with all his aristocracy of courts, and all the learning of the University of Leyden. The Treasurer [133] has less scholastic acquirements, but then he has a better knowledge of men and things, which, if he does not look at through the "spectacles of books," he perhaps observes more accurately and palpably, in the temper, real fitness, and consistency of our institutions.

If I have not taken Mr. Clay into the question, it is not that I do not highly appreciate his worth. His genius is peculiarly American, a combination of vast, but irregular powers. Sagacious in the smallest things, energetic to great ones, his views of our national policy, though opposed to our experience, are so beautiful in themselves, and supported with such candour, such eloquence, such a spirit of philanthropy, that we almost dread to come within the sphere of his fascination. But Mr. Clay's chance will not even carry him into the House of Representatives: and as his system of domestic policy [134] is at variance with the interest of the great majority of the people, they have never contemplated him as one among the probable *three.* Even if they had, I should oppose him, "not that I love Caesar less, but that I love Rome more." [135]

I now leave the trio (thank Heaven! no triumvirate) to the

chances of futurity. I am willing to rest my hopes upon a character that knows no disguise; a man who makes no promises for indirect bribery: who would not say the thing that is not, for the world's empire. A man of great practical knowledge, of rapid perception, of immense energy, of chivalric generosity. A man of the people; not more supported by the independent of the Republican party, than supported by the independent of all parties. A man of truth, *who would obtain "noble ends" by "noble means" and by no other.*

> "He would not flatter Neptune for his trident,
> Nor Jove, for his power to thunder." [136]

If Gen. Jackson become President of these United States, I anticipate a career of glory to my country. She has begun it, and what would stay her course, *he would remove.* Duplicity and adulation will be banished from her councils; talents and virtue will alone preside. Modest worth will be preferred to the noisy demagogue, *and guilt never escape punishment through ill-placed pity.* Ambition and success may spoil some men; but there is a peculiar, a rare intellectual character, in a few gifted individuals, which never *alters* but only *unfolds* its intrinsic excellencies. Few, indeed, whose minds are constructed of such costly materials, as was that of our lamented Lowndes.[137] Like the Pacific, it knew no storms; while its breadth touched the confines of either hemisphere, tinged and illumined with a rising and a setting sun. Few, whose souls are of such invulnerable mould as that of our Jackson. With him, ambition is virtue. The very atmosphere that surrounds him, would freeze the tempter

> "For he is constant as the Northern Star,
> Of whose true, fixt, and resting quality,
> There is no fellow in the firmament." [138]

With this, I conclude: That if, in these essays, I have succeeded in convincing the impartial reader of what is the true welfare of our country, and what the true characters of the candidates for the Presidency, I have succeeded in all that I proposed. I have no foes that I fear; no friends to favour. Too poor to possess influence over others, too proud to suffer it to be exercised over myself, I seek no other reward or pleasure but what I find in my *motives:*

> "JUSTITIA, *et mens sibi conscia recti.*" [139]

LXXI

Attacking the "Albany Regency," 1829-1832

Control of the Democratic Party in New York State had passed, before 1829, into the hands of a small group of party managers. These few men, led by Martin Van Buren,[140] William L. Marcy,[141] Azariah C. Flagg,[142] Silas Wright,[143] and Edwin Croswell,[144] were known under the name of the "Albany Regency."[145] Acting with almost complete arbitrariness, they determined party policy and directed the party's campaigns. They were by no means evil or self-seeking men; indeed, they were generally to be found on the side of reform, as that term was understood in the Jacksonian era. They fought against imprisonment for debt, to abolish which was one of the primary goals of the working men's section of the party. One of their aims was the extension of the suffrage; the Safety Fund Act of 1829 was one of their measures and they agitated for the Mechanics Lien Law.

Mordecai Manuel Noah, because of his political opposition to the upstate control of New York politics and his affiliation with the anti-Van Buren faction of Tammany, became tied up with the national opposition, within the Democratic Party, to the presidential ambitions of Martin Van Buren. Noah corresponded with Duff Green,[146] who was a leading advocate of the interests of John C. Calhoun, to prevent Van Buren from receiving Jackson's support. Their common antagonism to Van Buren did not, however, draw Noah away from his support of Jackson. Before the election of 1832, Noah announced a new paper, *The Evening Star*, which was to be pro-Jackson on the national scene and anti-Albany Regency in New York State. Letters from Duff Green to Noah, showing the tie-in between Noah's New York goals and those of Duff Green on the national scene, are printed below, together with an excerpt from the "prospectus" in which Noah announced his intention of publishing *The

Evening Star. Through these activities, Noah became the leading publicist of the anti-radical faction in the New York Democratic Party, tacitly joining forces with the followers of Henry Clay. Early in the correspondence between Duff Green and Noah, the former had advised the New York journalist not to let his conduct appear openly motivated by hostility to Martin Van Buren, and to consider carefully the degree to which it was safe to cooperate with Webb and the *Courier*,[147] representing an explicitly hostile viewpoint.

144. DUFF GREEN TO MORDECAI M. NOAH, 1829 [148]

Washington, April 21, 1829

It is now understood here that you and Swartwout [149] are acting in hostility to Mr. Van Buren and that the Courier have joined in support of Swartwout as the means of destroying Mr. V.B.'s influence. A little reflection must satisfy you that the President can not be induced to countenance any hostility to Mr. V.B. to appoint his own friends in prefference to those of Mr. V.B. is one thing and to appoint them in hostility to Mr. V.B. is another.

I do not see the propriety of your throwing yourself into this collision. If Mr. V. Buren does not sustain you against what he terms the party nominations he might nevertheless quietly acquiesce in your appointment as inspector if Mr. Ingham and the president express a wish to confer that office on you. Yet it is a question well worth your consideration how far it is *prudent* for you to act in any way that shall cause him to look on you as an enemy or to compell your friends to choose between you. . . .

All that you hear about division in the cabinet is not true. They have more pressing matters than the removals of a few unworthy men. Believe me that our strength consists in union I hope that I shall have some good news for you soon. Be prudent I am desirious to serve you but no man not even the President can controle *all* events. Stand upon your *own* claims and be careful to make no enemies. . . .   D. Green

145. DUFF GREEN TO
MORDECAI M. NOAH, 1830 [150]

Washington 24th March 1830

M. M. Noah Esq
New York

Dear Sir. . . . Your letter was not received until this morning.
You will see from the Telegraph of today that Webbs high authority
like himself is a little given to lying. I understand Mr Webb & those
who play the wires for him. I have no wish to hurt a hair of Mr
Van Buren head, so far from it I would save him from the follies
of his imprudent friends. As to Genl. Jackson, my answer to Webb
abuce of Saturday last is that President was consulted & approved
of my article of 16th before it went to press. You ask what is the
matter? The only difficulty which we have to encounter arises from
the impression so industrious circulated by Webb & other that Mr
Van Buren is the candidate of the administration. The people of
this country cannot beleive it respectful to Genl. Jackson that the
friends of one of his cabinet should at the same speak of him &
secretary of State as candidates. No one can beleive that Mr Van
Buren is sincere in the beleif that Genl. Jackson will be a candidate
whilst his friends are taking so much paines push his fortunes. It
is beleived that there are persons near the president who are industriously striving to make the President believe that Mr Calhoun is
his enemy & Mr Webb is the organ for the purposes of discord. As
to Webb I have spard him in mercy & in kindness to you, but I
advise you my dear sir to get your affairs with him in good train
because if the scoundrel dare attact me again I will riddle his
blankett. I know more of him than he suspects, & I will not hesitate
to give the facts to the world which will not onley destroy the
character of his paper but cannot fail to provoke the contempt of
every honest & honerable man.

The Senate are busily at work they are daily disposing of the
nominations, they are now engaged, as is understood on the treasury nominations & will of course in a few days reach your;& our
friend Swartwouts. Mr Calhoun is ardently the friend of both &

he can do more to serve you than any one else. Yet there are deep under curents, he did for a time entertane grat fear for the collector but I now hope that he is safe. This letter may contain too much feeling, but who situated as I am would not feel, if such a man as Webb could excite a suspicion with such men as your are.

Your friend   D. Green [151]

146. PROSPECTUS FOR "THE EVENING STAR," 1833 [152]

Hitherto, New-York politics have been a "by-word and reproach;" our high-toned, manly, and open-hearted brethren of the south did not understand us; our hardy and industrious fellow citizens of the east did not choose to confide in us; the west could not fashion itself to our political systems; all admired us; few imitated us; and none feared us. A state so populous, so gigantic, so wealthy, equal nearly, in numbers and resources, to the aggregate of all the old continental states, has no more influence, probably not as much, as states with one third of our population and resources. All the various parties which have hitherto existed, and do now exist, in this state, have been organized upon a contracted and exclusive basis. It has always been the besetting sin of this state, to have *idols,* before which, like the heathens of old, we prostrate ourselves. We have, in a population of two millions, for ever, our eye on *one* man, and we make that man our "favourite," toast him, swear by him, follow his directions, and make him our oracle and leader. It is in this exclusive and fickle spirit that we become clanish, and place the power of the state to the private credit and political speculation of a few selfish individuals. Where are the great men of the state of New-York? Where is the learning, the talent, the patriotism, and integrity of those who inhabit our fifty-six populous counties? Can any one name our great men? Are they known? Are they before the people, ready to serve their country with ability and fidelity? We *have* the men, we *have* the *worth,* and the talent, but it is all "cribbed, cabined, and confined." Unless it belongs to the "initiated," and is recognised by that select few, claiming to rule the destinies of this state, talent dare not peep from its hiding place, without being cuffed down. If men of judgment and integrity claim advancement, it must be secured by negotiation, and a surrender of manly independence. It must be obtained by consultation, and understanding, not with the great body of the party, but with the cabinet of leaders, which claim to hold that party in the palm of their hands.

The Albany regency, so called, and charged with the exercise of this proscriptive system, begins to attract general attention, not only from the prodigious power assumed and actually held by that irresponsible body, but from the fact, that what hitherto has been limited to the boundaries of this state, begins now to be felt in the general government; and, like the gradual progress of an epidemic, has broke out in several other states, and is likely to spread its deadly influence over the fairest portion of the empire. What is this regency? Who composes it? How is it organized and sustained? are questions very generally asked, and must now be answered. The Albany regency is a confederacy of persons, nearly all holding offices under the state government, somewhat masonic as to the confidential nature of their operations, though more limited in numbers than the fraternity. This regency, a self-constituted body, of probably less than a dozen persons, are men of character in private life, and of cleverness and address as politicians.

After a struggle of some years to obtain the ascendency in the state, the democratic party found it necessary to organize committees in the several counties, which committees, were to call meetings, get up conventions, make nominations of candidates for elective offices, publish addresses, and take care of the political concerns intrusted to them in their several counties. Albany being the seat of government, and all important political projects consummated at that place, the committee gradually extended their influence, and curtailed their numbers, and from being special in their powers, they soon became general in their operations, mingled in legislation, decided what bills should, or should not pass, took upon themselves to designate the speaker, and other officers of the assembly, obtained an influence in the choice of committees, decided what banks should, or should not be chartered, who should or should not be nominated to office by the Executive, and, in short, by address, perseverance, boldness, and threats of political denunciations against all who presumed to question their infallibility, became so powerful, and so tyrannical, that submission to their des-

potic sway was deemed inevitable. Strengthened by the cooperation
of the base, and the apprehensions of the timid, the Albany regency
amplified and extended their plans of operation, appointed agents
in the several towns and counties in the state, obtained the control
of banks and presses, mingled boldly in the nominations of members
of Congress, state senators, and members of assembly, decided who
should, or who should not be put in nomination; and what could
not be carried by persuasion, was driven through by bringing the
weight of party obligations to bear upon the subject. It will be
readily imagined, that by this gradual usurpation and consolidation
of power, the cabinet of office holders at Albany have thrown a
chain over the whole state, as galling and oppressive as any slavery
that has ever been submitted to by freemen. In this city, once free
from their influence, all their agents are known, and known to be
as servile as the serfs of Russia. No matter how pure the character,
how consistent the politics, how faithful the labours of a man may
have been, if he exhibits an atom of opposition to their will, he is
proscribed by this star chamber confederacy, and the presses under
its control are ordered to assail and hunt him down; and the worst
feature of this unholy league is in the fact, that the members composing it are avaricious stock jobbers, making every thing subservient to their private interest. It cannot be possible, that such an
unholy combination can much longer oppress the people of this
state, and I am convinced, that in the new political organization,
the great and triumphant party of this state hereafter will be the
anti-Regency Party, which is the true Republican and Liberal party,
calculated to give freedom to the people, to open the doors of promotion to the honest and talented, to put down faction, and de-
throne oppression. My zealous co-operation in this patriotic reform
will not be wanting; the regency and myself have been well acquainted for many years, but the dangers which now threaten the
general government, by the rapid and determined march of this
influence, admit of no further delay in arresting the evil. If the
regency penetrate the strongholds of the general government, this
country will be ruled from Albany.

Let me now come nearer home, to our own city, which constitutes
a tenth part of the population of the state, and has, for the last
fifteen years, decided, by its great majorities, every severely con-

tested election. In the course of my political labours and experience, I have seen many singular changes and transmutations, and have been compelled, by the force of party discipline, to endorse men to-day, who, apparently, but yesterday, were our opponents at the polls; and am now told, that certain doctrines we uniformly rejected as unsound, are, at this juncture, peculiarly safe and proper. The deep-seated popularity of Andrew Jackson was the signal of a general rush to Tammany Hall of men of all parties; and among the leaders who now give directions in our own wigwam, and prescribe terms to us in our own head quarters, are many federalists of the old school, who never, until this presidential election, ventured within the portals of that venerable mansion, and who are determined to hold possession of the ground, as if their conversion had been spiritual and miraculous. If I go over to Masonic Hall, I am sure to find, among the reputed "enemy," many sound, inflexible old republicans, who stood by their country during the late war, and stood almost alone in defence of free principles. I am told by these men, that they have been driven out of Tammany Hall, that they were proscribed, because they refused to follow leaders, or surrender the power of the party to the management of selfish individuals. We are too exclusive, and too proscriptive. We do not keep up with the change of times, and the claims of new generations. We cannot expect that a powerful party of young men, ardent, talented, and republican, will consent to submit to the control of individuals who have held undisputed sway for the last thirty years, and who are still determined, under every encouragement from the Albany regency, to maintain the power they have so long enjoyed. The time has arrived for the exercise of justice and liberality, when the doors of Tammany Hall should be thrown open freely to every republican, who agrees with us on principle, though he may differ with us about men. A crisis has now arrived, when we require a *union of honest men*, professing republican doctrines, more particularly to meet that important, delicate, and dangerous question connected with the presidential election. I am aware that, on this subject, there is a desire not to agitate the question at the present time, in order that angry passions may subside, and the present chief magistrate may be allowed an opportunity to carry into effect all the objects and intentions of promoting the public good. It is not, however, to be disguised, that there is an uneasy and fretful suspicion prevailing in the public mind, that management and address are to be substituted in the choice of a president, for the free, unbiased, and collected wisdom of the people. There is an apprehension widely afloat, that if the subject is untouched for two years, it will then be too late to collect and organize public opinion. "The deed will be done." The cannon will have been planted, and pointed in every direction, and the line of succession as distinctly marked, and to be followed with a submission as direct and abject as that which prevails in the monarchies of Europe. Removals will be made, and offices filled, with reference solely to this object. Great public measures, having in view the settlement of important subjects, connected with the prosperity and safety of the Union, will be subjected to the test of this "line of succession," and the president will be made at Albany, and not by the people throughout the United States. Here is the danger, the real danger, the true cause of our national troubles. I am quite certain, that Andrew Jackson will never, but with his life, abandon the post which the people has assigned to him, nor have I any reason to believe that he will ever directly interfere with the freemen of this country in the choice of his successor. But all our presidents have had some indirect agency in promoting the election of a favourite friend. This may have been done with patriotic and justifiable motives, but the general government is now so powerful, and its patronage so extensive, that the practice has become dangerous in the extreme, and every citizen in office may be made to feel that his safety depends not on his good conduct, but on his opinions relative to the succession; and thus we shall degenerate into servile, obedient, and dependent vassals and followers of power. It is unnecessary, at this time, to say who should be the candidate of the republican party for the next presidency, but it is essential that no time should be lost in showing who should *not* be the man. We stand on the crater of a volcano, and on the result of the next election our national safety depends. We must have peace in our domicile. No man must be permitted to intrigue himself into that station. The office must "not be sought for:" and public services, high and commanding talents, enlarged views of public policy, settled and well known opinions on cardinal points, general and acknowledged popularity, must be the passports to that high and important trust, instead of management, and the mere force of party discipline. . . .

In proportion to the real power of this state is the devotion and patriotism of the people. Whatever political dissentions we may have amongst ourselves, they have never until the present time, been pressed upon the nation, or the nation been made to feel the effects of our peculiar plans of state government. Secure in the enjoyment of our own internal prosperity, and in the vast patronage and power of the state government, desirous of affording a proper and necessary support to the general administration, the people of the state of New-York will never dictate to our sister states, or press any candidate of our own, whom the partiality of friends, or the hopes of expectants, may consider and call "a favourite son." We have many "favourite sons;" men of undoubted worth and ample talent; men of retiring habits and deserved popularity; men who are true to democratic principles, for the sake of those principles alone; men who have stood by the party, and the supporters of the party; men whose opinions on every subject are fearlessly and candidly avowed. We throw them all into the common scale, leaving the freemen of this country to select their candidate from any section they see fit. The president of the United States must be the choice of the nation, not of a state; and the democracy of New-York, will never hesitate to support the most worthy, meritorious, and popular candidate, no matter from what district of country he may come. How parties may organize on this important subject, what coalitions may grow out of sectional views and special interests, who of the old federal party is to be advanced, or the old democratic party proscribed, cannot as yet be clearly defined.

LXXII

The Nullification Controversy,
1832-1833

The two letters from Chapman Levy [153] of Camden, South Carolina to Joel Poinsett [154] report Levy's exertions in the struggle of
supporters of the Union against those hotheaded Carolinians who
favored unilateral nullification of federal tariff law even if that
course meant secession. Levy was one of the valiant supporters of
the administration of Andrew Jackson.[155] Jackson appreciated the
sincerity of Levy's support.[156] The first of the letters reports Levy's
readiness to bear a large part of the costs of having Jackson's proclamation against nullification printed and distributed in his district.
The second letter shows that an important part of the planter class
was still for the Union, suggesting that nullification was a movement
led by the merchant group, which was most affected by the Tariff
Acts of the Jacksonian era.

147. CHAPMAN LEVY TO JOEL POINSETT, 1832 [157]

Camden 22d. Decr. 1832

Dear Sir

Our members have returned from Columbia [158] & nothing has
been done to have the president's Proclamation printed for Circulation amongst the People. I have a Balance of about twenty Six
Dollars of the printing fund and upon this fund I have ordered 3000
printed by Landrun which will cost about $60. The balance I will
make up if no otherwise out of my own Purse. Five hundred of
those I will order Doct: Landrun to send to Edgfield. The Balance
I will distribute as follows Fairfield 1000. Marlborough 500. Kershaw 250. Sumter 500. A half Sheet will contain one Proclamation
and I put them in that form so that I can send them well wrapped

in small Bundles as News Papers. Barnwell & the Districts below and Marion and the Districts below as well as Abbeville ought to be Supplied.

I have written to Pendleton to Mr. Maverick [159] urging upon him the propriety of Supplying his District. He is a Staunch Union man and very wealthy, but I have little hopes of his doing much, as I appealed to him in the Strongest Terms last Spring & Summer, to furnish funds to supply his District. He sent me but twenty Dollars for which I sent him about thirty Dollars worth of extra News Papers with Select matter in them.

I think 4000 Proclamations exclusive of what will be printed in Columbia by Landrun will be Sufficient. Landrun will publish them for four Cents a Sheet each Sheet to contain two: That is one on each half Sheet.

I shall write to day to Euart of Columbia and to Col: Beaty of York urging them to Supply York, Richland & Lexington. I am in hopes in two Weeks to report good news to you. Our Chairman Col: Carter has not made a move. He has not organized a Committee or done one act. I have invited a meeting at Camden of the Delegates from Lancaster, Chesterfield, Darlington, Kershaw & Sumter Districts all contiguous so as to devise the best means to preserve the Country from Strife. Harmony amongst the people is to be preserved by the best means that our united Councels can devise.

Very respectfully   Yours &c.   C Levy

Joel A. Poinsett Esqr.

148. CHAPMAN LEVY TO JOEL POINSETT, 1833 [160]

Camden 25th. Feby. 1833

Dear Sir

I am now writing in my Chamber where I have been Confined for the last week with a Blister 8 Inches by 7 on my Chest. It is the third attack I have had of that provoking disease the Influenza or rather two relapses; for the last return of it as well as the former was brought on by addressing a meeting of the People, the last time on Saturday last a Week when I was not quite recovered. Talking now for 10 minutes irritates my Lungs. In health I can speak to a Congregation of 1000 for 4 Hours without inconvenience and without touching Water or any other Fluid. I recd. a Letter from Genl Blair [161] enclosing one from McDuffie [162] giving the lye to the Report contained in the Letter enclosed to you. Genl Blair had never any conversation with McDuffie on the Subject nor Shewn him any of my Letters nor had McDuffie written any thing of the kind to any person. How fertile are the Nullifyers in fabrication: But this is not new to us.

I have been so much indisposed since my return from Charleston that I have not been as useful as I desired.

On Sunday last a week I commenced an organization for Upper Salem Sumt: Dist: Bishopville head quarters. This is the East No. East part of Sumter bordering on Kershaw and Darlington. I think we will muster at least 100 there. On Saturday last a week a meeting was held at my Instance at Liberty Hill a Point in this District not organized and Fifty expected to attend. The People are ready & willing there but I was too unwell to go from my Plantation there 25 Miles. There was a meeting of one of the organized associations within 3 Miles of me to which I Ventured and address'd the People and in the evening went 6 Miles further on towards upper Salem to meet a part of the People of that Section on next day Sunday. My indisposition became so great next day that I could with difficulty get home on Monday when I was Bled, Blistered & took active medicine. I have given these facts as an excuse for not progressing as fully as I desired and you expected. But Sir be assured that my task is an arduous one not having any assistance from any one of our public men here and this entire District devolving on me unassisted.

In reply to your enquiry as to the numbers which may be obtained to attend the Union Convention, I can give you but little information being so much confined of late.

The Convention will be held at the most inconvenient time in the year. All the Idlers, Vagabounds & Dandies who inhabit Cities and live by their wits belong to the nullifyers. Our People are the Substantial yeomanry of the Country who in the latter part of March & in April are pitching their crops for the year. It is the busy planting Season & the success of the Labours of the whole year materially depend on the efforts in those months to get a good start. I may possibly muster Twenty from my District who will attend on paying their expences for they cannot afford it themselves for they will have to employ Some one to attend for them at home. Another difficulty is that the impression is gone forth that the Nullifyers have backed out & will do nothing and you cannot easily persuade people of the necessity of our keeping up our attitude. I have only guessed at the number I can get. All I can say is I will make all due exertions & if that is done throughout the State we may get a thousand there, especially if their expences are paid. I know that very many who attended our last Convention are what are called good comfortable livers but have families of Children to raise and educate and cannot afford to spend twenty Dollars a year on any other matter than necessary expences. If it is important you should press it on our people throught the State. If the people believed it essential, to the Cause of the Union & that there was a necessity for it they would make any Sacrifice; but believing as they now do that nullification is in its last agonies it will be difficult to get them to make the sacrifice of time at this important period of the year. Besides you have given a very short notice. Next week I attend Chesterfield Court, The week after the State convention which meets on the 11th. Excuse this incoherent Scrawl as I am in reality more a Subject for my bed at this moment than the writing desk.

Pray let me hear from you immediately and address your Letter to Chesterfield Court House where I expect to be on Monday next, develope fully your Views as none but the initiated can know its contents & very few of them.

Yours &c. C Levy

M[aybe] You perceive an exagerated account of the turn out of Volunteers in favour of nullification in Sumter. Believe it not. The Trick they play off throughout the State is to say to the Regiments: "Those who are friends to "South Carolina forward march." By this means they get out all parties. They have also swelled their lists of Volunteers by saying that there will be no fighting but is is necessary for every Nullifyer to Shew they are true to the faith by setting down their names. Calhoun passed thro' Camden on his way to congress, & reported as he went there was no danger of fighting, all would be Settled. Before that they could not muster twenty five Volunteers. If a conflict becomes necessary we will then see backing out.   C.L.

Joel R. Poinsett Esqr.
Charleston So. Cara.

LXXIII

Support of
President Van Buren, 1837

Martin Van Buren, despite his aristocratic birth, was probably the most radically democratic politician to have held the presidency of the United States. In his thinking, many of the inchoate and ill-defined trends of Jacksonian democracy were brought into a systematic whole. Central to his political thought was the struggle to achieve in practice the full rights that were held in theory by the American people. His economic program, related to the fight for popular rights, centered in the control of speculative tendencies in the economy. Van Buren was a "hard money" man, fighting always the inflationary effect of paper currency.[163]

We have seen [164] that Mordecai Noah was active in attacking Van Buren as a member of the "Albany Regency." In the following letter, we find another Jewish citizen of New York, Benjamin F. Hart,[165] giving expression to his enthusiastic support of Van Buren's program, as set forth in the President's 1837 message to Congress.

149. BENJAMIN F. HART TO
MARTIN VAN BUREN, 1837 [166]

New York September 6th 1837.

President Van Buren,
Highly Esteemed Sir,

Permit an humble friend (who feels tenacious of the rights of his fellow-citizens) after the perusal of your message to Congress, to return to you my most heartfelt and undisguised *gratitude* for the principles inculcated, and for the Simple & pure doctrines (which throbbed in the breasts of our Revolutionary forefathers) declared in this, one, of the purest documents ever emanating from the hand of the Executive. I rejoice that I live under them and that Martin Van Buren dare put them forth in the face of a proud aristocracy, and in the gloomy days of Panic & Presure. I fervently pray Heaven that his choicest blessings may crown your efforts in the herculean task at the helm of Government.

It is fortunate indeed for the people that you are at this time their executive officer and dare declare the pure & patriotic principles of the revolution at the formation of the Constitution in its Simplicity. and particularly for the welfare of the poor but honest labouring man. Our plain simple Federal form of Government as laid down in the Constitution, I see will now be brought back in its purity if Congress embrace your views. and then with watchful vigilence our Government will be founded on a Rock which no man or Set of Men through Sinister motives can overthrow.

The Collection & Care of the revenue in Gold & Silver, the disbursement of the same under the immediate Eye of the Executive is the only true principle that can be adopted in our Government, and the constant receipt and payment of those funds in Specie will be like a living spring of water or the dews of heaven to the American people. It will prevent overtrading and Speculation, and our Nation will evade that Mushroom groth which has Sprung up amongst us, give Stability to Commerce and commercial transactions, we Shall be permanently the most happy and flourishing government on earth.

There is not one word of the Message but I can see clearly the work of Sagacity, wisdom & patriotism. It is a document thousands will rejoicingly peruse, and you will witness the fruits of your disinterested patriotism in the firm and honest support of the Yeomanry, laboring, & Mechanical interests of our Country, Sustaining on this trying occasion triumphantly Your principles in every particular.

You would rejoice to witness the honest gratulations of your real friends here on reading your message—there is no fear but that you will be proudly sustained and when the time arrives for action depend on it that Democracy will rally round your Standard. May God long preserve you for future usefulness to our Country, and bless you with his choisest blessing, is the Sincere prayer of   Yours with High respect   Benjamin F. Hart

Martin Van Buren
President of the U. States

N.B. I shall visit Washington during the present Month, and you must gratify an humble citizen with a cordial Shake of the hand. It shall be the shake of a friend.

LXXIV

Party Struggles in
the New South, 1836-1838

Chapman Levy, whose services to the Democratic Party in South
Carolina have already been noted,[167] was later exceedingly active
as a Democratic partisan in the new states of Alabama and Mississippi. The Democratic Party had not yet achieved the strangle hold
on Southern politics that it was later to have. Indeed, in the late
1830s, the Democratic Party was still a fairly well balanced alliance
of northern, southern, and western factions, where the southern
interest was chiefly that of the yeomen and small planters. At the
same time, the Whig Party, though more heterogeneous, was supported in the South by the large cotton planters, who were dominant figures in Alabama and Mississippi, the sugar planters of Loui-
siana, and the largest merchants of the port cities. The two letters
below reveal the devotion with which Levy plunged into the task
of winning the still semi-frontier country of Alabama and Mississippi to the Democratic cause in the Presidential election year of
1836, when the Democrats won with Van Buren, and the "off year"
of 1838.

150. CHAPMAN LEVY TO
MARTIN VAN BUREN, 1836 [168]

Pickensville Alabama 6th Jany. 1836

Dear Sir

I am not known to you personally but am no less your Political
friend and my absence from my residence (Noxubee County Mississippi) during last Summer was very Seriously felt by the party.

I arrived at home one day before the Election and just in time to attend the most doubtful poll in the County and thereby secure the Election of a Representative who is your decided political friend. I reside within a Mile of the Alabama line and design operating in Pickens County Alabama (one of the most populous Counties in that State) as thoroughly as in my own State. In May next I shall commence my peregrinations and address the people at all Points in Pickens County as well as in this County (Noxubee Miss) and those adjacent. I receive any Communications addressed to Pickensville Alabama that being the nearest Post office. My object in writing is to ask information as we are in this County destitute of the journals of Congress. Please therefore to inform me whether you were in Congress at the period of the discussion of the Missouri Question, and if you were how did you Vote on that question. A certified Copy of the Journals on that Subject would greatly aid my purpose and if you were not then a Member a Certificate of that fact from the Clerk of the Senate would be of Service. You are aware that your opponents have reduced the propagation of falsehood to a System and that is the Subject wielded most to your disadvantage in this whole range of Country. Pickens will Vote between 16 & 17 hundred Votes and it is worth attending to, Besides the Votes of Noxubee & the adjacent Counties.

As you do not know me I beg leave to refer you to Governor Manning [169] who represents the District where I resided in So. Caro. untill within the two last years. Col: Claiborne [170] knows me by Character but Mr. Manning can inform you more fully whether I am capable of aiding the Cause to which I attach myself. Your Interest requires that I should be very speedily informed on this Subject. Altho I shall not enter the field of public discussion untill May I shall in the mean time not be Idle. I operated in the Elections of 1834 on the very ground I intend to travel over at the next Election and with entire success, beating our opponents in Pickens County upwards of 500 Votes, altho supporting the most personally unpopular Candidate. This Summer during my absence the Whig Candidates were elected. I can however give you the assurance that that County will be regenerated and I may if I have time extend my operations into Tuscalousa County. My plan of operation is to invite free discussion at the same meetings and have uniformly

Succeeded in that way. Pray Sir do not neglect this application as immediate use can be made of the information I desire.

Respectfully   Your Obedt Sevt.   C Levy

Hnble Martin Van Buren

151. CHAPMAN LEVY TO JOEL POINSETT, 1838 [171]

Columbus Mis: 8 Novr. 1838

Dear Sir

I arrived here two days past and was sorry to find we have been beaten in the several elections recently held in this county & in Noxubee & Kemper two of the Chactaw Counties which we claimed as our own. The enemy have for two years past had the field to themselves. Twice has Prentice taken the Circuit of the State unopposed & the People have heard but one side. This County holds a powerful influence on the Chactaw Counties and we have no one man here nor in the Chactaw Counties nearest to it who has the Talent and Zeal to harangue the People & make a great effort in the Cause. In Noxubee the County I formerly lived in Genl Grant was beaten by five Votes being the first triumph of the opposition in that County.

But let me assure you that the Cause is not hopeless. The Chactaw Counties have heretofore saved the democratic party & altho this retrograde in political sentiment has appeared in the above named Counties as well as others in the Chactaw Cession, yet all will be well. They will save the Party again. All the action has been on the other side. Governor Mc.Nutt [172] has been the only man of reasonable talent who has taken the Circuit of the State & addressed the people in favour of democracy. He is by no means a Strong man. So says our most judicious friends.

I now say to you the cause shall not be neglected within my range of Country so far as I have any Share of Capacity.

On yesterday I gave a Challenge to the man who they rank here as their Strong man to meet me at this place in free debate and the Challenge is accepted. I am on my way home and am to find the time on my arrival. there.

I have not addressed the people here since 1834 when I prostrated nullification.

There will be an immense concourse attend the debate. Since 1834 there has been a large accession here of Yankee merchants, and Georgia Nullifyers and amongst them several very *Talented Lawyers,* who are young, active and enthusiastic. They are all Whigs & have done much mischief.

The Struggle here will be a desperate one. The moment I arrived our democratic friends made strong appeals to me for help which induced me to give the Challenge.

I have no doubt of the result and that next November will see Mis: regenerated and fully restored to the democratic family.

I very much hope Mr. Holt [173] will turn out in lower Mis: Mr. Barton [174] will do his duty in the Chickasaw Country. I shall also visit as many of those counties as I can. But I will most specially attend to the Chactaw Country. I will have to ride 100 miles to this place to attend the debate here.

I have no kind of doubt whatever of entirely restoring the Chactaw Country. I know the Character of the People and the Talent opposed to me, and have discovered by the retrograde movements in Chactaw that the people must be attended to. I left the Political field in 36 and in the two years my political flock have squandered. New questions have arisen and new issues presented & the people want new information. Pickens County Alabama which now votes between 18 & 19 hundred has utterly gone over to Whigism. It is a county which in 1834 I rescued from the Nullifyers who had possession of it. We then beat them between 5 & 6 hundred votes. All their professional men are Nullifyers and Whigs & so are most of their merchants. I have arranged to address the People there at one Precinct before I leave here for Carolina. If I can by [any] possibility so arrange I will appoint for several precincts. I find myself fully again fully on the Political field, which I would most anxiously have avoided, had it not been apparent to me that our country at this time requires the exertions of every friend to our free institutions. I have been pressed again to accept the Democratic Nomination for Congress; But have again put my express negative on it. I am solicitous that Mr. Van Buren should not deem the cause hopeless in Mis:

The Battle has been fought principally on one side, and let him be assured that in the next Presidential Canvass he will carry Mis; most triumphantly.

Our Press in this place is very Poorly & injudiciously conducted. It is of no service to us altho the Editors who are also Proprietors are zealous in the Cause. They have some Tact in writing but they have no Talent to discuss the great political questions which now divide the Union.

They are obstinately bent on their own mode of conducting the controversy & will not republish the able Speeches which have been delivered by democratic orators. It would not do to establish a rival Press & we must bear the inconvenience.

I most sincerely regret the resignation of Judge Trotter.[175] It arose in consequence of the election of Whigs to the Legislature, in this & some other Counties who had Vacancies to fill occasioned by the resignation or death of Democratic members. Mis: is now in a false position but she will right herself.

I remain most truly Yours &c.   C. Levy [176]

P.S. I start to night for Kosciusko.

(2d. part of my Letter)

The Rivers are doun & paper Scarce here & I can only communicate in Scraps.

Another Piece of information I want to use in public debate.

Mr. Dent of Washington I think in my hearing related a decision of the Federal Court which was made in Washington & confirmed by the Supreme Court. It is highly important as a Set off against Chief Justice Marshalls & the Supreme Court decission on the Constitutionality of the U S. Bank. It will shew what authority is due to decissions by that tribunal, involving the principles which bear on Southern rights. I can wield it to good effect as an answer to the Judicial decission on the Bank question. The Case was this. A Gentleman of Virginia married a Lady in Washington who disliking her Virginia residence returned to Washington & there took up her abode. The good natured man let some seven negroes accompany her to wait on her but never surrendered by writing a settlement of any kind the Title to the Negroes. She made a will emancipating the negroes. He reclaimed them after her death and the Court of the District of Columbia by their decission Sustained their emancipation under the will; and that decission was confirmed by the Supreme Court, *Chief Justice Marshall* on the Bench. I want the *History* and *facts* and *name* of that Case with the decission of the Court, together with a reference to the Book of Reports. But as Books are scarce here I want a detailed Statement of the facts and the decission & name of the Parties.[177]

I know what is good material for the Peoples ears and I know you can speedily furnish me with this in a form in which I can use it.

C Levy

P.S. direct to Louisville Winston Cty. Mis:

LXXV

Democratic Prospects
in Florida, 1839

At the time when David Levy [178] presented the memorandum printed below to President Van Buren, Florida was about to change its status from that of a territory to that of a state. Its conditions were still largely those of a frontier region,[179] and the directions of its later development were still undetermined. Levy's wise suggestions asked that his party, the Democratic Party, should take an active role in leading the new state toward the future, even though winning the new state was not essential to immediate partisan aims. Levy urged his party to become a bulwark against speculative trends in Florida; land speculation, particularly in town sites, was already rampant.[180] Banking interests were already strong. These were forces against which the Democratic Party should fight. He pointed to various difficulties in the political organization of a new state, and suggested that the Democratic Party should build its organization around newcomers to the state, who were free from the ingrained thought habits of the territorial settlers. The memorandum reveals Levy's political shrewdness and his understanding of the economic and political conditions of Florida.

152. MEMORANDUM ON FLORIDA, 1839 [181]

Brief remarks concerning the Democratic cause in Florida, with a suggestion, respectfully submitted to the consideration of the President.

Florida is on the eve of taking her place among the States of the Union.

The administration under the auspices of which she is to be introduced owes to the Party of which it is the head, that so far as its influence is available she should take rank in the Union, as a *Democratic State.*

The future complexion of her politics will depend very much upon the direction given to them in the Start.

The Administration has it now in its power to give the proper impulse.

The new State must take part in the general politics *immediately* upon her admission. It is therefore of the *highest importance* that there should be full preparatory organization of the Democratic party for the strugle that will arise in the selection of the *first Senators and representative,* and the arrangement of her domestic Government.

Democracy rest[s] for its success upon abstract truth and disinterestedness of purpose. The progress of truth is slow. The opposition is sustained by the quickening principle of *Selfishness* & is therefore energetic and industrious in its action, and being based upon error, delights, like all other Factions, in suddenness and rapidity of movement. Upon the instant emergency it has the advantage. It is by slow approaches only that democratic truth subdues it. *If we go into the Union then unprepared, the Democratic party must fail.*

The *People* of Florida are in the main *radically* Democratic, but like all other people are liable to be decieved and lead off to false issues. With a proper direction they could be arranged almost *en masse* under the Democratic banner.

To the establishment of a Democratic party there, great obstacles exist

1st The people have been so long unused to look to general politics as a subject of concernment that it requires time and trouble to arouse them to attention and exertion.

The traces of their former political associations have become so much obliterated that new impressions must be made.

2ndly There is a great want of *leaders.* The disregard of all political landmarks in the legislation of a Territory operates as an invitation to reckless & unprincipled *speculators.* An abundant host of these have been attracted to Florida. These speculators have originated schemes which offering allurements of profit and power have drawn into their embraces all the fortune seeking or ambitious adventurers who constitute a large share of the emigrants to a new country. Thus the most intelligent and active of her citizens have become corrupted and gradually entangled in interests and associations altogether at variance with democratic principles and purity, *and are unfitted to serve as leaders to the honest laboring classes.*

3rdly Fearful influences are at work, which are spreading corruption through the country, and are eminently hostile to Democratic ascendancy and destructive of democratic principle.

Among the sources of these may be reckoned,

Three great Banking Monsters, one located in each District, the charachter & history of which institutions, and the connexion which in [   ] have with them would afford a clue to much that is mysterious in our politics.

The great land speculations that are on foot. In Middle Florida the vacant public lands have been mostly taken up on speculation by means of Bank facilities. In east Florida the public lands are all claimed under Yazoo grants.[182] The evil resulting is that to establish these *claims* in the latter district corrupt associations and conspiracies are necessary; and in the case of *both* districts the game is blocked upon that sort of emigration that would fill up the ranks of Democracy.

Town making Speculations which require the forcing aid of vicious and special legislation.

Innumerable Stock Companies &c &c &c

The peculiar and unusual interest which the corporate institutions of Florida have in opposing a democratic organization that would lead to reform, may be here mentioned. The charters are so shaped that they may bank altogether upon the public credit, *without any capital of their own!* They have by means of the immense scope of this chartered capital, & their extraordinary priveleges, *a complete monopoly* of the banking business for the next fifty years. Both these positions can be demonstrated beyond dispute. Besides, they have paid no *bonus* whatever, and are subject to no *tax* of any consequence. In the case of the Life Ins. & Trust Co. managed by Mr Lot Clark there is a still further extraneous cause impelling it to exertion in the struggle for political power, to wit its connection with a vast land scheme, the Hackley grant.[183]

4thly Another great obstacle in the way of democratic organization consists in the want of *inducements* sufficiently stimulating with the generality of the people to bring them forward in the cause. The banks and other corrupt associations have a direct pecuniary interest in the preservation of power to themselves. They can afford to spend time in politics. Politics is a necessary branch of their *business,* depending as they do upon corrupt legislation for the means of living without labor. They can afford to *pay* for electioneerers, and do it. Their members and favorites can spend their time *profitably* in active political warfare, and they have a strong incentive to spend both time and means in the destruction of all who attempt a demonstration in favor of democratic reform, and who cannot be corrupted. On the other hand, the laboring democrat who exerts himself in the cause, not only suffers pecuniary loss by the time abstracted from his regular occupation, but is immediately exposed to the deadly assault of the money power. A consciousness of disinterested service to the country is his only reward for the sacrifices he must incur, and the dangers of an exposure to the vengeance of the corporations and aristocratic classes. Ambition of place cannot be gratified for the people have no high offices to give, and pecuniary advantage is out of the question, for it is all on the other side. An effort is making to establish a democratic Party in Florida. For this no credit is claimed with the Administration; we are adventuring only in one [   ]. What we have done towards this end, I will not trouble the President with. We do not struggle for *power,* but for the *cause,* and we only ask *aid.*

My proposal is this, That to form a nucleus to the Democratic Party, afford leaders and infuse vigor into its organization *all the offices in Florida, from highest to lowest,* should be immediately filled with active thoroughgoing democrats mostly from the states. I should even say all from abroad, but some of the offices would be too small to induce persons to remove to Florida and some few selections of influential Floridians will be necessary to keep the people in humor.

In making the selections from abroad persons should be taken from such of the different states as have furnished most of the emigrants, that they may gather around them their respective clans. They should be persons too of a *stern* democracy, that they may not be seduced when they reach there, and who are well versed in the *tactics* of party, in which particular we are chiefly defective.

In aid of this the passage of the *Benton bill* would furnish us recruits for the rank and file *of the Party*.

In submitting the foregoing hasty and crude remarks I am guilty of a boldness which a conscious propriety of motive, and a cordial political interest in the present Administration alone justify to myself. Florida *may* be in the Union in time for the Presidential canvass, (tho' this may depend upon the application of Wisconsin), she *must* however be in before the next term of the present Admn will have expired. I wish her to come in as she should, *purely* democratic.

I charge that there is a large and powerful party in Florida which is secretly laying the basis of a general Whig party there. That their scheme is to veil their purpose till they are forced to unmask, but in the mean time to impress the public mind with sentiment, and create a *tone* of feeling, that will prepare the people to follow them off against the measures of the Administration when the time comes. This charge I could experience no difficulty in *proving*, for their movements are too palpable to those of us at home who watch the current of events.

The vote of Florida is not necessary to Mr Van Buren's success, therefore he can with a more evident disinterestedness render a service to Democracy and to human rights by using his power to establish a most pure party in Florida, that shall be a model to the rest of the Country. Let him take Florida under his charge, it affords a fine field for the exercise of his devotion to popular rights, and in the fruits of his attention give occasion to be gratefully remembered as a benefactor. Without the aid which the Government can bring to the cause, the people will be powerless and the enormous and startling schemes of fraud that are on foot, will prevail to the entire ruin of its best interests. They have become too strong for the people already, with the aid of the Govt they may be checked, in progress of time they will be beyond control.

If this suggestion of an *entire* reform in the offices in Florida be not acceptable, then I would take the liberty of suggesting *Secondly* that at least the Executive govt of the Terry. be placed in thoroughly democratic hands. *I can satisfy the Administration* that it is not now in hands at all likely to advocate or *advance its* interests * or to uphold the democratic movements. A good democratic Governor and Secretary would at least afford a *head* to the Democracy, and create a favorable influence. or else *thirdly*, send some one who has the confidence of the admn to Fla: and let him report the state of affairs.   D Levy of Florida

* a single number of the Govrs chief organ and the organ of the party he belongs to recd by the last mail from Tallahassee, will prove this.

Part Five
Stirrings of Cultural Activity

The first half century of national life in the United States can scarcely be regarded as a high-water mark in American culture. There were individuals who had been well-educated and had developed a measure of refinement in literary and artistic judgment. There were a few men of letters whose work retains its appeal. There was at least the beginning of an educational system. There were a few scientists and a large number of technologists. On the whole, however, the country was far too busy with the myriad of problems of establishing its national existence on a firm footing to have the leisure requisite for cultural activity on any considerable scale. Indeed, there were those who made a virtue of a necessity by trying to define the permanent values of American culture in terms of the practical manifestations that marked its first half century. Thus, Charles Jared Ingersoll, a distinguished leader in Pennsylvania politics, in an address before the American Philosophical Society in 1823, under the title "The Influence of America on the Mind," declared the genius of America to be practical. Its fruits would be seen in politics and applied science. Its possibilities for developing a literary culture Ingersoll dismissed with some scorn.

Yet, there were men, in Boston and Charleston, in Philadelphia and, a little later, New York, who were laying the foundations for the rich cultural life that was to grow in the United States—a cultural life that is only today beginning to be understood and appreciated. Never before in human history was culture regarded as anything but a prerogative of the upper classes; cultural standards were fixed in a leisure class mold. In the United States, there developed a cultural democracy, in which the literary and esthetic satisfactions of the mass became the touchstone. Ralph Waldo Emerson sensed this novelty of American culture when, in 1836, in his celebrated Harvard address on "The American Scholar," he asserted that "We have listened too long to the *courtly* muses of Europe." An aristocratic, "courtly" culture cannot grow naturally in a democratic soil.

If American culture in general, in the period with which we are concerned, was barely beginning to break through the surface, the best one can say of the culture of the Jews of the United States is that there were underground stirrings that betokened a later awakening. These first faint heralds were noticeable especially in Charleston and to a lesser extent in the other Jewish communities of the South. Massachusetts had only a handful of Jews, and they took no part in the "American renaissance" of the 1830s. Philadelphia contributed to the training of Jewish physicians and little more. New York's most distinguished Jewish literary figure, Mordecai Noah, was Philadelphia-born and his literary character was Charleston-formed. Indeed, Noah himself was aware both of the cultural deficiency of American Jews and of the leadership of southern Jews in whatever cultural activity there was. In his 1818 *Discourse* at the consecration of Shearith Israel's Synagogue, Noah had used the words, "We have genius and talent among us." When the *Discourse* was published, Noah added the following note: "This relates principally to the Jews in Europe; those in this country are too few to produce any remarkable traits of genius; their occupations and education being the same as those of other citizens, generally, they mix and commingle without any distinction. There may be a preponderance of genius among a few Jews in this country: the weight of talents, however, is in the southern states. There is a long list of illustrious men of antiquity; but commerce, in modern times, checks the advancement of literature." How far, indeed, commerce was the villain that Noah declared it to be is a matter of opinion; the fact is that very few Jews took part in the literary activity of the time, and that of these few, only two, Noah and Isaac Harby, achieved any distinction.

Even the field of Hebrew learning, which the Jews might have been expected to pursue with some measure of interest, was virtually neglected. There was more Hebrew scholarship among Christians than among Jews! Isaac Nordheimer, the only Jewish Hebraist of quality in America in this period, arrived in America in 1838 and took up a teaching position in what is now called New York University. I. B. Kursheedt had a considerable reputation for Hebrew learning, but it rests on no evidence beyond a few legal opinions of a later time. Meantime, there were Christian Hebraists of some stature at many theological seminaries and colleges throughout the country, including Clement C. Moore (better known as the author of "A Visit from St. Nicholas") at the Episcopalian General Theological Seminary in New York, and B. B. Edwards at the Congregationalist Andover Theological Seminary in Massachusetts. Moore's *Compendious Lexicon of Hebrew Literature* was published as early as 1809. A selection from Edwards's essay "On the Study of the Hebrew Language" is given below.

Part of the reason for this deficiency lies in the lack of adequate Jewish education. Meyer Polony's bequest to Shearith Israel to establish a Talmud Torah was designed to help alleviate the lack of educational facilities. It could, in the nature of things, not help much, because there was a lack of qualified teachers beyond the most elementary level. Gershom Mendes Seixas, Hazzan of Shearith Israel was responsible for the program of Polonies Talmud Torah; his own knowledge of Hebrew was so slight that, as has often been noted, the Hebrew address he composed for Sampson Simson to recite at the commencement exercises of Columbia College in 1800 is full of grammatical errors. Even much later, in the 1820s, when Jacob Mordecai, Parnass of Congregation Beth Shalome of Richmond wrote in reply to Congregation Mikveh Israel's letter of inquiry about possible candidates for the post of Hazzan (see Part Six, note 197), his reply said of Richmond's Hazzan and Hebrew teacher, Isaac Seixas, "he does not possess a Grammatical Knowledge of the Hebrew Language." Where the best teachers had so little to give their pupils, it is not to be wondered at that the pupils gained little.

In any case, the trend in our period was away from denominational schools and toward public schools. The completely non-religious public school was still in the future; the dominant tone of the schools in the early nineteenth century was what may be called a non-sectarian Protestantism. Even in the South where private schools were established by Jews—the Mordecai school in Warrenton and the Harby school outside of Charleston, for example —the schools were not concerned to teach any Jewish subject matter. During this period responsibility for supplementary denominational religious education fell on the churches and synagogues, and the Sunday School movement flourished. The American Sunday School Union was one of the great Christian organizations founded in the return to religion of the first two decades of the nineteenth century. Among the Jews, it was Isaac Leeser who, after an unsuccessful attempt in 1835 to establish a Jewish "all-day" school, took the first steps to create a Jewish adaptation of the Christian Sunday Schools. Rebecca Gratz was associated with him in this venture. Leeser went as far as to begin the production of textbooks for use in Jewish Sunday Schools. The Christian inspiration of his work is evident from the fact that the first text he produced was a catechism.

Considering the very small Jewish population in America and the tiny percentage of the general population that attended college, it seems likely, though accurate figures are unavailable, that Jews continued their education through college to about the same percentage as that of the non-Jewish population. But the impact of Jews on higher education was very slight. Nordheimer's teaching position at New York University has already been mentioned. Lorenzo da Ponte, who taught at Columbia, was born a Jew, but was converted to Christianity in his teens. Gershom Mendes Seixas was a trustee of Columbia College. These few items sum up the record.

There were a number of Jewish physicians in America, and some few of these contributed to the scientific development of their field of endeavor. Dr. David Nassy, who was elected to membership in the American Philosophical Society in 1795 and whose work on yellow fever in 1793 is advanced for its age, should perhaps not come into this record, since he carried on his practice in Surinam, rather than in the United States. But, in this period, the ophthalmologist, Isaac Hays, became editor of what later developed into the *Journal* of the American Medical Association, and Dr. D. L. M. Peixotto was one of the outstanding leaders of the medical profession in New York. In pure science, we do not find any Jewish participants, although Charles C. C. Cohen, who was an atheist, had studied chemical theory in his English youth and set up in New York in 1829 as an "analytical and manufacturing chemist." Cohen died in a chemical explosion in 1834, at the age of 27. On the other hand, there are records of a number of Jews who were concerned with various aspects of applied science.

Later in the nineteenth century, Jewish impresarios were largely responsible for bringing fine music to American audiences. In the earlier period, the only name worthy of record is that of the concert pianist, Daniel Schlesinger, who came to New York in 1836 and died in 1839. In his short American life, Schlesinger had much to do with changing musical taste in the country. With this exception, Jews made little impact on American culture in music, the plastic arts, or architecture.

LXXVI

Literary Pretentiousness, 1811

Jacob N. Cardozo's [1] *Oration on the Literary Character*,[2] delivered on the first anniversary of the foundation of the Methulogic Society of Charleston, is a thoroughly juvenile production. It is pretentious and sententious without any real substance. An extract is included here to illustrate the participation of young Jewish *literati* in the literary societies, especially in the South. Young Cardozo praised the enlightened spirit of free inquiry that was prevalent in what he still thought of as an age of universal toleration. He called attention to the impulse toward literary achievement that had been aroused in the younger generation by the spirit of the age, where by literary achievement he meant all forms of intellectual inquiry and artistic expression. He hailed republican institutions as particularly suited to the pursuit of the intellectual life and declared literary achievement to be the acme of human glory.

153. CARDOZO'S ORATION, 1811 [3]

My Friends,

The nineteenth century how illustrious an epocha in the history of the human mind! How animating the hope that the age which made it a prominent feature in its policy to subdue her spirit and energies, under the dominion of a most galling civil and religious tyranny, has forever passed away! A new and copious flood of light has burst in upon us, and the soul of man, throwing off every earthly incumbrance, has sprung with native elasticity to its proper sphere. Who will fail to see society in all this time blind to her most essential interests, when by successive persecutions she sought to crush every intellectual effort, and consequently all emulation in letters? She was impelled in a mad career, She was effectually depriving herself not only of the resources of a present security, but of one of the most efficacious instruments of a great and lasting renown.

She has now discovered letters and civilization to have a contemporaneous growth, if not a common origin. With a generous magnanimity she has recanted her errors by summoning the votarists of literature from the bosoms of their retreats to sustain her moral dignity, and perpetuate her empire. What a glorious attestation of the sovereignty of intellect! What an important era in the triumphs of learning! when the discoveries of her sons are no longer to be seen as heretofore blazing on the altars of fanaticism—and her laurels so often drenched in the tears of her votarists have ceased to be peace offerings to the intolerant spirit of her enemies. Which of us, interested in this great topic, who is not then proud of being a contemporary with this illustrious day, a day of literary success and exultation, a day memorable throughout the world for the interests of science, a day which shall be imperishable in the memories of men, for the great victories she has atcheived [sic] on all those scenes, where her sublime discoveries, had raised her up a multitude of oppressors. Who but must also recognize universal toleration, among the first of blessings, obtained by this noble conquest of reason over the madness of her foes? Yes! my friends, I may truly say the age of universal toleration has commenced, under the auspices of a spirit, which nothing has yet been able to impede in its rapid career, the spirit of free enquiry. It is this has thrown open the temples of science, and filled them with throngs of ambitious followers, pressing with the ardour of new made converts to the fountains of all light and truth, which, wherever it has appeared, has burst the prisons of oppression, and pierced the secrets of all tyranny, which spreading to the very ends of the earth, yet threatens to overwhelm in ruin every unnatural and monstrous fabric of human policy. What distinctions, are there not then due the class of characters who devote themselves to the cultivation and pursuit of this beneficent spirit, with an enthusiasm ever strong, and a courage ever daring? What rewards have governments in their gift too precious for the *literary character*, the grand source of all these liberal results? Where is the human calling so entitled as that of *letters* to the profound homage and admiration of the world? For I may ask on what other sphere have the efforts of man ever maintained a more unsullied dignity? Where is the profession exercising in the very bosom of society, so powerful an agency? one so all important in solidity of its services! On which of the theatres of human glory has the ambition of man struggling to immortalize its exertions, sought its way against a host of obstacles, through a succession of more heroical and hardy enterprize? and attested the lasting value of its successes, by a series of more splendid and honorable triumphs? When, though I speak of literature, I would embrace in the expression the whole compass of her efforts whether her followers be found in the paths of the historian, unfolding with the lamp of truth, the events wrap'd in the mists of time, or pursuing amid the blaze of science, a more luminous career, thro' a train of illustrious discoveries, whether their walks be those of poesy or philosophy, in whatever way their intellectual energies are concentrated, and applied to the elucidation of truth and in the transmission of its discoveries? How boundless the field which at once opens itself to our view! Who can describe the costs and sacrifices by which the man of letters maintains his rank the most pre-eminent and honorable on the rolls of fame? Who is there competent to trace him through every stage of his toils, thro' all the travails of his brain, and the painful gradations of his success?

LXXVII
Anti-Puritanism, 1828

Despite the Calvinistic, Puritanical heritage of the American colonial age, one of the first manifestations of nascent American culture was the emergence of a native drama in the major cities—especially Charleston, Philadelphia, and New York. To destroy the vestiges of Puritan opposition to the stage, it was necessary to defend the theatre as a beneficent moral influence. This, Isaac Harby [4] did, in his essay in "Defence of the Drama," [5] adding that the theatre is also a civilizing force, acting upon both young and old. He pointed out, wisely, that people do have passions and commended the theatre as a way in which these passions can find harmless expression. Harby's interest in the theater led him to write plays and dramatic criticism as well as this apology for the drama. [6]

154. DEFENCE OF THE DRAMA, 1828 [7]

But the great and prominent objects of the drama, and its world the stage, are not merely to supply curious critics with subjects for comparison and analysis, to sum up the tremendous difference between the styles of A and of B; these amusing themes are to be considered only as the auxilliaries [sic] of ambition, the flank companies to stir up and keep in countenance the advance of enterprise and talent. Emulation naturally begets excellence.

Nor are the amusements, the rational and tasteful amusements, of a Theatre to be regarded only as a relaxation from the toils of the day, *vivida vis* succeeding to the *tedium vitae*. Though, in this light, it is of no inconsiderable consequence. To see, and to be seen, to hear and to feel the busy hum. To mingle with those who hear and can *feel*, is at least a pleasurable contrast to the dull pursuits of a day of toil and business, or more properly (as the times are) of no business. [8] Every mental excitement is wholesome exercise; every intellectual pleasure innocent and improving; every pleasing sight, every pleasing sound leads to tranquillity, and "moves harmonious music" in the mind.

Nor is a Theatre, as the sphere where *The Poet* [9] lives and enacts his wonders, merely to be considered as the source of a people's rational entertainment, fitted only to the faded or luxurious mind. Not that this is not one among its attributes and excellencies; but it is not the only one. A Theatre, as the word implies, in its ancient (architectural) sense is a place where men *see around* various exhibitions, such as the painter, the machinist, the dancer, and the gladiator, can afford to the eye and to the fancy. But in its intellectual sense, that in which *alone* the great masters of Grecian Tragedy and of Roman Comedy viewed it, it is a spectacle of life, as it is, and was, and ever shall be. A representation, more vivid than any other art can create, of passion and of sentiment. The mirror of man "held up to nature!" a living, moving picture, pregnant with truth and animation.

In its wider and more magnificent application, the splendid genius of antiquity used a Theatre for almost every public spectacle. Whether the terrific inspirations of Aeschylus, the deep feeling of Sophocles (his pupil) or the pathetic power of *Euripides* (the rival of the latter) were to be pourtrayed, the stage was consecrated to the subject, and mask and music gave reality to the scene. Whether wild beasts were to be subdued by reckless men; or the last hope of some brave captive was to be suspended on the doubtful conflict, the hair-poised victory over many brave brothers in captivity; whether the *motion of the thumb* [10] was to decide the great palm, not only of breathing life, but of liberty and citizenship, the theatre was the appropriate arena. In these exhibitions the applauses and feelings of the multitude gave the approbation, while (as the case might be) a Consul or a Caesar, Brutus or Nero, furnished the enormous expenses.

And in our latitude and in our times, although the theatre was intended to be more limited in its sphere of operations, yet circumstance, fashion and the multitude have so controlled it, that its *subjects* are not confined to those great purposes which alone the dramatic poets of Greece and Rome cultivated and aimed to establish, but are extended almost as far as the amp[h]itheatrical grasp once extended, with this difference, however, without the patronage of government, the resources of an English or an American theatre must be gathered from the public, without political objects, neither family faction nor political power has much chance of bending the direct spirit of the drama to the purposes of ambition. The crimson gore of dying gladiators shall never again cement the tower of strength which some fortunate captain may wish to raise to his own popularity. The love for cruelty and taste for blood have passed away, have become unfashionable, except indeed in some few Byronic stanzas.[11] But that is mere affectation. No; our popular men, covered as they are with "golden opinions," *would not* if they could, and *could not* if they would, turn this tremendous engine to the purposes of personal aggrandizement. The temper and impress of the times, the character of our institutions, all would laugh at the effort. The stage is, indeed, a powerful engine; if its objects are more limited, they are not less effectually accomplished than those of the press. There have been instances, in which, appealing to the hearts of a people, its political impulse has been irresistible. It speaks with such fidelity, it is so direct in its passion, so vivid in its portraits, so full of life and mobility, that it can lift a weight quicker than, if it cannot sustain it as long as, the press. Instances in the revolutions of France and Italy attest this truth. In England a Foote,[12] in Paris a Le Sage,[13] in Athens an Aristophanes, made the stage a sphere for moral or for personal satire. Even the *Mimi* in Rome, whom Horace condemns as a race of buffoons, would sometimes exalt themselves into public accusers. Their tenacity or their thoughtlessness was wonderful. "The audacity of the Mimes (says Mr. Dunlop)[14] was carried still farther, as they satirized and insulted the most ferocious emperors during their lives *and in their own presence*. An actor, in one of these pieces, which was performed during the reign of Nero, while repeating the words "Vale pater, vale mater," signified by his *gestures*, the two modes of drowning and poisoning, in which that sanguinary fiend had attempted to destroy both his parents. The Mimi currently bestowed on Commodus, the most opprobrious appellation. One of their number, who performed before the enormous *Maximin*, reminded the audience that he who was too strong for an individual, might be massacred by a multitude, and that thus the elephant, lion and tiger, are slain. The tyrant perceived the sensation excited in the theatre, but the suggestion was veiled in a language unknown to that barbarous and gigantic Thracian."

It is, then, principally as a moral lever that the statesman and philosopher should regard the stage. Viewed in this aspect, who does not wish the drama to prosper? From the day so long gone by, when first the *Monologue* accompanied the sacrifice of a ram to Bacchus, through all its successive improvements of dialogue, story, passion and scene, to the closing labours of the great masters of comedy, the bold and pregnant Plautus, and the witty and elegant Terence, the drama has given to poetry what the prayer of Pygmalion imparted to his marble statue, life and beauty, a spirit to feel and "an understanding heart." The revilers of the ancients, forgot that Racine and Corneille and indeed the leaders of the French school, have drawn their spirit and their form, from the tragic writers of Attica, they forget that Moliere and even Shakespear himself have plundered from Plautus and Terence, plundered, it must be confessed, not like robbers, but like conquerors; while these latter themselves, as well as the other Roman dramatists, have taken largely from their Greek predecessors, particularly from Menander, the prince of comic poets, from Diphilus and Philemon, of whose excellencies we can only conjecture from a few fragments preserved in other authors, but sufficient to lead us to the well-spring, whence Plautus and Terence draw their delightful draughts. . . .

But it were vain to lay any stress, much more vain to enumerate all the legitimate consequences and the legitimate objects of the drama. There there unite talents in the actors and actresses, taste in the selection of dramatic pieces, and industry and judgment in the managers, what more does an enlightened community require? What more delightful than a well acted play? What more cheerful than a well filled theatre? The eccentricities of the stage are but the eccentricities of public taste: the application of it to other purposes than those to which it was peculiarly or originally intended, is but in obedience to the public will. He who opposes that will, weds his ruin. Our managers have no such "mad ambition." Those under whose direction our theatres are guided at present, have not only their interest to consult, but their *pride* to satisfy, in the arrangements they make. They have selected the best histrionic abilities, male and female, and every collateral aid of scenery, music and grace which industrious search, enterprize, talent and expense could accomplish. That these efforts will be met with a corresponding feeling, an enlightened and warm support and patronage from the community, is what friends and strangers, visiters and residents, must all unite in desiring; and of desiring they will not suffer that enterprize to perish: that talent to go unrewarded, and the vast expenses of a modern theatre with all its costly paraphernalia, to be held out in vain pageantry "mocking the air with colours idly spread." But, on the contrary, a liberal people will appreciate these toils, they will share in the pride they alone can nourish; in the design and execution they alone can adequately reward; and thus effectually and permanently give to the soul of their good wishes, a body and a voice, a tangible and material proof.

LXXVIII
Three Jewish Dramatists,
1820-1833

Many of the plays that were presented in the theatrical rebirth of the early national period were, of course, English. The growing sense of cultural nationalism, however, led many amateurs to try their hands at writing plays. The prefaces to the published versions of these plays reflect the need the authors felt for defending their creations in the light of the world, and especially English literature. The very frequency with which the defense was entered suggests the degree to which a sense of cultural inferiority persisted. Three Jewish writers—Samuel B. H. Judah,[15] Mordecai M. Noah,[16] and Jonas Phillips [17]—were among those who took part in this cultural nationalism by writing for the stage. The prefaces to four of their plays reveal the liveliness and turmoil, the spirit of competition and emulation, and the inevitable personal rancor that pervaded the theatrical atmosphere.

155. PREFACE TO JUDAH'S
"THE MOUNTAIN TORRENT," 1820 [18]

In writing the following dramatic trifle, I was not so foolish as to think to gain any literary distinction, or of giving it a lasting character; it was the offspring of a few days' labour, and my chief aim in writing it was to improve myself: and if any of those who see it performed gained a moment of pleasure and *gratification,* I feel myself fully repaid and satisfied for any labour there might have been in the composition. The dramatic authors on this side of the Atlantic have usually wrote a preface to their plays, sometimes of more real worth than the piece itself, railing against their readers and audiences for not truly estimating native talent; it is therefore totally unnecessary for me to tell over the old story of "stubborn prejudices," &c. &c. which, although sometimes very highly wrought, are nevertheless too true; but it becomes my duty to say, that although I had all these to combat, its reception, under every circumstance, exceeded its merits and my utmost expectations which shows plainly that though there are great prejudices in favour of the English drama, there are some *true hearts,* who can believe their country equally fertile in genius and learning, and are ready to foster American talent, whenever it shall bud forth.

In England there are a numerous tribe of dramatic writers, who make a profession, and sometimes a fortune of the drama; from youth they improve themselves in the dramatic writings of ages past, and drill themselves in every trifle. Neither time nor pains are spared; the laurel, rendered ten times more beautiful by the *golden* gems that deck it, awaits them if they gain the goal; no wonder then their pieces so far exceed ours. Yet with all these advantages, none or very few original are produced; they are mostly translations from the French or German.

I hope none of my friends suppose from this I intend to enter the lists, and become a combatant for the drama; in plain language, become a professed author; but they may rest assured, though I had the greatest talents for it, I should never commit such an act of madness, for otherwise I cannot call it. I am too well convinced, to use the language of the dramatist, "that fame, which the poet's heart creates his visionary mistress, is a fugitive, uncertain phantom, that tempts, but still eludes his living embrace, never to be yielded as a bride, till fate has chilled his human fires and the consciousness of his spirit has withdrawn to other worlds. Peace is the only real good and national monuments, shaded by the laurel and the bay, yield no dearer resting-place to him who fain would sleep for ever, than a turf grave clasped by osiers." No, truly; fame is a very good thing; but the *means* are better, and yet certainly do yourself more good by *living* on roasts, steaks, mutton chops, &c. than dying on bread and water all your *life time,* and living eternally *after.* Therefore, be it understood, that if I write again, it will be because the effort of composition amuses my mind, and perhaps it may please my friends; but *sat. est.* Have mercy, good critics!

I now print the *Mountain Torrent* as persented [sic] at the New York theatre with great success, not that it may be worthy of the press, but that it may be read by my friends, which was impossible while in manuscript; likewise as I expect it will sell well, to promote the *interest* of a worthy man, *Mr. Longworth.*

I have already trespassed on my reader, who I hope will pardon the length of this preface, but I cannot conclude without paying a debt of duty and gratitude: To *Mr. Simpson* [19] I owe much, "very much;" but it is in vain for me to attempt his praise. As an actor, a scholar, and a gentleman, he has been long before the public, and his worth is generally known, but those who are acquainted with him can appreciate him best in private life.

To *Mr. Maywood,* [20] likewise, I must return my most heartfelt thanks; and can safely say, in my own opinion, as well as on the authority of others, he never exerted himself more, or appeared to better advantage, than in his performance of *Baron Trevasi.*

To *Miss Johnson,* [21] the beautiful, the amiable *Miss Johnson,* I am highly indebted.

But it is in vain to speak of the merits of *each* performer that was engaged in this drama; it would swell this to a volume. Let me conclude, by saying, that *all* equally exerted themselves, and I owe the same debt to *all.*

S. B. Judah.

New York,
April 12, 1820

156. NOAH'S PREFACE TO "MARION," 1822 [22]

William Coleman, [23] Esquire, M.D.
Editor of The New-York Evening Post.
Dear Doctor,

I dedicate this play to you, being the only critic of pretensions who abused it without having seen it performed. [24] The originality of the design, as well as the novelty of the execution, fairly entitle you to a dedication; for who can say that you may not be pleased with a thing upon acquaintance, against which you directed your powerful canons of criticism.

Seated, the other day, in a comfortable chair, which I discovered was once the property of the Continental Congress, (there are several in the City Hall,) and reading an essay of your old friend, Sir Gilbert Blane,[25] on yellow fever, until I imagined I had all the symptoms, I heard a diminutive tap at the green blinds of my little cabinet, which half opened, and my printer thrust forward his honest face, and the following dialogue ensued:

Author. Ah. Long Primer, is that you? what do you want?

Printer. I want to know if you will let me have the manuscript of your last play, to publish it.

Author. Why you are mad—Coleman has abused it, called it "wretched stuff," said that he could not wish his bitterest enemy a greater evil than seeing it performed.

Printer. I know it, and that's the very reason it will sell; any thing that Coleman abuses must take with the public.

Author. But he abused it, acknowledging, at the same time, that he had neither read it nor saw it acted.

Printer. So much the better, sir, he is perfectly in character; so if you are not ashamed of it——

Author. Ashamed! oh no, though it cannot be expected that with my heavy occupations I can find time, an aptitude of mind, or, probably, sufficient genius, to compose an elegant play, yet a leisure hour of an evening devoted to a drama, founded on the glorious events of our revolutionary war, cannot create shame, though it may not produce confidence; besides, it is intended for the stage, not for the closet, we study effect only. But as a great politician in this state once said, "pray what am I to get by it?"

Printer. Why there is not much to be made by a small work— yet I will make you an offer for the copyright; I will give you ten loads of wood for the use of the prisoners in the debtors' apartment, this pinching weather.

Author. You are an honest fellow, Long Primer, and shall have it; and to convince you that I can be grateful for the generous spirit that dictated the offer, I will add a scene or two, and dedicate it to Coleman—that will make it sell.

Thus, Doctor, you are the cause of this publication; for as your old friend Polonius says, "this effect defective comes by cause," [26] and while I frankly tell the world that you condemned it without a hearing, I cannot deny myself the gratification of stating that

2,436 of our fellow citizens went to see it performed, and 3,000 would have been present could the house contain them, so the odds are rather against you. . . .

The world has attributed your opposition, to certain motives which I do not think exist. They say that our political differences have produced a personal excitement on your part, which breaks out in flashes against any thing that I may chance to write. Now, my dear Doctor, such suspicions are injurious to your good sense, for it supposes you capable of waging an imprudent warfare against the literary reputation of all your political opponents. Now, I fear, to speak technically, that the disease is deeply seated near the left ventricle of the heart. In confidence, let me whisper my suspicions in your ear: I fear that you never cordially approved the principles of our revolutionary war. I do not find fault with you; this is a free country, and men have a legitimate right to maintain their opinions; but I certainly doubt the policy of enforcing this opinion at this late day, and likewise very much question your prudence in pushing your hostility so furiously against the country during the late war. . . .

[M. M. Noah]

157. NOAH'S PREFACE TO "THE GRECIAN CAPTIVE," 1822 [27]

Several pieces have already been performed in England, relative to the present struggle in Greece,[28] and events dramatised, which 'tis said, have never occurred. This privilege of imagination is the peculiar property of the dramatist, who is not bound to wait for the tardy movements of armies, or the cold progress of cabinet negotiations, he is only to know that war exists in Greece, the cradle of the Arts, where Homer sung, where Themistocles conquered, and his fancy and invention must supply the rest; therefore, if eventually the Greeks should not recover Athens it will not be my fault, it was necessary to my play, and so I gave them possession of that interesting spot with a dash of my pen, being too far removed from the scene of action to take any part in fighting for it. I have also taken the small liberty of transferring Ali Pacha [29] from Joannina to Athens being a more extended field of operation and quite convenient, and have also made him the enemy of the Greeks, which he truly was, as his rebellion and hostility to the Sublime Porte were the only motives which induced him to favour the Greek cause.

We know the history of the fair Venetian, captured by Mahomet II. and sacrificed by him to appease the rage of his janissaries. The French have written a pretty melodrama on that subject, from which I borrow the incidents in the following piece.

We, citizens of a free country, cannot observe with indifference the present struggle for liberty in Greece. Though separated by a world of waters we are too familiar with the history of that country, with those illustrious events which mark the pages of her history, not to feel a deep interest in the success of that people, and the cause of freedom generally.

In writing plays on Greece we must bear in mind the theatres of Aeschylus, Sophocles, Aristophanes, and Euripedes. Despotism resulting from a frequent change of masters has impaired, if not destroyed, that great human energy, and those lovely blossoms springing from the cultivated mind, for which the Greeks were once distinguished, and celebrated. Still they are Greeks, and at this day we have the ruins of the magnificent Gymnasia, Odeum, Prytaneum, the Pynx, and all the glory of Pericles, left to admire; and we feel a deep interest for the present, in consideration of the glories of the past.

I believe I should apologize for this play being, after all but a poor play; but then the reply will be, why did you not write a better one? So let it take its chance with the rest of my little bantlings, which are vagabondizing over the Union, played in big and little theatres, adding a trifle to my reputation and nothing at all to my fortune. Wait till we have a publisher, who will give us one thousand guineas for a work, and then—

[M. M. Noah]

158. PHILLIPS'S PREFACE TO "CAMILLUS," 1833 [30]

This Tragedy was written during the summer of 1830, and, probably, would have remained in obscurity but for the friendly interest of H. G. Pearson, Esq.[31] who undertook the study and personation of Camillus and introduced it to public notice on the 8th of February, 1833, at the Archstreet Theatre, in Philadelphia the city of our mutual nativity.

Whether it is to this circumstance, or to any intrinsic merit the play possesses, I am indebted to the flattering reception it received, and the favourable notices of the critics of Philadelphia,[32] the public will now have an opportunity of judging; and in throwing myself upon the indulgence of its readers, I entreat them to bear in mind, that it is my *first* invocation of the tragic muse.

Though not present at the performance, its success and the established reputation of the actors, are sufficient guarantees that the respective parts were skilfully delineated; and I avail myself of this opportunity to tender my thanks to Messrs. Jones,[33] Duffy [34] & Forrest,[35] the managers of the Theatre,[36] and particularly to Mr. Pearson, for the care and attention bestowed upon its production. The unanimous award of praise to Miss Riddle,[37] who personated the character of Camilla, assures me that I have every reason to be gratified that the part was entrusted to one so capable of giving effect. One other fact I mention with pride, and which perhaps, an author has seldom had an opportunity of noticing, is, that my tragedy, an *American* production, was performed, and *well performed*, by American Actors.

To the gentlemen, who, though entire strangers, so kindly furnished the prologue and epilogue, I tender my most grateful acknowledgements, and only regret that in presenting the former to the public, I cannot announce the name of its accomplished author.

This Tragedy is now the property of my fellow citizens; and if its publication tends, in the slightest degree, to advance the cause of American dramatic literature, I shall be amply remunerated in having contributed, even thus slightly, to the promotion of an object of deep and heartfelt interest.

[Jonas B. Phillips]

New-York, July 18, 1833.

LXXIX
The First American
Jewish Poetess, 1833

Jewish men with aspirations to write could enter into the highly competitive field of writing plays. For Jewish women, this would have been an immodesty. Yet, inevitably, there were women of talent and creativity and the urge to publish to the world the fruits of their literary labor. The first Jewish woman to achieve a modicum of fame, Miss Penina Moise [38] of Charleston, chose to express herself, with the utmost gentility, in poetry, although it is clear from her verses that she had no poetic talent. The themes, especially those of social significance, that appear in her book, *Fancy's Sketch Book*, suggest that she might have done best as an essayist. These two poems illustrate how her mind was moved by social themes.

159. FEMALE PATRIOTISM IN POLAND [39]

"We have made cannons of our bells." "Yes, there are six thousand of us who have yielded up to our country all that we have left, all that women deem most precious in the world, our marriage rings."

> She gazed upon the golden pledge, oh! how could she forget
> When first upon her trembling hand, Love's glitt'ring seal was set;
> When Hope, upon the cherished link, a softened lustre shed,
> And she had thought, confidingly, on roses e'er to tread.
> Again she looked upon the ring, and faster flowed her tears,
> For in that fairy circle dwelt the memory of years
> The purity of bridal vows, the promise ne'er to sever,
> But in delight or peril still, cling to the plighted ever.
> And is it Freedom, before whom Felicity has flown?
> Yes! for that shrine my lord forsook his own domestic throne;
> The legends of his trampled land chivalrous deeds disclose,

And Kosciusco's [40] laurels late deprived him of repose.
The purple trail that Carnage leaves upon the blushing earth,
Will guide you to my hero's tomb, where victory had birth:
E'en Temples must, with mute appeal, to Piety invoke,
For now their brazen tongues resound but Liberty's bold stroke.

Shall I, degenerate, then reserve the trophy of my heart,
When even holiness, for this, must with her heralds part?
Away! and mingle with the pile that Patriotism's wand
Converts, by purest alchymy, to Freedom's fiery brand.
No fond regret shall sully now the glorious oblation,
The sanctifying sacrifice, that liberates a nation!

160. TO PERSECUTED FOREIGNERS [41]

Fly from the soil whose desolating creed,
Outraging faith, makes human victims bleed.
Welcome! where every Muse has reared a shrine,
The aspect of wild Freedom to refine.

Upon *our* Chieftain's brow no crown appears;
No gems are mingled with his silver hairs,
Enough that Laurels bloom amid its snows,
Enriched with these, the sage all else foregoes.

If thou art one of that oppressed race,
Whose pilgrimage from Palestine we trace,[42]
Brave the Atlantic, Hope's broad anchor weigh,
A Western Sun will gild your future day.

Zeal is not blind in this our temp'rate soil;
She has no scourge to make the soul recoil.[43]
Her darkness vanished when our stars did flash;
Her red arm grasped by Reason dropt the lash.

Our Union, Liberty and Peace imparts,
Stampt on our standards, graven on our hearts,
The first, from crush'd Ambition's ruin rose,
The last, on Victory's field spontaneous grows.

Rise, then, elastic from Oppression's tread,
Come and repose on Plenty's flowery bed.
Oh! not as Strangers shall your welcome be,
Come to the homes and bosoms of the free!

LXXX

Christian Reasons for
Studying Hebrew, 1838

In 1838, H. A. Henry,[44] a Jewish resident of New York, compiled
a Hebrew vocabulary on a new principle of arrangement. The
little book was published by J. M. Jackson [45] under the title *Imrai
Shaipher*.[46] Two pages of testimonials are included; only three
are from Jews—Mordecai M. Noah, Isaac Nordheimer [47] and J. B.
Seixas [48]—while eleven are from Christians. We may infer that
at this time Christian interest in the study of Hebrew was relatively
keen and widespread.

B. B. Edwards,[49] professor of Hebrew in Andover Theological
Seminary, was an advocate of an even greater interest in Hebrew
studies, especially by Christian ministers. The five reasons that
he brings forward may suggest to us why interest in Hebrew was
so prevalent: First, only where a great many students cultivate an
interest in Hebrew can an environment develop in which a few
outstanding scholars are able to achieve eminence. Second, recent
advances in German biblical scholarship can be fully appreciated
only by those who have mastered Hebrew. Third, knowledge of
Hebrew will strengthen the students' faith "in the genuineness
and divine authority of the Scriptures." Fourth, study of the Scriptures in the Hebrew original will have a beneficial influence on
the students' imagination and taste. Fifth, Hebrew is a valuable
adjunct to the missionary enterprise.[50] The extracts below, from
Edwards's address, "Reasons for the Study of the Hebrew Language," illustrate Edwards's arguments on these points.

161. THE STUDY OF HEBREW, 1838 [51]

I shall attempt, in the ensuing remarks, to adduce some reasons
why the study of the Hebrew language should be made a part of

a liberal education, and be put into the same category with Latin and Greek. There is no adequate cause for confining the study to a small part of one of the professions. Why should it not be considered as the common privilege of all the professions? I know of but one argument against its introduction into our present courses of collegiate study; they are already pre-occupied and crowded with other branches of learning. Were one or two additional years, however, allowed to the preparatory schools; were the elements of Latin and Greek thoroughly mastered at our academies, as they ought to be, and as they are at two or three of them, an opening might be found somewhere in the four college years for the histories of Moses and for the songs of David. No considerate man would dislodge the Latin and Greek classics from the place which they now occupy. Still, Isaiah is, in all respects—in simplicity, in fire, in originality, in sublimity—as worthy of study as Homer. The Lamentations of Jeremiah will not yield to the Elegies of Tyrtaeus. These things ought to be done, while the other should not be left undone.

1. An argument for the study of Hebrew may be derived from the fact, that great eminence in the pursuit, on the part of a few individuals, cannot be expected in the absence of a general cultivation of the language.

It has been argued, that we need a few men well-skilled in the original Scriptures to serve as defenders of the faith when attacked on critical grounds, while the great body of the clergy and of the educated laity may safely neglect or but imperfectly acquire the branch of knowledge in question. That this general position is untenable, it were perfectly easy to demonstrate. Of the ten thousand, or twelve thousand ministers of Christ in the United States, more than ten, or fifty, or one hundred, or one thousand ought to be intimately conversant with the original documents of their faith. Allowing, however, that a few men, well trained as original investigators would meet the exigency, still we contend, that this small number could not be raised up amidst a surrounding ignorance, or a general apathy, in relation to the pursuit. No one acquainted with the history of the world, or with the nature of man, can entertain an expectation so fallacious. . . .

In every department of labor, men are made for each other.

They need the cheering sympathy and the generous coöperation of fellow-laborers. Were there none to share the pleasures of success, one half of its value would be wanting. A modest man does not wish to acquire languages, that he may be stared at as the eighth wonder of the world. Ordinarily he will have no heart to labor, unless he is surrounded by a community who can properly estimate his productions. What motives has he to push his researches far beyond the point where they would be generally appreciated? What security, moreover, has the church, that he will not involve himself with them in errors and absurdities? He needs around him the safeguard of a vigilant, as well as the support of a sympathizing community.

2. My second argument for the more general study of the Hebrew is, that we may be better prepared to take all proper advantage of the immense stores of erudition on the general subject which have been collected in Germany. . . .

The Germans possess mines of inestimable wealth, which ought to be opened for the benefit of the world. They are now, comparatively, unworked or unknown. The social and political circumstances of the German States are such as not to admit of the employment and diffusion of their stores of learning in a thousand ways accessible to those who speak the English tongue. A large part, however, of their biblical labors are unappreciable by us. To use a favorite term of theirs, we have not reached the point of development. We are not able to grapple with their learning, nor sympathize with their spirit. Innumerable treatises, bearing on important points in the interpretation of the Old Testament, remain solitary copies in two or three of our libraries, because English versions of them could not be sold. Some of these essays would be of essential aid to all those foreign missionaries who are called to the office of translating the Scriptures. . . .

3. The importance of the study of the Hebrew language may be argued from its effect in strengthening the faith of the student in the genuineness and divine authority of the Scriptures.

The Roman Catholic binds up certain apocryphal books with the Old Testament. But it would seem hardly possible for a reader of common discernment not to perceive instantly that the claims of these books to inspiration rest on a very precarious basis. To render this obvious, they need only to be read in connection with the canonical books. These latter have the unstudied guilelessness, the transparency, the uniform dignity of divine truth; the former may have traces of proceeding from honest and pious minds, but the dignity is not sustained; the simplicity is an imitation; they contain, not unfrequently, jejune repetitions and puerilities. Their inferiority is rendered more striking by their position. Tobit would be a respectable story if it were not crowded in between Malachi and Matthew. But placed where it is, it is brought into most unfortunate proximity with the writings whose purity, decorum and consistency indicate their higher origin. Thus our confidence in the divinity of God's word is materially strengthened. It arises in part from feeling. We cannot describe the process. Before we are aware, the perception of the difference between the two classes of writing has become a part of our consciousness.

But if such is the effect in comparing the apocryphal books with our excellent English version of the Old Testament, the contrast is much heightened by examining the former in connection with the original of the latter. The Hebrew has the signature of a simplicity and a freshness, which no translation can fully copy, unless it be itself inspired. It is the freshness of Eden on the seventh morning of the creation; it is the simplicity of patriarchs and prophets; it is the innocent guilelessness of angels. Our translation is faithful to the sense of the original, and it will be an everlasting monument of the powers of the English language, especially in its Anglo-Saxon features. But it is no disparagement to the version to assert, that it does not give us all the vitality and beauty of the original. In reading the latter, we cannot but feel, that we have passed into the holy of holies; the proofs of divinity are thick around us. We do not simply *know* that our faith in these records is firm, we *feel* that it is. . . .

4. The influence of the study of the Hebrew Scriptures on the imagination and the taste.

The imagination is not a modification of memory or of any of her mental faculty. It is an original quality of the mind. It has the power of conferring additional properties upon an object, or of abstracting from it some of those which it actually possesses, and of thus enabling the object to react, like a new substance, upon the mind which has performed the process. It has also the power of shaping and of creating by innumerable methods. It consolidates numbers into unity and separates unity into numbers. "It draws all things to one, makes things animate and inanimate, beings with their attributes, subjects and their accessories take one color, and serve to one effect." [52] In its highest or creative power, the imagination belongs only to the few great poets. But the faculty is, doubtless, possessed by all men though, in some cases, it is faintly, or not at all developed. Whoever can read with intelligence and sympathy a genuine poet has imagination. . . .

The poetry of the Hebrews is sometimes represented as oriental, an eastern fashion, local, factitious, artificial, adapted to men living a migratory life, under an ardent sky, and not adapted to a severe European taste. But the Hebrew poetry is no such thing. It is European; it is occidental, for all ages and generations; it is universal in its character; it is everlasting as the affections of man. It furnishes food for that imagination, whose birth was not for time but for all eternity. Peasants can feel its force; philosophers kindle at its inspiration. Strip the Old Testament of its poetry, and it is not the old Testament; it contains truth, but not the truth which God revealed. Take out of it the element of imagination, that which makes it poetry, and the residue is neither poetry nor prose. It may be truth, but it is not the truth which we need. No error can be greater than to call the Hebrew poetry mere costume. There are some truths which are poetry in their very nature. Men, the world over, have imagination and love poetic truths, and these truths were necessary for them, and, therefore, part of the Bible is poetry. . . .

5. Another important consideration is the bearing of the study of Hebrew upon the missionary enterprise.

The one hundred and twenty-two ordained missionaries sent out by the American Board of Commissioners for Foreign Missions,[53] sixty-nine of whom were educated at this institution, have published, with the aid of their assistants, between fifty and sixty millions of pages, a large proportion of which are parts of the Scriptures. The number of languages employed is twenty-nine, nine of which were first reduced to writing by these missionaries. In all this wide department of labor, augmenting every year, an accurate acquaintance with the original Hebrew is, of course, indispensable. The missionary translator is not to repair to the Vulgate, nor to the Septuagint, but to the fountain head.

In the labors which are to be entered into for the conversion of the five or six millions of Jews, scattered over the world, the necessity of the Hebrew Bible is too obvious to need the briefest allusion. In respect to familiarity with its pages, the missionary himself must become a Jew.

The bearings of the subject upon those who speak the Arabic tongue may justify a moment's consideration. The great problem for the friends of civilization and Christianity to solve is the conversion of the millions who use the Chinese and the Arabic languages. These enlightened and saved, the world, comparatively, is evangelized. . . .

In promoting, therefore, the study of Hebrew in this country, we are taking a most direct means to spread the glorious gospel of Christ, not only where the Arabic is the dominant language, but wherever Islamism has penetrated, that is, from Calcutta to Constantinople, and from the Caspian sea to our American colony in Liberia. A thorough knowledge of Hebrew will remove at least one half the difficulty of acquiring the Arabic. It will introduce us to the same modes of writing and of thought, to the same poetic diction, and in part to the same material objects, the same countries, and the same historical associations. In this sense, the Hebrew is not a *dead* language. By its most intimate connection with the Arabic, and, I may add, with the Syriac, it is still spoken at the foot of Mount Ararat, on the site of old Nineveh, at Carthage, in the ancient Berytus, and where Paul was shipwrecked. It is reviving in Egypt, and the Bible and the Tract Societies are spreading its literature on the wings of every wind.

LXXXI
The "Book of Jasher," 1840

In introducing this translation, by an unknown translator, of the medieval Hebrew forgery of the *Book of Jasher* (*Sepher Yashar*),[54] one of the earlier "source books" to which the biblical text makes reference, Mordecai M. Noah revealed the limitations of his Hebrew scholarship. He insisted upon the authenticity of this fabrication and upon its right to a place among the historical books of the Bible. Noah was financially involved in the publication of this work, and he wrote the Preface—of which extracts are given here— but he seems to have had no hand in the making of the translation.

162. NOAH'S PREFACE TO
THE "BOOK OF JASHER," 1840 [55]

It is with pleasure that I am able to present to the American public the translation of the Book of Jasher, as referred to in *Joshua* and *Second Samuel,* which, after several years' negotiation with the owner and translator of the work in England, I have succeeded in obtaining.

There are many books named in the Old Testament, which are now classed among the missing books, or books supposed to have been lost amidst the many revolutions which have occurred in Judea. These books are not included in the Jewish Canons, and it is questionable whether there are any missing of what were considered as emanating from inspired writers; for, when the works enumerated in the Bible could not be found after the most diligent search, the inference was, that the names applied to other books, or that they were different versions of the same work.

Thus, the *Book of the Covenant,* (Exodus xxiv. 7.) was a mere collection of the injunctions and institutions delivered by the Almighty to Moses. So it might also be said of the *Book of the Law,* (Deut. xxxi. 9.) *The Book of the wars of the Lord* (Numbers xxi.

14.) cannot be found, and is every where spoken of as one of the missing books. Dr. Lightfoot,[56] in his Chronicles, thinks that Moses refers to a book of his own composing, written by command of God, (Exodus xvii. 14.) We think, however, that the Book of Judges is the one referred to as the *Book of the wars of the Lord;* because, in that book we have all the exploits of the Hebrews detailed at length. We find in Chronicles and Kings a number of books named, which are not to be found. The acts of David the King, written in the Book of Samuel the Seer, also in the Book of Nathan the Prophet, and also in the Book of Gad the Seer; the acts of Solomon are in the Book of Nathan the Prophet, and also in the Book of Abijah the Shulamite; the acts of Rehoboam in the Book of Shemaiah the Prophet; the acts of Jehoshaphat in the Book of Jehu. The journals of the kings of Judah and Israel; the three thousand and five songs, and a treatise on botany and animated nature, by this learned king, are lost; so also are the "Acts of Manasseh." These works, not having been found by Ezra, could not have been inserted in the Old Testament, and consequently cannot be considered as having been written by divine inspiration. Nevertheless, it would be assuming more than is required or necessary, to say that there were no other books in the time of Ezra, than those considered as divinely inspired. St. Austin [57] says, "The penmen of the Sacred Scripture writ some things as they are, men with historical lore and diligence: other things they writ as prophets, by inspiration from God." We thus have a classification of their labors, both as historians and as prophets. The negligence of the Jews in ancient days, and their constant transition from one country to another, occasioned many losses of the sacred writings. The Book of Deuteronomy was lost for a long time. There were many books rejected by the Canons which are still objects of curiosity, and venerable for their antiquity. The prayer of King Manasseh, Bel and the Dragon, the two Books of Esdras, the Book of the Maccabees, and the Book of Enoch, recently found and translated from the Ethiopic. The Book of Jasher, referred to in Joshua and Second Samuel, has been long an object of great curiosity. Some of the Hebrew writers contend that it was the lives and acts of Abraham, Isaac, and Jacob, and other patriarchs, who were called *Jasherim,* the Just. Dr. Lightfoot thinks it is the

Book of the Wars of God, and so the reader may think in perusing the various battles it recounts. Grotius [58] calls it a triumphal poem. Josephus [59] says, "That by this book are to be understood certain records kept in some safe place on purpose, giving an account of what happened among the Hebrews from year to year, and called Jasher, or the upright, on account of the fidelity of the annals."

It is known that such have been the curiosity and anxiety to discover this missing book, that several forgeries under that name have appeared from time to time; and the Rev. Mr. Horne,[60] in his Introduction to the Study of the Scripture,[61] has been at some pains to collect a history of the various fabrications of Jasher; the most remarkable of which was originally published in England, in the year 1750, by a person called Illive, and purported to be a translation from a Hebrew work of that name, found in Persia by *Alcuin*. It was republished in Bristol in the year 1829, and a copy is now in my possession. It is a miserable fabrication, occupying but sixty two and a half pages, with copious notes, making out Jasher to be one of the Judges, whereas the translation of the word is the upright, or the upright record. In the same work of Dr. Horne, a slight reference is made to the Book of Jasher, written in Rabbinical Hebrew, said to have been discovered in Jerusalem at its capture under Titus, and printed in Venice in 1813. This is the book now translated into English for the first time. . . . The printer's Hebrew preface to Jasher shows that it was a painful transcript from a very old and almost illegible Hebrew record, and printed by and with the consent of the great Consistory of Rabbins at Venice, who alone had the power of publishing such works from the Hebrew records as they deemed authentic. . . .

Whatever may have been written and published by commentators, relative to the fabrications of Jasher, I am persuaded they had no reference to this work, although this is the work slightly touched upon by Dr. Horne, as the publication in Venice, on the first discovery of printing; but of its origin and history he knew nothing beyond the rumor that it had originally been brought from Jerusalem. There are some events recorded in Jasher, that are found in the Talmud, no doubt copied from Jasher; for although we find in the Talmud, the Mishnah, and Gemarrah, many parables and fanciful tales, to effect moral and religious purposes, yet every thing that we have in Jasher we find recorded in the Bible, with this difference, that in Jasher the occurrences of the Bible are amplified and detailed at length. The celebrated philosopher, Mendelsohn,[62] expresses a high opinion of this work. There are, nevertheless, some events which are recorded in Jasher, which may create surprise, particularly a detail of the rape of the Sabines, which, at the first glance, I was disposed to consider as an interpolation; but a little reflection satisfied me that it was an event placed in proper chronological order. . . . If as Pizron says, the separation of the Sabines from the Umbrians took place 1500 years before Christ, it will not be far distant from the time at which Jasher places the rape of the Sabine women, in the 91st year of the life of Abraham. . . .

Without giving it to the world as a work of Divine inspiration, or assuming the responsibility to say that it is not an inspired book, I have no hesitation in pronouncing it a work of great antiquity and interest, and a work that is entitled, even regarding it as a literary curiosity, to a great circulation among those who take pleasure in studying the Scriptures.[63]

M. M. Noah

New-York, April, 1839

LXXXII
German-Jewish
Scholarship in America, 1838

Isaac Nordheimer was the first representative of nineteenth-century German Hebrew scholarship to come to America. He was named to the professorship of Oriental Languages in the University of the City of New York, now called New York University. Soon after his arrival, he published the first major work of Jewish scholarship issued in America, *A Critical Grammar of the Hebrew Language.*[64] In his Preface and Introduction, from which excerpts are given below, Nordheimer showed that he was an adherent of the scientific philology that was one of the new sciences of his age. He reviewed the revolution introduced by this new science, and its significance for the appreciation of the relations among languages. He maintained that it was no longer possible to consider the grammar of any language in isolation from that of other languages, thus illustrating the claim of scientific philology that all languages are subject to identical laws. He attempted to mediate between Gesenius's [65] overuse of parallels from other languages in place of explanations of difficult points in Hebrew grammar and Ewald's [66] emphasis on the universal rules, "frequently so vague and arbitrary," that Hebrew exemplifies.

When Nordheimer's article on "The Talmud and the Rabbies" [sic] appeared in *The American Biblical Repository* for October, 1839, it was prefaced by a page of "Introductory Remarks" by the editor of that journal. Among his other comments, the editor characterized Dr. Nordheimer in the following words:

"Dr. Nordheimer is not of that class of Jews who submit their consciences to the traditional authority of the Talmud, as a divine revelation. With him the 'Law and the Testimony' are the Old Testament Scriptures, and he feels no restraint in treating the traditional books of the Jews as merely human compositions, of no authority whatever excepting so far as they contain veritable history and sound instruction. He writes, therefore, not as an advocate of the Jewish traditions, but as a scholar, who, possessing the keys to this storehouse of learning, is willing to open it to that large class of our readers who have had less opportunity of becoming acquainted with its curious and interesting interior structure and history as well as with the accumulated mass of useless plenty which it contains." [67]

163. NORDHEIMER'S "PREFACE AND INTRODUCTION," 1838 [68]

The appearance of a Hebrew Grammar claiming to be a critical one, will not, it is thought, in the present state of philological science, prove entirely unacceptable. Indeed it might somewhat savour of affectation, were the author to offer any apology for the publication of his work in a period so productive in all the departments of literature; since it has been undertaken, and by the permission of the Almighty so far completed, with the design of meeting the urgent demands which the improvements effected in every branch of general philology now make on the cultivators of the Hebrew language for its further and more philosophical developement. With this view of the subject always before him, it has been the author's constant aim, to analytically investigate, and synthetically exhibit and explain, those laws which give rise to the phenomena of formation and inflection presented by one of the most natural and regular of languages; and at the same time incidentally to point out its surprisingly intimate connection, both lexicographical and grammatical, not only with the other Shemitish languages, but also with those of the Japhetish or Indo-European stock, thereby laying open to the view of the future investigator in this interesting field of research the rich mine of discovery which awaits him. How far the present work may have succeeded in effecting these important purposes, it must be left for the candid and impartial critic to state, and for time to decide.

The period has now gone by when a grammar was regarded as complete which exhibited the etymological and syntactical forms of a language as phenomena peculiar to itself, and whose sole merit consisted in the degree of diligence employed in collecting these facts, and the clearness of the arrangement in which they were displayed. In the present age, when philology, by means of the philosophical mode of treatment to which it has been subjected, is raised to the rank of a science, that grammarian will not be considered as having duly executed his task who does not enter upon the resolution of the phenomena of the particular language he undertakes to discuss, with the conviction that they are all necessary results of immutable and constantly operating laws, and with the intention of discovering and exhibiting those laws, and of applying them to the illustration of the whole body of facts which the language presents; at the same time showing for what reason and in what manner certain forms are made to serve certain grammatical purposes, and how these forms have arrived at their existing state. By this method of proceeding, the grammar of an individual language, which must otherwise prove a dry collection of lifeless, arbitrary, and loosely connected facts, is reduced to a completely organized system, connected in the most intimate manner by internal and eternal bands to an entire science.

The honor of creating this new and splendid era in philology has been reserved for the nineteenth century; the distinguishing characteristic of which is an impatience of the circumscribed limits within which our less enterprising forefathers were content to move, and an ardent desire to extend the moral, political, and literary horizon to its utmost stretch. In the general struggle of all classes of men for the advancement and elevation of their several pursuits, the philologist has not remained idle. For, as an aspiring youth, not satisfied with the one-sided view of men and things obtained by even the most intimate acquaintance with all that pertains to his country, travels through divers and far distant regions, and, after contemplating the exhaustless variety of their institutions and productions with the comprehensive glance of a world-historian, returns with his knowledge increased, his views enlarged, and his powers of observation sharpened, to his native land, where he meets with a thousand sources of interest and instruction which before from their very familiarity escaped his attention: so the philologist, to whose elevated aims the study of a few favourite tongues no longer suffices, turns his attention to that cradle of history, arts, and languages, the East, and, having reached the banks of the remote Indus, by investigating the venerable tongues there still existing, discovers the means and the manner of exchanging their ideas which men have employed from the birth of time; with the knowledge thus acquired, he applies himself anew to the examination of his native tongue and of those more nearly related to it, whose structure now presents to his delighted view a philosophical symmetry and beauty of which before he possessed not the slightest conception.

The revolution thus produced within the last thirty years in the science of philology, is one which for magnitude and rapidity has not been surpassed in the history of the human mind. When the scholars of Europe directed their intellectual vision to that newly discovered star in the East, the Sanscrit, now so brightly illumining the horizon of philology, and led on by its refulgent beams arrived at the classic soil of the ancient Hindu, where to their astonishment they recognised the scenery of their own familiar homes, and heard the well known accents of their native tongues, they began to anticipate a discovery of no less importance, than the means of demonstrating the correctness of those views of the fundamental connection existing between all languages, which had long pressed themselves on the attention of critical minds. For, knowing as they did that languages are the product of the movements of the organs of speech, which are originated and controlled by the emotions of the soul, . . . and also that, as human nature is in all times and places essentially the same, so consequently is human feeling, they argued with justice that these results of the operations of the mind, however concurrent circumstances might cause them externally to vary, must nevertheless bear a strong internal resemblance to each other.

The real conditions of the difficult problem the solution of which is the nature of that common bond of union between all languages whose existence has long been felt and acknowledged as certain, begin to be more clearly understood, now that the philologist, by a philosophical study and comparison of languages the most remote, is prepared to seek this intimate connection in something deeper than the mere outward form, viz. in the nature of the human mind,

the primary cause of all language and in the structure of the organs
of speech, the universal instrument by which it is produced. The
truth of the proposition is now fully established, that, as the logician
in undertaking to discover and explain the laws of thinking, (the
internal speech or language of the soul, depending indeed upon
words, but not yet incorporated into sounds,) must examine into all
the faculties of the human mind, watch with a deeply penetrating
look their movements, operations, and progress, and finally display
the results of his inquiries in a series of laws so systematically
progressive that each one may serve as the foundation for that
which succeeds it; in like manner the philologist, after an accurate
investigation and comparison of the various powers of the mind,
must discover in the relation of the physical senses to the external
world, how the internal man becomes excited to cause the organs
of speech to be set in motion, and in what manner these organs
are compelled by his feelings to the production of articulate sounds.

At the very outset of his inquiry, he will not fail to recognise
the important truth, that all the nations on which the sun shines
in his daily course, from the subdued and patient Chinese to the
untamed savage that roams the wilds of America, have the same
purpose in putting their organs of speech in motion, namely, to
embody in sounds the operations of their minds; and that those
ideas and feelings which one nation wishes to communicate, another
will likewise desire to convey. But that which remained undivided
and unchanged in the harmony of thought and feeling, and dependent for its form on the subjective character of each individual
nation, as soon as it steps out into the external world through the
agency of the organs of speech, becomes diversified in a variety as
boundless as the modifications which the voice and the movements
of the organs themselves admit. Thus the ideas must necessarily
break through their previous harmony in order to issue forth em-
bodied in sounds; and as these come in contact with the rest of
the external world, the reaction exerts upon their formation a
powerful influence. And hence the development of these sounds,
which are produced by changes in the position or configuration of
the organs of speech, as for instance the vowels, or by their actual
collision, as the consonants, although in all times and places essen-

tially the same, exhibits itself under varying aspects, not only in the different languages of separate nations, but also in the often numerous dialects of a single tongue. . . .

We may venture to observe, that while the stupendous exertions made to elucidate the Indo-European languages challenge the admiration of the learned world, to those of the Shemitish stock ample justice has not hitherto been done.

Ewald was the first who showed to any considerable degree that the modern improvements in philology have extended to the Hebrew—a language that has of late years attracted an increasing share of notice, particularly since its acquisition has been facilitated, and its importance to the philologist enhanced, by the learned labours of Gesenius. But the very attention thus drawn to the Hebrew caused it sooner to be perceived, that the illustration of its grammatical structure, even after the publication of the copious and well arranged Lehrgebäude of the latter scholar, was far from being complete. . . .

The grammarian who aims to be regarded as the philological investigator of a language, must first direct his attention to the discovery of its leading principles, which are few in number, and based on the nature of the human mind internally, on the genius of the language externally, and on the structure of the organs of speech, which form as it were the connecting link between them. From these the illustration of the phenomena he meets with must proceed, and to these they must continually be referred, in such manner that, each successive rule being exhibited as the consequence of what goes before, the whole etymology may be worked up into a gradually progressive system, in which the same mind that dictated the general plan may be seen pervading its minutest details. In this way grammar, instead of being converted into a means of overburdening the memory, is raised to the rank of a science, the study of which constitutes a mental discipline of the highest order.

Much it may be thought is here required, and much perhaps incidentally promised. These views, however, have not been adopted without mature reflection: they are the result of an enthusiastic study of the Hebrew and its cognate dialects, in addition to much time and labour devoted to the acquisition of a competent knowledge of the principal Indo-European languages. With the convictions upon his mind which such a course of study is calculated to produce, the author has applied himself more particularly to effecting improvements in Hebrew grammar; and if the solution of many difficult points, by some left entirely unexplained, and by others imperfectly and artificially illustrated, and the exhibition of hitherto considered exceptions and irregularities as the necessary results of the laws which regulate all language, demonstrate the correctness of the leading principles with which these investigations were undertaken, and justify the hope of having brought the subject of his labours nearer to perfection, he may be allowed to entertain the pleasing thought, not to have endeavoured in vain. If he might venture to intimate the light in which he could desire his work to be regarded in connection with the preceding labours of those two distinguished philologists, Gesenius and Ewald, he would remark, that while in forming his opinions he has remained completely independent of both, his aim has been to preserve a course intermediate to those which they have pursued. . . .

Thus, on the one hand, the author has not shunned the discussion of the most formidable topics that present themselves in the course of the etymology, even to the minutest particulars. Nor has he rested satisfied, in attempting their illustration, with adducing as a *ground form* some similar appearance in the Aramaic or Arabic; for, indispensable as a knowledge of the sister dialects certainly is to a thorough acquaintance with the Hebrew, the true use of such knowledge consists not in the bare citation of parallel cases, but in the application of the principles which regulate their phenomena to the illustration of the Hebrew within its own limits. A grammar is not like a lexicon. In the construction of the latter it becomes requisite to consult a variety of books in order to complete the list of significations in which words are employed, before we can arrive with certainty at their radical meanings; and when the literary monuments of a language are but few in number, so that some words may not occur in such connections as to render their import perfectly clear, recourse must be had to the cognate dialects, which may afford the information required. But the grammar of a language, which is the logic of speech, must be contained as completely in one book as in a hundred or a thousand.

On the other hand, the author has not allowed himself to be actuated by a mere thirst for novelty, or a desire to contradict all previous statements. His constant search has been directed to the attainment of truth and simplicity; and, as he believes, his inquiries have not unfrequently been rewarded by the discovery of new and important facts, which have enabled him to place matters that had been the subjects of such discussion in a clearer light. He has never lost sight of his principal object, which has been to render his work not only theoretically but likewise practically useful; and on that account, while he has spared no pains to reduce every part of grammatical formation and inflection to a comparatively small number of elementary principles, he has withheld many suggestions on points of minor importance which might have presented an artificial appearance. He trusts, therefore, that while his labours may not prove void of interest to the scholar already conversant with the language, they will render its acquisition an agreeable intellectual exercise for the learner.

LXXXIII

Proposals for
Modern Jewish Education, 1830

Dr. D. L. M. Peixotto,[69] in his *Anniversary Discourse* before the Society for the Education of Poor Children and the Relief of Indigent Persons of the Jewish Persuasion,[70] at the Society's second anniversary in 1830, made two suggestions for specific action in line with the Society's objective. The first was that a school be established to educate primarily the orphan children for whose benefit the Society was founded. Peixotto saw no reason, however, for limiting the benefits of the school to those orphans and he recommended that the school be open to others, of various ages and that instruction be organized on Pestalozzian[71] principles, with emphasis on scientific and practical studies, as well as on the study of Hebrew. Peixotto's second suggestion was that, in order to provide competent teaching in this school, the Society should join with other Jewish groups in financing the education of a young man for the combined offices of teacher and preacher, an office, that, the speaker noted, had theretofore been held by men of inadequate training. In addition to this educational discussion, a section of Peixotto's speech dealt with the general principles of Jewish philanthropy.[72]

164. PEIXOTTO'S EDUCATIONAL PROPOSALS, 1830 [73]

1. The first [proposal] is the formation of a school on principles similar to those of Pestallozzi. Let a few acres of ground be purchased at a convenient distance from the city, a plain neat tenement erected thereon, and here let a number of pupils be educated in the various branches of useful knowledge, and in the practical arts and sciences. It is not necessary that all the pupils be infants or mere boys. Those more advanced might likewise be admitted, and

from all who possessed the means, some compensation should be required towards defraying the expenses of the establishment. Nor should the rich disdain to mingle with the poor. It is the beauty and perfection of the plan of Pestalozzi, that all children, of whatever rank, are educated on equal terms, and brought up to a simultaneous knowledge of morality and learning. And here I trust I shall be pardoned if I step out of my path to recommend generally to all our brethren, both those who are members of our society and those who are not, the study of the practical sciences of life.[74] There is no individual, whatever the pursuit in which he may be engaged, who will not gain fast accessions to his means of happiness and usefulness, by extending the boundaries of his general knowledge. The means of accomplishing this important object are within every man's grasp. The "Society for the Diffusion of Useful Knowledge"[75] publish comprehensive but concise treatises on all the sciences, in numbers which can be had for the trifling sum of twelve and a half cents each. The introductory essay on the advantages and pleasures of science, from the master pen of Brougham,[76] should be universally perused.

In the school to be erected, I would direct that one of the first objects to be taught the pupil should be a knowledge of the Hebrew language. An acquaintance with the language of our forefathers and of our sacred laws, is the only guarantee we have for the preservation of our faith and our duty, and for the sacred bonds of a common descent.

Than a school such as I now propose, I know of no more effectual means to ensure the progressive and permanent advancement of our people. An eloquent writer of this country, illustrating the advantages of public schools, thus forcibly and beautifully expresses himself:

"If a stranger should enquire of me," says this philanthropist, "the principal cause and source of the greatness of my country, would I bid him look on the ocean widely loaded with our merchandise, and proudly ranged by our navy? or on the lands where it is girdled with roads and burthened with the produce of industry and ingenuity? Would I bid him look on these things, as the spring of our prosperity? Indeed I would not. Nor would I show him our colleges and literary institutions, for he can see nobler ones elsewhere. I would pass all these by, and would lead him out by some winding highway among the hills and woods, and when the cultivated spots grew small and infrequent, and the houses became few and scattered, and a state of primitive nature seemed to be immediately before us, I would stop in some sequestered spot, and directed by a steady hum, like that of bees, I would point to him a lowly building, hardly better than a shed, but full of blooming, happy children, collected together from the remote and unseen farmhouses, conning over their various tasks, or reading with a voice of reverential monotony, a portion of the word of God; and I would bid him note, that even here in the midst of poverty and sterility, was a specimen of the thousand nurseries in which all our children are taught of the Lord and formed, some to legislate for the land, and all to understand its constitution and laws, to maintain their unspotted birthright, and contribute to the great aggregate of the intelligence, the morality, the power, and the peace of this mighty commonwealth."

How, it may be asked, are we to procure a teacher? And this leads me to the second means which I would suggest.

2. Let this Society unite with the different congregations and societies of our people to contribute a mutual fund towards educating, in the most liberal manner, a youth of promise and character; let his heart be imbued with the great principles of our holy religion, and when he has attained to proper years, he may enter on the discharge of the duties of teacher of his brethren. With this duty should be blended that of expositor of the scriptures, and moral instructor to the congregation which support him; a duty which, in this country, has been hitherto only performed at intervals, and never by individuals expressly educated for its arduous and delicate discharge. That the members of our congregations would derive benefit from the adoption of this plan; and that the rising generation more especially, who are now threatened with a total want of religious and moral instruction, require an office of this kind to be instituted, must be self-evident to every one acquainted with the actual condition of our people, and anxious for its improvement.

LXXXIV

For Entertainment
and Instruction, 1820

When Isaac Gomez, Jr. (1768–1831),[77] of New York compiled an
anthology of selections, chiefly from classical sources, he did so
with the hope of encouraging the cultivation of sound literary taste
among Americans. In a sense, he may be said to have entered a
demurrer against cultural nationalism. His book appeared with
recommendations from Dr. Philip Milledoler,[78] one of the most
active members of the American Society for Meliorating the Condition of the Jews,[79] and Mordecai M. Noah, as well as from
teachers like Samuel L. Mitchell,[80] J. W. Kellogg,[81] John W.
Picket,[82] and E. Wheaton.[83] The prize recommendation, however,
was an excerpt from a letter from John Adams, ex-President of the
United States. The letters that passed between Adams and Gomez
are printed below together with the brief preface to Gomez's
Selections of a Father for the Use of his Children.

165. GOMEZ'S PREFACE, 1820 [84]

The following volume of Selections is published with a hope, that
it may prove entertaining to the old, and instructive to the young;
that it may beguile a few tedious moments, and improve a leisure
hour. Original essays are always deserving attentive consideration;
they mark the progress of American intellect, and develope the
taste, fancy and wisdom of American pens: but, as a young country,
we must not flatter ourselves with excelling in all the departments
of literature; and, therefore, we must establish a true taste upon
a firm foundation, we must select from the most approved authors,
and thus gradually lead to perfection of our own. Such motives
induces the publisher to give it to the world; and, he trusts, that no
part of it may give offence, for none could possibly be intended;

and, with these introductory remarks, he submits the work to the generous patrons of literature.

166. GOMEZ TO JOHN ADAMS, 1820 [85]

New York March 28th 1820

John Adams Esqr
Dr Sir

Pardon the liberty I take in addressing you a Gentn. with whome I have not the honour of a Personal acquaintance, but knowing the high rank you bear in the Literary World has induced me to request your polite acceptance of a work I have just published under the title of "Selections of a Father for the use of his Children,["] which have the goodness to give a reading & Sir shall feel highly gratified to be favd with your oppinion of the same, and the more so should such oppinion meet my wishes having formed & published the work for the purpose of giving support to my amiable family a matter in my mind of the highest importance to me as Husband & Parent, therefore your recommendation my Dr Sir (should my work merit it) would add greatly to my Interest in this affair. . . .

I have the honour to be   With due respect   Dr Sir   Your friend & Very hum svt   Isaac Gomez Junr

167. JOHN ADAMS TO ISAAC GOMEZ, JR., 1820 [86]

Montezello April 10th 1820

Sir

Your selection of a father for the use of his Children, are worthy to be presented by every father, to every Child—and deserve a place in every family, there is not an impure or mean thought in the whole Book. . . . But I regret that you have wholly omitted Cicero whose works abound in the most excellent moral Political Philosophy especially his Offices, His Essay on old age, on Friendship, his dream of Scipio his Letter to his Brother Quintas about to take upon him the third time the Government of Asia.[87] . . . The Book has solid merit, and I wish it were in the hands of every Child who can read it. To me it shall be a Manuel on my table, in which I can constantly find almost any of the most beautiful morsels, ancient and modern, which would take me hours in rummageing Volumes to find without it. . . .

I am Sir your humble Servant   John Adams

Isaac Gomez Junr
New York

168. GOMEZ TO JOHN ADAMS, 1820 [88]

New York April 17th 1820

John Adams Esqr
Dr Sir

I was made happy in having the honour of receivg your polite and much esteemed favour of the 10th Inst in answer to mine on the subject of my Publication, for the high encomium you are pleased to pass on my work, accept Dr Sir my most sincere thanks as well as for the friendly & Parental manner in which you are pleased to state your regret at my having omitted Cicero &c I regret it myself since I have recd your valuable opinion. . . .

I shall feel a Pride in placing amongst my list of recommendations Your polite mention of my publication and which I feel assured will not only add a lusture [sic] to my Book but will also I trust be beneficial to my Interest in the sale of my labourous production. . . .

Respected Sir   Yr Obliged friend &   Very huml Servt

Isaac Gomez Junr

P S respected Sir

In extracting from your amiable letter the recommendation you are pleased to give to my work I have taken the liberty of omitting the parts where you notice the Authors & Subjects you are pleased to regret my not having noticed.

LXXXV
The Polonies Talmud Torah,
1808-1811

Congregation Shearith Israel maintained some sort of Jewish school-ing from at least 1731.[89] By the beginning of the nineteenth century, however, the Shearith Israel school, called Yeshibat Minhat Areb, was in a very unsatisfactory state.[90] The will of Myer Polony,[91] who died in New York in 1801, left a bequest of $900 to the syna-gogue, the interest of which was to be used to establish a com-munal day school. Accordingly the name of Yeshibat Minhat Areb was changed to the Polonies Talmud Torah, in honor of its bene-factor, and some changes in curriculum were made to conform to its new status. In fact, the Polonies Talmud Torah was not as suc-cessful as was hoped, and it served chiefly as a charity school for a small number of pupils coming from the poorer class.

The preamble to its constitution of 1808, reproduced below, indi-cates the education objectives of responsible members of the syna-gogue and their ideas on how to achieve these ends. Although the Polonies Talmud Torah was an integral part of the common school system, by an oversight, deliberate or not, it did not receive the state subsidy that other denominational charity schools were given. In 1811, however, the Trustees of Shearith Israel petitioned the Legislature for this grant, and the authorization was given.

169. PREAMBLE, CONSTITUTION OF
POLONIES TALMUD TORAH, 1808 [92]

In the establishment of this institution, the following means are proper to be adopted for its accomplishment: firstly, to improve the understanding and to instruct the scholars, thoroughly, in the principles of religion and morality: and secondly, to have a strict attention paid to their actions, in order to make them conformable to the aforementioned requisites.

To accomplish the above object, the scholars are to be inspired with a sense of honor, a sense of shame, and above all, a sense of emulation.

As principles of religion generally accompany those of morality, an attention to the one insures the promotion of the other; their daily repetition of prayers can not alone constitute a strict adherence to religion; but it must be the knowledge of the Divine Origin of that religion, that can make them zealous adherents to every part of its tenets.

The task of informing their minds and maturing their judgment must necessarily devolve on the Teacher, who should by the plainest arguments, unassisted by those abstruse speculations that generally tend to distract the judgment and injure the memory, impress on their minds the excellencies of our *belief.* A certain time before or after the hours of study should be appropriated to *devotion,* and the usual service ought to be performed by one of the scholars competent to the task. A sense of decorum during divine worship must be strongly inculcated, and a certain grade of punishment should be instituted for inattention to this observance.

The encouragement of a sense of emulation, should be the primary object of the teacher and superintendants of the school, to inspire it honestly in the breasts of all the scholars, would be the most certain means of insuring improvement in their studies, a favourable report to the inspectors of their assiduity and conduct, advancing them to the honourable post of monitor to the junior classes, removing them to a higher order of study, and the presentation of a medal at the annual public examination, are the rewards that should be held out to them as incentives to assiduous application.

Crimes or vices should, in every respect, be treated in a different manner from faults occasioned by idleness or neglect of studies; the punishment of the former should, at first, be by enjoining extraordinary tasks, and a degradation from the rank they hold in a class, to a lower one; when these methods prove ineffectual, and the scholar is found to be of an incorrigible nature, he certainly can be no longer a fit companion for the rest, and therefore should be reported to the inspectors, who may adjudge the punishment according to the crime, and, if the nature of it warrants the necessity, he should, for example sake, be publicly expelled [from] the school. Those faults occasioned by idleness or inattention, should be punished in a lesser degree, according to the discretion of the teacher.

It is also absolutely necessary, that the most profound respect should be paid to the preceptor, and a want of it should subject the delinquent to the severest penalty the rules can inflict.

The punishment of the scholars for appearing unclean in person and dress, the manner of conducting themselves, suppressing bad habits, &c. should rest entirely with the discretion of the teacher.

A strict and uniform adherence to the foregoing remarks, which are solely made with a view to benefit the institution, must ultimately tend towards promoting the chief end in contemplation, viz. To instill in the youthful mind a love of learning, a veneration for religion and morality, and an attainment of useful instruction, whilst all visionary and impracticable schemes should be rejected on the one hand, just and salutary maxims ought to be adopted on the other.

170. PUBLIC FUNDS FOR THE TALMUD TORAH, 1811 [93]

January 3, 1811: Mr. N. Judah [94] presented the draft of a memorial to the legislature received from Mr. Dewitt Clinton [95] which was read as follows:

To the Honorable the Legislature of the State of New York

The petition of the trustees of the Congregation of Shearith Israel in the City of New York most respectfully represent:

That from the year 1793 a school has been supported from the funds of the said Congregation for the education of their indigent children. That on the 8th of April, 1801, certain school monies were distributed among seven charity schools of the said city, supported by religious societies. That the free school of the Roman Catholic church and that of your memorialists were overlooked in this benevolent distribution. That on the 21st of March, 1806, a law was passed placing the school of the former on the same footing as the others. That your memorialists also made application to the legislature, but did not succeed owing as they presume to the pressure of business. Your memorialists fully persuaded that the Legislature will look with an equal eye upon all occupations of people who conduct themselves as good and faithful citizens, and conscious that nothing has been omitted on their part to deserve the same countenance and encouragement which has been exhibited to others, do most respectfully pray your Honorable body to extend the same relief to their charity school which has been granted to all others in this city. Ordered that the clerk prepare a copy of the same and hand it to the President of the Board for the signatures of the members thereof, and that when completed, it be delivered to Mr. Dewitt Clinton to be by him presented to the Legislature, with the certificate of the school being supported from the funds of the Congregation attached thereto.

April 22d. 1811: The Mayor's compliments to the Trustees of the Congregation Shearith Israel and sends the enclosed section of an act which passed the Legislature for their benefit. 19th of April, 1811.

Extract from the act entitled an act of the payment of certain officers of government and for other purposes passed April 9, 1811.

"And be it further enacted that it shall be lawful for the Mayor, Aldermen and commonalty of the City of New York to pay to the trustees of Shearith Israel in the city of New York the like sum as was paid to the other religious congregations respectively by virtue of the act entitled "an act for directing certain monies to be applied for the use of free schools in the City of New York" and the act entitled an "Act respecting the free school of St. Peters Church in the City of New York" the monies so paid to be applied according to the directions of the first mentioned act, and the treasurer of this State is hereby directed to pay to the said Mayor, Aldermen and the Commonalty of the City of New York the sum so paid by them, out of the unappropriated money arising from the duties on sales at auction in the said city."

LXXXVI

The Philadelphia Story, 1833-1840

The documents below illustrate the difficulties faced by Isaac Lee-ser [96] in his attempts, over a period of years, to furnish adequate instruction in Hebrew and in the Jewish religion to children in Philadelphia. Leeser's conviction, not only at this time but also years later when it became a frequent editorial topic in his periodical *The Occident*,[97] was that Jewish children attending the public schools were being indoctrinated with Christian ideas and beliefs. For this reason, he was eager to maintain an all-day Jewish school where Jewish indoctrination could be substituted for Christian. His letters to the members and leaders of Congregation Mikveh Israel reveal how disappointed he was with his attempts to carry on such a school.[98]

Under the sponsorship of the Female Hebrew Benevolent Society,[99] and with the devoted assistance of Rebecca Gratz, however, Leeser did establish a Sunday School for the supplementary religious education of Jewish children. The two documents in the group below are the preface to Leeser's *Catechism for Younger Children,* the first attempt in America to reduce Jewish teachings to this form, and his review of the history and background of the first permanent Jewish Sunday School.

171. LEESER'S MEMORIAL ON SUNDAY SCHOOLS, 1840 [100]

Sunday schools are nothing new among our Christian neighbours,[101] as many sects of them have had such establishments for shorter or longer periods. Among our people, however, the case is very different, as far as the knowledge of the writer extends; and only at Richmond, Va., had the attempt been made, with but partial success, by the late Isaac B. Seixas,[102] (then minister of that congregation, and since then of the synagogue *Sheerith Israel,* at New York,) and the writer of this memorial, before several of our ladies, feeling that something might and should be done to improve the religious character of the Jewish children, and to give them at least an elementary and comprehensive idea of their duties, resolved on founding a school for the promulgation of religious knowledge on the first day of the week, it being a general day of leisure, and as it could be devoted to this pious object without interfering with the exercises of other schools, and the avocations of the teachers. This plan, which promised to be so beneficial, soon found many willing to co-operate; and the zeal of the teachers, was seconded by the eagerness of the children to avail themselves of the opportunity to acquire a knowledge of their religion. The school was at first commenced under the patronage of the Female Hebrew Benevolent Society of Philadelphia; but unless he errs, the writer thinks that it never had to depend for support upon that excellent charity, as from the first outset donations were freely offered for the furtherance of this blessed undertaking.

The first assemblage of the scholars took place at the house No. 97, Walnut street; but when the ladies had to give up the room they there occupied, the Franklin Institute,[103] with a commendable spirit of liberality, permitted them to take possession of a spacious apartment in the old Masonic Hall, in Chesnut street, where the weekly meetings have taken place now for more than eighteen months.

As may easily be imagined, some prejudice was at first manifested by various persons, who fancied that they discovered an objectionable imitation of gentile practices in this undertaking, forgetting that it is the first duty of Israel to instil knowledge of divine things in the hearts of the young, and this institution was eminently calculated to bestow this necessary blessing alike upon rich and poor without fee or price. It is but seldom that so noble an aim has been sought after, begun solely for the glorification of our Maker and the well-being of his people; it is therefore gratifying to record, that this unfounded prejudice has nearly died away, and one cannot give a better evidence of the fact, than that now fully one hundred children are enrolled, and what is more, that nearly all attend whenever the weather is at all favourable, and this despite the great distance which many of the scholars and teachers have to walk, living as they do in almost every part of the city and suburbs.

Another great difficulty, and one far more formidable, was the scarcity of suitable books to be placed in the hands of scholars, since those published by the American Sunday School Union, although admirably written, and having a powerful tendency to impress the minds of children, contain so much matter of a sectarian nature as must almost banish them from a Jewish school, where it is of importance to inculcate those principles which are the foundation of our religion. The only other books within our reach were the Elements of the Jewish Faith, by Rabbi S. Cohen,[104] and the Instruction in the Mosaic Religion, arranged from the German of Johlson, by the writer of this.[105] In this emergency the Child's Bible Questions, by the A.S.S. Union, was of necessity but partially adopted, there not being a similar book and one more free from sectarian matter at hand; but it is pleasing to remark, that an adaptation of this little work after our own manner is now in the hands of a young lady of this place, and will, it is hoped, see the light soon, and this with the consent of the A.S.S. Union, who have waived their copyright in our favour; [106] this, too, is a highly gratifying fact, and it speaks loudly and emphatically of the enlightened views of the board of publication of that powerful institution, and especially of the kindness of John Hall, Esq.,[107] through whom this polite offer has been conveyed.

Last spring the first anniversary examination took place. The day fixed upon was one of anxiety to many a little heart; and fathers and mothers too, looked forward with some thrill of hope and fear to the probation of their children. It need not be told, that the exercises were highly pleasing, and the liberal contributions, which were voluntarily made without any solicitation, proved more clearly than words, how pleasing an object our brethren had witnessed that day.

In the mean while the example set in this city was followed in New York [108] and Charleston [109] about the same time; and there, as well as here, the superintendence and teaching are in the hands of the ladies. The endowment, likewise, in both places, has been quite liberal; and there can be but little doubt, that the commencement so happily made, will not fail to produce all the good results which could reasonably be expected. It is manifest, however, that such imitation abroad could not do otherwise than stimulate to perseverance the first authors of this good; and they have not disappointed the hopes formed of them. They have gone on improving their charges by careful training, and these have for the most part proved by an acquisition of knowledge and more correct deportment, especially at public worship, that the labour bestowed upon them has been well bestowed.

The increasing demand for religious information induced the writer, immediately after the above examination, to finish and to commit to the press the Catechism for Younger Children; and he mentions it with sincere gratitude that it has already been introduced in the three Sunday schools mentioned above, in several private institutions, and for family reading; it was more than he could have expected within nine months after its appearance; especially since he had so often claimed the support of his fellow-Israelites in his former publications. Yet he says it without affectation, that his issuing the two school-books, already mentioned, appeared to him like the launching of a frail bark upon a stormy sea; but the promptitude with which many of the answers were given by the scholars in their examination on yesterday, has inspired him with the hope that the frail bark may be made instrumental in bearing some devoted spirit to the haven of righteousness by the blessing of Him who imparteth knowledge, and giveth to man wisdom and understanding.

It was yesterday that the second examination of the scholars of this nursery of piety took place: [110] it was natural to expect some improvement upon the progress of last year, but the result far surpassed the most sanguine expectations. The northern half of the ground-floor of the synagogue was reserved for the scholars, each class headed by its teacher; and the steps leading to the ark were occupied by the youngest class, and certainly formed a collection of happy faces, which no one could look on without pleasure; and these little ones, when called upon to answer their Bible-questions, acquitted themselves in a manner highly gratifying to their parents and creditable to their youthful teacher. The other classes, as they were called up in succession, also showed that much care had been profitably bestowed; but it would be invidious to mention particulars where the whole was so satisfactory. The writer knows not how others felt, but he can truly say that he felt rejoiced and gratified; and to judge from the countenance of the many that thronged the place of worship, he may freely affirm, that never a public exhibition left more favourable impressions upon the hearers, and that the words of congratulation every where uttered must have sprung from hearts convinced that a good work had been done in Israel.

We were lately gratified by the arrival among us of the Rev. Moses N. Nathan,[111] Minister of the German Congregation, Shangaray Yashshar, of Kingston, Jamaica, who visits this country in quest of a renewal of his own health and that of his amiable companion. As the annual examination was so near at hand, Mr. N. was invited to address the congregation at the conclusion of the exercises; he kindly consented, and returned from New York, whither he had gone to the relations of his wife. He has conferred an additional favour by permitting us to have his address printed; [112] and it is to be hoped that its admirable sentiments will be long remembered after this interesting stranger shall have been restored to his home and station.

It only remains to be added, that at the conclusion of the address contributions for the school-fund, more liberal than last year, were made; and we may look forward to a long continuance of the usefulness among us of the religious enterprize of our benevolent sisters, and that it will every year lay a stronger hold on the affections of all the Israelites of this city; and all that then will be left is to hope that this example of righteousness may be universally followed, and cause the spread of truth and grace among all the seed of Jacob. . . .

Monday, March 30th. [1840]

172. LEESER'S PREFACE
TO HIS CATECHISM, 1839 [113]

The present is one of the series of books for the promotion of religious knowledge among the Israelites, whose vernacular is the English language, which I announced in my first publication about nine years ago. Although as yet the sale of my works has been scarcely adequate to defray the expenses: I have never given up the pleasing idea of supplying at convenient intervals, according to the best of my limited abilities, the lamentable deficiency of devotional works, which is on all sides admitted to exist among us. I would, however, do injustice to my feelings were I to let the present opportunity pass without acknowledging the kindness which has been extended to my various efforts, even in distant parts, by persons entirely unknown to me. Such indulgence, to the many defects discoverable in my writings, whilst it encourages me to persevere amidst many difficulties which need not be made public, claims my sincere thanks, and demands of me greater care and unremitting labour for the future, to prove that I have not been altogether unworthy of the kindness extended to me. But to Him above, who has not withheld from me his light and his manifold blessings, my heartfelt gratitude is justly due in a high degree, for having permitted me to accomplish what I have done, without much human assistance.

It is but justice to acknowledge, that, although this little book appears as an original, it is, nevertheless, founded upon a German work, by Dr. Eduard Kley,[114] of Hamburg, which appeared at Berlin in 1814, under the title of Catechismus Der Mosaischen Religion. For several years past there have appeared in Germany a number of Catechisms, all more or less valuable; and in thinking over the best plan for the present undertaking, it struck me that Dr. Kley's was the most suitable, even in preference to the one I originally entertained of giving it the form of a conversation on religion, which, however, I occasionally introduced, as will appear from inspection. I retained the division of subjects, nearly all the questions, and occasionally an answer of Dr. Kley. Still this book is no translation; because, in the first place, it contains fully double the quantity of the Doctor's book; and, secondly, not to mention that several important points had been omitted or too obscurely given by him, he had imparted a peculiar colouring to his ideas, which unfortunately have become rather too famous, since his connection with a society of schismatics, to whom he has borne the relation of pastor for many years past. Nevertheless, I would not detract the least from the merits of this learned and eloquent man despite of his errors; and I gladly admit that my labour was much abridged, by having so excellent a guide as he has furnished, which I preferred following, than be too anxious for entire originality, by which this Catechism could have gained nothing in value.

It has been my endeavour to make myself understood by children of from eight to fourteen years old; yet I fear that I may have failed, oftener than I should do, of rendering the subject-matter sufficiently clear. I trust, however, that teachers and parents will not put the book into the hands of their pupils and children, without giving at least a cursory explanation, which, it is confidently hoped, will be enough to assist the learner.

Occasionally a subject has been introduced more than once, which originated in the idea that it is better to have all the points connected together exhibited at one view; for children are but too apt to forget what they have learned some weeks back. So likewise were several Bible-texts quoted more than once, when it was thought that the same text would be the best applicable to explain or elucidate different subjects. This quoting twice may in a few instances have arisen from inadvertence, which is very likely to occur in a work so difficult to compose, on account of the youth of the persons for whose instruction it is intended; but generally it was done designedly for the reason given. I trust that some allowance will be made, if I have not succeeded in imparting all the interest, variety, and polish, such a work might have received by others better acquainted than I can pretend to be with the operation of the youthful mind; but the reader may be assured of one thing, that not a passage or a word even was allowed to pass without much care and anxious reflection; it was my endeavour to teach the truth, and the truth only.

Believing that as the scholar advances in a work, the matter may with advantage be a little more elaborately given, in order to require always a sufficient degree of application and study: I have not hesitated to use language a little more complicated and rather longer paragraphs in the latter than in the first chapters. Still, if thought too difficult, the chapters on the Moral Law, the Messiah, and the Life after Death and other portions, may be advantageously deferred till a second reading, as they are not absolutely necessary to an understanding of the whole subject.

With the confident hope that this unpretending work may have its useful effects, to awaken in the young a spirit of devotion and piety, I commit it to the care of the Great Teacher, who bestowed on us his law, as a guide to our souls, unto the haven of that happiness which He has destined for those who fear his name and lay hold of his covenant, to obey his will all the days that they live on the earth.

Philadelphia,

[Iyar 23d, 5599
[May 7th, 1839

LXXXVII

The First Jewish Trustee of Columbia College, 1814

The service of Gershom Mendes Seixas as trustee of Columbia College reveals the high regard in which the "minister" of Congregation Shearith Israel was held by the entire community. Seixas was the first of a long series of Jewish leaders in America to have conceived of his role as resembling that of an ambassador, representing the Jewish viewpoint in a non-Jewish, though friendly, environment. Seixas's career, especially in the post-Revolutionary era, anticipated the interfaith movement. It was based upon the idea that mutual understanding between religions was a sound basis for religious coexistence.

Even in this early period, Columbia College, though it was an Episcopalian foundation, accepted Jewish students and was ready to welcome a Jew to its Board of Trustees. Columbia's first president, when it was known as King's College, was Samuel Johnson.[115] Johnson was an enthusiast for the study of Hebrew and something of a Hebraist himself. To the extent that interfaith activity requires mutuality, a readiness on both sides to explain and attempt to understand, the attitude of the College was the necessary concomitant to Seixas's self-appointed task as Jewish ambassador to the Christian community.

When Seixas resigned his trusteeship, he was not replaced by another Jew. His election had been a tribute to his personal qualities, not a recognition of the Jews of New York as a group apart.

173. SEIXAS'S RESIGNATION, 1814 [116]

New York 7th Novr 1814

Sir

Will you be pleased to acquaint the honorable Board, that my Infirmities prevent me from the necessary attendance at their meetings. I therefore beg them to accept of my resignation.

That the Institution may continue to flourish, will always be (as it has ever been) the sincere desire of   Sir   Your most obd't Servt

Gershom Seixas

Richard Varick Esqre [117]
Chairman of the Board of Trustees of Columbia College

174. ACCEPTANCE OF SEIXAS'S RESIGNATION, 1815 [118]

At a Meeting of the Trustees of Columbia College held at the City Hall of the City of New York on Monday the 2d day of January 1815. . . .

A letter was read from the Revd. Gershom Seixas resigning his place as Trustee of Columbia College, whereupon

Resolved that the said Resignation be, and the same is hereby accepted.

LXXXVIII
Preparation for College, 1815

When full biographical studies of early American Jews have been completed, we may be able to work out reliable statistics on the number of Jewish youths who attended college in the years from 1789 to 1840, and also to give accurate information about which colleges they attended. For the time being, the information that is available is not sufficient for any detailed statement to be made. Isolated college students and graduates are known; no general statement is possible.

The interesting letters below tell of the preparation of Nathan Nathans [119] for admission to college. The first, from Nathans to his sponsor, William Meredith,[120] raises the question whether Nathans's religion will be a handicap at Harvard College, and whether, if this is so, he should not aim rather at admission to the University of Pennsylvania.[121] The second letter, a progress report from Nathans's tutor, also goes into the question of religion. We learn from it that the compromise that Nathans worked out was to observe both the Jewish and the Christian Sabbaths.

175. NATHAN NATHANS TO HIS GUARDIAN, 1815 [122]

Brighton, May 21st, 1815.

Wm Meredith Esqr.
Dear Sir.

There is one thing that I neglected mentioning in my last letter. I would wish to know wether it is your wish for Doctor Allen to prepare me, for the Cambridge Collegge or the University at Philada as I think there will be some difficulty about my religion at Cambridge, as I understand they are very strict; I think that it will be much better for me, to be prepared for the University at Philada as it will be much more agreeable to myself & family.

& I therefore hope it will meet your approbation. Give my best respects to Mr. Gratz, & be pleased to write me soon as school will commence the 29 this month.

I remain   Dear Sir,   Your affectionate ward,   Nathan Nathans.

176. REPORT OF A TUTOR, 1815 [123]

New Hope, Decr. 14, 1815

Wm. Meredith Esqr.
Dear Sir,

Agreeably to your request I drop you a few lines relative to the young gentleman whom you have placed under my care. It affords me real pleasure that I am able to give you so good an account of him. He has behaved with the strictest propriety in every respect. In his conduct he is respectful, & in his application to his studies, he is assiduous. I found him defective in his acquaintance with his Latin Grammar, owing I suppose to his having been permitted to translate Latin without sufficient previous acquaintance with it: but this defect I hope will ere long be remedied. I had feared lest there might be some difficulty on account of the peculiarities of his religious sentiment, & the regulations of my School relative to the observance of the Christian Sabbath; but I am happy to say there is none. He is permitted to observe his own Sabbath; & of his own accord, without any requisition from me he has regularly attended with the other young gentlemen under my care at the Church in which I preach, on our Sabbath. The moral & religious instruction which the young gentlemen who are with me receive on the Sabbath has a very beneficial influence on their conduct & their attention to their studies thro the week & I therefore consider it a matter of great importance strictly to attend to it. I hope to visit the City between Christmas and the New Year, & will then do myself the pleasure of calling on you: at present I shall only add that I am much pleased with young Mr. Nathans & I hope that his future conduct may prove as correct as is his present. Be pleased to present my respects to Mrs. Meredith & your family.

With sincere esteem & respect   I remain   Your Obdt. Servt.

Saml. B. How.[124]

LXXXIX

A Jewish Medical Writer, 1793

In the late eighteenth century, two schools of medical thought were in sharp opposition. One school was rationalistic in its approach, attempting to solve the problems of disease and to discover their treatments by logical inferences from the writings of earlier medical theorists. The other school was experimental, emphasizing the clinical description and trial-and-error cure of disease. Dr. Benjamin Rush,[125] at this time an outstanding leader of the medical profession in Philadelphia, advocated a method that was a synthesis of these two approaches. His theories of the nature of fever were, however, far less clearheaded than his ideas on method. He considered all fevers as the product of irregular action of the arteries; to remedy this condition, he advocated purges and bleeding. When he put this regimen into practice during the 1793 epidemic of yellow fever, he became a target for bitter attacks from other physicians.[126]

One of his opponents, David Nassy, a Jewish physician from Surinam, in the West Indies, was of the experimental school.[127] He was in Philadelphia at the time of the yellow fever epidemic of 1793.[128] He wrote, in French, his *Observations on the Cause, Nature and Treatment of the Epidemic Disorder, Prevalent in Philadelphia,* a careful description and clinical account, which was published, with a parallel English translation, in Philadelphia late in November, 1793.

Two years later, Dr. Nassy was elected to membership in the oldest American scientific society, the American Philosophic Society of Philadelphia, founded by Benjamin Franklin. His letter of acknowledgement, in French, dated June 19, 1795, speaks of his gratification at the honor, of the necessity for his return to Surinam, and of his intention to regard himself as a correspondent of the Society while in his own country.[129]

177. DR. DAVID NASSY ON YELLOW FEVER, 1793 [130]

Many Physicians have published in the newspapers of this country, their methods of preventing and curing this disease, which may be ranked as one of the most destructive and fatal; but none of them have yet thought of favoring the public with an accurate account of the nature, and particular symptoms of the fever, that makes such cruel havoc.

Never agreeing among themselves, they have mutually opposed the opinions of each other, and have often bestowed reciprocal offence. The result of this difference of ideas, always dangerous for suffering humanity, has been, that each prescribed according to his own manner, as well for preserving persons against the contagion, as for treating the disease, by bleeding, drastic purges, by stimulants, by diluents, by demulcents, by antiseptics, and by tonics, without pointing out, in the smallest degree, the circumstances or particular cases, wherein such medicines might be employed or rejected.

The most credulous amongst the people, alarmed by the public papers, and by the numerous precautions advised to be taken against the pretended pestilence, began to administer medicines to themselves, and in order to avoid imaginary evils, produced real ones; some by having recourse to the heating regimen, gave additional fire to their disease, and thus created their own graves; other applied to physicians, who, smitten with fear, thought that they perceived pestilential appearances in a common disorder, and ordered medicines, which could only add to the evil. Of consequence, those who did not fall a sacrifice, recovered with difficulty. Hence the number of the sick and dead have amazingly encreased; and the sentiment of fear operating upon every mind, has made the greatest part of the inhabitants to leave the city, and forsake in it, without attendance or assistance, the sick, who were not able to quit it.

Would to God, that instead of that fear carried to excess, the citizens of Philadelphia had imitated the Turks! thus behaving like them towards those, would not have abandoned their children, nor the children their parents, the servants their masters, nor friends each other; but every one would have contributed to comfort and solace one another. The physicians were frequently compelled, by motives of humanity, to become nurses to the sick, who were unable of themselves to take the medicines.

These remarks may sound harshly, but they are founded upon my own experience as well as that of several other physicians, who whilst others were arguing on the means of preserving the city from the contagion, were courageously treading in the path of practice, solicitous to fulfil the sacred and religious duties of their profession.

In order to make up as much as in my power lies, for the void left by those who have spoken of that disease in the public papers, I shall endeavour to express my ideas as clearly and precisely as I can.

I may have mistaken the inductions with which the diagnostic signs of the disease have furnished me. I may also have mistaken the proximate and distant causes of the present epidemic. But what I am to advance, shall be less founded on theory, which often deceives, than on practice, and my clinical observations. Thus, I will only say what I have seen, or believe myself to have seen, in my patients. I shall neither exaggerate nor disguise any thing. I only seek for truth, and I write but for the good of humanity, without intending to give my observations for incontestable decisions. Hippocrates has said of medicine, *Ars longa, occasio celeris, experimentum periculosum, et judicium difficile.* I have, then, no other aim but to stimulate my colleages, more learned than me, to enlighten the public. It is our duty likewise to undeceive the physicians in other parts of this continent, and of Europe, concerning the specifics recommended in the newspapers of North America, which may be very fatal to mankind. . . .

The result of all that I have said is that in the cure of this disease, no regular system can be followed: Therefore, I followed none, nor have I adopted any one medicine in preference to another. My prescriptions were only regulated by the conjectures which I have drawn from the examination of my patients, and the informations they could give me concerning their constitutions, and the state of their health before they were taken ill.

After that, here is a summary of the method I have followed, and still constantly follow, with such successes, that compared, with the

number of patients, whom I fear to have been the unfortunate victims of the means used in vain to cure them, confirms me more
and more in the resolution I have taken to follow that practice.*

As soon as I was called to visit a patient, and as soon as I perceived the least sign of inflammation, I, first of all, ordered him
to be bled once or twice, and regulated the quantity of blood to be
let, according to his age, and the strength of his constitution. If it
was the first day of the sickness, and the inflammation was not likely
to be of consequence, and if the patient inclined much to vomiting,
I administered to him either a vomit in a large quantity of water,
or some purgative of senna, manna, cream of tartar, and salt of
seignette to cleanse the first passages. If he complained of a head
ache, which did not lessen, or if the inflammation began, I pre-

* I have visited and attended, during the course of this disease, that
is to say, since the 28th August to this day, more than 160 patients of
whom 117 were really attacked with the fever, which it would be difficult to call by a very characteristic name. Of that number I had the
misfortune to lose 19. To eleven of these I was only sent for on the 2d,
4th or 5th day after they were taken ill, after they had been treated by
other physicians, after they had taken violent vomits, cathartics, tincture
of bark, with liq. laud. as they themselves informed me. Every one complained of beating pains on their stomach already much swelled.—
Eight others who sent for me in the beginning of this sickness, had
on the second or third day of my treatment, considerable vomitings of
a black matter, the jaundice, pissed blood, and died on the 4th, 5th 7th
or 9th day.

I do not mention other patients whom I have visited and treated during that time, the number of which exceeds fifty. Many had but little
remittent, or colliquative fever. A greater number were affected more
in mind than body, having consulted me, the more I attributed their
uneasy situation to the fear they were seized with, and the more that
I assured them they were not sick, the less they believed me. I was
obliged, in order to cure them, to make use of an innocent stratagem,
by giving them some agreeable potions concealed under the disgusting
appearance of medicines; and though they were only made with a few
grains of cooling powders of stahl, they operated on them, by the merit
of persuasion, by restoring to them the tranquility of mind they had lost.
[Nassy's note]

scribed bleeding after the purgatives,† and during that time until the third day, I only prescribed plentiful and cooling drinks, and in proportion as the strength failed, or I suspected a beginning of dissolution in the humours, I did not spare cordials, or the most softening astringents, mixed with mucilages and antiphlogistics; not forgetting, when occasion required, antiseptics, for which I used the alexipharmic essence of stahl, and the camphoric tincture of besoard; I also prescribed blisters, when I perceived the least sign of sleepiness. I have never purged any patient, excepting those who took physic on the first day; but about the sixth day of his illness, or when I perceived, by his urine, that the coction was made, I never used bark, which I look upon rather as a good strengthener than as an antiputrid, before the disease is abating. As to children, all I prescribed for them was bermifuges [sic] and glysters made of milk and honey, and every one evacuated a considerable quantity of reddish worms.

Amongst all the melancholy symptoms of this cruel disease, I found none so difficult to calm as vomitings, and hiccup. Acids composed of dulcified marine, and vitriolic salt, had but little success. I succeeded much better, as well against continual vomitings as against bloody evacuations, with a strong mucilage made of flaxseed, gum-arabic, honey, and cinnamon water, of which I directed my patients to take a spoonful every ten minutes.

Topics of emollient herbs boiled in strong wine, vinegar applied warm on the stomach, the lower part of the belly, and the reins, have also been of great service with me against the pains of those parts. I used no narcotics. If the patient, when the disease abated, was tormented with a want of sleep, I only administered to him almond-juice very thick, mixed with diacodium. In fine, my whole treatment was at first only established upon the inflammation, which

† None of my patients were bled more than twice, and they lost but 6 or 8 ounces of blood at a time. My well grounded fear of the dissolution of the blood, made me to be very cautious about bleeding, which I prescribed but in case of need and according to the signs I perceived in my patients. Thus many recovered without having been bled. [Nassy's note]

I always believed to be the origin of that disease, and afterwards on the dissolution of humors which followed; and therefore I made the application according to circumstances, and the different shapes in which the disease presented itself, and of the best advices given us by the most eminent authors who have written on physic.

But is, or is not this disease contagious? A question which I think I am only able to answer by a distinction, which experience seems to justify. It is contagious for those, whose organical constitution has great homogenity with the air of this country. The affinity and relation existing between their constitution, and the impression of this atmosphere, gives them a nearer disposition to receive the impressions of the putrid miasmas, with which the air is impregnated, and which alter and trouble, more, or less that equilibrium of the solids and liquids, so necessary to maintain good health. The disease is not contagious for foreigners, whose constitutions have little homogenity with that dry air. We are convinced of it by the prodigious numbers abounding in this city, none of whom were attacked with that disease, whilst the most part of the natives, and those used to the climate, were taken ill with it.[131]

The relations of man with all that surrounds him, and the influence of the air on the constitutions, cannot be described. We see the effects of them without often being able to penetrate the causes. We can give but conjectures on that head; and I only ground this, upon this certain fact, that men accustomed to a climate, are much more subject to the hurtful variations and influences of its atmosphere, than those, whose complexion, through a physical propensity, is still subject to the nature of the climate that they have just quitted. From thence arise endemic diseases, which do not affect foreigners, and from thence also the peculiar diseases which attack new-comers, without affecting the natives, as experience has often shewed to us in our colonies.

XC

Dr. Moses Sheftall on
Yellow Fever, 1795

Dr. Moses Sheftall of Savannah studied for his medical degree under Benjamin Rush.[132] The letter printed below was written to Rush and concerns the younger physician's reading of his teacher's paper on the 1793 yellow fever epidemic.[133] Although, in some minor matters, Sheftall was critical of Rush, the pupil accepted his master's basic view of the nature of the disease. Perhaps, Sheftall's defense of Rush against the attacks of other medical writers was not wholly ingenuous, since the letter also contains a request for the use of Rush's influence to win Sheftall a federal appointment as physician of the port of Savannah.

178. MOSES SHEFTALL TO
BENJAMIN RUSH, 1795 [134]

Savannah January 24th 1795

Doctor Benjamin Rush
Sir/
It is with pleasure, I have perused your publication, entitled an Account of the Bilious yellow Fever; as it appeard in your City, in the year 1793. 'tis not for me to Comment or say much upon it, but, Sir the world I think must ever feel herself obligated to you, for Introducing into practice what has been by some called the new mode of healing the Yellow Fever;

I beg you'll excuse me, for not proceeding in a Regular manner, through your publication on that Epidemic; as it was but a hasty view, that I had of it; I had long ago from Publications which I frequently seen, in the News'papers, of yours as well as other Gentlemen of the faculty, felt myself satisfied, that the disease, then spoke of was one of those diseases, that might be truly Called Inflammatory; but Sir when I Come to See the Volume; published by you, giving, an Account of the other diseases; such as the mumps the Scarlatina, &c. putting on those Inflammatory appearances; had there been the least doubt in my mind, it must have been immediately removed; for the previous, Heat & dryness, of the weather no doubt Contributed greatly to Increase the Inflammatory disposition of the diseases. Doctor Sydenham [135] attributes a highly Inflammatory, State of the Small Pox; to a previous Heat and dry Summer; these observations, and many others, that are mentioned in your piece, with the Method of Cure; must fully Convince every reasonable man, that the disease, was of the Inflammatory Kind; it will do well to observe here that I do agree with you in opinion, with respect to the Name of this disease; which you say you've adopted the term *Yellow* from its being more frequently used, I am of opinion, that a more proper and Suitable one might be Found; for I Can assure you, that almost every Fever, which prevails in this Country in the lower parts of it particularly, where there is low and swampy grounds and with Easterly winds, there is a yellowness of the skin, as too appearances a suffusion of Bile; it surely would be the Height of Imprudence, for the Safety of our Citizens and peace of their minds, to Call those Fevers the yellow Fever; I beg you'll excuse my suggesting to you whose many years experience in the Science of medicine, must long Since, have put it out the power of So young a Practitioner; to Suggest any thing new, or entertaining; but from my Knowledge, of your disposition, to listen with attention to Such as may, address you, and put them to Rights, when they err; I have ventur'd to Call this the Inflammatory Bilious Fever; this new name, alone would Induce practitioners of medicine in different places, to immediately have recourse to the antiphlogistic remedies, laid down by you; then this vague, and absurd Idea of Putrefaction of the Circulating blood; would not be thought of But every man of any medical information, would know, that unless this Inflammatory affection was speedily removed it would fall on, Some Vital parts and there in a short period of time, would undergo the Same Changes that all other Inflammations do; he would not think of pouring in Bark wine, & Laudanum, from his knowledge of the impropriety of such remedies in those diseases.

although it would be more proper at Some other time, to bring into View; the authors referred to by you, I must beg leave here to Say that with respect to Tertians spoke of By Doctor Cleghorn,[136] whose own words, I will here Insert "These Tertian Fevers have as a good right to be Called Contagious, as the Measles, Small pox, or any other disease; for although in that Season there Certainly is a peculiar disposition in the air to affect numbers; in the Same way; yet those who are much Conversant among the sick are most liable to Catch the distemper Page 132 I must differ with him; that Tertian Fevers are not contagious, I would prove by asking this question, are not persons much Conversant among the sick of any disorder [much] more liable to take that disease than any other? by being much; debilitated by Fatigue, anxiety, night watching, &c. if So Surely Tertians are no more Contagious than Pleurisy Peripneumonys or any other Complaints that occur during the year;

Your Fever I think was takeing by Exhalation from the Coffee, and then propagated by Contagion, as appears plainly from Mrs Leamings takeing it from her sister; it is impossible for me to travel through your history of the Yellow Fever, and give it its Just merits; the Calumnies raised against you by Many of the Medical Faculty can only in my opinion; tend to endear you more to your Fellow Citizens; as they are fully Convinced of the utility of the mode of treatment; pursued by you; and the destruction brought on by a Contrary mode of practice. as for Doctor Kuhn's [137] Conduct on the occasion I know not what to Compare it too; but that of A General officer, flying from his standard; I think he should be brought to a Court Martial and tried for desserting his post in time of Danger; was I one of his Court; I should surely Cashier him and render him incapable of ever Serving in the Field of medicine.

These lines Sir are intruded on you from no vain motives, they are wrote for the purpose of receiving a letter of Instruction and Information, in return for them as they can afford no further satisfaction than to know that your Former Students; who attended your medical and useful Lectures, however distant, they may be; always feels a pleasure, when they peruse a work done by you; particularly where they so precisely see the difficulty which you must labourd [sic] under, and the Satisfactory manner in which you triumphed over your Enemies; and the readiness with which you Forgive them for the Calumnies they raised against you, tis truly expressive of your Goodness of Heart.

Permit me to beg your attention for a moment to my business; as tis generally believed that Congress will in their present Session; make some arrangement with respect to Hospitals for the reception of Sick seamen in the different Ports of the United States, I must beg of you to use your best endeavours to get me appointed visiting Physician for this Port; my recommendations have been laying for some time in the hands of my Brother in Law Doctor Bush,[138] to whom I have wrote, requesting him to deliver them to a Mr Baldwin [139] a member of the House of representatives from this State, if you can Serve me, I shall ever gratefully acknowledge it.

Before I bring this to a Conclusion; permit me most sincerely to condole with you on the loss of your amiable Sister, and worthy Students; losses which no doubt, must long make a lasting impression, on your mind, of the Fatality of your late Contagious Fever. with my best wishes for your future Health, and may the great Author of all Beings long preserve and protect you and increase the number of your years that you may long be a lasting evidence and scourge to pestilential Fevers, should your City be ever again visited, which Heaven Forbid is the Sincere & ardent prayer of Sir your most obedient and very   Humble Servant   Moses Sheftall

PS: Be pleased to present my best wishes to Doctors Mease [140] & Woodhouse; [141] and tell either of them I will be thankfull if they will forward me Mr Seybarts [142] Inaugural dissertation, and other late Medical publications; particularly that of the College of Physicians of your City,[143] with the Cost, and I will by the first opportunity remit them the Expence of the Same.

XCI

Raising Standards in the Medical Profession, 1831

Dr. Daniel L. M. Peixotto [144] was not only a physician of ability and distinction, and a benevolent and practical philanthropist.[145] He was also one of the leaders in the organization of the medical profession for its own improvement. Although, as we have seen, there was an opportunity for formal medical education in the United States in the 1790s, in Philadelphia, graduation from a medical school was not required as a condition of entering medical practice. The old system of apprenticeship to a practicing physician was retained well into the nineteenth century. One of the ways in which the more devoted members of the profession tried to raise standards was that of self-policing through medical societies.

In 1831, when Dr. Peixotto was called upon to address the Medical Society of the City and County of New York,[146] he took as his major theme the proper objectives that should be pursued by a medical society bent on improving professional standards. Among the methods that he mentioned were the encouragement of the foundation of other medical societies and associations, the establishment of a medical journal and the publication of the transactions of the society, the development of an adequate library, and the suppression of quackery by rigid licensing requirements. It is interesting and characteristic that Peixotto, an ardent Jacksonian Democrat [147] and advocate of laissez-faire, should have emphasized the role of the medical profession itself in fixing licensing requirements rather than suggesting that these requirements be set and policed by the city or state government.

179. D. L. M. PEIXOTTO'S ADDRESS, 1831 [148]

By the remarks on which I have now ventured with the object of elucidating the true character of the medical society, and of vindicating it against the aspersions of its enemies, I hope I shall not be misunderstood as indulging in an overweening conceit of an excellence which is foreign to it. Much yet remains to be done before this society will have accomplished all that may reasonably and confidently be hoped from the enterprise, the intelligence, and the researches of its numerous members. Essentially identified with the great mass of the profession, its honor and its advancement are their own. Now it cannot be denied that the standard of professional character is not so high amongst us, as our wishes may justly aspire to; and the remark might be extended to almost every portion of our country. The qualifications necessary to constitute a physician, whether he enjoys the title by a diploma or a license, are not sufficiently numerous; they do not keep pace with the advancement of science and the progress of the intellectual achievements of the age. Too great an apathy pervades the members of our profession, too striking an indifference to scientific pursuits, and too great an absence of public spirit. The causes of this inferiority it were curious though difficult to investigate. Perhaps it will suffice to point out a few of the means by which it may be removed, and which, more or less, must have relation to the former.

1. One of the first means which I would suggest for the improvement of the condition of the medical profession, is the encouragement of medical associations. The institution of literary and scientific societies is acknowledged, after an experience of nearly two centuries, to be one of the most successful instruments ever devised to promote the advancement of knowledge, and diffuse a general taste for intellectual improvement. The communion of enlightened individuals, devoted to the pursuit of one great object, is admirably calculated to awaken the dormant mind to exertion; to enkindle the spirit of honorable emulation, and induce habits of accurate observation, extensive reading, and cautious research. Facts are elicited, opinions are interchanged, and an impulse and a direction are given to inquiry, at which the solitary efforts of an insulated student would

never have arrived. *Ex singulis fere nihil,* as Scaliger [149] hath it.
The sublime efforts and magnificent results of unaided genius, are
exceptions, but genius is rare indeed, and the most knowledge is
diffused, the rarer is it likely to be. . . .

2. A second means to elevate our professional character may be
derived from the published transactions of all institutions devoted
to medical objects, and endowed or patronized by the state. Among
the sources from which medical science has received its unbounded
and vast accession of facts within the last thirty years, and to which
it is mainly indebted for its rapid strides to improvement, the reports of medical observation and experience emanating from the
hospitals, lunatic asylums, and infirmaries of Europe, must be
ranked as the most prominent. Physicians and surgeons enjoy no
sinecures in these institutions; for where the law does not exact
a strict and detailed account of their professional labors, their own
spirited zeal and the dread of being kept in the back ground, prevents their inactivity, and urges them to contribute some mite to
the accumulating stock of information. Why are not our institutions
rendered equally subservient to the cause of humanity and knowledge? I have heard it said, We want good practitioners and not
good writers in our eleemosynary institutions. Are the ordinary qualifications requisite to enable a physician to note down in correct
language the result of his daily observations on the diseases submitted to his control, and on the methods of treatment he pursues,
incompatible with the character of an able and successful practitioner? The idea is absurd in the extreme, and has its origin in selfish
and contracted motives. Bacon [150] has justly said, that every member
of a learned profession should be a writer. The great end of all
institutions devoted to the sick poor, is undoubtedly the immediate
good of the unfortunate. But the attention paid to them may be,
without injury to themselves, converted into means of remote utility
to those who come after them. Or must a narrow and short-sighted
policy ever keep establishments munificently endowed by the government, and supported by the money of the people at large, as so
many sealed books? In the present age of inquiry and mental activity, it is a stain upon the character of any enlightened physician not
to render any public situation he may be called on to fill, useful in
contributing materials, upon which the ultimate perfection of medi-

cal science must depend. It is time that the physicians of New-York looked to this object. . . .

3. When I adduce a successful periodical work as one of the means of improving the condition of our profession, I may be deemed by some to be actuated by selfish motives. It requires less experience than I have had in conducting journals, to ascertain the well established fact, that little is the profit which can accrue from even the most successful work of this nature. . . . It is in reference to the honor of the profession at large that I would urge the claims of a journal, provided it be conducted with ability and discretion, indulge in no personalities, embark in no local questions unconnected with the true interests of science, and in short, be independent and useful. Such a work would defy opposition.

4. The suppression of quackery. I can anticipate the smile of hopeless incredulity, when I express the belief that the last head of this hydra monster may still be reached. It will never be, however, by coercive laws.

L'atrocite des loix impede l'execution, says Montesquieu: [151] the severity of laws prevents their enforcement. And of this we have abundant proof in our present medical law. No, gentlemen: if we would reach the evil, we must aim at its root. Cut down the branches and the trunk, and they will grow up again, and with renewed luxuriancy. Public opinion must be convinced of the dangers and follies resulting from unskilful and blind ignorance; and public opinion can only be reached by popular addresses. For this purpose, I would recommend the appointment of committees by the medical societies, whose duty it should be, in imitation of that excellent institution, "The Society for the Diffusion of Useful Knowledge," to prepare and circulate a series of popular observations on subjects most immediately connected with the preservation of health, the signs of disease, and with a knowledge of the qualifications indispensable to those who would exercise the art of preserving the one, and removing or mitigating the other. By such a system, wisely and prudently conducted and adhered to, more might be done than by laws more severe than those of Draco, or even as mild as those of Numa.

5. The qualifications at present requisite to procure a license and diploma, should be more extensive, and be more rigidly enforced.

No youth should be allowed to commence the study of our profession who had not received a previous liberal education. By this I do not mean to include what is strictly called a classical or collegiate course, although I am fain to confess that my opinion is in favor of the pre-eminent advantages attending even such preparation for a professional course of study. The opinion of Rush is often cited to the contrary, and the example of Franklin often adduced, in proof of what may be done without a knowledge of the ancient languages. But allowance is to be made for the time in which the illustrious father of American medicine lived: and Franklin acknowledges that he formed his simple nervous style by a close imitation of the writers of queen Anne's reign; and they are close models of the imperishable monuments of Grecian and Roman literature. Leaving aside this disputed ground, it cannot be denied that a knowledge of our own language is absolutely indispensable. And yet, how many students do we not encounter, nay, with how many full-fledged physicians do we not have the pain of conversing and corresponding, whose knowledge of the rules of orthography are often in an inverse ratio to their medical success. This is disgraceful; and our societies and our colleges should unite in abating the nuisance. Many other branches of knowledge should be possessed by every candidate for medical pupilage; such as mathematics, natural philosophy, and a tolerable proficiency in the modern languages of Europe. Great exception would undoubtedly be taken against the oppressive demand of such a regulation; but the event would vindicate the wholesome propriety of the enactment in the improved aspect of the medical community. And if it somewhat thinned the ranks of applicants for pupilage, would any loss be incurred? Surely not by the profession at large, however it might affect particular teachers. On the subject of medical education, much might be advanced; but I withhold for the present, sincerely hoping, that when it is taken up again for discussion by this society, a liberal and catholic spirit, candor, and all absence of invidious feeling, will be manifested, and that whatever is decided on may be effected without injury to any, but with a true and single aim to the public good.

6. Libraries are indispensable to the successful and unrestricted cultivation of science. They are the shrines on which are treasured up the oblations of the innumerable votaries of learning of all ages

and from all countries. We may suppose them to have been dimly shadowed forth in those temples of antiquity devoted to the god of health, upon the walls and pillars of which were sacredly recorded and preserved the accumulated and diversified experience of all who resorted to them with the great object of increasing the resources of the healing art. Long since recommended to this society, little success has as yet attended the attempt to form one worthy of the character of our city, or adequate to supply the wants of an extended medical community. The time has, however, arrived, when we may, without exaggerated hopes, set about instituting a New-York Medical Society Library. The mere number of our members is now so great, that a very small contribution from each, either in books or money, as an outfit, would form a respectable nucleus, which would not fail to be augmented by additional supplies. These would be furnished partly by individual liberality, partly by small annual contributions from each member, and perhaps we might venture to hope, not altogether vainly, by public munificence. The distinguished incumbent of this chair, to whom I have already had occasion to allude, long since promised to exercise his usual liberality in the promotion of this great object; and I sincerely believe that he is only prevented from evincing his munificence by the indifference of the society, and by the want of suitable accommodations to receive and preserve valuable books. Other resources will not be wanting, I know, to enrich the collection. I respectfully suggest the adoption of immediate measures to enforce the success of so desirable an object. To this effect, let a separate fund, to be entitled the "Library Fund," be forthwith instituted; and for its accumulation we may confidently rely on the generous zeal no less than the notorious wants of every member of the profession.

Lastly, gentlemen, to the successful improvement of professional character, the possession of public virtue is indispensable. Intellectual superiority is enviable, and vast learning is honorable and honored; but a society which should be distinguished by these qualities, eminent as they are, and yet should not possess the higher attributes of moral excellence, would be like the fabled statue of Prometheus, before the fire of heaven had animated its being and inspired it with a soul. Its proportions might be exquisite, its outlines graceful, and its workmanship complete; but it would be cold marble still. Endue it with a soul, and with moral energies and responsibilities, and with what superior charms would it not be invested! How admiration of the lifeless statue warms into rapture! On the medical profession the duties springing from an active and disinterested morality, are peculiarly enjoined as beings accountable, first by their knowledge, secondly by the mode in which they apply it to practice, and thirdly, by the vast opportunity afforded them of exercising all the dearer charities of society, and of cultivating all the pleasures which so abundantly spring from a useful and well-spent life.

XCII

Commercial Possibilities
in Science, 1790-1808

The documents collected below illustrate three relatively early instances of Jews concerned in the practical technological applications of scientific knowledge. It is not entirely accidental that, in all these cases, the recipient of the communication was Thomas Jefferson. When Jacob Isaacks (1718–98) [152] of Newport wrote to Jefferson, who was then Secretary of State, about his process for distilling drinking water from sea water, he thought he had made a genuine discovery; Jefferson's report to the House of Representatives of November 21, 1791, advising against a federal bounty to Isaacks, recapitulated the history of the sort of experimentation that Isaacks had done and denied the petitioner's claim to novelty.[153] Isaacks did not accept the decision with grace. Francis Da Costa's [154] communication of his discovery of a lead mine on his Pennsylvania farm was addressed to Jefferson as president, an address that was motivated by Jefferson's well-known interest in applied science; we do not know whether Jefferson replied to Da Costa. Jefferson was still President when Abraham Cohen [155] wrote to try to interest him in promoting a company for the bottling of artificial mineral water; the President, though addressed as "The Patron of Arts & Sciences in our Infant Country," tactfully denied any authority to judge the value of Mr. Cohen's product, and recommended that the opinions of the physicians of Philadelphia should be sought.

180. JACOB ISAACKS TO THOMAS JEFFERSON, 1790 [156]

Newport August 17th 1790

Sir

The inclosed copies of certificates Signed By Severel Gentlemen of *this* Town Will Inform You Respecting a discovery that I have Recently Made, and which if encouraged will I flatter myself be highly beneficial to Mankind, and Particularly to those concerned in navigation as the apparatus is so simple, that an extraction can be performed on board any Vessell at a very trifling expence.

A Bottle of the water extracted agreeably to the last Certificate, I am emboldened from the Regard you have ever Shewn to the usefull discoveries of Americans to have presented to you, and ardently wish it may Meet your approbation and patronage.

I have the honor to be Sir   Your most Obedient Humble Servant

Jacob Isaacks

181. ISAACKS'S TESTIMONIALS, 1790 [157]

We the Subscribers do Certify that we have Seen Mr. Jacob Isaacks of this town distill by a very Simple apparatus, Nine pints and half of fresh water from ten pints of Ocean water, and that it was freed from the ill taste and disagreeable Marine Qualities of sea water so as to answer either at Sea or on the land for all the Common and Culinary purposes of fountain or River Water.

Newport State of Rhodeisland
July 22d 1790

Isaac Senter [158]
Nich P Tillinghast [159]

We the subscribers having attended a process made by Mr. Jacob Isaacks of extracting fresh water from salt water, do thereon certify, Report, and declare that notwithstanding the apparatus by which the process was effected was of a bad construction, Yet in the Course of one and an half Hour, he extracted from Ten pints of Salt Water, Eight pints of fresh water.

Newport Rhodeisland April 8th 1790

Caleb Gardner [160]
Moses Seixas [161]
William Ellery [162]
Geo Sears [163]
Saml Vernon Jun [164]

182. ISAACKS TO JEFFERSON, 1791 [165]

Newport Novem 4 1791

Hond. Sir

I take the liberty to address you on the Subject of taking the fresh water from the Sea Water, notwithstanding I met not with the encouragement by Some that attended at the time I made the tryall before you, tho' they were pleased to tell me that my Method was not New, Still it was their Oppinion that I was entitled to have Some gratuity allowed me even for Renewing the Same, but I can Say with truth, that I never read any books on the Subject untill I had tried many experiments to bring it to pass, in many of them I fail'd, but have now to inform You that I can take off by Calculation in 12 hours, with not half the fire I did it at Philadelphia, & much less trouble, 60 Gallons of pure good fresh Water free from any Salt whatsoever & on tryall will not be Milky or terbulent as Doct: [   ] was, as is Said in the Books that his best distilled water on tryall proved to be Milky & terbulent & had a portion of Sea Salt, whereas this of mine has not any I have Some by me that I distill'd the 22d. July 1790. & is now clear & Sweet without any Settlements in it, there is some gone forward to Europe, & doubt not but it will meet with approbation, there, and as Soon as I Receive any accounts from thence, I Shall let Mr Bourn [166] Know, & much desire you'll be So Kind as not to make any Report on my Memorial, untill I have the Answer from Europe, but I Remain with much esteem, and have the honor to Subscribe Myself   Your Honors most hble Servt   Jacob Isaacks

P. S Please to take notice that I exceed my memorial in taking off much more fresh Water then I mentioned in the Said memorial therein I say 8 parts out of 10. Whereas I took 11 out of 12, & on the Second tryall 23 fresh out of 24 Salt

183. ISAACKS TO JEFFERSON, 1792 [167]

Newport Monday
March 19th 1792

Honor'd Sir

I received yours with the Report [168] and was sorry to find you was Hastety in Making the same so soon Publick as it has proved greatly detrimental to my Interest altho' you were not in possession of my secret which I am fearful wou'd have shared the same fate. You must be thoroughly senseable of the injury that report has done me by making it of Publick Use without any Advantage to the Disscoverer, and I am now deprived of Selling my Secret to Private Persons many of whom had made me Good offers before I presented my Memorial, but have since withdrawn their proposals by your making the Disscovery Publick, for which I must again entreat your aid and Assistance in getting my Petition Granted & secure me such a Compensation as the Honble Congress shall think just & reasonable. Having a large Family to support at my advanced time of Life, will I hope be sufficient without any other motive to gain yours and the rest of my Good Friends Interests for which I shall ever greatfully remember the Obligation that I may succeed in my Petition is the Constant Prayer of Sir   Your most Obedient Humble Servt   Jacob Isaacks

184. FRANCIS DA COSTA'S LEAD MINE, 1804 [169]

Thomas Jefferson president of the United States
Sir

The interest you have constantly manifested for all discoveries, connected more or less with the prosperity of the United States will I hope make you forbear the liberty I have taken of Sending you the Sample of a lead mine discovered on my plantation and which I caused but lately to be opend. The vein has appeard off the Surface of a Hill almost eighty feet above the highest rise of a creek at the bottom of it: at first the vein went down under an angle of about 40 degrees, but altered very Soon to a course almost perpendicular encreasing So much in about nine feet depth as to have enlarg'd from two to fifteen inches Solid ore duly walled in on each Side with the mineral Stones usually enclosing real veins of ore. Having made a regular opening to ascertain the Course direction and thick[n]ess and broke down the mineral bank, about two tons of fine ore was collected in less than four hours, one ton more remaining at the bottom of the pit. The sample I have the honor to send you has been been taken from a piece of pure Galena weighing nine hundredweight at least. the Strata of the Country is a Specie of red Slate in this the vein has been discovered. Other places on the plantation have evident Signs of the Same mineral So as to induce a belief that the vein I have been upon is a branch only of one more valuable and running to a Considerable extent. My farm lays at the mouth of perkiomen Creek, County of Montgomery, State of Pensilvania, distant about twenty two miles from Philadelphia. The ground being much broken abounds with Springs which and the never-failing-water of the Creek will admit extensive water works to carry on the extracting of lead and its manufacturing in any nature or Shape whatsoever.

This Short account of this Discovery I have thought is due to the Eminent Philosopher and naturalist I have the honor of adressing and Should it prove acceptable I request it may be Considered as a proof of the great respect with which   I am   Sir Your Most obedient   & Humble Servant   Frcis Da Costa

Philadelphia the 20th November 1804

185. A. H. COHEN TO THOMAS JEFFERSON, 1807 [170]

Dec. 21, 1807

His Excellency Thos. Jefferson
Honoured Sir

Regarding you as the Patron of Arts & Sciences in our Infant Country. I am Led to Take the Liberty of offerring to your Notice an Institution which If favoured with your Approbation will I flatter myself produce a Publick Good. as Such am Confident it will Need no other Commendation to Merit your Patronage. The Beneficial Effects derived from the Use of Mineral Waters which have become Celebrated by affording Relief in Cases where most other Remedies have failed has Induced the most Celebrated Chemists to Ascertain by a Correct Annalysis these Beneficial properties & by Chemically combining those Traits. to produce by Art. what Nature hath so bountifully bestowed and so far have they Succeeded. as to Merit a decided preferrence of the Artificial to the Natural Waters by Increasing their Active properties and Excluding foreign particles not Necessary but Rather detrimental to Health. You Respected Sir who are so well Acquainted with the principles of Philosophy are well aware of the difficulties. Attending this process in order to Sufficiently Impregnate the Waters with the Gaseous & which is Indeed the most Active principle in most of the Celebrated Waters. How far I have Succeeded in this difficulty have Taken the Liberty of Submitting to your Inspection by forwarding you a Specimen of the Balls Town, Pyrmont & Soda Waters. and also Refer you to the Hon. Lemuel Sawyer [171] (to whom we had the Honour of forwarding an assortment.) for some of the Seltzers of which am at present out of a Supply. this being the most highly Impregnated Water containing from 250 to 300 [   ] of the Carbonic Acid Gas. a Quantity Seldom attained or Exceeded by any Attempt in Europe. The Happy Effects derived from their Use have been already Evinced by an approving Publick & Testimonies of the most Celebrated & Eminent Chemists & Medical Characters in this City. Yet in order to Give it all the Advantages that Might Result It Requires the aid of a Larger Capital than in my power to afford. to Render it of that Extensive Utility. to prove a Publick Benefit the aid of a Capital from 10 to 15000 doll. would Accomplish the Object of Erecting a Suitable Building in which fountains would be Placed as the Waters are now delivered and would be Sufficient to furnish a Supply to the United States or also to furnish them Gratuitously to the Poor, to whom the Physicians Might deem it Necessary.

Under your Auspices & favour Respected Sir this might be Amply Effected. & the Name of a Jefferson Recieve an Additional [   ] to the Debt of Gratitude from his fellow Citizens already so Largely Incurred. those fountains of Health flowing through his Patronage would Claim the benediction of Relieved Sufferrers, and thus Afford an Additional Solace to a Retirement where the Prayers & Gratitude of the Worthy & Good will always follow you. I now Submit an Outline of the Plans for [your] Approval, the above Sum to be divided into Shares of 50 dol. cash payable in Installments, the Subscribers to be Entitled to Exclusive privilige. & recieve the amount to themselves or order in Mineral Waters at a deduction of 20 [per ct.(?)] from the Selling price. your Approval & patronage Joined to the Respectable characters in this city will fully Enable me to accomplish this object. and dedicate an Institution to you Whose Virtues an Applauding Mind will Never cease to Emulate and which the Voice of Envy cannot Tarnish. Nor Shall any Exertions on my Part be wanting to Render the Establishment Worthy of this Honour & prove the Gratitude of Yr Respectfull & Obt Serv.   Abraham Cohen

Phil: Dec. 21. 1807.
No 31 So. 2d Street

186. JEFFERSON'S REPLY, 1808 [172]

Washington Feb. 10.08

Sir

I have not been able sooner to acknolege the receipt of your letter of Dec. 21. which did not come to hand till Jan. 27. nor to return you my thanks for the mineral waters which came with it. I am happy to learn that these productions of nature can be successfully imitated by art, and that something may thereby be added useful to mankind. of the degree of that utility I acknolege myself not a judge, being little acquainted with the composition of these waters, and still less with their effects on the human body, a consciousness of this would make it too presumptuous in me to suppose that any connection of my name with an establishment for their preparation would be a recommendation of them to the public. they would be sensible that it is out of my line and would view it as neither favorable to myself or the medecine. the names of the celebrated Physicians of Philadelphia are those which would give a just reputation to these waters, and present them with authority to the notice of the public. giving every just praise therefore to the efforts you have so meritoriously exerted in perfecting a preparation which may relieve the afflicted from some of their sufferings. I feel it a duty to leave it's fortunes & it's direction in the hands of those so much better qualified to promote it's success: and I pray you to accept my best wishes for that, & my respectful salutations.

Th. Jefferson

Mr: Cohen.

XCIII

America's First Significant
Jewish Musician, 1836-1838

The development of musical culture in the United States has been greatly furthered by Jews, who contributed to the shaping of musical taste in America as impresarios, as performers, and as composers. For the most part, however, these services to American cultural life came at a later period than the one with which we are here concerned. Only the brief American career of Daniel Schlesinger [173] can be used to illustrate this aspect of American Jewish culture. Schlesinger, a concert pianist, came to New York in 1836. On his arrival he found a musical public whose taste was predominately for vocal music, largely because they had had little opportunity to hear instrumental virtuosi. He was responsible for beginning to turn the tide toward instrumental music; but he died in 1838. The memorial notice from which extracts are reprinted below set forth clearly both Schlesinger's distinction as a pianist and his impact on musical taste in America.

187. OBITUARY OF DANIEL SCHLESINGER, 1839 [174]

It was on the sixth of October, 1836, that the good ship President brought Daniel Schlesinger to these shores, where, had Listz [sic] landed on that day, we question if he would have found any one to recognize him in so flattering a manner. He would have found a public exclusively attached to vocal, and comparatively ignorant of instrumental, music; in whom his marvellous power would have excited but little enthusiasm. . . .

Were he to visit us to-day, after the lapse of three years, he would encounter a far different reception; would be courted and admired, and command an abundant audience; with warmth of feeling heightening in proportion as he disclosed to them the great masterpieces; whilst their susceptibility to musical impressions would atone for their want of discernment. We forbear to enhance the picture, and yet cannot but believe he would, moreover, find both character and concert among the members of his profession, and feel that, henceforth, it only depends upon themselves to render it an honourable one in this free land.

Much of this change in the musical condition of our society we are proud to attribute to the influence of the artist we are lamenting. The first man of the old Helvetian Wedge penetrated the enemy's ranks at the cost of his life, and opened the phalanx for his comrades. Mr. Schlesinger seems to have perished by a similar destiny. Can we present a more concise and graphic epitome of the valuable services which a few years enabled him to render the public, as well as his profession?

His first appearance was at the National Theatre,[176] on a benefit night, when his performance created little sensation amidst the histrionic parade, and, though nothing so beautiful as the *variations* upon the *march in Tancredi* had been heard on this side of the Atlantic, they produced no *retentissement* in our circles. By degrees, however, it became known to a few lovers of music that there was "one Pianist more;" and we must do our amateurs the justice to say that, at various *reunions,* his talent soon came to elicit their unfeigned admiration.

It was on such an occasion, one evening in the winter of 1836, that our ears were first gladdened, at the abode of a German patriarch, by the sonorous inspirations of Mr. Schlesinger. The impression is ineffaceable. We were entirely unprepared to meet such an artist out of Europe; where, in the course of a long and earnest pilgrimage, we had worshipped at every musical shrine that lay in, or near, our path; which he had never crossed, as our stay in London had been brief and in the unmusical season, and the enthusiasm of the British metropolis is periodical. Excited by the brilliancy of his variations from Tancredi we hastened to make the acquaintance of the modest artist; with whom a few minutes conversation convinced us he was no ordinary man. His expressive countenance was marked by character and genius; his forehead, broad and lofty, with significant expansions, rose above brilliant and remarkably prominent eyes which pierced you as you spoke, not with cunning to penetrate your motive, for he was childlike, but to divine your meaning. His features were muscular, collected in their repose, and singularly playful in their animation. "His soul seemed made up of harmony; and he never spoke but he charmed his hearer, not only with the clearness of his remarks but all his words, and his very tone and cadences were strangely musical." His manner was polished without affectations, and reflected upon you his self-respect; his address gentle and his person gentlemanly. He was of moderate stature, compactly built; black curly hair surmounted his white brow and harmonized with his dark complexion. Owing to great near-sightedness his countenance often took an anxious cast, and it was difficult to say what those broad eyes were gazing at until their smile lit upon you, and warmed you like a sunbeam, or they opened still wider to interrogate you. His use of English was easy and faultless, and his humour required earnest conversation. Therefore was he troublesome to the frivolous, suffering no word to pass unnoticed; and was never satisfied as long as an equivocal remark remained unexplained. Was not this an *original man?*

In the course of the above evening, he was invited by two ladies to extemporize upon the piano. Each furnished a theme, and left him to choose between *"Lützow's Wild Hunt,"* and *"The Rhine."* He took his seat before the instrument, and, after a majestic prelude, opened the great Rhine chorus; then commenced a series of variations of the highest brilliancy and most finished execution, pursued the air through many a hazardous modulation and intricate measure until the time changed, the tone softened, the chorus seemed winding off in the distance, you questioned your ears? Is that *"The Rhine?"* No! " 'Tis the hunt of Lützow the free and the brave." A burst of applause welcomed "the chase," as its swelling tones came nearer and nearer, until they poured upon the ear their jet of notes and martial rythm, and made the heart leap with joy. On, on he carried us with the hunt, which serpentined through harmonic mazes and leaped from measure to measure until his left hand, gaining fast upon the right, compelled it to slacken its wild pace and sounded, heaven knows how it was accomplished! the Rhine, the Rhine, the Hunt still resounding, and the dissimilar melodies flowed harmoniously in one silver stream, to their journey's end.

Mr. Schlesinger's performance, and the pleasure it afforded us on that memorable evening, were types of the talent he displayed and the delight he gave on many a subsequent occasion. We had then never witnessed an impromptu so alive with inspiration, so spontaneous, so opulent in harmony, which enhanced instead of stifling the free flow of melody; and its novelty heightened the zest of our gratification. It was musical eloquence, poetry, genius. Nothing embarrassed him. He defied all keys, all measures, and was truly admirable. He never hesitated or paused, but went on as if an angel were holding before him a bright page which he hastened to interpret before it melted away.

These improvisations were deemed, by many, his brightest excellence. They were unlike his compositions and could not be recalled. The night after one of them, you might give him the same theme, and listen in vain for the exquisite variation you longed to hear once more. His mood, and with it his view of the subject, had changed; but they who never heard him cannot realize with how lavish a hand he poured forth the treasures of his art. At times fantastic and capricious, he inspired an air with the *badinage* of a *Scherzo;* at others earnest and melancholy, he clothed it in the solemnity of an anthem. To-night he would compose with *non piu Andrai* a waltz, in which the left hand played the air one beat behind the right, so that on whichever side of the piano you stood, the melody was distinctly audible; next week pour forth a brilliant fantasia upon Don Juan with two and at times even three of the airs of that inimitable opera simultaneously wooing the ear.

One night some artists, who had just arrived from New-Orleans, met him in a small *soiree musicale.* Among them was M. Boucher,[177] subsequently his warm friend and constant companion. After several concerted performances, Mr. Schlesinger sat down to clothe Yankee Doodle in music, which never before made its appearance in so imposing a garb. The new-comers gathered around him amazed, to see the process by which he constantly seized the air in whichever modulation it sought to elude his grasp. Suddenly looking up from the instrument at the French group behind him, he smiled; and it was amusing to see their bewildered faces as he convinced them that the air they had been mistaking for Yankee Doodle, was their own national air, Gretry's [178] *Vive Henri IV!* It resembled the process by which a learned philologist derives a familiar word from some unexpected Greek type; and the dexterity of the juggler who performs the *volte,* with the pack of cards your eye is fixed upon, and whistles, as the queen of hearts becomes the knave of diamonds. Need we add that the exclamations of admiration with which his musical brethren greeted each transition and metamorphosis, served, though they were not wanting, to confirm all present in their estimate of his singular genius, his fertile invention, and his felicity of expression. We recollect his once harmonizing the American with the English national air so that they seemed to appertain to each other; and yet the imagination may be challenged to paint two more opposite melodies than Yankee Doodle and God Save the King.

Let us not omit to mention, how eagerly Mr. Schlesinger sought to collect our native melodies, and how it disappointed him to find the feeble air we have just named, an agreeable one compared to most of its comrades, Hail Columbia, The Starspangled Banner, and that class of tunes called the African melodies, to which our patriotic troops march bravely, on parade days. He studied it, however, very deeply, and enriched it with some remarkable variations which, unfortunately, with his habitual disregard of fame, he never wrote down. Do not dream that there was aught of preparation in these impromptus. He was ever ready to prelude upon any theme proposed, or to vary the same in innumerable shapes. One summer's evening in 1837, two distinguished artists, *premiers prix* of the Parisian *conservatoire,* came to hear him play. He asked them for a theme, about which, they hesitating, he chose the chirp of the cricket that was heard through the open window, and played upon it during three hours a series of variations so novel, strange and abundant; so wild and yet so closely embroidered around the subject, as to dismiss them equally astounded at his talent, and perplexed to know why such an artist should bury himself here.

Of his playing we may here remark that his touch was of singular force and ease and his tone of the richest quality. He played with extended fingers, and it was wonderful to see the self-possession with which they sported among the black and white keys. He had a beautiful hand for the piano, which he never placed on the keyboard without spanning a *tenth*. This gave his chords a plen[i]tude and grandeur that made it seem another instrument.

We have said Mr. Schlesinger landed in our city on the sixth of October, 1836. Need we recapitulate the too familiar events of the last three years, to show how unpromising a prospect of employment he encountered at his arrival. Or need we unfold the process of acclamation, so familiar to the experience of many, to illustrate, what they must already feel, that, but for the consolations of his art, and the patience acquired in the years of his noviciate, gloomily indeed would flow the dreary hours of an artist's expectation here. During the winter Mr. Schlesinger numbered but three pupils. Besides the scarcity of money, the price of his instruction deterred many from employing him, who thought what was customary in London and Paris, exorbitant at New-York. He never abated his terms, and, as we shall shortly see, had subsequently no reason to be dissatisfied with his share of patronage.

It was pleasant to visit him in his comfortless lodgings during those months of uncertainty, and see how cheerfully he awaited with his wife and children the rising of the tide. You generally found him at the piano studying Bach, Beethoven, or Hummel. He would continue or intermit his playing at your option; and, however much his music delighted you, you were sure to be charmed by the natural and easy flow of his conversation. It was a curious contrast to traverse Broad-street and its hurried throng in the busy hours of the day and find at one extremity that calm, hopeful and happy artist, inhabiting the gardens, palaces and wildernesses of the land of sound, unconscious of the thousand cares and miseries which tortured human existence around him. Music was for him a spell of hope; cast by genius the enchanter.

One night, having been compelled to find rooms in an adjoining house, they were all nearly suffocated by the fumes of some charcoal which had been carelessly left unextinguished in their new abode. It was only in the spring of 1837 that they entered the dwelling in which they lived so happily until within a year of "the end." It was about this time, on the thirteenth of April, that Mr. Schlesinger performed a second time in public, in a concert given by Mr. Russell, where he was warmly applauded. The entertainment he himself contemplated offering the public soon after, was injudiciously postponed until the sixth of June, when such a *programme* as had been rarely seen here drew but a moderate audience together. The season was unfavourable; and the chief attraction of the evening, Hummel's *Concerto in A Flat*, presented little inducement to the passer-by, who knew it not, with its two movements respectively heading the first and second acts. His execution of that magnificent production was enthusiastically received; as well as the variations on an "American national air," which he then played for the first time, and which we have now to regret are lost for ever.

Among the projects suggested during the summer by his fervent desire to improve the musical taste of our community, was one whose very failure entitles it to a place in this narrative. It was the organization of a series of *Chamber-Concerts* to be given during the winter, under his direction, at intervals of a fortnight. The idea was a happy one could it have been realized; but the result proved it premature. These entertainments were designed to resemble those by which Mori [179] communicated an impulse to the fondness of the British public for instrumental music, in a manner so profitable alike to his patrons and himself. As the enterprise involved the labour of preparation and the responsibility of expensive engagements to secure its successful execution, it became necessary to ascertain, through subscriptions, how far it was likely to receive encouragement; and Schlesinger accordingly placed in the hands of various influential friends, lists headed by a modest proposal to do all in his power to render these concerts worthy of his art—with the promise that, in the combination of music and of artistical talent, they should surpass any hitherto offered on this side of the Atlantic. We recollect remonstrating against the extremely guarded language of his prospectus, without influencing his conscientious resolve not to hold out even as tempting inducements as he might have surely commanded. Heralded by no puffing extraordinary, unattended by the fashionable *prestige* which is so apt to generate enthusiasm, and presented, with the simple attractions of his art, to a public in whom even Beethoven's name could not have then awakened a glow, it is not surprising that this project enlisted few subscribers. Nay, it is worthy of record, that thirty-eight veritable amateurs were found to enroll their names upon a list to which two hundred signatures were indispensable. So far as memory serves us, it was Mr. Schlesinger's intention to have directed in person these performances, in which his piano was destined to take but a moderate part. Such an occasion for the display of fine orchestral music he deemed too valuable to be appropriated to solo performances.

His fourth public appearance was in a concert which he gave at the City-Hall on the twenty-fourth of November of the same year. The musical world, enthralled by a new vocalist, assembled in small numbers to listen to Hummel's splendid *Concerto in A Minor* which, with Thalberg's [180] *Fantasia* upon the "Capuletti and Montecchi," and a beautiful solo by Boucher, were the evening's chief amusements. His having been the first to introduce here the music of Hummel and Thalberg, were of itself a merit, and deserves a record in the musical annals of a new land, as much as the early representations of the legitimate drama; for, when the musical vaudevilles of our day shall have been sacrificed to human caprice, the great instrumental composers, fewer in number and mightier in genius, will survive the mutations of opinion, and, in lieu of inspiring the initiated only, will resound in the hearts of the multitude.

A concert he was encouraged to give at the "Stuyvesant Institute," on the twenty-first of March, 1838, met with better success than any of Mr. Schlesinger's previous efforts to please the public. His *Quatuor*, two movements of which were played and well received, was first introduced here on this occasion. He little thought its echoes would next mingle with the tones of his requiem. This, with Thalberg's *Fantasia* upon *Don Juan*, and Weber's "Invitation to Dance" constituted his share of the programme; but the evening was marked by an unexpected and characteristic trait. On entering the room a mourning-card was placed in our hands. It purported that, "intelligence having been that day received of the death of Ferdinand Ries,[181] his ancient master, Mr. Schlesinger begged permission of his auditors to open the concert with the 'Marcia Funebre' of Beethoven's Sonata in A *flat*, as a slight tribute to his memory." It was a touching circumstance; the voice of Beethoven

summoned to mourn his only disciple, by one who has since joined
them both in Paradise! Let us not forget to mention, that four
members of the Concordia, a musical association of German amateurs, of which the deceased subsequently became leader, laying
aside, for a compatriot's sake, a reluctance natural to the occasion,
added two very agreeable quartettes to its pleasures. From this
period, up to the opening of last winter, the flow of our artist's
existence was smooth and uneventful. He had acquired many
warm friends; and now counted pupils sufficient to give a tone to
his life and hopes. He never failed to inspire those who knew him
with a lasting respect, alike for himself, his talent, and the art it
illustrated. Over many he exercised a singular control, for no one
that saw forgot him. To such as have followed his path thus far,
the causes of this influence will be no longer a secret. His was an
uncommon union of attributes. A wonderful artist, whose talent was
spontaneous; a man whose firmness was only surpassed by his
rectitude, and whose modesty equalled his self-respect; cheerful
without effort, and winning without familiarity, neither stooping
to offer nor to receive adulation, each trait in his character bore
testimony to the earnest singleheartedness that had carried him
through life. You felt that he was an exalted being; incapable of
a sordid action or unworthy thought; whose motives would bear
exposing, nor discredit a child's simplicity.

His mind, exercised in thought and never wasted upon futilities,
had been disciplined by the severe studies of his profession; and
was of so truly original a stamp as to have often attracted persons
of intelligence to converse with him both here and in London,
upon the most intricate topics. We recollect an evening in the
summer of 1837, where a distinguished divine, who had been
charmed by his musical invocations, became engaged at a late
hour in a religious discussion with Mr. Schlesinger; whose clear and
striking views interested him so deeply as to prolong the argument
till near day-break. A remarkable readiness at mathematical calculation, which doubtless proved highly serviceable to him in the
combinations of musical science, was another prominent trait in
our artist's intellectual character. And did we not forbear to multiply such instances, many occasions might be cited, where this talent
was strikingly displayed. But to the simplest as well as the ab-

strusest subjects, you felt that he brought one precious element of knowledge, the experience of himself. Perhaps as you met him picking his way so collectedly in the street his intellect was framing harmonies to some suggestion of his fancy; for he constantly thought in music, although like Paisiello,[182] his happiest inspirations came to him in the morning, before he rose; when he was accustomed to perfect his designs, which he never inscribed on paper until they needed no further change. His head was stored with musical lore; a kind of learning more difficult to retain than what is usually termed erudition. In this economy of the notions he had acquired by labour, he was an example to the student; and from his patient gestation of his own ideas until maturity, the author might derive instruction.

XCIV

Choral Singing at Shearith Israel, 1818

Gradually, the standards of the Protestant culture with which they were surrounded began to influence the patterns of thought and life of the American Jews. As this took place, there developed, insensibly, a demand for the adaptation of various aspects of the internal, Jewish culture of the Jews of the United States to that of the surrounding milieu. We have already seen [183] how Jewish adaptations of Protestant Sunday Schools developed in the early national period. Religious results of the changed patterns of thinking will appear hereafter.[184]

In 1818, there arose in Shearith Israel a group which suggested that choral singing would be a healthy innovation, contributing an atmosphere of decorum to the synagogue services. The suggestion was met by the objection that choral singing would be a break with the traditions of synagogue worship. In spite of this and other objections, the innovation proposed was adopted by the Trustees of Shearith Israel in a tentative and modified form.[185]

188. COMMITTEE REPORT ON CHOIR, 1818 [186]

The Committee to whom was referred the letter of a number of Young gentlemen of the Congregation, who propose forming a class, with a view to improving the Singing in the Synagogue, and for that purpose to rehearse occasionally in the meeting room of the same and asking permission of the Board thereto. Report that they have consider'd the same and before entering into the subject matter of the application, beg leave to state, that they are of opinion that the gentlemen associated are entitled not only to the thanks and approbation of the board, but of the whole congregation for their good intentions, and consider that it affords full evidence of their ideas of the propriety of conducting our worship in a manner different from what it has been heretofore performed, and to give to the service that solemnity that our prayers and psalms should have, It however must not be concealed that all innovations on customs and forms established for a long series of years, however reasonable they may appear, should be approached with great caution and defference, We should be careful while endeavouring to cure an evil, not to create another and one perhaps of greater consequence than the existing one, We must view the application in all its bearings, its disadvantages as well as the advantages to be derived and if possible find a remedy for the one and gaurd against a result totaly different from the intentions and wishes of the applicants, the Trustees, or the Congregation, In stating what we now do, we certainly cannot mean to suppose that any of the applicants have an idea of doing any thing that may tend to the injury of our holy place of worship, but we have seen enough of the [   ] and jealous disposition of mankind to know, that there are persons in all associations, who from private pique and resentment, or other cause, permit their passions and feelings to get the better of their judgment, so far as often to do a material injury to the very plan of which they were the original founders; and if in process of time this association from practice and talents acquires so great a control, over the rest of the congregation, that the whole or the greater part of the services should by general consent devolve on them, what we ask would be our situation, when as before observed, for private pique, jealousy, resentment, or other cause, several of the association should refuse to continue longer members of the same, but withdraw themselves and even discontinue their attendance at Synagogue Another objection is, that they may be called from this City to reside elsewhere, and as the number is small, sickness or other casualty may prevent their attendance and from a discontinuance of the old form, we might find ourselves in a very unpleasant situation much more than at present. A whole congregation should never rely on the gratuitous services of any number of persons, it is uncertain and often attended with great inconvenience, Your committee are therefore of opinion, that it would be inexpedient to grant the request in the manner as we conceive is contemplated by the association, whom they are convinced never considered it in the light that your committee have, They are however of the opinion, that the association may do great good, and for that purpose invite them to commence their rehearsals without delay, with a full and entire understanding that any member of the congregation, may attend the same, join therein, as well as in the Synagogue, under such rules & regulations as shall be adopted We shall thus acquire a harmony in singing and give a general solemnity to our service, offend none & prevent any thing like discord in shool, by some singing who have been under rehearsal, & others endeavouring to drown their Voices who have not had an opportunity of attending the rehearsal and who may disapprove of a select number singing in shool, Your Committee therefore recommend that a Copy of this report be sent to the association, and that a committee of the Board be appointed to operate with them under the direction of the Board of the Trustees, all which is respectfully submitted

signed   N Phillips [187]

E S Lazarus [188]

Aaron Levy [189]

XCV
Synagogue Architecture, 1839

After the destruction of the old building of Congregation Beth Elohim of Charleston in 1838,[190] plans were drawn up for a new synagogue which was completed in 1840. The specifications set forth in the contract for this building, excerpts from which are given below, reveal another way in which the environing culture unwittingly influenced Jewish life: the building looked like a Protestant church, at least from the outside. Furthermore, in consonance with the generally neoclassical architecture that prevailed in the construction of public buildings, and even some private mansions, in the South, the building planned for this synagogue utilized neoclassical elements. The architect was not Jewish; he was Cyrus L. Warner [191] of New York. Characteristically, the building committee of the congregation took it upon itself, possibly with the advice of the builder, to introduce modifications in Mr. Warner's plans.

Although Charleston was no longer the leading Jewish community of the country, as it had been about fifteen years before the construction of this building, that it was by no means a poor and struggling community is indicated by the cost ($32,500.) of this building.

189. SPECIFICATIONS FOR A SYNAGOGUE, 1839 [192]

Dimensions. Length of enclosed part of Building Eighty feet three inches. Portico Fourteen feet nine inches, whole length of building ninety five feet. Breadth of Building Fifty six feet two inches. Whole Height from the surface of the ground to the apex of the roof forty six feet three inches. Foundation below the surface of the ground Four feet the committee reserving to themselves the right to have the same more or less by paying for any thing over said depth and claiming a deduction for any thing under. . . .

Portico & Columns. As per elevation and plans, the cornice pediment &c to be work'd in Brick the floor to be paved with dark Blue or Black and White marble tiles not over Ten inches Squares to be laid on brick arches to be constructed to receive the same. Columns as per plan, the flutes to be work'd in the brick work

West End. As per plan with the addition of one window on each Side of the door of Same Size and to correspond with the other windows of the building, to have a flue built in the wall to receive Stove pipe from the upper room of Vestibule

South Flank. As per plan entire, with the exception of Single instead of double antaes. See alterations

Granite. From the surface of the ground to the top of the base moulding all round the building as laid down in plan to be of granite ashlar. All window and door sills and lintels, Steps and buttresses, caps to columns and antaes and architrave to portico extending from column to column, which are to be workd full depth as laid down and in two thicknesses, door Sills to be eight by twenty four inches Window Sills eight by twelve inches all cut wash. lintels to extend in Width into the wall not less than two inches beyond the window frames. The whole to be of blue granite cut in the best manner, laid in cement and well Secur'd

Brown Stone. The corona or crown moulding to pidiment on each end and broad sides to be of best Connecticut brown Stone, the gutters to be cut in the stone forming the corona, to be elevated in the centre carrying off the water to each end there to empty into copper leaders of five inches diameter to be work'd in the Antaes and led off by Shoes to the ground. All the Stone work to the building to be cleand off before the Scaffolds are Struck

Iron Work. All Anchors, collars, Knees, Straps, bolts &c to be of best quality Sweeds Iron and placed to make the building Secure

Plastering. All the walls, partitions, ceilings &c to be lath'd with Sawd laths four feet long to be put up with five nails to the lath, to have three coats plastering of Strong lime sand and hair Mortar, the third coat to be a hard finish, The ceiling to be as per plan

Cement. The out side of walls columns antaes, cornices and pediments to be cemented with best roman cement not air slack'd, prepared with coarse sand and fresh water gravel, the joints of the bricks to be well cleand from loose mortar and the walls made Sufficiently wel before the plastering is put on, the plastering of cement shall neatly devellope the fluting of the columns of the portico and be finishd in the best possible Manner. All out Side cementing must be done between the first of May and first of August. . . .

Dome & Ceiling. To be furred down to receive plank ribbs and furred for five nails to the four foot lath, and naild Securely to ranging timbers, and as per plan. The pannels in the Spandrels to be Sunk Six inches, the Mouldings planted in to be a four Inch Moulding to leave a Margin of two Inches from the Moulding to the face of the rails round the pannels. The pannels in the dome to be sunk Six Inches at the bottom or lower end of the pannel and four and a half Inches at the upper end. The mouldings to be four Inches at the lower end of the pannels and diminish'd in the Same ratio of the Sinking of the pannels at the upper end. The ceiling of each Story of the vestibule to have a plain centre piece

Gallery Columns. As per plan to be made of clear White pine to be fluted and glued up and to have plank bases, height to be not less than Nine feet

Stairs. As per plan to be made of Yellow pine boards clear of Sap and Knots one and half Inches thick and moulded to be plough'd and tongued together, glued and block'd and Secret nail'd, Scotias plough'd and glued in, Steps housed into String well wedged and glued, Steps not to exceed seven Inches the entire rise, to be five feet long and to have winders if necessary the brackets to be continued around the well hole, to have a closset under each flight of Steps opening into the vestibule to be lined inside with narrow boards and enclosed with clear northern pine narrow boards, beaded on both sides each to have a grecian pannel door one and half Inch thick with locks &c to correspond with the rest of the building, the clossets to be as large as the Space will admit one of them to have as many drawers of six by fifteen Inches as can be placed convenient to be got at the other to shelved. Stairs to have an eight inch newel, Moulded rail and fancy turned two Inch ballisters, to be polished and varnished and made of St. Domingo Mahogany, all to be made Secure with a Sufficient number of Iron ballisters for the Same

Gallery. As per plan, the seats to be elevated with backs and doors to be framed and pannell'd with one and a quarter Inch northern pine. Seats to be of White pine clear of Knots, the backs to be capped and moulded with St Domingo Mahogany pollishd and varnish'd the doors to be hung with two and half Inch butts and fasten'd on the inside with brass buttons on plates. . . .

Ark. As per plan with S.D. Mahogany doors to slide in back boxing doors to be pannell'd the sides Markd H H on plan to be of Mahogany pannell'd and to be shelved inside as small clossets in the pannel door to each. All the doors to Ark to have best brass tumbler locks and Keys. The whole ark including the foliage to be of best St Domingo Mahogany. The ceiling over platform to be of White pine pannell'd or in Stoco work as may be directed by the committee. The two tablets top of the Ark mark'd D D and the freize Marked M to be of purest white Italian Marble with the ten commandments in Hebrew ingraved in Gold letters on the tables, and each other inscription in Gold letters on the freize as the committee may direct: The carpeting on floor and steps to be inserted (carpeting to be furnish'd by the committee)

Pulpit. As per plan all above the floor of which, Say Desk, Bench, Ballisters and Capping to be of best St D. Mahogany pollishd and varnishd.[193]

Part Six
The Strains of
Religious Adjustment

Of all the adjustments that had to be made by the Jews of the United States, none has been more difficult and productive of greater tensions than their religious adjustment. For it must be remembered that religion is, and has been throughout the existence of the Jews, the vital center of Jewish life. Whether in acceptance, in modification, or even in rejection, Judaism has been the dynamic factor for Jews at all times and everywhere. This is not to suggest that the Judaism that has served Jews dynamically has itself remained static, for to assert this would be to deal in paradox. On the contrary, variations and modifications of basic Judaism have developed in every land in which Jews have at any time found a home. Every Jewish group has developed its own *minhag*, its own customary pattern, with more or less rapidity, depending upon the conditions under which it lived, the non-Jewish culture by which it was surrounded, and the type and extent of interrelatedness between the Jews and their neighbors.

The reasons for the difficulty of Jewish religious adjustment in the United States are implicit in what has been said thus far. Even in the period with which we are concerned, a period of relatively small Jewish population, the Jews of America came from a number of different European Jewries each differing in some degree from every other. There were Jews of Spanish and Portuguese descent (*Sephardim*). Some of these were representatives of families that had been expelled from the Iberian peninsula at the end of the fifteenth century and that had never abandoned their ancestral religion. Others came from families that had nominally accepted conversion to Christianity to avoid expulsion, but had retained a secret attachment to Judaism (Marranos, or crypto-Jews). When a return to Judaism became possible, in Holland or in the New

World, the Marranos had availed themselves of the opportunity to revert, but they came back with special traditions of their own, developed during their half-life. All of these accepted the *minhag* of the Sephardic congregations in Europe and, for a time at least, maintained Spanish or Portuguese as a semi-sacred language. They pronounced Hebrew in a different fashion from that of other Jews. There were certain characteristic Sephardic customs with regard to synagogue arrangement, the order of prayers, and congregational government. Every synagogue organized in the United States prior to 1795 followed the Sephardic *minhag*. Yet, numerically, the Sephardic Jews were in a minority in America as early as 1730.

The Ashkenazic Jews who thus early outnumbered their Sephardic brethren emigrated from England, Holland, Poland, and various parts of Germany, and, to an inconsiderable number, from France. They brought with them their different local variations of the Ashkenazic *minhag*, and although they became members of the Sephardic synagogues and even, after a time, officers, there remained a difference, especially keenly realized by Ashkenazic immigrants of the post-Revolutionary years. One part of this difference lay in the fact that for these later arrivals, it was not the Iberian languages but usually German (occasionally, though not often in this early period, a Judeo-German form of Yiddish) that had a semi-sacred character. Furthermore, by Ashkenazic standards, even the most conforming of the Sephardim were regarded as religiously lax, while the general indifference to organized religion that marked the post-Revolutionary period, until 1798, in Christian America extended into American Jewry as well. The first difficulty of Jewish adjustment was, then, that there was no single pattern of Judaism that all the Jews of America were prepared to accept as a norm. Several varieties were jockeying for position and prestige.

A second major difficulty was created by the very ease and frequency of association between the Jews and their Christian (and, in this period, Deist) neighbors. On the one hand, the determination of Americans, far more marked in the early national period than it is today, to maintain full freedom of religion was one of the liberal features that attracted European Jews to immigrate to America. On the other hand, the lack of sharp boundaries defining the limits of association made it difficult for the Jewish group to exer-

cise control over its members. Many more Jews had the experience
of close friendship with Christians than had ever had such experience in Europe. They were able to see how their neighbor
lived; there were temptations to eat their neighbor's food, or to woo
and wed his sister or daughter. Some Jewish children might go to
school with their Protestant neighbors, and even imbibe a little
Protestant Christianity in the process. Their parents occasionally
attended churches, and, even if they did not attend, were aware of
what went on in the churches and how it differed from worship in
the synagogue. The "wall of separation between Jew and non-Jew,"
which with minor breaches was characteristic of European life at
this time, had been almost completely broken down in America.

Out of this background came many of the demands for changes in
patterns of worship that began to split Jewish unity in the 1820s.
Christians had a decorous pattern of worship in the churches; the
synagogues should abandon their traditional pray-as-you-please
policy, with its Oriental and "barbaric" suggestions, and introduce
a less chaotic pattern. Worship in the churches (almost all Protestant, at this time) took place in English, so that all the congregants
could understand the prayers; for Jews, even for those who knew
no Hebrew, Hebrew was a sacred language to be retained in prayers, but the Hebrew prayers could be repeated in English translation and thus made intelligible. Christian ministers delivered regular sermons, expounding matters of faith and morals; synagogues,
too, should have preachers or lecturers, to perform a similar ex-
pository function for the Jewish community. To all these and other
suggestions, the traditionalist would often answer that things simply
had never been done that way before. Such a rigidity of outlook
could produce nothing but an uncomprehending stare from those
who, however recently they had come to America, had already
seen many things done, in many areas of life, that had never been
done that way before and yet were done successfully.

For the United States was an experiment in pioneering, not only
geographically but in all other respects as well, and it did not take
a newcomer long to fall into the prevailing mood of regarding that
which had never been done before as not only preferable, but even
in some sense morally superior to that which had been done. And,
with the adoption of this attitude, there began a passion for innova-

tion in Jewish religious life that was not brought to fruition before 1840. Its most dramatic expression in the early national period was the short-lived Reformed Society of Israelites in Charleston, but the documents below reveal that this was not its only manifestation and that, indeed, it may be regarded as a pervasive current in American Judaism in the early nineteenth century. The new attitude was a first product of Americanization; each new immigrant or immigrant group repeated the process. First, there was a shocked horror at what passed for Judaism in the United States, accompanied perhaps by a firm resolve not to permit oneself to yield to the unholy religious atmosphere. Then came the yielding, point by point, to Americanization in attitude and to Protestantization in practice. It is only fair to add that, to the extent that America was physically and geographically a land of pioneering, the Jews who immigrated were, by and large, those who might hope to gain a foothold in a pioneer society. They were the relatively rugged and relatively bold, not the scholars, not the men of learning. They had to be those who were ready to take a chance. It was not until years later, when there was a comparatively stable life into which they could enter, that the rabbis and the Jewish scholars came to America.

In spite of the three major difficulties to which attention has been called, there did develop a synagogal life in the United States, following population trends, establishing itself during our period in newer communities in the middle west. The synagogues were regularly chartered under the laws of the state in which they were established. They printed constitutions and by-laws, and had more or less democratically elected officers and trustees. Financial difficulties arose and were met with ingenuity. "Ministers," usually men of little education who were able to lead the services, were hired and fired. To make possible the observance of the dietary laws, synagogue authorities hunted high and low for men qualified to take office as *Shohet*. The synagogues also made arrangements for the baking of *matzoth*. Men competent to perform circumcisions were rare in the United States; there were cases in which fathers circumcised their own sons, and many others in which no circumcision was performed. At first only on occasions, but later on every Sabbath, sermons were delivered, though the most distinguished religious addresses surviving to us were those of laymen rather than those of professionals. Questions of religious law arose and were decided, whether with or without formal authority. The injunction to charity was honored both through the synagogues and by the formation of philanthropic societies. There was, in short, however inadequate it may have been by European standards, a Jewish religious life in America.

Somehow or other, by compromise between factions or by duplication of institutions, in spite of indifferentism and ignorance and of the small and widely scattered Jewish population in America, the tradition of Judaism was carried on, so that not only were Jews naturalized as citizens of the United States, but their religion was also naturalized as part of the complex and pluralistic religious situation in the United States.

XCVI

Family Records in a Lunar
Calendar, 1801-1830

The keeping of family records of births, marriages, and deaths in a treasured religious book is a widespread custom. For the most part, records of this sort are to be discovered in old family Bibles or in prayer books. The family of Levy Solomons [1] discovered a substitute in the first American printed calendar of Hebrew dates (*Luach*), compiled by Moses Lopez [2] of Newport, Rhode Island, and printed in that city in 1806. Gershom M. Seixas,[3] minister of Shearith Israel in New York, checked and approved the work of Lopez, which must, indeed, have served a useful religious function in the United States.

The Solomons's family notations, ranging in date from 1768 to about 1869, tell the story of a family that remained faithful to the Jewish tradition in their migrations from place to place in the New World. Until her death (in 1852 at the age of 84), the record was kept by the matriarch of the Solomons clan, Catherine Manuel Solomons, wife of Levy Solomons. Many of the entries have a touch of poignancy, as child after child passed away, leaving the old mother to record the sad fact.

190. TITLE PAGE OF THE
LOPEZ CALENDAR, 1806 [4]

A / Lunar Calendar, / of the / Festivals, and Other Days in the / Year, / Observed by the Israelites, / Commencing Anno Mundi, 5566, and / ending in 5619, / Being a Period of 54 Years, / Which by the Solar Computation of Time, / begins September 24th, 1805, and will / End the 28th of the same Month, in the / Year 1859, / Together with other Tables useful and / convenient.

The Whole of which having been carefully examined and corrected, its utility has obtained the voluntary acknowledgment and approbation of the Rev. Mr. Seixas. the respectable Hazan of the K.K. Shearith Israel, in New-York.

By Moses Lopez, of Newport, Rhode-Island.
(*Copy-right Secured.*)
Printed at the Office of the Newport Mercury, 1806.

191. RECORDS OF THE
SOLOMONS FAMILY, 1801–1830 [5]

[1] Levy Solomons born Montreal Canada 23 December 1771
[2] Catherine Manuel his wife born in London 1st January 1768
(In 1824 she was aged 56 years old.)
[3] Where the above couple were Married In New York by the Revd Gershom Mendes Seixas Hazan of that Congregation on 29th July in the year 1801
Menakim Ab 5561
[4] First Daughter Still Born 24th June 1802
[5] A Son Born 7th October 1803 Named Lucius Levy Solomons in New York the 30 day of May 1804. at Eight months old.
[6] A Son Born 27 December 1805 Named Adolphus Asher Solomons in New York 25 May 1806 at five months old C[6]
[7] A Son Born Saml David Solomons January 11th 1808 Named in New York on 19 Day May 1808 at nearly Six months old
[8] A Son Born 24th March 1810 Named at five weeks old in New York Named Levy Solomons
[9] All the five children of Levy Solomons Where born In Albany and the four Sons all named by Revd Gershom Mendes Seixas Hazan of the New York Shool for 51* (*49) years,[7] and Brother In law to me.[8]   Cathe Solomons
[10] Lucius married at Phila 31st march 1824 to Selina Seixas by Levy Phill[ips] [9]
[11] Lucius has a Son born on 23 Decr 1824 In the Same year of his marriage named in New York by Mr I B Kursheedt:
Levy Solomons

I was his God mother but being in Albany. Sally Kursheedt [10] acted for me

[12] On 22nd Novr 1826 Lucius had twins born In Montreal Canada the boy was first-born. than the Daughter, who is Named after me, In the New York Shool. by Revd Mr Peixota,[11] Catherine Manuel Solomons & named also in Montreal where the child was born. (by Joshua Mendes Seixas) my nephew [12]

[13] My poor dear Levy [13] departed this Life, on Sunday Morning a little before 2 on 8th July 1832, late on the Shobas afternoon on 7, which was the Eve of his death he Calld on our heavenly father has a Witness, that he had always loved Cherished and Obeyed his all Surviving Parent [14] and prayed for her happiness. On the Monday morning Saml [15] accompanied his Brother's corps to the house of Cousin R. Judah and Aaron H. Judah, and on the Tuesday was buried, his last orders, with his last wish was to be Sent to Aaron In N york, Mariam Judah, with myself Said the Shamong [16] at his last moment
Cathe Solomons

[14] our poor dear Lucius [17] Died on 5th March 1830 In Montreal, on the Same day (friday) Son Levy and Self got there, Saml Seixas,[18] Son Levy,[19] and self was present at his last, and all Repeated the Shamong, was Sencible to the last, was buried on the Sunday afternoon. His last sweet babe, Lucius, must have been only two months Old when at time of his Death
Cathre Solomons

[15] Mrs Rebecca Solomons [20] of Montreal departed this Life In her Chair at the table while giving the agoda [21] first night of passover. on 27 March: 1812

[16] Levy Solomons Senior [22] departed this Life In Montreal on the 18 May 1792, about 62 or 63 years of age

[17] Sarah McCord [23] departed this Life In Montreal 13 June 1812, aged 42 or 43

[18] My Dear Husband. Levy Solomons [24] departed this Life of Woe on the 11 June 1823. In New York for Several Years previous, his afflictions and Sufferings were Great which he bore with the Greatest fortitude, age when he Died, 52 Years, 5 months, & 4 days.

[19] My Dear Child Adolphus [25] departed from us on Sunday

morning the 15th June 1828 at about 10 minutes of Three OClock Aged. 22 years. 5 months & 19 Days

Cathre Solomons

Albany 11. Jan 1829

[20] my Child bore his afflictions throughout, with his Usual Sweetness of Disposition till the last   Cathre Solomons

XCVII

A Public Lottery and
Synagogue Finance, 1790

The post-Revolutionary years were a time of considerable religious indifference in America, and the handful of Jewish congregations undoubtedly suffered from the disorder that beset the Christian churches. Certainly, there was a financial stringency in the affairs of Congregation Mikveh Israel in Philadelphia [26] that led to the attempt to ease their straits by holding a lottery,[27] as described in the circular reproduced below.

The scheme is fully described in the circular. It is of interest to note that the object is stated as that of "paying off some pressing demands against a religious House," that a special enabling act of the General Assembly was passed to permit this lottery,[28] that the object is presented as one that will commend itself to "all pious persons of liberal sentiments," and that, unlike commercial lotteries, the prizes to be disbursed equal the total amount to be realized by ticket sales, the promoters' need for funds being met entirely by a twenty-five percent "house cut" on the prizes.

This lottery could not have been oversuccessful, for two years later, Mikveh Israel was still forced to plead poverty.[29] That it was not a complete failure is, however, indicated by the fact that, some years later, in 1808, Philadelphia's first Ashkenazic congregation, Rodeph Sholom, also attempted to use the lottery method of raising funds for its needs, but did not receive the permission of the authorities.[30] In New York, Congregation Shearith Israel found itself in economic difficulties as a result of building a new synagogue. It was rescued by philanthropic bequests and the sale of property.[31]

192. NOTICE OF LOTTERY, 1790 [32]

A Lottery, For raising the Sum of Eight Hundred Pounds

To enable the Hebrew Congregation in the city of Philadelphia to extricate their House of Worship from its present incumbrances, agreeably to an act of General Assembly of the State of Pennsylvania, passed the sixth day of April, one thousand seven hundred and ninety.

The Scheme.

1	Prize of	1000	Dollars, is	1000	Dollars.
1	do.	500		500	
1	do.	300		300	
1	do.	200		200	
1	do.	100		100	
10	do.	50	are	500	
4	do.	40		160	
8	do.	30		240	
16	do.	20		320	
32	do.	10		320	
72	do.	5		360	
2013	do.	2		4026	
	First drawn Ticket			400	
	Last drawn,			214	
2160	Tickets at 4 Dollars			8640	

The Prizes to be subject to a deduction of twenty five per cent.

This Lottery being instituted for the sole purpose of paying off some pressing demands against a religious House, dedicated to the worship of Almighty God, it is to be hoped that all pious persons of liberal sentiments will encourage it especially there is no blanks, of course the risk is inconsiderable: Andt although the low prizes are less than the price of a ticket, yet the adventurers do not loose the whole of their disbursements (as is the case in most Lotteries) whilst for the small sum of Two Dollars and one half, which they do venture in this, they have the chance of drawing a prize of One Thousand Dollars, or even Fourteen Hundred Dollars, besides the satisfaction of having contributed to an object so pious and meritorious.

Ticket may be had of Manuel Josephson,[33] Solomon Lyon,[34] William Wister,[35] John Duffield,[36] and Samuel Hays,[37] of Philadelphia; and Solomon Etting,[38] at Lancaster, who are appointed, by law, managers of the Lottery.

A list of the prizes will be published immediately after the drawing is finished. And payment made by orders on the Bank of North America, where the money will be deposited for that purpose.

The Managers of the above Lottery beg leave to inform the Public that it was their full expectation to draw the same on the day at first advertised, which from the rapid call for Tickets they were warranted to hope would be the case; but as a considerable number of Tickets has been sent to several of the States on the Continent, for which the remittances have not yet come to hand, they are under the necessity to postpone the drawing until the second Tuesday in October next, when the Public may be assured, it will then positively take place, with out any further delay or notice, at the Court-House in Market-street, (by permission of His Worship the Mayor of the city.)

As the few Tickets remaining on hand, are not the object for which the drawing of the Lottery is put off, but solely for the reason aforesaid, it will be expedient in those who incline to become adventurers to be speedy in their application for Tickets, as by delaying it to the last they may be disappointed of their intention.

Monday, Aug. 9, 1790.

XCVIII

Representative Government in the Synagogue, 1793

The small documents brought together here tell the story of a charge of usurpation of powers brought against the Parnass (president) of Congregation Mikveh Israel by the members of the Junto (council). Synagogue government by the laity was a tradition of the Sephardic congregations [39] that was carried on in all the early American synagogues (all of which, until 1802, followed the Sephardic pattern). This representative form of government was reinforced by the type of government established in the United States under the Constitution. However unwise the decisions made by Benjamin Nones, acting unilaterally, may have been, his major folly lay in his disregard for the elected representatives of the congregation.

193. THE JUNTO OF MIKVEH ISRAEL TO BENJAMIN NONES,[40] 1793 [41]

In Junto

Saturday Evening Feby 23 1793

The Junto met to know if an answer had been recived [sic] from Mr B Nones Parnass to a letter they wrote him dated the 15th Instant requesting of him to Call the Junto on Business of Importance but finding no answer had been received by either of the Junto therefore Resolved that another Letter be wrote to the Parnass requesting his attendance to morrow afternoon at Mr Cohens [42] where the Junto will meet & receive such Business that Mr Nones may have to lay before them and that a Copy of this resolve with the Letter be sent to Mr Nones.   Jonas Phillips [43]

Levy Phillips [44]

Moses Nathans [45]

Saturday Evening 23 Feby. 1793

Sr

The Indignity you have treated us with as Representatives of this Congregation wou'd have been resented by us in the manner it deserves but having the welfare of the Congregation at heart and wishing to live at peace with every Individual we will pass it in silence and now request that you will meet us to morrow afternoon at 4 OClock at Mr Cohen's on Business of the Utmost Consequence to the Congregation. if you Still persist in your Obstinate refusal in meeting us we Shall agreeable to Law Reason & Equity proceed On Business with out you We are Respectfully Sr your most Obedt humble Servants   Jonas Phillips

Levy Phillips

Moses Nathans

P.S. No Verball answer will be received.

194. THE JUNTO OF MIKVEH ISRAEL TO BENJAMIN NONES, 1793 [46]

[To Mr. Benjamin Nones, Parnass]

At the Meeting of the Juntas of K. K. Mikve Israel on Sunday the 11th Nisan 5553 Corresponding With the 24th day of March 1793 . . . Present—   Levy Phillips

Moses Nathans

Jonas Phillips

The Junta Met to deliberate Wether the parnass has done his duty in regard of his Office & Wether he has acted for the Wellfare of this Congregation Which he ought to have at heart. Resolved that it is the opinion of the Junta that Parnass has taken on himself sundry Liberties of the Utmost Consequence to this Congregation which he ought not to have done without the approbation and consent of the Junta it is therefore resolved Unanamous that the parnass is suspended from his Office & that he is not to officiate as Parnass Untill he has had a meeting of the Junta or the Congregation & given his reason for his Illegal Pro-

ceedings Resolved that a Copy of the above be Sent to Mr Nones
for his Government.   Jonas Phillips
                                                  Levy Phillips
                                                  Moses Nathans

Mr. Benjamin Nones
SIR: The above is a copy of Resolve entered into by us you will
please to observe that as we the representative of this Congrega-
tion are in duty bound to discharge the trust reposed in us as
Juntas of this K. K. Mikve Israel if we have acted out of Character
in the above resolve we are willing to leave the matter to the
Whole Congregation at Large for its decission.[47]
   We are respectfully Sir Your Most Obedie[n]t. Serts.
                                                  Jonas Phillips
                                                  Levy Phillips
                                                  Moses Nathans
Philada. 24th. March 1793.

XCIX

A Plea for Leniency, 1796

Congregation Shearith Israel must have appeared as complainant against the husband of the writer of this pathetic and plaintive letter. Beyond the fact that he had offended by going to the Synagogue, we know nothing about the case. Had he perhaps disrupted services? Was he "drunk and disorderly"? Was there some anti-semitic impulse behind his visit? Whatever it was, he was jailed on the complaint of the congregation, and his wife made this plea to the officers, asking leniency for her own sake, and promising to keep her husband away from the synagogue in future.

195. MRS. G. PHILIPS TO
SHEARITH ISRAEL, 1796 [48]

To the Pornas & Trustees of K K. S. Israel
Gentlemen

I beg you will take into Consideration my present Situation & Distress I am in at this present time from the Behaviour of my husband. I acknoledge he deservd Some punishment, but as you have punished him with Confinement I hope it will bee the Means of his Better Conduct in future, I beg the favour of you Gentleman to release him from Confinement being the first Offense I do promise in future to keep him from going to Synagoge any more. Consider Gentleman I am left Without a Husband & a friend to provide for me Nesesirais of life in my present Situation. By Complying with the Above you will Oblige your Destresed friend

G Philips

N York April 26th 1796

C

A Synagogue Constitution, 1805

On March 27, 1801, the Legislature of the State of New York passed "An Act to Provide for the Incorporation of Religious Societies." The third section of this act provided specifically for the government of the "estate and property" of religious societies by a group of trustees, chosen by an election in which "every male person of full age, who has statedly worshipped with said church, congregation, or society, and has formerly been considered as belonging thereto, shall be entitled to vote." The act prescribes the manner of announcing elections and of holding them, and goes on to place limits on the financial holdings of incorporated religious societies, and to define their competence in temporal affairs. Soon after the passage of this act, in 1805, Congregation Shearith Israel of New York revised its constitution and bylaws in strict conformity with the state law.[49]

From this constitution and the accompanying bylaws, which are typical of synagogal regulations of the period, we can learn a great deal about the strength of the synagogue in Jewish life. So, for example, although in the fourth article the right of the Parnass to punish offenders is stated, the specific punishments noted in the bylaws, in articles 2 and 4 especially, are relatively few in number. There is no specification of punishment for infraction of religious laws, as there was in earlier Shearith Israel constitutions.[50] The absence of such provisions may be taken as a measure of the extent of laxity of religious observance.[51] We should also note that in the third article of the constitution provision is made for the occasional introduction of an English sermon, and that Article VIII of the bylaws includes four provisions for maintaining decorum during services in the Synagogue. Thus two of the objectives for which later reform movements were started were taken into consideration in the Shearith Israel Constitution of 1805.

196. CONSTITUTION OF
SHEARITH ISRAEL, 1805 [52]

Constitution, &c.

Article I. The Congregation of [Shearith Israel] in New-York, heretofore known under that stile and title, shall be continued under the same name, and become a body corporate.

Article II. Sec. 1. There shall be six persons elected to serve as Trustees, according to the manner and form prescribed by the act of the Legislature, providing for the incorporation of religious societies, to take charge of all the temporalities and of all matters relative to the interior government of the congregation.

Sec. 2. It shall be the duty of the said Trustees to elect from amongst the members of their Board a [Parnass] or [Parnassim], he or one of them presiding in the Board, and possessing all the powers out of it, that may be granted by the laws to be established.

Sec. 3. There shall always be a [Shohet, Hazzan,] and [Shamash] chosen by the congregation, to perform the services required of them in their several departments, subordinate officers to be chosen by the Trustees.

Article III. The fixed prayers the [Torah we-Haftaroth] shall forever be read in the Hebrew language, according to the [minhag Sephardim] but the Board of Trustees may on a public thanksgiving or other special occasion, direct the [Hazzan] or any other suitable person, to deliver an address, sermon, or moral lecture in English.

Article IV. The [Parnass] or [Parnassim] may at all times cause any offender or offenders against this constitution, or any of the laws of this Congregation, to be punished in such manner as may hereafter be provided.

Article V. Sec. 1. The Synagogue and burying places shall ever be the joint property of all Israelites, who are or may hereafter become electors of this Congregation; and the same shall never be sold, mortgaged or shut up, by any person or persons under their authority, nor shall any of the leases of that part of the property of this Congregation adjoining the [Beth Hayim] now on lease, be renewed for a longer term than twenty-one years.

Sec. 2. Should the Board of Trustees deem it necessary or con-ducive to the interest of the Congregation to dispose of any other real estate, they shall cause the electors residing within the juris-diction of the Corporation of this city, to be duly notified by written or printed notices at least one week previous to holding said meeting, stating the object thereof, to assemble at the usual place of meeting, or such other place as they may appoint, when two thirds of the members present agreeing shall be considered a majority.

Article VI. This Congregation shall forever be supported by the sale or taxation of seats in Synagogue, and by free will offerings; but no poll or income tax shall ever be assessed on the members of this Congregation.

Article VII. Whereas by the last will and testament of Myer Polonies a legacy was left to this Congregation for the express purpose of establishing a Hebrew school, it shall therefore be the duty of the Board of Trustees, to form such a school under some suitable teacher or teachers, with such regulations as they may think proper; and that a free will offering may be made in Syna-gogue for the benefit of such establishment, in such manner as the Trustees may direct.

Article VIII. Whereas there is established in this Congregation a [Chevra Hased we-Emeth] the same is hereby recognized, under its present constitution and laws.

Article IX. No person shall hereafter be an elector, unless duly qualified agreeable to the act of incorporation.

Article X. It shall be the duty of the Board of Trustees to enforce by law the payment of all monies due to this Congregation, arising in any manner whatsoever within three months after the same shall accrue. And it is hereby expressly understood, that all fines arising from default under this constitution and bye laws are included in this article.

Article XI. Sec. 1. No alteration, addition or amendment shall ever be made to this constitution, but in manner following, that is to say, whenever seven electors of this Congregation shall deem an alteration, addition or amendment necessary, they may apply in writing to the President of the Board of Trustees for the time being, stating the proposed alteration, addition or amendment, whose duty it shall be to convene the electors within fifteen days after such application, giving them at least ten days written or printed notice, in which shall be contained the alteration, addition or amendment proposed; at which meeting, two thirds of the electors residing within the limits of this city shall be requisite to form a quorum; that a final decision shall not then take place, but a second meeting shall be called and held, within one month after, and in like manner as the first, at which time the proceedings of the former meeting shall be taken up and finally decided on; provided, two thirds of such quorum as aforesaid vote for such alteration, addition or amendment.

Sec. 2. And should the President of the Board of Trustees refuse or neglect to convene the electors in manner and form as aforesaid, that then the said seven electors may thereupon exercise the duty enjoined on the President by this article, any thing contained in this constitution to the contrary notwithstanding.

Bye Laws of the Congregation of [Shearith Israel]

Article VI. Every male person of the age of twenty-one years, and upwards, professing Judaism, and residing, or having resided within the limits of the corporation of the city of New-York, and does not sign the constitution, and bye laws, within three months after the adoption and ratification thereof, or within three months after the return of such person or persons who were absent at the time of its adoption, he or they shall be barred, of and from having or enjoying any of the rights, benefits and immunities, for, during, and until the expiration of three months after signing the same. . . .

Article VIII. In order further to promote solemnity and order, during the time of our worship, without which, prayers cannot be acceptable to Almighty God,

Sec. 1. It is hereby declared, that every member of this congregation shall, previous to the singing any psalm, or prayer, remain silent until the [Hazzan] shall signify the tone or key, in which the same is to be sung, and those who are so inclined may then join therein, with an equal voice, but neither higher or louder than the [Hazzan].

Sec. 2. That no children of either sex under the age of three years be admitted in Synagogue under any pretence whatsoever, except in cases of [Berith Milah u-Birhath Gomel] or the naming of a child, and that all children of the female sex be confined to that part of the Synagogue appropriated for females.

Sec. 3. That all umbrellas and canes, excepting canes carried by lame persons, shall be left at the door, and that all garments taken off shall be deposited in the free seats near the door, unless the owners thereof put them in their own seats.

Sec. 4. That any person or persons leaving the Synagogue shall retire in a quiet and orderly manner, and avoid going out together or in bodies; and more particularly during the reading of the [Torah] and [Haftarah] and that if any person or persons shall act contrary to this law, they and each of them, shall be considered as having committed an offence, and punished accordingly.

Article IX. That all applications to have the name or names of any deceased person or persons recorded in a book to be kept for that purpose by the clerk of this congregation, for the privilege of an [Ashkabah] shall be made to the Board of Trustees, a majority of whom shall decide on the same, and if granted, they shall charge therefor, for the benefit of this congregation, the sum of twelve dollars and fifty cents.

Article X. It is also declared, that all and every person or persons who shall have been considered of the Jewish persuasion, resident within the limits of the corporation of the city of New-York, that do not commune with us under the constitution and bye laws now established, shall be assessed and charged by the Board of Trustees ten dollars per annum, and in case of refusal to pay the same, shall not be entitled to any of the rights, benefits and immunities, granted to the electors and members thereof, until he or they shall have paid up his or their arrearages, and the consent of the Board of Trustees had thereto.[53]

CI

A Breach of Decorum in the Ladies Gallery, 1825

The particular sort of disorderly violation of synagogue decorum that is described in the following letter may perhaps be attributed to the egalitarian mood that was coming into prominence in the Jacksonian era, although the existence in earlier synagogue constitutions of provisions for the punishment of offenders suggests that disciplinary difficulties were chronic. The *shammash* of Congregation Mikveh Israel of Philadelphia certainly faced a difficult task in attempting to persuade some young ladies to occupy their proper seats instead of taking other people's seats in the front of the ladies gallery. It was especially hard when the brother of the displaced females threatened physical harm to the poor fellow, who was only trying to do his duty and to enforce congregational rules.

197. ABRAHAM ISRAEL [54] TO ZALEGMAN PHILLIPS, [55] 1825 [56]

Dear Sir

With Great Reluctance I am Persuaded to bring before your honnor what has passed the last day of Pesah when I as shamas found my Selve obliged to inforse the Rules of the Congregation. I went up in the Gallery I Adress my Selve to Some Ladies that the front seats cant be occupied by them, and have Satisfied me to Go to a place which I have Give to them, Afterward I Address my Selve to the young Ladies of Mr. Andrews [57] and told them as before, but one maight keep the front seat in place of her mother butt no Reply has been made and still kept in the same for to Prevent disturbance in the devine Worship I. went down, and when I went out to see if any boys are About to ordre them in Mr. Jos J.

Andrews [58] Came up towards me, and Asked what I have done up stairs by his Sisters I. told him to Request one to move out from the front seats that she is not Entiteled to seat thier, he boldly told me I order you, never to go up Again to my sisters or I will Drag you down, I Replyd I have to due my duty as Long I will be shamas and preforce the Rules of myn Supirior he said he dare the Parnass or any one to ordre his Sisters out of the front seats he will spent a hundred dollars to See it, with Ohter Abusive Expression so well to the Superior officer as to members of KKMI this is only to know how I have to Act in future on my Part for the Remainder it is left with your honnor to Judge According, I have to Repeat Again that I am Sory that I have to bring information of any member of this Congregation before your honnor butt my duty Compels me of Doing so

    Sir I Remain your humble Sert   Abm. E. Israel shamas KKMI

Zalegman Phillips Esqr
Parnass K K M Israel
Philadelphia April 11th 1825

CII

Synagogal Responsibility
for Kashruth, 1805-1836

During the early national period, the American synagogues retained responsibility for supervising the ritual slaughtering of meat for Jewish use. The *shohet* (slaughterer) was a synagogue employee. It was up to the trustees of the synagogues to hire a *shohet,* having previously examined his qualifications and certification. The limited number of available candidates made the problem of selection a difficult one, and when a *shohet* fell sick or died there was considerable confusion. The four documents collected below illustrate various phases of the problem of maintaining synagogal responsibility for *kashruth.* The insistence on the importance of keeping up the tradition and the stress on its centrality to Jewish life in the selection from the minutes of Congregation Shearith Israel in 1825 reflects the fact that that year was a critical one, in which challenges to the established synagogal order were beginning to arise everywhere.

198. AARON LEVY [59] TO SIMON GRATZ, [60] 1805 [61]

New York 14 Jany 1805

Mr Simon Gratz
Dear Sir
    The bearer Mr Isaac Lazarus [62] I have had examin'd by the Shohet of our Congregation [63] and Mr Jacob Hart [64] an old and respectable member of our Society whose Opinions, I herewith transmit you. Mr Lazarus has also a Certificate which he brought with him from Europe. Mr Kursheedt [65] (who has seen it) inform'd me it was a good one and knew the Signature to be from a respectable person. as for the Character of the young man, I can say

nothing he being a perfect Stranger in this place, and without any money in his pocket. his willingness, to get in employ and his general Appearance are in his favor and *I think?* I may venture to recommend him to you as the person, who is calculated for the Shohet of your Congregation. the terms will be left with yourself, all he at present asks for, is a sufficiency, to keep him above board. He will deliver you a Cheese Sent Mr Moses [66] for your father. Should Mr L answer the purposes you want him for, I shall feel happy that I had it in my power both of serving you and promoting his Interest. I am with Sentiments of esteem your friend

Aaron Levy

199. FINDING A TEMPORARY SHOHET, 1825 [67]

[August 17, 1825]

The Committee appointed at the last Meeting on the subject of the Shochet, report, That they have visited Mr Mark Solomon [68] and find that he will not be able to attend to his duty of Shochet for at least two weeks, that they advised him not to go out until he was well and that when perfectly restored for him to address a letter to the Parnass advising him thereof and of his readiness and ability to reasume his business

The Committee also report that Mr Abraham H Cohen [69] has been since the sickness of Mr Solomon performing the Duties of Shochet, assisted in the labor part by Marcus Van Gelder [70] by the directions of the Parnass, As Mr Van Gelder was a stranger to the Committee they considered it adviseable to have him examined as to his capability for a Shochet & Bodeck, the result of which examination is hereunto (annexed) attached

Having thus far executed their duties the Committee deem it proper to state that they are of opinion that the present mode of supplying the Market with Cosher Meat as well as the manner of remunerating the Shochet might be placed on a more eligible footing; the Office of Shochet made more respectable and more independent of the Butchers than at present, The Mode that appears preferable to the Committee, is, that the Trustees should agree with a sufficient number of Butchers to supply the different Markets with Cosher Meat, each of them to pay such Sum as may be agreed on in lieu of all perquisites now given to the Shochet. Should this Mode appear eligible to the Trustees an understanding with the Butchers might then take place as to what sums they would be willing to Pay, and in what manner a legal and sufficient supply of Cosher Meat might be calculated on in the different Markets

As the business is at present the Committee would recommend that Mr Cohen be continued to perform the Duties of Shochet until the recovery of Mr Solomon & assisted by Mr Van Gelder in such way as Mr Cohen may think proper to employ him, and that the President of the Board be authorised to draw Warrants on the Treasurer for such sums as may be deemed Adequate and reasonable for their Services.

Mr Solomon has served the Congregation in the Office of Shochet about 28 years his advanced and consequent increasing infirmities point out to the Committee the propriety of calling the attention of the Trustees to such measures as may be necessary to persue on such a religious subject, It is of itself the foundation of the ceremonial part of our institutions and the most sacred of our rituals. It therefore behoves us as the repositaries of the power of the Congregation not to look with indifference on the situation we may be placed, in the event of Mr Solomons being incapable hereafter at any period to perform the duties of Shochet, added to which the encreased number of our Bretheren, and also the probability of many more comeing to reside in this City greatly encreases the labour of the Shochet, and from the Scattered situations of the Butchers, render it very problematical whether one Shochet will be sufficient for this Kahal

Having thus brought this very interesting Subject to the view of the Board, the Committee refrain from offering an Opinion as to the measures that should be taken, Wishing rather that the individual Views of the Members may be elicited in relation to the same

Signed   N. Phillips [71]

Committee

M L Moses [72]

New York 16 Augt 1825

200. DANIEL SOLIS [73] TO
ZALEGMAN PHILLIPS, [74] 1832 [75]

Philad July 19. 1832

Sir

On the 13. of this Month I Called on You in person to Dedfend [sic] My self in answer to Yours of the 10 [?] and You them [sic] told Me that You would Not have any thing to Do with the Butchers and all I had to Do was to find Meat for the Congregation Now Sir as this Day is a Day Huminiation [sic] and prayres [sic] with the Gentiles it was Not known whether the Butchers would go to Market

I Did Not Know it till Late but I Did killed one Calf and three Lambs alls one Ox but it proved trippa [76] which You will allow is Not My fault it will hppen [sic] to any Man. I have killed this Day a plenty there will be Beef on three Stalls besides veal and Lamb and the Markets will be suplied Every Day for the future I hope I Do Not flatter Myself if I Say that there is but few Schocket would have gone to kill to Day being as unwell as Myself for Not to Leave them without Meat for [Sabbath]. Sir I hope I am in No ways Deficient in Respects to You as a Gentlemen in or out of Your Office

I remain Yours &c

Daniel Solis
Schocket
K. K. M I

Mr Z Phillips
Parnass

201. NAPHTALI PHILLIPS [77] TO
LEWIS ALLEN, [78] 1836 [79]

[New York, May 10, 1836]

Mr Lewis Allen
Dear Sir

After the last examination of Mr Solis [80] I took upon myself never to be again engaged on a like purpose: the Obligations attached to that Service are of too high a nature, for a person of my age to undertake, at least I think so, in respect to myself, and *Sixty three Years,* admonishes me that I am subject to want those qualifications, & which I may not be sensible of. I therefore am compelled to decline the examination. I refer you to Mr Solis, for what I have done to promote the Object of his Visit here.[81] Praying that you & your family may enjoy health & prosperity. I remain Dear Sir   Your H Servt   N Phillips

N York 10 May 1836

CIII
Synagogal Concern
for Matzoth, 1825

The long excerpt from the minutes of Congregation Shearith Israel printed below illustrates clearly another way in which the synagogue took responsibility for preserving traditional Jewish observances and for guaranteeing that the legal requirements connected with these observances would be properly met. In this instance, what is involved is the arrangements for supplying the Jews of New York with properly prepared *matzoth* for use during Passover. In full detail, these minutes record the contract with the baker, the experience of previous years, and the deficiencies of the product that had been prepared under previous contracts.

The value to the baker of the contract for baking *matzoth* is well-illustrated in a letter of 1834 from a young firm of bakers, Netlad and Hyatt, in Philadelphia, to "the President and Manager of the Hebrew Congregation." In this letter, soliciting the business of the congregation, the new firm pointed out that they had leased the establishment of the baker with whom the congregation (Mikveh Israel) had previously had contracts, that "we have employed all journeymen who have heretofore been accustomed to your mode of baking." [82]

202. BAKING MATZOTH, 1825 [83]

March 1, 1825

The Committee appointed to make arrangements for Bakeing Matsot [84] made the following report

The Committee appointed to procure a suitable place to bake Matsoth for the endsuing Pesach report that they called on Mr Speir [85] the person employed last year for that purpose, who is willing to undertake it again provided he is paid at the rate of

Seven *Cents* per pound, last year he received Six *pence,* but from a statement which accompanies this report, it appears that he received in all the sum of $323 5/100 and that he expended for

34 Barrels flour		229.50
7 Loads Wood	—	14—
For Men	—	68—
		311.50

which left him a gain of $11 $^{55}\!/_{100}$ for his trouble, use of his Bake House and wear and tare of his Oven, and which appears to be too small a recompense and which would at once have induced them to accede to his proposition of Seven Cents per pound had it not been that he has discontinued Bakeing in the Patent Oven, and now has the old fashioned oven the use of which for Bakeing Matsoth would cause the introduction of the former Mode of Shingles Board &c against which so many objections exist. . . .[86]

The Committee finding themselves thus situated made application to Mr Hunter who had for several years with the exception of the last Baked the Matsoth. they fully stated to him what would be required as per Memorandum herewith, he is willing to undertake the business on the condition therein mentioned. . . .

[*March 27, 1825*]

The Committee state in addition to the foregoing communication to the President that they had conferr'd with the Revd Mr Peixotto [87] appointed by the Board on the same subject, that Mr. Peixotto addressed to them the following letter which induced them to settle on the Bake House of Mr Speir with whom they made a written agreement combining all the necessary particulars contained in said letter, that the Committee accepted the services offerd by Mr. Peixotto. . . .

M L Moses   Esqrs   Committee for Baking Matsoth
N Phillips

Gentn

In compliance with your resolution appointing me to examine the patent oven of Mr Hunter and likewise that of Mr Speir and to report to you which I should recommend as most suitable for the baking Matsoth so that the ordinances of our Religion may not be infringed, I have the honor to report

That a variety of considerations should be had in regulating the baking of Matsoth which are not sufficiently attended to and which my duty as your Hazan compels me to enforce upon your special notice these more especially relate to a number of improper circumstances which are allowed to occur in the baking and which it is our duty to see forthwith corrected

The difficulty it appears to me does not exist in a choice of the ovens, either may answer provided a proper regard be paid to certain points which shall presently be mentioned.

Cleanliness must of course be a principal object, then the method of baking should be carefully attended to, that pursued heretofore is altogether improper the making of the dough being too much accelerated, often-times a piece of dough of mostrous [sic] size is laid on the table and there allowed to remain ¾ of an hour before it is worked into cakes, Then the cakes again are left lying another half hour or more before the same are put into the oven so that it is quite impossible the oven should contain as much cake as the workmen are preparing in the meen time with the greatest acceleration. The only method of correcting this evil will be to prevent the dough from being made in such large quantities and so soon in succession as to expose it to lay on the table beyond the proper time. I am credibly informed that in Philadelphia no mass of dough at any one time exceeds 14 lb of flour.

Secondly, The Bake Oven of Mr Hunters which I have today examined according to your wishes, is *unfit*, It must not be used unless the Copper be replaced by one entire piece. The Copper now in use is broken and conceals many particles of Dough which cannot be properly extracted

Lest one of the most solemn precepts be transgressed I beg leave to submit to you my opinion relating to the most effectual method of correcting the evils complained of.

1st The time allowed to bake the Matsoth is not sufficient Mr Hunter or any other person employed in baking consults only the means most likely to conduce to his own Interest and is little solicitous to see our ordinances enforced now I am persuaded that the quantity of Flour mixed at each time is too much and hence the Cakes already made accumulate and are allowed to lay on the table, There should be no more Flour mixed then the oven can contain for the time being without the Dough being left to lay

2nd The Dough ought not to be removed from Breaker but there remain and a person be kept constantly working it, and that the quantity taken thence to be made into cakes at each time be small instead of being removed at once from the Breaker and placed at the working table in such case the Dough might be made in larger quantities, *provided it remain working at the Breaker and not be removed to the table and there left to be*

The person entrusted with this weighty care ought to be empowered to stop the working forthwith, and not to proceed on the least dereliction on the part of the Contractors. I would willingly (should you desire it) devote one or two days in the beginning of the work so as to instruct and regulate the mode of proceeding in order that your desire of doing what is right may have effect and to obviate incurring transgressions of one of our most weighty Commandments being no less than [kareth].

And if to obtain this object greater expenses will be incurred, as longer time will be required to perform the baking, it must nevertheless be attended to notwithstanding the additional expence

Whichsoever of the ovens may be made choice of cleanliness and great attention are required as respects the oven & the Vessels to be used, I may further mention that as Mr Spier has two ovens if he would agree to have both used at the same time much difficulty might be obviated. All which is respectfully submitted by Yr obedt Servt   signed M L M Peixotto

On motion Resolved that the thanks of the Trustees be presented to Mr Peixotto for the services rendered by him to the Congregation at the Bake House.

CIV

On Wearing of the Tallith, 1825

A critical question of religious practice was raised in Shearith Israel by the increasing number of synagogue attendants who failed to conform to custom by wearing a *tallith*.[88] When the question of permitting this deviation was raised in the meeting of the Trustees of the congregation, it was acknowledged that the constitution and bylaws of the congregation made no mention of the wearing of a *tallith*, and that there was no discoverable religious imperative that prescribed its wearing. It was pointed out, however, that the *tallith* was a custom sanctioned by age-old tradition and that its use ought to be continued. As a faint herald of reformed thinking, it should be noted that one of the members of the Board, Joseph L. Joseph,[89] voted in the negative with respect both to the acceptance of the committee report on the subject and to the proposed resolution to require the wearing of the *tallith* as a condition of being called to the reading of the Law.

203. SHEARITH ISRAEL ACTS, 1825 [90]

The following report was presented by David Hart [91] and Moses L Moses [92]

The Committee appointed by a resolution of the Board of Trustees to report on the subject of persons not wearing the Talez in Synagogue have had the same under their deliberate consideration, & after a careful examination of our Constitution & bye laws, they cannot find any law relating to this particular subject, nor can they ascertain that the wearing the *Talez* is a law of imperative religious obligation, but inasmuch as it has allways been strictly observed in this Congregation from its first establishment, the Committee cannot but view a departure from it, as an innovation, which if permitted to pass unnoticed may lead to other deviations, and Ultimately to the subversion of all the venerable & established usages of this Congregation, In order therefore & as far as lies in the power of the Trustees to remedy such evils, the Committee submit the expediency of a Law to the following effect that no person either a Member of this Congregation or otherwise who in our holy place of Worship wilfully neglects to wear a *Talez* at the times & periods it is the Custom so to do shall not be entitled to any Mitsvot whatsoever

All of which is respectfully submitted

Signed   M. L. Moses   Committee
David Hart

October 26, 1825

On Motion the Report was accepted with the exception of Mr Joseph L. Joseph who voted in the Negative, and in conformity with the aforerecited Report the following Resolution was adopted (with the exception of Mr. Joseph L. Joseph who voted in the Negative) That the acting Parnass be directed not to call to reading of the Sepher or give any Mitsvot in Synagogue to any person wilfully neglecting to wear a Talez at the times and periods it is the custom so to do.

CV

Defiance of

Synagogue Discipline, 1825

At a different time and under other circumstances, the refusal of Barrow (i.e., Baruch) E. Cohen [93] to make the standard offering for charity on being called to the reading of the Law might have seemed like a pointless and, indeed, somewhat childish defiance of authority.[94] But the year in which the incident occurred was 1825, a year when, as we have already seen,[95] the seat of authority in the Jewish synagogues in America was shaking. Moreover, in Shearith Israel, it was a year in which any incident might serve to crystallize the mounting struggle between the older families who dominated the life of the synagogue and a growing number of newer arrivals, of whom Cohen was one. There is no doubt that Barrow Cohen's defiance of authority was used as a test case by both parties. The victory of the synagogue authorities was one of a number of specific incidents that led to the first secession from Shearith Israel and the starting of New York's first Ashkenazic synagogue, B'nai Jeshurun.[96]

204. THE BARROW COHEN CASE, 1825 [97]

[*April 13, 1825*]

It having been manifested to the Board that Mr B. E Cohen did on the eighth day of Pesach when called to the Sepher, committe an offence against a law of this Congregation which makes it obligatory for every person called to the Sepher to offer at least two Shillings to the Sedaka fund which Mr Cohen did not do

On motion of Mr Moses [98] seconded by Mr Phillips [99] Resolved that Mr Cohen be called before the Board to answer for such conduct. Carried Unanimously with the exception of Mr Hayem M Solomons [100] who voted in the Negative

Ordered that Mr B. E Cohen be Notified to appear before this Board on Tuesday evening next at 7 O Clock & that a Copy of the above preamble and Resolution be sent to him. . . .

Motion Resolved that Mr Phillips & Moses be appointed a Committee to draw up the necessary interrogatories & or order of proceeding. . . .

April 17, 1825

There not being a sufficient number to form a quorum, the meeting was adjourned to assemble on Wednesday evening (next (the 27 Instant) at 6 O Clock Mr B E Cohen having attended agreeable to notice. . . .

April 27, 1825

The Committee appointed in the case of Mr B. E Cohen have agreed to the report herewith and recommend the following as Rules to be observed in the investigation

1st A Chairman to be appointed by ballot, and when he has taken his seat, Mr Cohen to be called in The Chairman shall read the report to Mr Cohen The Clerk shall write down his reply If any Member of the board is desirous of asking a question of Mr Cohen, he shall commit the same to writing and hand it to the Chairman

If the Chairman should be of opinion that the Question is improper Mr Cohen shall be requested to withdraw and the board shall decide whether the said Question shall be put or not, and Mr Cohen shall be called back

2nd No Member of the board shall make any observations in relation to the subject matter before the Trustees when Mr Cohen is present, A Violation of this rule to subject the Member to a fine of Ten Dollars Mr Cohen may call in any Congregator to give evidence in his behalf

Signed   N. Phillips
             Moses L. Moses   Committee

We also present the following letter to be read to Mr B. E Cohen

Mr Baruch I. Cohen

Sir

The President of the board of Trustees of Congregation Shearith Israel and parnass of the said Congregation has laid before them a statement of your conduct in the Synagogue on the eighth day of Pesach, from which it appears, that you was called to Sepher on that day; that you declined making any offering, notwithstanding you was informed by the Hazan that it was obligatory on you to make at least an offering for the Congregation, that you drew from your pocket a Book or paper with an apparent view of shewing the reason or cause for the course you was about to persue and that finally you withdrew without making an offering for the Congregation

This being contrary to the resolve of the Trustees of the 6th day of September 1820 and which was published in Synagogue on the two days of Roshashana thereafter constituted the offence for which the Trustees have deemed it proper to require your attendance here

With a view of affording to you every proper means to explain to the Board the reasons or causes that induced you to act in the manner now stated to you, the Trustees are ready and willing to hear and consider any thing you may have to alledge in defence of the conduct displayed by you when called to the reading of the Seaphar on the eighth day of Pesach. . . .

Mr B. E Cohen admitted and the Chairman Mr Naphtali Phillips elected on the above motion read to him the foregoing Document, on being questioned in relation thereto he admits he was called to the Seaphar [sic] as said in the charge and retired without making an offering for the Congregation, and in his defence alledged that he acted according to the Constitution of this Congregation, and as he has seen others do, If the Trustees proceed against him contrary to the Constitution that he will apply elsewhere for redress. . . .

Then the following Questions were put to Mr Cohen by the Chairman

Have you not allways made an offering for the Congregation
and Parnass

Answerd Yes, except in the present instance

? Did you not know that it has allways been customary to offer
for the Parnass & Congregation and that you concientously believed it was your bounden duty so to do till the day alluded to

Answer he knows nothing about it. I have done what others have
done. . . .[101]

How came you to have the Book of Laws in your Pocket on the
8th day of Pesach

Answer he declines Answering at present

Was you the owner of that Book on the first day of Pesach

Answer he declines Answering

What was your inducement for not offering on that day at the
Seaphar

Answer that as a Congregator his rights were taken from him.
but did not know that it was intended as an insult and as such did
not feel himself bound to support the Congregation as he had done
that he afterwards made an offering before the Hechal in consequence of the proclamation of the Parnass, not wishing to insult
the Congregation

did you tell any person that you would never Duchen at the
Haechal, If so how could your rights be taken from you

Answer. I did tell a person so

Whether he recollects that he signed the Book of the Constitution
& bye laws

Answer yes he did. . . .

May 8, 1825

The President stated that Mr. Joseph Samuel [102] had informed
him that he had for many years been acquainted with Mr B. E
Cohen in England & that during that period he had not known the
said as a Cohen who has been officiating as such in our place of
worship

Therefore Resolved that Mr Joseph Samuel be requested to
attend at the Board at the present meeting

Mr Samuel appeared and Stated that he lived in Gosport
England and was acquainted with Simcho Abrams the Father of

B. E Cohen (about one) for 14 years and was also acquainted with B. E Cohen about one or two weeks before he left England— never knew him as a Cohen, but does not know that he is not— Mr Samuel then retired. . . .

A letter of this date was recd from Mr Hayam M Solomons resigning his Seat as a Trustee of this Congregation, which resignation was accepted & on motion resolved that notice thereof be given to the Hazan

Mr John I Hart [103] attended agreeable to the request of the President who stated that he had known Mr B E Cohen for many years they having been School Mates and knows that he is a Cohen having seen him and his Father officiate in that Character often— therefore it is considered the further interference of the Board unnecessary.

The Board proceeded to the Consideration of the case of Mr B. E Cohen as stated on the Minutes of the last Meeting & having fully considered the same are of opinion that the Defence of Mr Cohen does not form a full excuse for the Conduct alleged against him, but the Trustees are inclined to the opinion that Mr Cohen acted from a mistaken view of the Law and not from any desire to insult the Congregation as stated by himself and which was proven by his going before the Hechel and making several offerings including one for the Congregation

Therefore Resolved that the Clerk transmit to Mr Cohen a Copy of this Minute with this declaration, that the Trustees expect Mr Cohen will hereafter conduct himself when attending Divine Worship in such a manner as to comport with the Character of a good Member of the Congregation.

CVI

Division in the
New York Community, 1825

In the minutes of Shearith Israel for May 31, 1825, the following
passage appears: "The letter . . . requesting the use of our place
of Worship and Sepharim [scrolls of the Law] at times different
from the usual hours of Service, the Management of the same to be
intirely under the control of a Committee to be chosen by themselves being under consideration and the Trustees having given the
same the most serious attention, adopted the following Resolution

"Resolved Unanimously that the application contained in the said
letter cannot be granted and that a Copy hereof be sent to the
said Applicants." [104]

The story behind this brief entry is that the dissatisfied elements
in Shearith Israel made an attempt to retain the unity of the Jews
of New York by proposing to hold their own separate services in
the synagogue building. Once this request was denied, secession
was the only road that lay open. A religious society under the
name of *Chevra Chinuch Nearim* was organized and became the
parent organization out of which Congregation B'nai Jeshurun
developed. In the original constitution and bylaws of the *Chevra
Chinuch Nearim*, Sephardic practice was prescribed.[105] The constitutional provision that most clearly reflects the religious probings
after innovation characteristic of the decade of the 1820s is the
eighth article, which calls for the establishment of a regular preaching ministry. Apparently this society was unable to establish the
regular preaching that it sought, but the significant point here
is that the demand should have been so clearly voiced. The provision for frequent rotation of officers [106] indicates both the more
democratic mood that prevailed at this time [107] and the fact that
the newer arrivals and younger men who formed this society were

not in a position to devote as much time to volunteer service as were the better-established older families who dominated Shearith Israel.

205. THE OPENING GUN, 1825 [108]

[*May 1825*]

To the Trustees and Parnass of the Congregation Shearith Israel.
Gentlemen,

The undersigned in behalf of themselves and a number of their brethren, actuated with religious motives, respectfully request the use of our place of worship and the Sephorim, on the Sabbath mornings during the summer months, in such a way as will no wise interfere with the time now devoted, to the residue of the Congregation.

As it is merely our desire to say the prayers at an early hour on the mornings of Sabbath as well as on other mornings of the week before breakfast observing the same minhog that has always been observed in the congregation,[109] and as the custom which we intend to follow is now and has been practised in Europe and other parts of the globe,[110] among Yehudim; therefore it is earnestly requested, the Trustees will promote our undertaking.

In the performance of our early prayers, it is not expected by us that any trouble should be given to the officers of the congregation; as a relief to them, the management of the service, will be entirely under the controul of a committee, to be chosen from among and by those attending the early worship—and for the furtherance of this reasonable favour, which we feel every assurance will be granted without hesitation; it is determined by us, that all offerings shall be under the same rules, and for the like purpose, as they are now; and it shall be the explicit duty of the same committee, to charge and keep a regular account, of all such amounts of offerings, that they may be given to the clerk of the congregation, and be added to the usual bills.

As the favour is one to which there can be no grounds for refusal: as we have no doubt the trustees will cheerfully concur in the promoting of our zeal and attention to the worship of our holy religion, we shall consider that we are allowed to put in practise our design the ensuing Sabbath (4 June) unless notified to the contrary.

We are gentlemen,   Yours &c

Signed by the Committee appointed in behalf of a number of the Congregation.

206. CONSTITUTION OF
CHEVRA CHINUCH NEARIM, 1825 [111]

Preamble

Whereas, many Yehudim residing in this city and belonging to the Congregation of [Shearith Israel] have, in respectful terms applied for the use of the [Beth ha-Keneseth] [112] for the sole purpose of early morning prayers, as received by divine command, and according to the undeviating usage of all our brethren of other parts of the world, which service, they declared should not interfere with the saying of the prayers by any other part of the congregation, and have been refused that right: and,

Whereas, many members and others belonging to our Nation, having an ardent desire to promote the study of our Holy Law, and the better to extend a knowledge of its divine precepts, ceremonies, and worship among our brethren generally, and the enquiring youth in particular and anxious to carry their intentions into effect, have subscribed their names hereunto, and associated together in order that a society shall be known and distinguished by the name of [Chinuch Nearim] and in order to make manifest their intentions more effectually, have bound themselves to conform to the following as primary articles of their *Constitution,* and each member has accordingly subscribed his name . . .

Constitution. . . .

Article 3d. There shall be a committee consisting of five members who shall serve for three months to manage the affairs of the society, spiritual as well as temporal, whose duties and power shall be expressed in the By-laws, and at the end of which time said committee shall account to a general meeting, for all matters which they may have acted on during the time of their service, and all monies appropriated, shall be at the disposal of the society, after which an election by ballot shall take place for a new committee to serve for a like period, and no person shall be re-elected three terms in succession. . . .

Article 5th. The service shall be performed in [minhag Sephardim].[113]

Article 6th. No person can be a member of this society, unless he strictly adheres to our religion as regards the observance of our holy Sabbath and Holidays; and it is a further requisite that he possesses a good moral character. . . .

Article 8th. It shall be a further duty of the governing committee if possible, to procure a suitable person or persons, who in Hebrew and English shall explain and descant on the service, prayers, ceremonies and customs, as used among our nation, at least once a week. . . .

Article 11th. All meetings of the officers of the society shall be open to every member to see and hear the proceedings, but none except the members of the committee shall have a voice at such meetings. . . .

Bye-Laws. . . .

Article 2d. Section 6th. The committee shall provide a suitable person or persons, to officiate as reader, who, for the time being, while engaged in the religious duties of the society, will not be distinguished in his habit from any other member, except at the proper times by wearing the [tallith],[114] at any other period, out of the meetings of the society he is not to assume, or perform any function or service, other than that of any other private individual of the society. . . .

Article 4th. Section 1st. Any member of our religion, competent by the 2nd. and 6th. articles of our constitution, wishing to become a member of this society, shall signify his intention in a letter to the chairman, who shall at the next meeting lay it before the society and, if the applicant receive a majority of the votes present, he shall be considered as having been admitted. This rule is not intended to exclude any brother Yehudah from attending at the hours of worship for the purpose of joining therein, provided he conduct himself with propriety: but none other than a member shall be admitted to hear the afternoon discourse in english unless introduced by a member.

207. LETTER TO SHEARITH ISRAEL, 1825 [115]

New-York June 30th. 5585 [1825]

To the Parnass and the Trustees of the Congregation of Shearith Israel.

Gentlemen,

A Society having been formed for the purpose of instruction and explanation in the ceremonies of our ancient laws and religion and for the performance of early prayer by the name of [Chinuch Nearim]

We the undersigned in behalf of the members of the said society, being a committee appointed to regulate the affairs of the same, have taken the liberty of addressing you, believing no doubt, with ourselves, you are equally interested, in the promoting of an object, which strikes us, not only as highly laudable, but of great moment, to the Hebrew Community at large: as tending to encrease the respect of the worship of our fathers.

We therefore respectfully request that you will loan to the society, one of the [sefarim] [116] now in use and belonging to the congregation.

We farther solicit for the same object, as many benches belonging to the old shool as you can conveniently spare: also the old [tebah] [117] and [heichal], [118] and what other articles you may suppose will assist our intentions.

The effects enumerated we are led to understand remain in your hands of no use at present, and as they will be of great service to the society in its early stage. for their safe return, in at least, as good condition as they are at the time we receive them, the members of the society collectively, and individually, bind themselves.

We farther deem it proper to state, that the object of the society is purely religious; and to do away all ill and unfavorable impressions that may have been made on your minds against our association: as our constitution and bye-laws have not yet been printed we think it necessary to detail briefly, the governing principles on which we have formed ourselves.

First. Early attendance to our prayers, the room in which the same is to be performed, to be freely at the service of any other part of the congregation after the service of the society. and during the service of the society, the doors to be open to our brethren.

Second. Conveying religious instruction to our youths.

Third. Our city having become very large and yearly increasing in size, and our brethren scattered in every direction it is therefore one of our first duties to multiply facilities in order to afford all an opportunity of paying that adoration to our benificent [sic] creator, which is the duty of life to return him for his manifold mercies, that are every hour extended to us. Now, gentlemen with these ideas before you, we confidently believe you will grant the seeking of the society, and by so doing we believe you will be performing that which is the part of every follower of the House of Israel: the lending a mite towards the erection of a dwelling of the Living God! whose temples should be spread in every corner, and multiplied by his people.

N.B. It has been omitted to mention that the society intend in no way to create distinctions, but each member is to fulfil the duties in rotation, having no Parnass nor Chazan.

CVII

The Younger Haym Salomon
on Religious Laxity, 1825

On June 23, 1825, Haym M. Salomon, son of the great Revolutionary figure, Haym Salomon, wrote to the Parnass and Trustees of Congregation Mikveh Israel the following letter: "Having understood that the Sepher Torah which my Father (olav hashalom) [119] had imported at considerable expence, and which was lodged in the philadelphia Shule as our property, had in Consequence of being unopened for the long time while the Shule was rebuilding so dimned the Ink of its writing that in many places it has become quite obscure

"Wishing to have it perfectly repaired, I have found a very competent friend who has undertaken to have it remedied compleatly here and prevent its becoming Pausul.[120] Please therefore hand it carefully over to my Nephew Joseph J Andrews.[121] who will forward it to me without delay for that object." [122]

More than three months later, on October 2, 1825, Zalegman Phillips, Parnass of Mikveh Israel, was directed by his Board to write Salomon informing him that the scroll was regarded as the property of the synagogue and that it needed no restoration.[123] It was November 30 before Salomon had the chance to write the following letter, reasserting that title to the scroll remained in his family, and commenting on the high degree of religious laxity in both Philadelphia and New York. Salomon was one of the few prominent leaders of Shearith Israel to identify himself with the *Chevra Chinuch Nearim*.[124] He was, apparently, a stern traditionalist. Furthermore his comments in this letter make it seem likely that he wanted the scroll not only for restoration but also for reading at the services of the secessionist *Chevra*.[125]

208. HAYM M. SALOMON TO
ZALEGMAN PHILLIPS, 1825 [126]

New York Nov 30 1825

Mr. Z. Phillips Esq
Dear Sir

I have been waiting several days for a private opportunity to reply to your answer pr mail of the 13th inst.

It is much to be reggretted [sic] that the board of managers should have formed conclusions upon such untenable premises. many circumstances exits [sic] which renders it quite improbable they could be in possession of the requisite information to form there determination on with true judgment & justice. & which in shewing my unquestionable claim to the sepher in behalf of our estate will evince the moderation & reasonableness of my request

Allow me my dear Sir to acknowledge the kind mention you made of the known exertions my father made during his residence in your city to promote the due observance of our religion. But you must remember also that the same kind of Escaba [127] is made for the other gentlemen who were assistant founders of the shule in common with him & that for the large sum he advanced towards erecting the first shule in Philad They made him the usual & appropriate mishaberach [128] on Kipur day [129] annually previous to his death and even without his having given a sepher to the shule

I need not remind you how indifferent after his death his survivors were in keeping up a regular attendance on the shule
It is well known that for years scarcely minyon at the proper times of service & many respectable persons where not seen in shule more than once in a year

It were well perhaps for our posterity that the present generation should show that defference [sic] for the memory of munificent & departed individuals as you have expressed in your last esteemed letter but I fear we are as is the trite saying "fallen on evil times."

The Lord, I fear is taking his countenance from off us in america I mean as it regards the govt of the old shules both in New York & Philad so disgusted have numerous true followers of our faith become with the management both temporal & spiritual here that on the sabbath eve not more than three heads of families are sometimes found to join in prayer with the reader of the old shule on friday night

It has been stated to me that it is only since the breaking down of the former building with you that the people have renewed their attention to our divine worship in Philad

What extraordinary folly! Would you credit it sir, that in the oldest settled places where there are shules the most ancient & decayed those shules are treated with the most religious reverence & attention In conclusion dear sir, I beg you to use your endeavours to convince the board of managers that I would not apply for the sepher in question, If, Firstly, I was not justly equitably entitled to it &

2ndly which is most of consequence I want it principally to read in before a praying assembly of yehudim [130]

3dly I will be willing to give a bond of indemnity to the trustees (if they will send it without a prosecution that no one can lawfully claim it except *through me*)

If you can offer me any thing in reply encouraging to my expectation you will confer an obligation on me as well as others

Whishing you health & happiness   I remain yours &c &c

Haym M Salomon [131]

For the State of the govt of the Jews here See the National advocate of Monday 5 Decr.[132]

CVIII

Synagogue Authority in Charleston, 1820

Of all the revolts against established synagogal authority that occurred in the 1820s, by far the best known was that in Charleston. Here the secession took place for reasons of reform of ritual as well as for reasons of dissatisfaction with prevailing authority. It must be remembered, too, that at this time Charleston still contained the largest Jewish population of any American city, and was at its peak as a center of trade, commerce, and literature.

We can only speculate as to the degree to which dissentient ideas were already prevalent in Charleston before 1820. If there were such ideas, the constitution adopted by Congregation Beth Elohim in 1820 could only add fuel to the fire of dissatisfaction. Although only excerpts from the constitution are available, they clearly reflect the stultifying atmosphere of religious authoritarianism in the life of this congregation. Beth Elohim was jealous of its exclusive position; its constitution denies the right of any other synagogue to exist "within five miles of Charleston." Although Charlestonian Jews were apparently formally observant, a clause like this suggests that there had already been talk of establishing another congregation, and that it was this threat that the constitution of 1820 was designed to forestall.

209. BETH ELOHIM'S CONSTITUTION, 1820 [133]

The Parnass Presidenta shall have the sole direction in the Synagogue, during divine service, and all officers under pay shall be under his control. . . .

He shall be authorized to call before the Private Adjunta any person or persons, who may misbehave either in Synagogue, its enclosures during divine service, or other legal occasions of meeting, and moreover shall make it his indispensable duty to support, protect, and defend this Constitution, and call any one to account who shall violate the same. *Rule VI.*

And if any new and unforeseen case shall arise and come before them, for which this Constitution does not expressly provide, they shall be empowered to investigate the same, according to their best judgment, and discretion, and if necessary for the good example and advantage of this Congregation, the said Private Adjunta shall place the offenders under disabilities, and inflict a fine not exceeding one hundred dollars; and all persons whatsoever coming under the penalty of the Laws, shall absolutely be deprived of their honors, rights and privileges, in and out of Synagogue, until he, she, or they comply with the fine, disabilities, or otherwise be reconciled to the Congregation. *Rule VII.*

No person or persons shall be sanctioned to combine for the purpose of erecting any other Synagogue or for uniting in any other unlawful Minyan, within five miles of Charleston; nor shall any person or persons, under the jurisdiction of this Congregation, be permitted, under any pretence whatever, to aid, join, or assist at any such unlawful Minyan or Combination.

All strangers arriving here, who do not, after the lapse of time affixed by the Constitution, become members of the Congregation, shall be liable to all the penalties and restrictions that members are subject to, and shall not be admitted members, until such restrictions are removed. And if any person under the jurisdiction of this Congregation, be guilty of such an atrocious offence, as either to be concerned, aid, or assist as aforesaid, he shall on sufficient proof thereof before the Private Adjunta, forfeit all his rights and privileges in this Congregation, and be subject to a fine not exceeding two hundred dollars; and such offender or offenders, shall never be reinstated into his or their rights and privileges, and moreover be deprived the right of burial inside of the Beth Hiam,[134] until he or they by themselves, executors, or administrators, relations, or friends, pay up and settle the fine that they may be inflicted. And any person or persons placing themselves into such a predicament, shall incur the penalty, inasmuch as the same, either in joy or in sorrow, shall extend to the whole family under his or their control and jurisdiction. *Rule VIII.*

All Israelites now in Charleston, who are not Yachidim,[135] and such as may arrive hereafter, after one year's residence shall be bound to subscribe to the subscription list, and provide themselves and wives (if any) with seats as aforesaid. . . . This law embraces all persons indiscriminately above twenty-one years of age, under an obligation, as before stated, to give their support towards this Congregation. *Rule XII.*

No person being called to the Sepher, having Portos-Hechel, or going up there to offer, shall leave the same, without offering at least one shilling for the Parnass Presidenta, and prosperity of the Congregation, nor shall any ridiculous or unusual offering be permitted.

Any person offending in either of these cases, shall be called before the Private Adjunta, and at their discretion fined, or dealt with according to the nature and aggravation of the offence, and shall continue under all disabilities in and out of Synagogue, until such decision is complied with. *Rule XIII.*

This Congregation will not encourage or interfere with making proselytes under any pretence whatever, nor shall any such be admitted under the jurisdiction of this Congregation, until he, she, or they produce legal and satisfactory credentials, from some other Congregation, where a regular Chief, or Rabbi and Hebrew Consistory is established; and, provided, he, she, or they are not people of color. *Rule XXIII.*

Any person or persons being married contrary to the Mosaical Law, or renouncing his or their religion, shall themselves and their issue, never be recognized members of this Congregation; and should such person or persons die, they shall not be buried within the walls of the Beth-Hiam, unless he, she, or they shall have reformed, at least one year previous to his or their death, and undergone such penance as is prescribed by the laws of our Holy religion.

Nor shall any person, desirous of consummating a marriage with any female who has lived as a prostitute, or kept a disorderly house, be permitted such marriage under the sanction of this Congregation, but should such person or persons so marry without its jurisdiction, and after having lived some years a moral and decent life, he or they shall be entitled to the same right of becoming Yachidim as all strangers arriving in this city. *Rule XXIV.*

Any person or persons publicly violating the Sabbath, or other sacred days, shall be deprived of every privilege of Synagogue and the services of its offices. He or they shall also be subject to such fine and penalties as the Parnassim and Adjunta may deem fit, nor shall he or they be readmitted to the privileges aforesaid, until he or they shall have paid the fine and suffered the punishment to be inflicted under this law. *Rule XXV*.[136]

CIX

The Attempt to Reform
from Within, 1824

In 1824, reform Judaism asserted itself in Charleston. The discontented memorialists who presented the statement reprinted below to the parent congregation Beth Elohim were largely of established Jewish families of Charleston.[137] They were in revolt against the persistence of meaningless traditional forms of worship, against what seemed to them the ossification of their religion that followed from many of its practices and forms having become unintelligible to the worshippers.[138] Their own statement makes it clear that these Jews were aware of the reform movement that had arisen among German Jewry,[139] and yet it is equally clear that this was no mere imitation of a movement born elsewhere. The demands for change made by the reformers were all on the level of religious practice, not of theological dogma. They insisted upon the need for a shorter service, with improvements in decorum. For intelligibility, they asked that an English translation accompany the Hebrew recitation of certain basic prayers. They called for the adoption of an English sermon as a means of religious education. They urged the elimination of unintelligible benedictions and flourishes in Spanish. Finally, they suggested that the unseemly practice of making offerings at certain times during the service should be abolished.

When Beth Elohim declined to consider these proposals, the dissidents established the first American reformed synagogue, the Reformed Society of Israelites.

210. PETITION TO THE
CHARLESTON CONGREGATION, 1824 [140]

To the President and Members of the Adjunta of Kaal Kadosh Beth
  Elohim of Charleston, South Carolina
Gentlemen,

The memorial of the undersigned, showeth unto your honourable
body, that they have witnessed with deep regret, the apathy and
neglect which have been manifested towards our holy religion. As
inheritors of the *true faith,* and always proud to be considered by
the world as a portion of "God's chosen people," they have been
pained to perceive the gradual decay of that system of worship,
which, for ages past, *peculiarly* distinguished us from among the
nations of the earth. Not unmindful, however, of the various causes
which regulate human conduct; and at the same time, unwilling to
shield themselves from any censure to which their actions may
justly entitle them, they have ingenuously investigated the reasons
which may have led them from the Synagogue, and are now seriously impressed with the belief, that certain defects which are
apparent in the present system of worship, are the sole causes of
the evils complained of.

In pointing out these defects, however, your memorialists seek
no other end, than the future welfare and respectability of the
nation. As members of the great family of Israel, they cannot consent to place before their children examples which are only calculated to darken the mind, and withhold from the rising generation
the more rational means of worshipping the true God.

It is to this, therefore, your memorialists would, in the first place,
invite the serious attention of your honourable body. By causing
the Hasan, or reader, to repeat in English such part of the Hebrew
prayers as may be deemed necessary, it is confidently believed that
the congregation generally would be more forcibly impressed with
the necessity of Divine Worship, and the moral obligations which
they owe to themselves and their Creator; While such a course,
would lead to more decency and decorum during the time they are
engaged in the performance of religious duties. It is not every one
who has the means, and many have not the time, to acquire a

knowledge of the Hebrew language, and consequently to become enlightened in the principles of Judaism; What then is the course pursued in all religious societies for the purpose of disseminating the peculiar tenets of their faith among the poor and uninformed? The principles of their religion are expounded to them from the pulpit in the language that they understand; for instance, in the Catholic, the German and the French Protestant Churches: by this means the ignorant part of mankind attend their places of worship with some profit to their morals, and even improvement to their minds; they return from them with hearts turned to piety, and with feelings elevated by their sacred character. In this consists the beauty of religion, when men are invoked by its divine spirit, to the practice of virtue and morality.

These results, it is respectfully submitted, would be sufficient of themselves to induce the alterations requested. But your memorialists cannot fail to impress upon the minds of your honourable body, the singular advantages this practice would produce upon the habits and attention of the younger branches of the congregation; besides the necessity of good behaviour, which the solemnity of the service should impose, they would become gradually better acquainted with the nature of our creed, the principal features which distinguish the Jew from every other religious denomination, and the meaning, and the reason, of our various forms and ceremonies. Believing, at the same time, that the above views of what is indispensable to the preservation of our faith, will meet with the approbation of every reflecting and liberal mind. They repeat, that they are actuated by no other motive, than to see our Synagogue in a better, a more wholesome, and a more respectable state of discipline; to see it elicit that regard from Jew and Gentile, which its great character deserves, and should always command; and finally, not to destroy long standing institutions, but to accommodate them to the progress of time, and change of situation and circumstances.

With regard to such parts of the service as it is desired should undergo this change, your memorialists would strenuously recommend that the most solemn portions be retained, and everything superfluous excluded; and that the principal parts, and if possible all that is read in *Hebrew*, should also be read in *English*, (that being the language of the country,) so as to enable every member of the congregation fully to understand each part of the service. In submitting this article of our memorial to the consideration of your honourable body, your memorialists are well aware of the difficulties with which they must contend, before they will be enabled to accomplish this desirable end; but while they would respectfully invite the attention of your honourable body to this part of their memorial, they desire to rest the propriety and expediency of such a measure, solely upon the *reason* by which it may be maintained. Your memorialists would further submit to your honourable body whether, in the history of the civilized world, there can be found a single parallel of a people, adressing the *Creator* in a language not understood *by that people?* It is indeed surprising, that heretofore no innovation has even been attempted, although it is readily admitted your honourable body may boast of many very enlightened, liberal and intelligent members.

Your memorialists would next call the particular attention of your honourable body to the absolute necessity of abridging the service generally. They have reflected seriously upon its present length, and are confident that this is one of the principal causes why so much of it is hastily and improperly hurried over. This must be evident to every reflecting mind, when it is seen, that notwithstanding the evil complained of, the service of the Sabbath, for instance, continues until *twelve* o'clock, although usually commencing at *nine.* It is therefore manifest, that, according to the prayer of your memorialists, should the service be in future conducted with due solemnity, and in a slow, distinct, and impressive tone, its length would certainly occupy the attention of the congregation until two o'clock, if not later.

The *Offerings* will next command the attention of your honourable body; and upon this part of our memorial, we would respectfully crave the favour of a patient hearing, while we clearly set forth the entire uselessness and impropriety of this custom. In the first place, your memorialists earnestly protest against the unwise and absurd practice of rendering in the Spanish language, any offerings which may be intended to benefit the Synagogue, or which may be otherwise identified with our holy religion. Besides the free scope which the practice of offering in a language understood by few, affords to mischievous and designing men to pollute the holy altars by gratifying their evil intentions. We certainly think it highly inconsistent to select for this very purpose, the language of a people from whom we have suffered, and continue to suffer, so much persecution. But forgetting for a moment this consideration, your memorialists would further suggest to your honourable body, whether the arrangement recently made in the financial transactions of the congregation, would not altogether supercede the necessity of any offerings whatever? This is most seriously and strenuously desired by your memorialists, because they are prepared to show, by an act of your own body, that the practice of offering is not the result of any imperious necessity, but merely intended as an idle and absurd indulgence. By the 11th Article of the Constitution of your honourable body, it is provided, that such offerings as are made by any member of the congregation, shall, at the end of the year, be *deducted out of the amount of his annual subscription, as well as that of his wife, if he be a married man.* According to this part of the Constitution, a revenue is *created independent of the offerings which are subsequently made and deducted out of the amount of subscription at the end of the year.* Your memorialists would, therefore, inquire, wherein exists the necessity, under this arrangement, of any offerings whatever? How, and in what manner, the support of the congregation *depends* upon them? and, in a word, whether the above article is not a tacit admission by your Constitution, that so much of the offerings as may amount to the annual subscription of a member, was never intended as a means of supporting the congregation, inasmuch, as the whole amount is *already* anticipated long before a single offering is made! In fact, many persons, when their amount of assessment is exhausted in offerings, are induced to go out and remain in the Synagogue yard, to prevent being compelled to offer against their will, a practice irregular, indecorous, and highly to be censured, because it sets an ill example to our children, and draws upon us the eyes of strangers.

Your memorialists are aware, it may be said, that some few subscribers offer *more* than the amount of their annual subscription. But to this it may be answered, that it is certainly not difficult for the general body, in their wisdom and discretion, to devise some means equally profitable to the congregation, and at the same time, as well calculated to meet the views of the *liberal,* without resorting to a practice, which only interrupts the worship of God, and is productive of so little good. Your memorialists therefore respectfully suggest, that the addition in numbers to your body, which it is expected will shortly take place, will greatly aid in the funds, and serve as an additional reason why the offerings should be abolished; but as a further inducement for their entire abolishment, your memorialists would respectfully recommend, the propriety and expediency of addressing to the understanding of the people, and more particularly the younger branches of the congregation, appropriate discourses, *in the place and at the very time the offerings are usually made.*

According to the present mode of reading the Parasa,[141] it affords to the hearer neither instruction nor entertainment, unless he be competent to read as well as comprehend the Hebrew language. But if, like all other ministers, our reader would make a chapter or verse the subject of an English discourse once a week, at the expiration of the year the people would, at all events, know something of that religion which at present they so little regard.

It is also worthy of observation that a number of Israelites, whom it should be the special care of your honourable body to bring back under your immediate protection and influence, are now wandering gradually from the true God, and daily losing those strong ties which bind every pious man to the faith of his fathers! In these individuals, your honourable body have fair subjects for the holy work of reformation; by moulding our present form of worship to suit their comprehensions, you will instantly receive them among you; they will collect under your especial care and guardianship; they will aid in the pecuniary resources of your holy institution; and if, from among the whole number now scattered about our city and state, either through irreligion, through disabilities imposed, or any other cause, you are enabled to make but one convert, it will add much to those laudable ends which it should be the principal desire of your honourable body to accomplish. It should also be remembered that while other sects are extending the means of Divine Worship to the remotest quarters of the habitable globe, while they are making the most zealous efforts to bring together the scattered of their flock, offering the most flattering inducements to *all denominations,* we, who may be termed the mere remnant of a great nation, are totally disregarding the fairest opportunities of increasing our own numbers, and at the same time neglecting the brightest prospects of enlarging our resources, and effectually perpetuating our national character.

Your memorialists trust, that they have been perfectly understood by the foregoing observations, that they entirely disclaim any idea of wishing to abolish such ceremonies as are considered land-marks to distinguish the *Jew* from the *Gentile;* they are wholly influenced by a warm zeal to preserve and perpetuate the principles of Judaism in their utmost purity and vigour, and to see the present and the future generations of Israelites enlightened on the subject of their holy religion, so as by understanding, they may learn the nature of its Divine source, and appreciate its holy precepts; that they would not wish to shake the firmness of any man's faith, or take from his devotion towards it; that they will always fervently and zealously support it as the first and most ancient of religions.

The alterations above submitted, being all your memorialists can in reason and moderation require, they would beg leave, in concluding, to bring to the notice of your honourable body, the reformation which has been recently adopted by our brethren in Holland, Germany and Prussia. The following is an extract from a German paper entitled the *"Frankfort Journal."*

"The functions relative to Divine Service, such as the rite of taking the Law out of the Ark, the promulgation of the Law, etc., shall no longer be sold by auction in the Synagogue. The Rabbis, and the Elders of the Synagogue, (the first in their discourses) must endeavor to put an end to the custom of *see-sawing* during the prayers, and to that of repeating the prayers in too loud a voice; all profane tunes during Divine Service are prohibited. The ceremony of striking the *impious Haman* at the festival of Purim, is most strictly prohibited. Children below the age of five years are not to be taken to the Synagogue. All unsuitable pleasantries, in which the young people sometimes indulge in the Synagogues on the eve of some festivals, or on the festivals themselves, as well as the distribution of sweetmeats by the women to each in the Synagogues, are strictly forbidden. Some of the religious ceremonies must be accompanied by a German discourse [that being the vernacular] on a Hebrew text, in which the meaning of these solemnities shall be *explained, and on the Sabbath a discourse shall be held in German* in every Synagogue after the reading of the prescribed passage of the Law, and a chapter of the Prophets."

Thus, from the above extract, it appears, that no climes, nor even tyranny itself, can forever fetter or control the human mind; and that even amidst the intolerance of Europe, our brethren have anticipated the free citizens of America in the glorious work of reformation; Let us then hasten to the task with harmony and good fellowship. We wish not to *overthrow*, but to *rebuild;* we wish not to *destroy*, but to *reform* and *revise* the evils complained of; we wish not to *abandon* the institutions of Moses, but to *understand and observe them;* in fine we wish to worship God, not as *slaves of bigotry and priestcraft*,[142] but as the enlightened descendants of that chosen race, whose blessings have been scattered throughout the land of Abraham, Isaac and Jacob.

And your memorialists will ever pray.

(Signed by forty-seven Israelites of the City of Charleston.) [143]

CX

Isaac Harby's
Anniversary Discourse, 1825

On November 21, 1825, the first anniversary of the foundation of the Reformed Society of Israelites was celebrated in Charleston. The feature of the occasion was a beautiful speech by Isaac Harby,[144] one of the leaders of the group. The speech was very well received both by its immediate auditors and by those who read it later.[145] Harby reviewed the principles and significance of the society in the light of developing liberal tendencies. He prophesied that reform would triumph in Europe as well as America, even before the full political emancipation of the Jews.

For the next few years, Charleston reform flourished and its anniversaries were marked by the delivery of addresses of comparable quality by other eminent Charlestonian Jews.[146] Towards the end of the decade, however, and especially after Charleston's trade had felt the effect of the Tariff of 1828, the city began to decline as an important center. As the city declined, the Reformed Society of Israelites lost its momentum in the early 1830s, and was formally dissolved in 1833, by a notice in the following form sent to subscribers: [147]

Charleston, 7th May, 1833.

Sir:

The Reformed Society of Israelites at a meeting held on the 2nd inst. having abandoned their intention of building a new Synagogue in the City of Charleston.

Resolved unanimously, "that such sums of money as were subscribed by their fellow citizens for that purpose, be forthwith returned, with the interest which has accrued thereon." Your name appearing on the lists appended to the sum of five dollars, we herewith inclose the same with interest, and the thanks of the Society for the liberal feeling which prompted the donation.

"Your obedient servants,

Abraham Moise [148]
I. N. Cardozo,[149]
Isaac Mordecai,[150]
Michael Lazarus,[151]
Thomas W. Mordecai,[152]
Committee.

Donation $5.00
Interest 1.68
                          ――――
                          6.68

Sept. 6, 1833

The force of reform was not entirely dissipated. Under the ministry of Gustave Poznanski,[153] in the late 1830s, Beth Elohim adopted some of the modifications suggested more than a decade earlier. The earlier intransigence of Beth Elohim drove the reform element into secession; the later reforms led to a secession of the strict traditionalists. It was already impossible to please both extremes.

211. HARBY'S DISCOURSE, 1825 [154]

It is almost superfluous to inform you, my respected friends, of the purpose for which you are this day assembled. It is to celebrate the first anniversary of a society, whose existence, whose name alone, forms an era in the history of your race, gratifying to every philanthropist. The great cause of Improvement in government, in religion, in morals, in literature, is the great cause of mankind. Bigotry and despotism may rear their "miscreated fronts" to thwart your way, but the consuming beams of truth must drive them back to their original darkness. In this happy land, however, you have no such obstacles to oppose; equality of laws and freedom of conscience leave you a wide and cheerful field to act upon. You have no enemies then, but the inveteracy of habit, and the timidity of ignorance. Against these you have already struck a noble blow;

be true to yourselves and the victory is yours. The man who meanly crouches to mental oppression, is an object to be pitied by the good, contemned by the courageous; but he that nobly breaks the intellectual chain, and stands forth the champion of reason and of virtue, is a being honourable to the earth from which he sprung, and approved of by that heaven to which he aspires.

In the short revolution of a single year, what a spectacle does your society present! You began your career with only a handful of men; some of them not yet determined how far their fears or their wishes might carry them. Your opponents falsely prophecied that this "handful" would soon melt away, and the "Reformed Society of Israelites" dissolve into air. But the spirit of the constant among you has been diffused throughout the whole mass, and you can now enumerate a respectable number, trifling indeed for the purpose of moving mere "brute matter," but one of immense *moral force* in the cause in which we are embarked. The pen of Luther was the great intellectual lever which shook the papal supremacy to its foundation, why may not the virtuous example of a few Israelites, then, shake off the bigotry of ages from their countrymen? Your principles are rapidly pervading the whole mass of Hebrews throughout the United States. The progress of truth, however slow, is irresistible; and I should not wonder if the principles I speak of, were to settle permanently among the Jews of Europe, even before the despotic governments of that portion of the globe extended to our countrymen the political privileges of their other subjects.

But the consideration of what may be effected abroad, is but of minor importance to the great and *practical* objects we have in view. Our sphere of action is at present limited to *home*. It is in Charleston, and, in its more immediate consequences, in the United States, that we are to look for the experimental developement of our system. What is it we seek? The establishment of a new sect? No; never. Let other systems of religion split into a thousand schisms; let other modes of faith present to your eyes the motley scene at which philosophy may smile, and the true piety must weep, brethren instructed in a religion of mercy warring against each other by the arm of flesh and the weapons of theological pride. Let these examples of human error be seen in other religions—but it is the glory and test of the Jewish faith that its followers worship One God, that when they raise their hands to veil their eyes, and repeat, "Hear O Israel, the Lord our God, the Lord is One," they regard only the God of their fathers, the Lord of all creation, the Supreme Jehovah. This be your boast, this be your bond of union.

What is it then we ask of the Hebrew Vestry? The abolition of the ancient language and form of Jewish worship? Far from it. Those who have thoughtlessly opposed our efforts, are well aware that neither in the petition, which first convened this respectable assemblage of Israelites, nor in the constitution which grew out of the rejection of that petition, unheard and uncanvassed, and which constitution stands at once the monument of your firmness and your moderation, was any such abolition contemplated.[155] They well knew that every prayer, every ceremony, calculated to add dignity to external worship and warmth to true devotion, was the ardent wish of the members who compose your society. Our desire is to yield every thing to the feelings of the truly pious Israelite; but to take away every thing that might excite the disgust of the well informed Israelite. To throw away rabbinical interpolations; to avoid useless repetitions; to read or chaunt with solemnity; to recite such portions of the pentateuch and the prophets, as custom and practice have appointed to be read in the *original Hebrew;* but to follow such selections with a translation in *English,* and a lecture or discourse upon the law, explanatory of its meaning, edifying to the young, gratifying to the old, and instructive to every age and every class of society. Is this abolishing our mode of *sacred* worship? Is this sapping the foundations of our venerable faith? No; my friends; this is stripping it of foreign and unseemly ceremonies; divesting it of rubbish, and beautifying that simple Doric column, that primeval order of architecture, which raises its plain but massy head amid the ruins of time and the desolation of empires!

It is remarkable, and it is well it should be so, that the human mind is prone, naturally prone, to suspect every thing mysterious to be founded in fraud, every thing dark to be surrounded with danger. The bigot tells you, seek not to understand what is above your comprehension; seek not for reason, where you have only to exercise faith. But the learned king has said, "Wisdom is too high for a fool, but those who seek wisely, shall find good," and the proverb of the heaven-gifted Solomon is confirmed by the doctrine of philosophy, which tells you, that *faith* is the result of rational *demonstration*, not of blind acquiescence.

The object then, which we have in view, is too obvious to be misrepresented *with effect*, for any space of time longer than that necessary for giving the inquirer an opportunity to undeceive himself. Let that inquiry be made in the spirit of candour, and we fear not the result. Every enlightened friend of religion must approve our cause.

It is not intended to impugn the motives of our opponents. They shall not be charged with the weak ambition of holding a power they know not how to exercise, or of grasping tighter those reins which they fear may soon be snatched from their hands. But it is intended to call upon the good and the wise and the pious, out of this society, to aid us in our virtuous exertions—to open the door to reason—to welcome, with the welcome of brethren, those who desire to add dignity to their religion. This can only be done by the union of candour and patience and fortitude. Once done, we ask no more. The temperance of our proceedings shall disarm hostility; and the authority, the true legitimate authority of the Bible on which alone we act, will lull the vigilance of bigotry to sleep. It is but little we demand: To abolish the profane offerings and not insult us with bad Spanish and Portuguese; to admit an English discourse, explanatory of the *Parasah,* or portion of the law appointed to be read; to discard the idle comments of the Rabbins which have no connection with the ancient Hebrew worship; to be more dignified and more emphatic in reading, or singing the effusions of the Psalmist and the Prophets; and to select the sublimer portions of these (appropriated to the day) and such other prayers as taste and piety can approve, to be said or sung in the *English language.* We wish to abstract, not to add; to take away whatever is offensive to the enlightened mind; but to leave in its original grandeur whatever is worthy to be uttered by man, and to be listened to by the Deity.

CXI

An Early American
Jewish Sermon, 1803

In the earliest days of American-Jewish settlement, when there were no members of the congregations with any scholarly pretensions whatsoever, it was a matter of good fortune if a community had even one or two men well enough versed in Hebrew to be able to conduct services. Later, when Gershom M. Seixas became Hazzan of Congregation Shearith Israel, even his meager scholarly attainments seemed substantial to a community totally without Jewish learning. Seixas was the first Hazzan to use the title of Minister; he represented the Jewish community with dignity on many occasions, and even served as a trustee of Columbia College.[156]

At this point, our concern with Seixas is that he was the first American Jewish religious leader to preach in English in the synagogue. He did so only on special occasions, like days of national thanksgiving or humiliation. The sermon from which excerpts are printed below was delivered on a day of thanksgiving for the passing of the yellow fever scourge in 1803.[157] There is no artistry in the construction of the sermon. It is a simple review of the vicissitudes of his congregation during the trying years in which this plague was a frequent and disastrous visitor. The good fortune of American Jews in living in a land of religious freedom is emphasized, and ultimate hopes for a miraculous return to the holy land are expressed. There is an intermingling here of religious, patriotic and prudential themes.

212. A SERMON BY SEIXAS, 1803 [158]

To declare the Providence of an all merciful Creator, to glorify his holy name, to render praise & thanksgivings for the benefits we receive, are amongst the most important duties of Man. It is for this purpose we are assembled this day that we may express our gratefull thanks for the many & various blessings that have been graciously bestowed on us during the last Season, & for the more special care of Divine Providence, in withholding from us, the visitation of an epidemic disease, which of late years has proved so fatal to our fellow-citizens, and that the evil arising from the malignity of its influence, has been considerably lessened in a neighbouring City. Although the horror of mind, & the many inconveniencies in consequence thereof, have been experienced by the inhabitants, so as to have driven them from their respective dwellings, to seek for shelter among the more remote Villages of the State, that the evil is now subsided, and they are again re-established in their former places of residence, enjoying domestic happiness in health & peace, we sincer[e]ly thank thee Oh God! and we are truly sensible that it is not from any merit of ours, but altogether proceeding from thy mercies & thy truth, as it is said by king David in Ps[115]

Not unto us Oh lord, not unto us, but to thy name give glory, for thy mercy & thy truth. . . .

In examining the words of our text, you will find the disinterested benevolence of our Creator, that is ever extended towards us, and by endeavouring to imitate Him, we attain that peace of mind, which is the sure result of Virtue, this naturally leads in the road of perfection, & fits us to meet the rewards of a future State, when our immortal Souls shall be freed from this unstable tenement of flesh. and were it not for the hopes, and promises of an hereafter, who would desire to be a creature of this transitory existence, where troubles & disasters continuall arise, unsought for & unexpected, the best among us are not exempt from pains, and none can expect to pass through life, without encountering its vicissitudes, the aged & and the young[,] the rich & the poor, are alike subject to sickness & mortality, & we often see those who abound in all worldly good, suffering the agonies incident to human-nature, whose relatives are oppressed with anxiety, and in continual apprehension of a greater evil; from whom then can we receive consolation? Can it flow from any other source, than from the fountain of all perfection? whose everlasting mercies alone can give comfort to the afflicted mourner, or administer relief to the helpless Invalid. it is to Him we must look for fortitude to support us under our trials, and it is He alone who tempers our minds with resignation, when we ask it of Him in truth. it is by His efficient grace that we conquer the ills of life, and obtain the blessings we possess; to His will we become submissive, and cheerfully acquiesce with His dispensations.

It is more common for Man under these trials, to call upon His maker for aid, than when enjoying the Luxuries of this world, not considering, that the (sa)me Providence who grants, can withhold, and [   ] are thankfull for the benefits we possess, they can be withdrawn, in the most sudden manner and when least expected. . . .

Were it for no other reason that we join in celebrating this day with the other inhabitants (of) this city, it would be of itself sufficient, but as we are so peculiarly situated in our captivity, that I conceive we are more specially called upon to [r]eturn thanks to benign Goodness, in placing us [i]n such a country, where we are free to act, according to the dictates of conscience, & where no exception is taken from following the principles of our religion, a religion founded on the very nature of our existence, & whose laws are uniformly calculated to make us wiser & better & happier, these are circumstances that should always be considered, & it rests with every individual to examine his own conduct, & to discard such propensities as would lead him to err, to subdue the passions of his carnal appetite, and to be governed by the spirit of truth, which is an emanation of eternal Wisdom. the sacred scriptures abound with Lessons of morality, & it is but looking, to find them, we therein see the duty of Man to God, the obligations we are under to obey His commandments, & the respective mutual duties that subsist in a State of Society. connected with the various blessing(s) we have experienced in the course of the present year, we may be thankfull for the establishment of a Seminary, which is yet in its infancy, where our children may be instructed in the holy language, & in process of time may become acquainted with the literary writings of our ancient Sages, whose works are altogether corroborating proofs of divine revelation, as handed down to us in a regular succession, from our great & wise legislator, through the Prophets to the grand Sanhedrim, & conveyed by them to the heads of the great Synagogue, the exposition & explanation of our holy Law, is only to be found in their writings, & many passages that appear to be contradictory to each other, in the written Law, are in the oral Law thoroughly reconciled & made to agree. may the supporters of the Institution, live to see the good effects resulting, from so excellent an establishment. beside this, another institution is erected, for (the) benefit of our Society, whose services have been [al]ready experienced, & the promoters thereof are in hopes of its becoming more extensively usefull. Surely [then,] we have every reason to be thankfull for the benefits we have received from an indulgent Providence [in] common with the people of the country, in preserving us in health, and for the special blessings attending this small congregation, in procuring the means of defraying the additional expences incurred, in consequence of establishing such commendable Institutions. the satisfaction arising from a consciousness of having performed our Duties in the several stations, to which we have been called is an happiness of itself, for which we should be truly gratefull, and we should be forcibly impressed with the Idea, that we are only instruments in the hands of Providence, to answer His designs & to fulfill His purposes. let us now implore His divine succor to perfect the work we have began, that our Youths may know that the Omnipotent God of Israel, is ever ready to assist them, when called upon in truth, let us prostrate ourselves before Him and supplicate Him to take them under his immediate care, that they may grow up to fear & to love Him and that they may know that we are the works of His hands, that He hath made us, & not we ourselves & that we are His people, & the Sheep of His pasture. . . .

We will here take a comparative view, of the [late] season, & the former, when the epidemic disease prevailed throughout the city, when every mind was filled with anxiety & terror, when numbers were constrained, to leave their peaceful abodes, to seek an asylum from contagion, to have seen the distressed situation of families, weeping & mourning over their sick & dying relatives, unable to afford relief or consolation, & see them now abounding in health, blessed with the fruitfull production of the earth, enjoying the pleasures of peace. exercising the priviledges of religious worship, without restraint & under the auspices of a lenient administration of government for all these bene[fits] we are indebted to the Omniscient Creator of the universe, whose "tender mercies are over all His works" and we his creatures are bounden to adore Him for His divine goodness, "& to serve him with all our Hearts, & with all our Souls" according to the monition of Moshe Rabenu [of blessed memory], who ordained it to the children of Israel, to be obser[ved] for ever, Is it not then a duty incumbent on us, to assemble & return thanks for the mercies [we] have experienced? and to render praises for the unbounded goodness of our God, most devoutly we pray unto thee Oh Lord, that thou wouldst hear us, and grant us a continuance of thy providence, that we may be endued with the precious blessings of peace & health, plenty & prosperity [both] national & individual, we humbly thank thee for placing us under such a Magistracy, [who] are disposed, to sanction every religious mode of worship, & who so readily conform to the recommendation of those whose duty it is to watch over the cure of Souls, & who no doubt were actuated by the most disinterested motives, [s]eeking only the wellfare of their fellow Citizens, rejoicing for their temporal advantage & earnestly endeavouring to promote their spiritual happiness. Such are the general blessings in a free government, such advantages, we should strenuously maintain, by conforming to all Rules & recommendations, that do not interfere with the precepts of our religion. . . .

From what has been said in the preceeding pages, you will readily observe the propriety of sanctifying the day, as a tribute of thanks justly due to our heavenly Father for the kind display of His providential care, during the last season in protecting us from the malignant disease that hath prevailed in former seasons, for his enabling us to carry into effect, the institutions that have been established, within the year, & for the general, & special blessings, we have enjoyed in peace. you will likewise find the necessity of prayer, to continue us under His all powerfull protection, that we may at all times, so conduct ourselves, that we may not incur his divine wrath, but always be sensible of His power & glory that we may publish to the world. that through His mercies & truth, we are brought safely to this period of our lives, and not from any merit of ourselves, and according to the words of our text let us declare with king David, Not unto us, Oh Lord! not unto us, but unto thy name give glory for thy Mercies & thy truth.

Let us then cheerfully unite in praises & thanksgivings, to our God, the God of Israel, & humbly invoke Him, to pour forth His holy spirit upon us, that we may be made perfect in the law of obedience to his divine Will, that we may be accustomed to good works, & that we may ultimately receive the blessing of Life ever-lasting. We humbly beseach thee Oh Lord our God, & the God of our Fathers, to hear our supplications when we call upon thy inef-fable Name, grant us thy blessing on the institution established under name of Polonys [Talmud Torah] and may you my dr Chil-dren, who are now under my tuition, be reared as an honor to the Institution and as ornaments to Society. may the promoters & bene-factors live to see their offspring, grown up in the love & fear of God, and may you all receive the pleasures arising from a con-sciousness of duty. grant to the Inhabitants of these States the United States of America the blessing of health, the increase of prosperity, succeed them in their lawful pursuits whether agricul-tural or commercial, let peace and harmony prevail in their terri-tory. Bless & preserve the Rulers & Administrators of the govern-ment, remove far from them, the evil spirit of discord, let no cause of jealousy persist among them, to injure the wellfare, of their respective constituents, may union of sentiment ever preside in their councils, teach them to respect themselves, that they may always be respected among the Nations of the earth, may each one in his own department, act so as to deserve the approbation of all, And may the Magistrates of this Metropolis, be ever vigilant in their duties, and may they long practise the calling of piety and ever be attentive to the true principles of Virtue.[159]

CXII

A Physician's Sermon,

1820

Another of the handful of addresses on religious occasions by American Jews that has been preserved to us from the early national period is the discourse delivered by the physician Jacob de la Motta [160] at the dedication of the building of Congregation Mikve Israel of Savannah, Georgia, on Friday, July 21, 1820 (the date corresponds with the 10th of Ab, 5580). It seems singularly appropriate to have scheduled this celebration of the erection of a new synagogue building on the day following the traditional Jewish fast day and day of mourning for the destruction of the First and Second Temples. Dr. de la Motta was not only the featured speaker on this occasion; he also took a major part in making arrangements for the impressive procession and exercises.[161]

De la Motta's Discourse was very well received, and justly so, for it is a good if somewhat florid speech. It is interesting to note that this address and the anniversary address by Isaac Harby,[162] both delivered by laymen, are far superior in style, if not always in content, to the sermons by Seixas [163] and Leeser,[164] the religious professionals. De la Motta stressed the benefits of equality that the Jews of America were experiencing and contrasted the American-Jewish situation sharply with that of the Jews in other lands.[165]

213. DISCOURSE BY
DR. JACOB DE LA MOTTA, 1820 [166]

The objects embraced in this celebration, are of the first magnitude to liberality and religious toleration, its effects beneficial to mankind. It discloses to the enlightened, the devoted state of a people, freed from the house of bondage, and willing to attest it, by an offering of the incense of gratitude, at the shrine of their God. A people! invigorated by the resplendent rays of their faith, would willingly undergo severer probations, than resign their trust. A people! dwelling in a land abounding with "milk and honey," and avowing in the utmost ardency of expression, the blessings they enjoy. A sect! exulting in the privileges guaranteed by the tutelar Goddess of Liberty, to worship God, according to the ritual of their ancestors. A Nation! whom [sic], while appreciating the benefits granted by a spotless constitution, cast an eye to their brethren in foreign lands, writhing under the shackles of odious persecution, and wild fanatacism [sic]; with the fondest hope, the measure of their sufferings will be soon complete; that the gloom of bigotry will be displaced by the light of reason; and that a scattered race, may enjoy the privileges and immunities, *God* intended all should participate. A Nation! who have suffered for their transgressions, but never will be forsaken by *Him*, who appeared and led the way in a "cloud by day, and a pillar of fire by night."

Assembled as we are, to re-establish by commemoration, the *Congregation* of this remnant, or small portion of the house of Isreal [sic]; your expectation of a brief sketch of our History, and particularly as connected with a primeval residence in this City, and for many years past, even down to our own time, shall be realized; and may I trust, it will not be uninteresting, as it will include the well known fact, that many Jews struggled, and sacrificed their dearest interest, for the independence of this country.

The emigration of Israelites to this City,[167] from the best records and information, is traced to the earliest period of its settlement. The enterprising adventure[r]s, who accompanied the first Provincial Governor and Commander in Chief, James Edward Oglethorpe, had not long arrived within the River Savannah, when an additional number, including about twenty respectable Jew families, landed on our shores, on the 11th July, 1733, corresponding with the 16th *Tamus*, 5493, of the Hebrew Calender [sic].

Persecution sustained by bigotry, and strengthened by intollerance [sic], compelled many of our nation to abandon their precarious and gloomy abodes, in Spain and Portugal, and leave their possessions, families and friends. Threatened on all sides by a turbulent storm portentous of complete annihilation, no alternative was left, but flight, torture or death; and the most convenient port was their dernier refuge. Striken by contumely; assailed by the keenest invectives, the aged and youthful driven from their home; were willing to engage in new adventures, that should promise security, tranquility and liberty. Uniting their destinies and common interest, with many respectable German Jews; they left Europe to sojourn in a foreign land; inspired by the benefits, that encourage prospects, and a transatlantic clime, offered their migration. At this period the Government of Great Britain, under George 2nd, was transporting to the new country, many individuals, who were allured by proffered possessions in a rich soil, the luxuriant productions of which by proper cultivation, and a ready exportation, held out the means of amassing wealth; independent of the settlement and extension of a distant section of the habitable Globe. To effect this object, several under the munificence of their sovereign, were sent free of expense. Not so with the Jews. Their easy circumstances and high toned dispositions, placed them above the level of incumbents. They came unassisted by bounty. The distributions of land to the new settlers, gave a portion to each, and certain tracts are still retained by the descendants of those, who possessed the original grants. For respectability, "even tenor of conduct," correct deportment, and a zealous attachment to the prosperity of the country; the Jews stood on the same eminence with other sects, and by the privileges extended to them in a civil capacity; they were bound by no common ties, for the general weal. Thanks to the protectors of our liberties, *here* we still continue to boast, and enjoy the same rights. Many Jews removed to other places; several died; and those who remained, continued firm in their attachment. These gradually diminished in 1757 to three or four families, branches of whose posterity are within the sound of my voice; and have acquired as a legacy from their progenitors, that love for the soil, which can only cease with their existence, when the same soil shall have received their mortal remains. Those who deserved the appellation of inhabitants, were soon attached to a place, that from the inducements it afforded, altho' thinly settled, and the advantages to be derived, endeared it to their best regards. Participating alike with all Religions, those benefits the laws then in force enjoined, placed in such respective functions, as tended to elevate and dignify; a union of action kept pace, with a union of sentiment;

and in order to strengthen the bonds of society, whose links were rivetted in one general chain; an association was formed, to keep alive the social compact; to extend the commiserating hand of Benevolence; and to evince those noble qualities of the heart, that exalt and adorn our species. A Society was at once established, now aged in years, as well as aged in the best of services, that enrolled as its founders, an Episcopalian, a Catholic and a Jew. From such a union of opposites in mode of worship, hence the name, but it was a union, predicated on preeminent virtues, and devoted to the best interest of humanity. From this institution, many have derived the substantial advantage of well cultivated minds, to laud that liberality, which disregarded particular tenets, when united for universal good.

The dawn of the Revolution, opened to their view, new scenes; and they revolved in their minds, the condition of their forefathers, who toiled and suffered under the yoke of servitude, during the reign of Pharoh. They saw in prospective, what would probably be their lot. They panted for Liberty and an enjoyment of equal rights, that "nature, and nature's God" intended they should partake. Resolving to separate from the standard of Tyranny, they united with freemen for the general good; contended for the independence of the states, and none were found more zealous, more active, more brave, and more patient, amidst the sufferings, that the fortune of war, the cravings of hunger, and the merciless breast, had daily subjected them. Their distresses and privations during the struggle for freedom, constituted conspicuous incidents. When the trump of war marshalled all classes to the tented field, Georgia produced her quota of Israelites, who were found equally as zealous, brave and enterprizing, as others of a different persuasion. The most stubborn inflexibility, the most unshaken integrity, the firmest attachment to American glory, acquired for the Jews the countenance, confidence and esteem of the General Government. Some obtained commissions, and others conspicuous appointments, that at once placed them on the same eminence with other nations; and there yet remains a few of those worthies, to testify their efforts in the general cause. They alike with others, were the theme of applause—the theme of admiration. . . .

Turning from the review of degradation, casting the mantle of oblivion over the frailties and enormities bordering on proscription, that have darkened the path, and sullied the fair prospects, and successful advancement of the Israelites in distant climes; it must be inexpressibly pleasing to the Philanthropist, whose bosom is the receptacle for the generous feelings of humanity, to consider their present condition.

On what spot in this habitable Globe, does an Israelite enjoy more blessings, more privileges, or is more elevated in the sphere of preferment, and more conspicuously dignified in respectable stations? where can similar instances be noticed of the various appointments held by so great a majority of a few of the persuasion? Have we not ample cause to exult? but it is the exultation of grateful hearts, bounding by the impulsive action of transcendent feelings. Sensations of gratitude to Him, who rules the destinies of man, and compasionates the children of misfortune. Gratitude to Him, who has extended his protection to the "gathering or hope of Israel."

Attentive to the admonition which exhort us to continue worthy of Divine favor, we must not forget those duties, which we owe society as well as ourselves. This is to be maintained, by a proper regard for, and attendance to his House of God; in which we are to render ourselves acceptable in his sight, and deserving his countenance. Were we not influenced by religious zeal, a decent respect to the custom of the community, in which we live, should actuate us to observe public worship. But we need no greater incentive, no stronger inducement, than the imperious mandate contained, and forcibly expressed in our sacred Decalogue. Remember the Sabbath Day. On that day the people of Israel should rest from their labors. Who can expect his soul to rest, who will not rest with his God? On the seventh day he ceased from his great work, and sanctified it; and it was promulgated to all nations of the earth. May it hereafter be perpetually observed: and may it be among this remnant of Israel, as a holy convocation.

In directing our attention to the privileges and benefits proffered to all in this country, and so strenuously aspirated by that palladium of our rights, the Constitution; we are led to forget those days of anarchy and bloodshed, which has stained the annals of other times. *Here,* a liberal and tollerant [sic] spirit, pervades every individual. *Here,* unbiased protection, and friendly co-operation, are alike extended, without consideration or reference to particular faith. *Here,* Justice presents her scale to public view, and guards its preponderance from the touch of illeberality [sic]. *Here,* a union of friendship and fellowship is promoted and encouraged. *Here,* the light of learning discloses the errors that mankind imperceptibly encounter; and it is by this light they are relieved from the vices and follies, incidental to weak-minded bigotry and blind superstition. It is *here,* that we are reasonably to expect the enjoyment of those rewards for our constancy and sufferings, as promised by the word of God, when he declared he would not forsake us. Be it then our care, to merit a continuance of that favor, which has already been extended, to insure a completion of his promise, by a rigid adherence to his commandments, and an undeviating pursuit of that path, which by his protection, leads to that eternal and exalted kingdom, the haven of benignity.[168]

CXIII

A Professional Sermon, 1831

Isaac Leeser, who became Hazzan of Congregation Mikveh Israel of Philadelphia in 1829, was the first American Jewish minister to institute regular preaching in English as a feature of the Sabbath services.[169] The sermon from which extracts are reprinted here, on "Confidence in God," was Leeser's first sermon; indeed, the young preacher felt it necessary to begin with an apology for his limitations of form and substance. He had good reason to apologize.

It may be that Leeser's limitations as a preacher account for the fact that he did not, at any time before 1840, feel secure in his position with the Congregation. When J. J. Lyons,[170] a Hazzan from Surinam,[171] visited Philadelphia in 1837, the Parnass of Mikveh Israel [172] notified Leeser that Lyons had expressed a desire to conduct the Sabbath services. Leeser's reply reflects his insecurity and casts an interesting sidelight on the struggle between minister and lay leaders.[173] In courtesy, Leeser granted Lyons the right he sought, but he indicated that the request should properly have come directly to him from Lyons. He insisted that the secular officers of the congregation were without authority in the matter. There is an undertone of suspicion in Leeser's note, as if he felt somehow that the lay leaders of the congregation were trying to undercut his position. Similar indications that Leeser's relations with his congregation were troubled arose in connection with his efforts to establish a religious school.

By far the clearest evidence for a lack of harmony is to be found in a letter Leeser wrote to his congregation on May 15, 1840.[174] His term of appointment was about to expire, and his reappointment was due to come before the congregational meeting. At this time, Leeser was certainly the outstanding Hazzan in American Jewish life.[175] Whatever his limitations of training may have been in 1829, when he first came to serve Mikveh Israel, by 1840, when he wrote this letter in review of his eleven years in the

employ of the congregation, he had overcome some of his deficiencies by hard work. Yet, on the testimony of the letter, he felt
that his years of faithful service and his scholarly attainments had
been rewarded by injustice, even by trickery and deceit. From the
very beginning, he said, he was paid less than he had been given
to expect, and his position, even after eleven years, carried no tenure. The officers of the congregation had, in the opinion of the
minister, showed a callous disregard for his welfare. If only a
fraction of the accusations he charged to the congregational account
were true, he certainly had good reason to complain. Of course, the
letter gives only one side of the story; there may have been reasons
for everything that Leeser considered as maltreatment. This letter
may be described, however, as the first American Jewish plea for
better employment conditions for religious leaders. As such, it
shows Leeser as the proponent of a more generous and responsible
attitude by laymen toward religious functionaries.

Justice to the congregation requires the statement that, at no
time in his career, if we may judge by his published volumes of
Discourses,[176] was Leeser an inspired or inspiring preacher. His
sermons, in his maturity as well as in this specimen from his youth,
read like student essays. There is, too, a stiffness, almost a pom-
posity, in their style and language, with no touch of warmth and
color or any originality of conception or freshness of exposition to
them. He must have been very dull to hear.[177] Perhaps the redeeming quality of his sermons, for the auditor as well as for the reader,
is the obvious sincerity with which Leeser struggled to express his
simple faith and piety, the confidence in God that is the theme of
this first of his sermons.

214. LEESER'S FIRST SERMON, 1831 [178]

Brethren of the House of Israel!

It is with extreme reluctance, founded upon a knowledge of my
inability to advance any thing which may be generally interesting,
that I now, for the first time, venture to address you. I feel too little
confidence in my attainments (and I hope that no one will accuse
me of affectation for so saying) even to imagine that I could do
justice to our holy religion by anything I am going to say. Before

I begin, therefore, I am constrained to tell you, that only in obedience to the repeated solicitations of persons who really feel an interest in the welfare of our nation, I persuaded myself to attempt teaching that, which I deem to be the essential parts of our faith. After this candid avowal, I trust, that you will pardon any defect which you may discover, and be a little indulgent to my first effort at public speaking. It is highly probable, that most of you, if not all, may have heard all which I can advance; but then I must beg of you to consider, that known truths may often be but faintly remembered, and that we may derive great and lasting benefits by having them presented to us in a light, in which perhaps we had never before viewed them. It is for this reason expedient, that occasional lectures on religious subjects should be delivered in our Synagogues, although I cannot deny that many members, perhaps the greater number, of our society are sufficiently acquainted with their duties, and need not be reminded of them by any preacher, however, eloquent. Having premised thus much, let us proceed to the consideration of the following verse, from the XXVth chapter of Isaiah:

"And it will be said on that day: Behold this is our God in whom we have trusted, and he will save us; this is the Lord in whom we have trusted, we will be glad and rejoice in his salvation." Isaiah XXV.9.

God is great and mighty, nothing is too great for his power to accomplish, nothing is hidden from his searching view. For if we look around us and behold the stupendous works of creation; when we see the regularity and order which reign in every thing; and when we turn our view within ourselves, and consider the nature of the living soul which we feel to animate us: we must be convinced, that the One above is powerful beyond compare, and wise beyond all measure. And if we descend from a contemplation of the greatness of God, as displayed in his creation, and reflect with care and candour upon the individual fortune of every human being: we will discover, that his providence and goodness are no less displayed in the details of life, than his power and wisdom are shown in the structure of the universe. . . .

It should be enough for us, that we are doing our duty; that we are obeying the will of our Father: and this consciousness will strengthen us to bear up against all worldly ill; for animated by a true confidence in God we must feel, that He is mighty enough to repay us our losses, remunerate us for our toil, and protect us from any injury to which we may be exposed. If therefore we are truly impressed with the knowledge of the power and goodness of the Lord, we must be his willing servants, and practice that readily which we are taught by Him to call wise and good, independent of all considerations of personal gain or aggrandizement unswayed by fear of loss or persecution.

But as it is undeniable, that we Israelites have at present no national government; as our number is but small and unimportant when compared with the mass of mankind: the pursuit of our religion may appear unprofitable to many among the worldly-minded, since it can bring them no temporal advantages, for there are none in authority who may bestow on them offices of trust and profit for their attachment to the ancient faith; and the system which we uphold makes often strong demands upon our personal convenience and upon the riches we may possess. Perhaps the strict observance of our law may prevent us from participating in the distribution of certain offices, the duties of which may compel us to transgress the divine precepts. Again, some one may be induced to plead necessity as an excuse for not adhering very strictly to the religion of his forefathers; and he may imagine to himself a sufficient number of excuses to lull his conscience to sleep, whilst he transgresses the commandments of his God. Nevertheless he will assert, that he is a good and truly religious man, since he observes what is commonly called the moral duties; and alleges that he fulfils every thing which God can in reason ask of him; but he forgets in his self-gratulation, that interest alone, sordid meanness, groveling avarice, and a yielding to selfish desires are the true motives of his conduct. And can this be religion? is this a display of pure faith? an entire reliance on God's omnipotence? No! Let me tell him that he has not true religion in his heart, that his soul has not the proper reverence of the Lord, that his confidence is not entire in the God who created him. And although it is natural that we should be startled at the sight of what is called necessities, and although we are very apt to view every obstacle as insurmountable, provided we can excuse ourselves thereby for not doing our duty: we cannot call ourselves good and religious, we cannot be said to confide in God, as long as we are deterred from obeying Him by the dread of evil we may have to suffer here, and withheld from engaging in his service by the sight of difficulties which we have to encounter; for we are not then kindled by that devotion to the will of the Lord which will enable us to make personal sacrifices, and to submit to dangers in our endeavours to serve Him.

But, brethren, if interested motives tend so powerfully to weaken our confidence in God, there is yet another feeling, which may aptly be called *self-sufficiency,* against which we are to arm ourselves by every means of which we are masters, if we wish to lead a religious life. For there are many, who, inflated by success in their pursuits, are misled to esteem their strength as sufficient to enable them to combat every obstacle, to shield themselves against all vicissitudes, to break down all the barriers which may oppose their success; and, therefore, rendered selfish and proud, they neglect to pay due deference to religious duties.

CXIV

Intersynagogal Cooperation, 1792-1839

The documents collected below illustrate some of the ways in which synagogues in various communities were called on to help each other. In our period and throughout American Jewish history, established synagogues did help when circumstances allowed. In May, 1792, Congregation Beth Elohim of Charleston applied to Mikveh Israel of Philadelphia for financial assistance in building a Temple; [179] the request was turned down because Mikveh Israel was itself in financial straits.[180] In 1825, Mikveh Israel invited Congregation Beth Shalome of Richmond to participate in the exercises in dedication of their new Philadelphia building; [181] the Parnass of Beth Shalome replied with best wishes and the promise that prayers for the success of their Philadelphia brethren would be offered in the Richmond services on the dedicatory Sabbath. An undated letter from Beth Shalome to Mikveh Israel regrets the inability of the Richmond congregation to help in finding a Hazzan for Philadelphia.[182] In all these cases, the original letter of request must have been sent to many congregations, in the United States and abroad. They may, indeed, have been printed circulars, like the 1839 request of Shearith Israel for aid in finding a competent Hebrew teacher able to assist the Hazzan at need; it is interesting to note that the salary offered was as large as that which Leeser received at this time for his services as Hazzan in Philadelphia.[183]

215. BENJAMIN NONES [184] TO CONGREGATION BETH ELOHIM, 1792 [185]

[*September 9, 1792*]

Sirs

The absence of some Members Composing our Ajunto is the cause of delaying an answer to your favr. of 22d. May Last.

It affords me great pleasure to be informed of your prospect to effect the "building a Temple in which the name of the only & great God of Israel is to be adored & revered"

But it is a mortifying Circumstance that we have it not in our power to answer your zealous and polite application in such a manner as the exigency of the Matter demands & our inclination would prompt us. You Can't be unacquainted with the dilemma this Congregation was in, the Year before last; that had not the Legislature of this Commonwealth been activated by the principles of benevolence & Liberality to grant us the instituting a Lottery to extricate us from the difficulties we then were involved in we should in all probability have had our House of Worship torn from us and converted to profanation.

The Congregation at that time was Small, and to our great regret its Numbers have since still decreased, and having no fund—the burthen of Supporting a Hazan, Shochet and other unavoidable incidental Charges is intirely borne by 9 or 10 individuals by Subscription. This being the case, its obvious that our abilities are not equall to our inclination, for which we feel a Most painfull regret. Hoping that the more wealthy Congregations abroad will exert themselves in Liberally assisting your pious and Laudable undertaking, that the great & holy God of Israel May Support you & Crown your Zealous endeavours with every desired Success Speedy to accomplish the good work you have begun. May he grant you peace & Concord in your habitations, and register you in the Books of Long Life and prosperity, are the wishes of your Sincere Brethern and very Obedt. Servts.　　B. N. Parnas [186]

Philad. K. K. Mikva Israel. 22.
Ellul A. M. 5552 9 Septr. 1792

M.J.[187]
B.G.[188]
S.L.[189]　　　　　Junto [190]

216. JACOB MORDECAI [191] TO
CONGREGATION MIKVEH ISRAEL, 1824 [192]

Richmond 15th June [1824]

To B. Phillips,[193] Simon Gratz,[194] and Isaac Hays,[195] Esquires, Committee & ca.

Gentlemen

I have received the communication with which your honoured me in behalf of the KKMI. The paucity of our number in this place enables me/ without delay/ to ascertain that no person can be found here, who combines the qualifications you require, or who would in any wise answer your purpose as Mr. Isaac Seixas [196] forms the only exception; and he does not possess a Grammatical Knowledge of the Hebrew Language. We should relinquish this Gentleman with much regret, indeed were we deprived of his services, our Synagogue must be closed. Great as this sacrafice [sic] would be we should readily bow to circumstances that would ensure to him a permanent and desirable income.

I very cordially reciprocate your personal good wishes, and pray that your respectable congregation may soon be enabled to dedicate their new Synagogue, and obtain a pastor who shall completely answer their purpose. May your Society be distinguished in Israel by the Union and Zeal of its members in promoting that Piety, Charity, and Brotherly love, so strongly inculcated in the precepts of our great and distinguished ancestors.

I have the honour to be   most Respectfully   Jacob Mordecai
                                                 P. KKBI

217. JACOB MORDECAI TO
ZALEGMAN PHILLIPS, 1825 [197]

Richmond 11th January / 25

Sir

I am honoured with your communication of the 5th instt. This congregation is duly impressed with the courtesy and the fraternal motives which induced the "board of managers" to extend their kind invitation to them. In their behalf I beg you to present to those Gentlemen the expression of their individual acknowledgments, in which permit me to unite. On the Sabbath of your dedication we shall offer up the prayers of this K.K. to the God of our fathers, beseeching his merciful kindness and choisest [sic] blessings on your meritorious endeavours to promote the worship of his holy name, and thus publickly adhering to his almighty command to be his "witnesses" the witnesses of his perfect Unity, with the nations among whom we are scattered. May your Society increase the national respectability by the Unity of their measures, and by their regular attendance on the worship of God in the house they dedicate to his service. Accept my thanks for the cordial terms in which you have been pleased to communicate the desire of the board of managers.

I have the honour to be with great respect.   Your obedient servant
Jacob Mordecai Parnass
K.K.B.S.

Z. Phillips Esqu.
Parnass K.K.M.I.
Philadelphia

218. CIRCULAR, 1839 [198]

New-York, January, 7th 1839.

To the Parnassim and Elders of the Congregation, in Congn Mikve
    Israel   Philada [199]
Gentlemen.

The Trustees of the Congregation [Shearith Israel] in this city, the oldest in this country, aware how much the congregation has suffered from a want of a person every way competent to teach the hebrew grammatically, and to translate it in a manner to be perfectly comprehensive to the pupil; have adopted a resolution, authorizing and empowering the undersigned to address a circular to several congregations, making known their wants, and applying for the service of a competent person.

They desire therefore to know whether there is in your congregation the prospect of obtaining the services of a well educated young man, or one with a small family, capable of teaching the Hebrew, with the spanish and portuguese pronunciation, and also the rudiments, if not the more advanced parts, of an English education. It is also necessary that the person thus qualified as a teacher, should be able to aid our [Hazzan] in the discharge of his duties, as occasion may require: as in case of sickness &c for which purpose he must understand the manner of chaunting the prayers and reading the [Sefer Torah] according to the [minhag Sephardim] and be possessed of a clear voice and distinct enunciation. Our main object is to procure a teacher, and one able to aid the [Hazzan] in one person.

It is needless to say that he must be a man of unblemished morality and piety, strict in his religion, devoted to his duties, and of good temper and address. To a person thus qualified, an income of one thousand dollars per annum, may be calculated on; with a prospect of doing better, should his services be every way acceptable, and his course of conduct popular with the Congregation.

Should you know of such a person in your district willing to come to this city, and answering, in every respect the qualifications required, you would essentially oblige the congregation by addressing either of us on the subject, detailing all the particulars, at your earliest convenience, accompanied with such vouchers as you may deem necessary, in order that the trustees may be able to come to an immediate conclusion.

We are, Gentlemen, your humble servants,

Samuel N. Judah,[200]
Tobias I. Tobias,[201]
Aaron L. Gomez.[202]   Committee

CXV
Questions and Answers
on Jewish Law, 1793-1840

The traditional method for resolving practical community problems in the application of Jewish law was by submitting questions on particular cases to ordained rabbis.[203] It must be remembered that the rabbi was not originally anything like the Christian minister; he was, rather, an expert on Jewish codes of law and customs.[204] In America, however, in the period of our history, there were no rabbis.[205] Hence major questions were submitted to the Jewish religious authorities in London; from the Sephardic congregations, usually to the Sephardic *Haham*[206] or *Beth Din,*[207] and from the Ashkenazic congregations to the Ashkenazic *Beth Din,* or later, to the Chief Rabbi. Minor questions were, as a rule, decided by the most scholarly lay members of the congregation—men like I. B. Kursheedt,[208] for example—or by the Hazzan. Actually, even the more important questions posed by the American synagogues were not of a very profound character. Essentially they were comparatively involved applications of very simple principles concerning marriage, burial rights, and problems of bastardy.

The examples printed below are typical: a query to the London *Beth Din* from Philadelphia, and a *responsum* to a New York question by the British Ashkenazic Chief Rabbi, Solomon Hirschell.[209]

219. BENJAMIN NONES [210] TO THE LONDON BETH DIN,[211] 1793 [212]

To the Beth din of K. K. Sha..nar a Shamaim [213] of London, whom god augment.

Philadelphia Augt. 7th. 1793

Gentn.

We the Parnass and ajuntas of K. K. Mikvey Israel of this City have the honor to address your respectable Board on Business of importance to Jewdaisme at Large, and to our Young and Rising Congregation in Particular; and we flatter ourself you will as Soon as it may be Convenient favor this Congregation with your answer and advice, the Case is this:

A (Yehid) [214] of this Congregation has Lived in a Public way with a (Goyeh) [215] woman who has Kept (House) for him about (eig)ht Years and has had By her three Children two of which are boys which he had (Ge-mulim) [216] at the 8th. day, the Same Person *now* applies to us with the Consent of the Woman to make her a (g-yo-reth) [217] as also grant him Permission to marry Said woman with (Chupuh u-kidushim).[218]

We must Say in favor of the above (Yehid) that he has and does Keep up as far as we know to our Rules; and Contributes toward the Support of our Congon. as others do.

We have represented to the best of our Knowlidge the Case and Conduct of the person. and therefore request your opinion on the Subject and what we have to do, your answer will much oblige this Congregation in whose Behalf we are Gentn. Your most obedt. Hble. Servts.   Benjamin Nones Esq. Parnass

220. SOLOMON HIRSCHELL TO B'NAI JESHURUN,[219] 1839 [220]

To the Wardens and Committee of the Jewish Congregation, New York.

Gentlemen,

It having been intimated to me that a certain individual of your city, by the name of . . . , is anxious to marry his daughter to a man of the name of . . . , I lose no time in informing you, that such a marriage cannot by our law take place, the said . . . being a [mamzer]; [221] and I understand that he has represented to you, that he has been married in England [kedat Moshe we-Israel].[222] I beg to inform you that such could not have been the case, unless the said . . . must have imposed upon us, or have been married without authority by some unworthy character.[223]

I hope this will arrive in time to stop the contemplated marriage between the parties, and trust that you will endeavour to do all in your power to prevent the union taking place elsewhere, so that the Vineyard of the Lord of Hosts may be kept from diverse seed.

Wishing you prosperity, and long life to all the leaders of your congregation, I remain yours, &c. &c.   (Signed)   S. Herschell
Chief Rabbi.

May 12th 5599 [1839], A.M.

CXVI

The Synagogue as
Philanthropic Agency, 1800-1814

One of the central expressions of the Jewish religious spirit is philanthropy. By expressing and exercising concern for fellow human beings a Jew shows his concern for God's handiwork. Philanthropic expressions may be individual, and the record of personal philanthropy among American Jews is a distinguished one. In Jewish custom, however, a considerable part of philanthropic activity is a community affair, exercised through agencies of the community.[224]

In the early national period of Jewish life in America, the synagogue was still an important philanthropic agency. It had not yet been supplanted by specialized organizations, although these were beginning to develop. The constitutions of the synagogues made provision for regular contributions to their funds for charitable purposes. In the first instance, at least, these funds were used to prevent members of the congregation from becoming public charges. Beyond this, the synagogues assisted Jewish non-members when possible.[225] The documents below illustrate this philanthropic aspect of synagogal activity.

221. KEEPING A JEW OFF
PUBLIC CHARITY, 1800 [226]

Mess. Abrahams [227] & Judah.[228] a committee appointed for the purpose of reporting to the trustees what provision was necessary for the support of Michael S. Hays.[229]

Reports that from his being a Cripple he is quite Incapacitated to obtain a livelihood They are therefore of opinion that the sum of Forty pounds pr. annum for which they can obtain him board & lodging ought to be allowed for his support out of the fund of the Zadaca.[230] To alleviate the distresses of the unfortunate as far as we can is our first duty as Men. To prevent a Yehudah from going to live among goyim at the poor house (which would be the case if the recommendations of your committee are not adopted) should be the first duty of The Trustees of this congregation

Mr. B. Hart[231] moved & seconded by B. Seixas[232] that Thirty pounds p. annum be allowed him which was carried as follows, Benj. Seixas, Isaac Abrahams. Bernd Hart for and Naph. Judah against it.

Resolved that Mrs Rachel Hays[233] and Mr. Solomons[234] be allow'd at the same rate for the two & Mr Hays boarded with them, first deducting all moneys they have already received on that account and Mr Solomon's Shool bill.

222. AARON LEVY[235] TO BENJAMIN PHILLIPS,[236] 1814[237]

[Benjamin Phillips, Esq.]

Dear Sir

I once spoke to you about poor old Mr Solomon[238] to move you to give him something out of the Charity box but I have not had the pleasure of seeing you since nor have I heard that he has got anything. I have now to inform you that I do not believe they has a spoon or a plate to eat with or off of and as the Hollidays are approaching I would wish you to give him a few dollars that he may buy some good victuals to eat during their continuance. If I was not convinced that they are in a state of the most abject distress and that they have scarcely had bread to eat during the winter I should not take the liberty to trouble you so much about this business but I do not believe there is a person in the Congregation or even in the City more deserving of your bounty than he is. He has received 50 weight of Passover Cakes.

I am yours &c   Aaron Levy

March 30th 1814

CXVII

Philanthropic Organizations,
1801-1820

Among the early philanthropic organizations that developed in the United States, at first to supplement and ultimately almost to supplant the synagogues as a vehicle of philanthropy, the best known were mutual aid societies of various sorts—loan societies, societies for the assistance of members in sickness, cooperative burial societies.[239] As time passed, however, and some members of the Jewish group achieved stability and even a surplus, organizations for direct aid in various contingencies came into being. One of the earliest of these was the Hebrew Orphan Society of Charleston; the Preamble to the constitution of this society is reproduced below. Again, philanthropic activity was regarded as a noble way for Jewish women to occupy their leisure. In Philadelphia, for example, the Female Hebrew Benevolent Society was organized in November, 1819, and the roster of its officers and "managers" reads like a "Who's Who in Philadelphia Jewry."[240] Extracts from the constitution and the first annual report of this society are also reprinted below.

223. CARING FOR ORPHANS, 1801 [241]

Whereas, at a meeting of Israelites held in Charleston on the 15th day of July, 1801, it was resolved that a Hebrew Society should be formed, for the purpose of relieving widows, educating, clothing and maintaining orphans and children of indigent parents; making it a particular care to inculcate strict principles of piety, morality and industry; and designing at the same time to cultivate any indications of genius they may evince for any of the arts or sciences, that they may thereby become qualified for the enjoyment of those blessings and advantages to which they are entitled, kind Heaven

having cast their lot in the United States of America, where freedom and equal rights, religious, civil and political, are liberally
extended to them, in common with every other class of citizens;
and where, no longer oppressed by the contracted policy and intolerant spirit which, before the happy dawn of liberty and philanthropy had circumscribed those natural rights granted by Almighty
God to the great family of mankind, they can and may freely
assume an equal station in this favored land with the cheering
conviction that their virtues and acquirements may lead them to
every honor and advantage their fellow citizens can attain.[242]

224. FEMALE BENEVOLENCE, 1820 [243]

Preamble, &c.

In all communities, the means of alleviating the sufferings of the
poor are considered of high importance by the benevolent and
humane. The ladies of the Hebrew Congregation of Philadelphia,
sensible to the calls which have occasionally been made in their
small society, and desirous of rendering themselves useful to their
indigent sisters of the house of Israel, agree to establish a charitable
Society; and in order to make the benefit permanent, adopt the
following

Constitution. . . .[244]

Article III. The Society shall be regulated by a Board, consisting
of thirteen Managers, to be annually elected by the Society; out
of which number shall be chosen a first and second Directress, a
Treasurer, and a Secretary. . . .

Article VI. All life subscriptions, legacies, and donations, exceeding ten dollars, shall be invested in some productive property, to
form a permanent fund, the interest arising from which shall be
added to the amount of annual collections for general expenditure.

Rules and Regulations
For the Government of the Female Hebrew
Benevolent Society of Philadelphia. . . .

Visiting Committee. A committee of Managers shall be appointed monthly, to investigate the situation of applicants, and

administer to their relief. They shall visit pensioners, make inquiries respecting their characters and conditions, and in all cases provide them with necessaries, rather than with money.

Pensioners. The pensioners of the Society shall be Israelites, residents of the city or county of Philadelphia, of good moral character. Assistance may also be given to sojourning Israelites, in clothing or small sums of money.

To educate the children of indigent families, will be a desirable object of the Society, when their funds will permit.[245]

The Board of Managers shall have power to fill all vacancies occasioned by the death or resignation of any of its members, and to make by-laws for their own regulation.

Report

In compliance with the fifth article of the Constitution, the Board of Managers of the Female Hebrew Benevolent Society, make their first report; and though they have rather to express anticipations of future usefulness than to record benefits already conferred, they hope enough has been done, to give assurance that the benevolent purposes of the Society will be fully answered when time shall mature their plans, and their funds become adequate.

From the organization of the Society in November until the present meeting, the Board have met once a fortnight, and every application for assistance has been attended to by the visiting committee. One or two cases may have been attended with disappointment to the applicants, as upon investigation it was thought necessary to reject one altogether, and to give but little to another. The Board would not trouble the society with these particulars, but they are desirous to explain the principles on which they act. The funds elicited by charity they consider a sacred trust, to be distributed only where the purposes of charity can be effected. They could not, consistently with this bestow upon the idle and improvident, although their poverty may excite to pity. An indigent family, who are frugal, industrious and grateful, have been assisted during the winter. They bless the Society for many comforts, which had else been strangers to their dreary habitation.

It is to modest worth, pining in obscurity; to the indigent who are "ashamed to beg;" to the sick, and to the infirm that the assistance of this society will be most freely given. And that every delicacy may be secured to those who have "seen better days," a select committee will be formed at the next session, through whose hands relief may be secretly bestowed on reduced families, should such unhappily be found in our congregation.

The Board, likewise desirous of establishing a reciprocal service to the industrious, and the infirm, propose that persons willing to attend on the sick or to assist in performing the last charitable offices for the deceased, should leave their names, with the president of the society; [246] that when occasions among our poor occur, they may be called on and remunerated by the Society. Females who wish employment as seamstresses, and those who want them, may also make application to the president, who will keep a register for the accommodation. The Board have the pleasure to state, they have received, and accepted the offer of professional services from Drs. Phillips [247] and Hays,[248] for the sick among their pensioners, and also the use of the Hebras' contributions to the city and Northern Liberties dispensaries. They have expended by the visiting committee forty-one dollars and thirty cents, and deposited in the savings bank three hundred dollars until a purchase of United States six per cent. stock can be made on favourable terms; reserving at the disposal of the Board, fifty-four dollars and seventy cents, for present purposes.

In making this first communication to their patrons the Board are duly impressed with the importance of the trust reposed in them; and feeling the deepest interest in the success of the Institution, they pray that the God of Israel may give them understanding equal to their zeal, so to conduct its concerns as to benefit the distressed and do credit to those who have "stretched forth their hands to the poor and needy."

CXVIII

The Spirit of Philanthropy, 1830

When Dr. Daniel L. M. Peixotto [249] spoke at the celebration of
the anniversary of the founding of the Society for the Education of
Orphan Children and the Relief of Indigent Persons of the Jewish
Persuasion,[250] in New York in 1830, he soon rose beyond specific
matters to discuss the pervasive spirit of philanthropy in the early
nineteenth century. He illustrated this pervasiveness by referring
to the number of societies to meet every human need and purpose
that were being formed. Indeed, it is true that the multiplicity of
Jewish philanthropic societies reflected a widespread pattern of
voluntary organization in American life as well as a continuation
of a deep-rooted tradition of Jewish communities all over the world.
Peixotto, an ardent Jacksonian,[251] influenced deeply by the Jacksonian demands for freedom from interference,[252] also spoke of the
danger that these many societies would go too far in attempting
to reform their fellowmen.

Jewish philanthropic labors, he pointed out, are founded not
only on the spirit of the age but also on the Scriptures. The limited
objects of Jewish societies are not due to illiberality but to the
practical and particular considerations of where the responsibilities
and capacities of the Jewish groups can best be utilized. The
selection reprinted below may be regarded as a typical expression
of the religious and philosophic considerations that lay behind
Jewish philanthropy in the early national period.

225. A PHYSICIAN ON PHILANTHROPY, 1830 [253]

The objects of this Society are twofold: the diffusion of knowledge,
and the dispensation of charity among the ignorant and the indigent of the House of Israel. These objects, it will be perceived,
are in strict accordance with the spirit of the numerous societies
instituted for benevolent purposes, which are, at once, the boast

and the pride, at the present day, of every civilized country.

The age in which we live may be emphatically termed the age of benevolence. Not all the useful discoveries, the rare and splendid inventions, which have been brought to light by the "spirit of improvement that is abroad upon the earth;" not all the vast accessions which have been made to the physical and intellectual resources of men, giving him a dominion over the powers of nature, and furnishing him with innumerable comforts and luxuries of which his ancestors could scarcely form a conception; not the rapid communication and extensive diffusion of knowledge, by means of the press and the wonderfully increased facilities of [intercourse] between the most remote countries of the earth; nor even the glorious reformation which has been achieved and is still being achieved in the civil and political constitution of most nations; not all these honourable and gratifying evidences as they are of the progressive career of our race are so characteristic of the spirit of this enlightened age, as its grand designs and unbounded plans of philanthropy. There is scarcely a civilized country in which there are not to be found associations, instituted for the benign objects of relieving the distresses of the needy, enlightening the ignorance of the uneducated, and redeeming the idle and the vicious from the grasp of crime and degradation. Neither confined in its reach, nor stinted in its bounty, the benevolence of our times is not satisfied with doing good at home, but often goes abroad in quest of objects, among whom it may scatter the profusion of its kindness, and dispense the blessings of its sympathy. The numerous societies for the relief of the poor, the destitute sick, the orphan, the widow, and the aged; the humane societies for the recovery of persons suddenly and incidentally deprived of life; those for the education of the deaf, and the blind; the mechanics' societies and institutes; the societies for the diffusion of useful knowledge; the Philhellene, Colonization, and Manumission, the Sunday School, Tract and Bible societies, are all of them fruits of the benevolent spirit which so peculiarly illustrates the character of the present century. I am aware that to the objects of some of the associations which I have enumerated, there will be many, very many, found totally indifferent, if not hostile; that, with the peculiar sectarian feelings and opinions sought to be propagated by some of them, few will feel any congenial sympathy; and that the overabundant zeal, so often displayed by their founders and friends, will be condemned by all liberal and humane minds, whenever it is carried to the extent of an officious interference with the conduct, and an arrogant condemnation of the sentiments of their fellow-men who differ from them, and who, alike with themselves, are dependent upon the gracious mercies of a just but forgiving Creator. Censure equally awaits those designing men, who, availing themselves of the appeal to popular favour afforded by an ambitious display of strained virtue and overwrought piety, seek access thereby to the highest honours and the most ready fortunes. But while we may differ about the value of the objects of particular institutions; while we condemn the coercive, inquisitorial, and invidious measures too often pursued by their overzealous promoters, and frown indignantly upon the hypocrisy, selfishness, and cunning, that would convert them into engines of personal aggrandizement, we must, nevertheless, accord the cheerful testimony of our approbation to the disinterested zeal, the exemplary self-devotion, the willing and immeasurable sacrifices so frequently exhibited in their cause. In the indulgence of these exalted feelings, the refined and the high-born, and even the more delicate sex, do not disdain to thread the filthy alleys of the crowded city, to enter the miserable and noisome hovels of the wretched poor, and minister to their present wants and permanent happiness. To gratify this noble ardour in the cause of humanity, the acute statesman and the polished scholar exercise their talents and task their scientific ingenuity that they may open up and render familiar to the lower classes the avenues to knowledge and moral improvement. Actuated thus, the missionary quits the dear scenes of his home, resigns, without a murmur, the comforts and blandishments of civilised life and the charms of intellectual society, and braving the dangers of the seas, roams to far distant and untrodden lands, to diffuse the blessings of knowledge and religion among the untutored sons of the forest, the jungle, or the desert.

Imbibing this spirit, in its most active influences, from the great Law which was announced to them, amidst the awful thunders of Sinai, by the Creator Himself, the Israelites have never been found wanting in yielding their ready assistance to promote and extend its operations. It may, however, be urged against them, that their benevolence is confined in its exertions to themselves; and the very title of this Society would seem to lend countenance to the charge. It is not, however, founded in fact. The ear of the Israelite can never be deaf to the cry of the sufferer; his heart can never refuse to sympathise with the distresses of his fellow-man; nor can his door ever be closed to the hospitable reception of the destitute, whatever be their creed, origin, or complexion. The first law impressed on his heart, and engraved upon his memory, by his religious teacher, is to love his neighbour as himself, and not to afflict the stranger that is within his gates.

If it then be asked, why are the objects of *this* Society limited? The answer is ready: Not from any illiberality of feeling have the founders of this institution circumscribed the sphere of their exertions, but from an honest conviction that charity, to be efficient, must be limited to a definite number of objects, and of those objects only with whose peculiar claims and wants it is best acquainted. An indiscriminate and vague dispensation of relief is ever destructive of its own end. It is a received law in moral and political economy, that the first duty which a citizen owes to the community of which he is a member, is to provide for his own wants; in other words, to prevent those wants from becoming a burden to the public. After these wants are satisfied; after this first duty has been discharged, then it will be time to assume new responsibilities and charges. Now, the same rule which applies to individuals will also apply to *associations* of individuals, or to sections of the community. *Their* first duty is to protect their own body from suffering; and, if they succeed in doing this, if they subtract all the evil that falls within their own immediate sphere from the general charge, they will, in reality, do more to contribute to the public good, than if they were, with utopian zeal, to attempt to grasp the universe in their ideal benevolence. The proudest *badge* of any sect is, and should be, that none of its members are dependants on the public eleemosynary institutions. Not then, I repeat it, from illiberality does the limitation of our benevolence proceed; but from a sincere desire of rendering that good which is in our power, efficient and conducive to the general weal. It is not in the United States of America that a Jew can cherish illiberality. It is not in the land where the very term toleration is exploded, and which acknowledges him as equal of his fellow-creature man, that the Jew can regard that fellow-creature with indifference, or a contracted spirit.

Notes

The following abbreviations have been used throughout the notes.

A.J.A.	American Jewish Archives, Cincinnati, Ohio
A.J.H.S.	American Jewish Historical Society, New York
DAB	*Dictionary of American Biography*
Elzas, *JSC*	Barnett A. Elzas, *The Jews of South Carolina*, Philadelphia, 1905
Executive Journal	*Journal of the Executive Proceedings of the Senate*, Washington, 1828
Ezekiel and Lichtenstein	H. T. Ezekiel and G. Lichtenstein, *The History of the Jews of Richmond, 1769–1917*, Richmond, Va., 1917
Goldberg, *Major Noah*	Isaac Goldberg, *Major Noah: American-Jewish Pioneer*, Philadelphia, 1936
JE	*Jewish Encyclopedia*
Makover, *Noah*	Abraham B. Makover, *Mordecai M. Noah: His Life and Work from the Jewish Viewpoint*, New York, 1917
Odell, *Annals*	G. C. D. Odell, *Annals of the New York Stage*, New York, 1927–1949
PAJHS	*Publications of the American Jewish Historical Society*
Phillipson, *Letters*	David Phillipson, ed., *Letters of Rebecca Gratz*, Philadelphia, 1929
Pool, *Old Faith*	David and Tamar de Sola Pool, *An Old Faith in the New World*, New York, 1955
Pool, *Portraits*	David de Sola Pool, *Portraits Etched in Stone*, New York, 1952
Reznikoff	Charles Reznikoff with the collaboration of Uriah Engleman, *The Jews of Charleston*, Philadelphia, 1950
Schappes	Morris U. Schappes, *Documentary History of the Jews in the United States*, New York, 1952
Stern	Malcolm Stern, *Americans of Jewish Descent*, Cincinnati, 1960
W. & W.	Edwin Wolf, 2d, and Maxwell Whiteman, *The History of the Jews of Philadelphia*, Philadelphia, 1956

Notes

Part Four. The First Jews in American Politics

1. The Treaty of Peace between the United States and Great Britain, ending the Revolutionary War, was signed at Paris, Sept. 3, 1783, by David Hartley, John Adams, Benjamin Franklin, and John Jay. It was ratified by Congress on Jan. 14, 1784 and proclaimed on the same day. For text, see Hunter Miller, *Treaties and Other International Acts of the United States, 1783–1855* (6 vols., Washington, 1931–42), II, 151–57; for discussion of the international implications of the Treaty of 1783, see Samuel F. Bemis, *A Diplomatic History of the United States* (New York, 1936), pp. 45–64. See also Andrew C. McLaughlin, *The Confederation and the Constitution, 1783–1789* (New York and London, 1905), pp. 18–34.

2. During the diplomatic negotiations that accompanied the crisis between the United States and France, 1797–1801, unnamed French go-betweens, referred to only as "X," "Y," and "Z," proposed payments of a large bribe as a condition for settling issues. This proposal was indignantly turned down by the American commissioners and resented by the American public. For texts, see Herman V. Ames and John B. McMaster, eds., *The X.Y.Z. Letters* (Philadelphia, 1900); for discussion of the American mission to France, A. J. Beveridge, *Life of John Marshall* (Boston, 1916), II, 214–334. See also John S. Bassett, *The Federalist System, 1789–1801* (New York and London, 1906), pp. 226–37.

3. President John Adams acted as a moderating force to keep the United States from declaring war on France, despite the pressures of public opinion. However, an undeclared naval war was more or less halfheartedly waged on both sides, 1798–1800. The explosive situation was mitigated by the fact that Great Britain, which was then at war with France, was no less indifferent to American maritime rights than was France. See Gardner W. Allen, *Our Naval War with France* (New York, 1909), and U.S. Office of Naval Records and Library, *Naval Documents Related to the Quasi-War . . . February 1797–December 1801* (7 vols., Washington, 1935–38).

4. Benjamin S. Judah (died 1831) was the oldest of twelve children of Samuel and Jessy (Jonas) Judah. Samuel Judah died in 1781, at the age of 53, at which time all the children were in their nonage. Young Benjamin became the nominal head of the family. He had taken part in the Revolutionary War; after his return from action, he continued his father's interest in Philadelphia's Congregation Mikveh Israel. In 1783, Jessy Judah and her numerous brood returned to New York. Through

the rest of his life, Benjamin S. Judah was active in the affairs of Congregation Shearith Israel, despite a slight alienation over his sisters' seats in the women's gallery. For details see W. & W., *passim;* Pool, *Old Faith, passim;* and Pool, *Portraits,* pp. 392–94, and *passim. Census,* 1790, New York, p. 117, Dock Ward, records Benjamin S. Judah as head of a household consisting of 3 free white males over 16 years of age, 2 under 16, 7 free white females, and 2 slaves.

5. Benjamin Judah to Alexander Hamilton, London, Sept. 5, 1798; MS., Alexander Hamilton Papers, Library of Congress.

6. Jonathan Dayton (1760–1824), soldier and congressman, was Speaker of the House of Representatives in the Fifth Congress and later a member of the Senate from 1799 to 1805. *DAB,* VI, 166.

7. Judah was probably referring to Thomas Henderson (1743–1824), physician, soldier, and public servant, who served both in the New Jersey State Assembly and in the National Congress. See *DAB,* VIII, 532.

8. Philip Van Cortlandt (1749–1831), Revolutionary officer and Congressman, commissioned as brigadier-general in 1783. Elected to the House of Representatives in 1793, he retained this position for 16 years. *DAB,* XIX, 162–63.

9. Joseph Hart Myers was a son of Naphtali Hart Myers, Warden of the Great Synagogue in London and a prominent personage in Anglo-Jewish communal life. According to Cecil Roth, Joseph Hart Myers was "the first professing Jew to take a degree in the normal course of events at a British University." The degree was in medicine; the date was 1779; the university was Edinburgh. Roth, "The Jews in the English Universities," *Miscellanies* of the Jewish Historical Society of England, Part IV (1942), p. 108.

10. Ephraim Hart to Department of State, New York, Jan. 1, 1815; MS., RG 59, General Records, Department of State, Miscellaneous Letters, Jan.–March, 1815, National Archives. James Monroe was Secretary of State at this time.

11. Harriet Judith Hart, daughter of Ephraim and Frances (Noah) Hart of New York, married Benjamin Hart of Canada. See *PAJHS,* IV (1896), 217.

12. Benjamin Hart (1779–1855), son of Aaron Hart, was a wealthy Canadian colonist. See *PAJHS,* IV (1896), 217; *JE,* VI, 242.

13. Ephraim Hart (1747–1825), a wealthy stockbroker, served as State Senator in 1810. He was one of the organizers, in 1792, of the New York Stock Exchange. At the time of his death, he was a partner of John Jacob Astor. His services to Congregation Shearith Israel were numerous, and included its presidency in 1794. See Pool, *Old Faith, passim.* His wife, Frances (Noah) Hart, was a sister of Manuel Noah, and, therefore, aunt of Mordecai M. Noah. See Pool, *Portraits,* pp. 289–90. Ephraim Hart is listed as a householder in the South Ward of New York City in *Census,* 1790, New York, p. 131.

14. Samuel Myers, see Part Two, *passim*.

15. Samuel Myers to John Quincy Adams, Norfolk, Jan. 17, 1820; MS., RG 59, General Records, Department of State, Miscellaneous Letters, Jan., 1820, National Archives.

16. Samuel Myers to John Quincy Adams, Norfolk, Feb. 2, 1820; MS., RG 59, General Records, Department of State, Miscellaneous Letters, Feb.–March, 1820, National Archives.

17. Mordecai Myers (on whom see Part Three, note 67) seems most likely to be the "M. Myers" of this letter.

18. M. Myers to Department of State, New York, June 3, 1808; MS., RG 59, General Records, Department of State, Miscellaneous Letters, Jan.–June, 1808, National Archives.

19. Moses Myers, see Part Two, *passim*.

20. Richard Forrest, born in Maryland, was apparently employed in the Department of State as a clerk before adequate records of civil jobholders are available. As early as Dec. 22, 1809, he was nominated by President Madison for the United States consulship at Tunis; more than a year later, after grave and repeated consideration, this nomination was rejected by the Senate on the ground that it was not "expedient" for the United States to have a consul at Tunis. See *Executive Journal*, II, *passim*. Later, in 1816, Forrest was a clerk in the Department of State, employed in Washington at an annual salary of $1150. See *Register of Officers and Agents. . . . ,* p. 5.

21. Moses Myers to Richard Forrest, Norfolk, Dec. 23, 1817; MS., RG 59, General Records, Department of State, Miscellaneous Letters, Dec., 1817, National Archives.

22. Robert Montgomery, originally nominated as United States Consul at Alicant, Feb. 19, 1793, with confirmation Feb. 20, 1793, apparently held the same position till his death (1823 or early 1824) at which time he was replaced by his son, also named Robert Montgomery. *Executive Journal*, I, 130, 131; III, 366.

23. Haym M. Salomon (1785–1858) was the son of the Revolutionary patriot, Haym Salomon. Scattered references to his activities can be found in Goldstein, *A Century of Judaism in New York;* Pool, *Old Faith;* Grinstein; W. & W.; and *PAJHS*.

24. Henry Clay (1777–1852) was at this time Secretary of State in the administration of John Quincy Adams.

25. Haym M. Salomon to Henry Clay, New York, Jan. 26, 1827; MS., RG 59, General Records, Department of State, Miscellaneous Letters, Jan., 1827, National Archives.

26. Cortland Parker of New Jersey was nominated by President Monroe to be United States Consul in Curacao, March 1, 1819; the Senate confirmed this nomination, March 2, 1819. *Executive Journal*, III, 180.

27. See this Part, Documents 119, 120.

28. For Isaac Harby, see Part Five, note 4.

29. Langdon Cheves (1776–1857), was a Democratic-Republican congressman from South Carolina, and one of the "War Hawks" before the War of 1812. In 1814–15, he was Speaker of the House of Representatives. Later, from 1819 to 1823, he was President of the Second Bank of the United States. *DAB, IV, 62.*

30. Isaac Harby to Langdon Cheves, Charleston, S.C., Feb. 8, 1815; MS., National Archives.

31. David Rogerson Williams (1776–1830), one of the pioneers in manufacturing in South Carolina, served as a Democrat from his state in Congress, 1805–9 and 1811–13. In 1814, he was elected Governor for a two year term. *DAB, XX, 253.*

32. For details of the appointment, presented from a strongly partisan, pro-Noah, and filio-pietistic position, see A. B. Makover, *Noah,* pp. 10 ff., and Goldberg, *Major Noah,* pp. 70–108. How far the situation had changed between 1809, when the Senate had found it not "expedient" to have a consul at Tunis (see this Part, note 20) and how far Tunis was regarded simply as an out-of-the-way spot for getting Mordecai Noah out of the way is a matter of doubt and guesswork.

33. Certainly, there are many documents of an official character bearing on Noah's financial mismanagement in the National Archives.

34. Naphtali Phillips (1773–1870) was Noah's uncle and political sponsor, as well as one of Noah's favorite correspondents. Letters to Phillips and extracts from other letters are printed in Goldberg, *Major Noah, passim.* Phillips also owned the *National Advocate,* and employed his nephew as its editor. For about thirty years, from 1822 to 1853, Phillips served in the Customs House, as appraiser and, later, inspector. He was active in the administration of Congregation Shearith Israel and was "repeatedly" its president. See Goldberg, *Major Noah, passim,* and Pool, *Old Faith, passim.*

35. Abraham A. Massias (1772–1848) of Charleston, S.C., began his military career in the New York militia. In 1802, he was commissioned as ensign; 1804, lieutenant; 1807, captain. In 1809, he resigned his New York commission to become a captain in the United States Army. He played a heroic role in the War of 1812, being promoted to his majority in 1814. At the end of the war, in 1815, he was discharged, but in 1820 he returned to military service as paymaster with the rank of major, and served until receiving his honorable discharge, Sept. 23, 1842. He was an active member of the Charleston Synagogue, to which he bequeathed $3,000 as residuary legatee in his will, probated in 1848. See *Universal Jewish Encyclopedia,* VII, 408; Heitman, *Historical Register . . . U.S. Army,* I, 696; Elzas, *JSC,* p. 195, n. 63; and Reznikoff, pp. 104, 286.

36. Stephen Pleasanton (not "Samuel") of Delaware was at this time a clerk in the Department of State. If salary is taken as the standard

of rank in the Department, he was the third ranking employee, topped
by James Monroe, the Secretary of State, and John Graham, Chief Clerk.
Pleasanton later moved into the Treasury Department where he had a
long career as Fifth Auditor. See *Register of Officers and Agents . . .
1816,* p. 5; see also Part Two, note 194.

37. James Monroe to Mordecai M. Noah, April 25, 1815, as printed
in Goldberg, *Major Noah,* pp. 111–12.

38. James Madison.

39. Isaac Harby to James Monroe, Charleston, S.C., May 13, 1816;
MS., RG 59, General Records, Department of State, National Archives.

40. *Correspondence and Documents Relative to the Attempt to
Negotiate for the Release of the American Captives at Algiers: including
remarks on that regency* (Washington City, 1816).

41. Richard R. Keene, a native of Maryland, had become a Spanish
citizen. Noah contracted for Keene to use his services as agent in the
ransoming of American sailors held by the Algerines. The text of the
agreement betwen Noah and Keene, Nov. 13, 1813, is given in full in
Goldberg, *Major Noah,* pp. 91–92. Some of Noah's difficulties stemmed
from his responsibility, as principal, for the expenditures of Keene as
agent. See Goldberg, *Major Noah,* pp. 92–95.

42. Richard B. Jonas, U.S. Consul at Tripoli, praised Noah's zeal and
firmness in defense of the rights of American citizens and asserted that
Noah "had reasoned wisely, and acted courageously." Andrew C. Gier-
lieu, Danish Consul-General to the Algerine states, wrote a personal
letter to Noah on his dismissal full of regrets and expressions of esteem.
See Makover, *Noah,* pp. 33–34.

43. Virgil, *Aeneid,* Book VI, lines 726–27. "A spirit from within sus-
tains; and mind, permeating the members, moves the whole mass, and
mingles with its mighty frame."

44. "Simple, at least, and single."

45. "The obnoxious letter of dismissal could not be removed from
the files of the State Department. 'Delays, red tape, and other causes
have prevented its removal even to this day,' wrote one of his biog-
raphers some years ago. But the letter is no longer in the official files
of the government, although this fact does not indicate necessarily, that
it was withdrawn. It merely indicates that the letter cannot be found, or
has been lost, but it may be properly said that it has mysteriously
disappeared." Makover, *Noah,* p. 34.

46. Naphtali Phillips to James Monroe, New York, Oct. 20, 1816;
MS., RG 59, General Records, Department of State, National Archives.

47. Congregation Shearith Israel.

48. On Dec. 30, 1816, Attorney General Richard Rush handed down
a long review of the Noah case which had been referred to him for
consideration. With the report, he sent a note (marked private) addressed to Mr. Monroe, explaining the length of his report: "You will

not, I hope, be alarmed at the apparent size of the paper I send in Mr Noah's case. As it presents several points, as it is possible that it may excite attention, and moreover as my convictions became more clear as I gave it a more critical examination, I thought that I would present the whole in the shape of an argumentative opinion, contrary to my usual and to what perhaps, in a general way, is the most proper course. The whole case is made up of so many parts as to fact, that I could not well be shorter, attempting to reason it at all." R. Rush to James Monroe, dated "Tuesday evening", MS., RG 59, General Records, Department of State, Miscellaneous Letters, Dec., 1816, National Archives. While Rush's opinion suggested that Noah may have been unwise, it certainly did not suggest that Noah's actions were in any way dishonest. As an immediate result of this vindication, Noah received the following letter from the Department of State: "Sir: Your account as Consul of the United States at Tunis has been adjusted at this Department, in conformity with the opinion of the Attorney General of the 30th December last, of which you have a copy; and a balance of Five Thousand Two Hundred and Sixteen Dollars Fifty-seven Cents, reported to be due you, will be paid to your order, at any time after Congress shall have made the necessary appropriation. A sum of One Thousand Six Hundred and Sixty-four Dollars, besides a charge of thirty-five per cent. loss on the disbursement of your agent at Algiers [Keene], is suspended, for reasons mentioned in the account of which you have been apprised." This letter, dated Jan. 14, 1817, was signed by S. Pleasanton. See Goldberg, *Major Noah*, pp. 125–28, and especially the text of the letter, p. 128.

49. A. A. Massias to Stephen Pleasanton, Savannah, Ga., Dec. 15, 1816; MS., RG 59, General Records, Department of State, National Archives.

50. Massias's claim against the government was for "various services performed by me (other than military) during the occupancy of East Florida by the Troops of the United States." This phrase is taken from the letter of Massias to James Monroe, Savannah, April 5, 1816; MS., RG 59, General Records, Department of State, National Archives. The State Department Archives contain a number of letters of various dates to Monroe and to Pleasanton pressing this claim.

51. The Governor of Georgia was territorial Commissioner for the United States in East Florida. In Jan., 1816, the Secretary of State had addressed to the Governor of Georgia a letter of inquiry relative to Massias's claim. Massias's reference here is to the reply to that letter of inquiry.

52. Massias's activities on behalf of the government did not meet with the immediate reward that he had anticipated. On Jan. 22, 1817, we find him again writing to Pleasanton—still miscalling him "Samuel" —"Five weeks has elapsed since I had the honor to address you & I am yet without your favor, when I last had the pleasure of an interview

with you, it was your request that I should interest myself in this matter, on the subject of Mr. N. affairs, and endeavour to do away *impressions,* this I have done, particularly as you said it would be agreeable to the Secry." A. A. Massias to Stephen Pleasanton, Savannah, Jan. 22, 1817; MS., RG 59, General Records, Department of State, Miscellaneous Letters, Jan.–Feb., 1817, National Archives.

53. The complicated interrelations of the Jews and the politicians in the matter of Noah's recall from his consulship were by no means completely ended by the machinations and vindications displayed in these documents and notes. In 1818, another phase of the story began with a demand from the Bey of Tunis for $1,000. rent for two years of the house that Noah had occupied while in Tunis. This bill was forwarded by Mr. Anderson, the Consul in Tunis to whom it was submitted, to the Department of State, now headed by John Quincy Adams; Adams sent the bill, under date of Feb. 20, 1818, to Noah. Noah's reply (M. M. Noah to John Quincy Adams, Albany, March 4, 1818, and subsequent letters; MSS., RG 59, General Records, Department of State, National Archives) suggests that the Bey was attempting a persecution of Noah; that enough property was left by Noah in the hands of a chargé d'affaires, Ambrose Allegro, to answer for all legitimate demands.

54. Nathan Levy, a resident of Maryland, and for many years United States Consul to the island of St. Thomas has left little personal trace on the record. Leon Hühner, "David L. Yulee, Florida's First Senator," *PAJHS,* XXV (1917), 2, suggests, on the basis of Committee Report no. 705, 24th Congress, First Session, vol. III, that Nathan Levy may have been related to Moses Elias Levy and David (Levy) Yulee, but this is not borne out by Malcolm Stern's genealogical researches. The most likely identification, on the basis of Stern, p. 109, is Nathan Levy (1759–1846), son of Benjamin Levy (1726–1802) and Rachel (Levy) Levy (1739–94), who were residents of Baltimore. In 1818, Nathan Levy was named U.S. Commercial Agent in St. Thomas; see Nathan Levy to John Quincy Adams, Baltimore, July 15, 1818; MS., RG 59, General Records, Department of State, Miscellaneous Letters, National Archives. By Dec. 23, 1818, Levy had been in St. Thomas for a month and submitted his first report (Nathan Levy to Secretary of State, St. Thomas, Dec. 28, 1818; MS., RG 59, General Records, Department of State, National Archives). His formal appointment as Consul seems to have come in 1826. Even after he had left the consulship, his troubles were not over. Lawsuits brought by shipowners were decided against him, and he had to petition Congress for payment of the damages assessed against him. In 1836, 1837, 1839, and 1840, the House Commerce Committee recommended that Levy be reimbursed on one of these accounts, and presented a resolution to that effect. The resolution apparently was not passed, since each year the identical report was made by the Commerce Committee; see *Reports of Committees,* no.

705, 24th Congress, First Session, vol. III; no. 87, 25th Congress, Second Session, vol. I; no. 238, 25th Congress, Third Session, vol. I; no. 72, 26th Congress, First Session, vol. I.

55. Joseph O'Reilly to John Quincy Adams, without place or date; MS., RG 59, General Records, Department of State, National Archives.

56. Robert Monroe Harrison of Virginia had served in the United States Navy during the Quasi-Naval War. He was promoted to a lieutenancy, Oct. 14, 1799, and was discharged July 8, 1801 under the Peach Establishment Act. Callahan, *List . . . Navy*, p. 249. In 1816, he was named Consul at the island of St. Thomas (*Executive Journal U.S. Senate*, III, 29, 31); in 1821, he was named Consul for the Island of St. Bartholomews (*Ibid.*, III, 257, 260); in 1823, named Consul for the Island of St. Christopher and Antigua (*Ibid.*, III, 337, 338); in 1827, back to the St. Bartholomews consulship (*Ibid.*, III, 573, 576); in 1831, he was named Consul at Kingston, Jamaica (*Ibid.*, IV, 146, 147, 151).

57. James H. McCulloch of Maryland named Collector of the Port of Baltimore on nomination of Thomas Jefferson, 1808 (*Executive Journal*, II, 79); again named by John Quincy Adams in 1825 (*Ibid.*, III, 463, 470); reappointed, Andrew Jackson, 1830 (*Ibid.*, IV, 63, 64) and 1834 (*Ibid.*, IV, 375, 378, 392).

58. Robert Monroe Harrison to James H. McCulloch, Saint Thomas, March 10, 1820; MS., RG 59, General Records, Department of State, National Archives.

59. A bribe.

60. Nathan Levy to Martin Van Buren, Saint Thomas, Nov. 29, 1830; MS., RG 59, General Records, Department of State, National Archives.

61. There is a very large number of letters from and about Levy to his State Department superiors in RG 59, General Records, Department of State, National Archives, dating from 1820 to 1834. A rapid and incomplete check has noted about forty items. Several of the letters, in addition to the one printed here, include Levy's replies to charges made against him. Had these charges been solidly grounded, it is hard to believe that Levy would have remained so long in his consular post. The official records reveal no ground for the volume of protest except Levy's insistence on the letter of the law. Representative of the rigor of his approach is Levy's letter of April 12, 1827, to Henry Clay, then Secretary of State: "Every possible avenue have I pursued to obtain some restraint, over the conduct of the American Ship Master and Crew whilst in Port, respecting the former landing, discharging and leaving behind his seamen &c., the latter running away from there [sic] respective vessels, and falling ultimately on this consulate sick for support; some remedy is highly requisite to prevent such imposition on the liberality of the United States; and as far as I can possibly give check, my duty I presume imperatively calls on me to do so. The register &c. heretofore dwelt too much on by self, still is with-held, the plea for so

doing, that the security to the Customs for duties &c. would be weakened if relinquished, is one that looses by consideration. This Port is so fortified by four several Batteries that the movement of a vessel could be frustrated at any moment, especially if under way, either by day or night, the winds most prevalent here, are Easterly, to proceed to sea, a Southerly direction must be pursued by all vessels, a merchant vessel frequently requires from ¾ to an hour before she is without the range of Cannon shot, therefore could not escape without conforming to the municipal laws, of the place, independent thereof the Register would be holden by your Consul untill a clearance was exhibited from the Customs in accordance to the laws of the U.S. If, Sir, an opinion was permitted me to express without possessing proof sufficient to substantiate the fact, I should say, The nefarious proceedings allowed and carried on here, under the American flag with or without papers to designate a nationality, makes it a solicitous policy with the authorities to keep your Consul hoodwinked, this, Sir, is the clue which with all due respect, I submit to your reflection to pursue; the accompanying copies of a letter to His Excellency the Governor from me, and his reply thereto will fully elucidate my intention to guard if possible, the trust placed within my control. It is not agreeable to be reminding Government so frequently of my official grievances and complaints. . . . It only requires the interference of the Honorable Secretary to alter things for the better" (RG 59, General Records, Department of State, National Archives).

62. Morris Goldsmith, a member of Congregation Beth Elohim and of a Masonic lodge in Charleston, was made Deputy United States Marshal in 1819. He was one of the organizers of the Reformed Society of Israelites when that group broke away from the parent congregation and he served as Secretary of the Reformed Society in 1825–26. He was the compiler of the *Charleston Directory for 1831*, which lends added interest to the account of the Reformed Society of Israelites that appeared in that volume. See Elzas, *JSC, passim,* and Reznikoff, *passim.*

63. John Drayton (1766–1822) was twice (1800 and 1808) elected Governor of South Carolina, on each occasion for a two-year term. In 1812, President James Madison appointed Drayton judge of the United States Court for the District of South Carolina; in this judicial position Drayton served until his death. *DAB,* V, 444.

64. Charles Pinckney (1757–1824), a prominent political leader in South Carolina, twice elected to the General Assembly of the State, governor, member of State assembly, and United States minister to Spain, was at this time an elected representative from the state of South Carolina to the House of Representatives. See *DAB,* XIV, 611.

65. John Drayton to Charles Pinckney, Charleston, Jan. 28, 1820; MS., RG 59, General Records, Department of State, National Archives.

66. The enclosed petition reads, in part, as follows:

"To the Honorable The Judges of the Circuit Court of the United States for the District of South Carolina

"The Petition of Morris Goldsmith Respectfully Shewith That Your petetioner in January last was Ordered to Execute a Bench Warrant against Sundry persons charged with Piracy being part of the Crew of the Ship Louisa. That your Petetioner employed some persons to aid him in the Execution thereof and paid them together with Contingent Expenses attending said duty $30.$\frac{50}{100}$ That at the last Special Court Your Honors was pleased to Certify the Account and it was transmitted to the Secretary of State, but Your Petetioner has heard nothing more of the same, That Your Petetioner after Six Nights & Days labour, Succeded in Arresting Eleven of the Crew, That in the Month of August last Your Petetioner was again Ordered to Execute a Bench Warrant against certain Persons charged with Murder & Piracy. That Your Petetioner was thirteen Nights engaged in Searching for and Arresting the said Pirates That he Succeded in arresting Nine of them, That from the Exertion used by Your Petetioner in the discharge of that duty he got the Feaver, and was Confined to his bed upwards of a Week in addition to incurring the Expence of Medical assistance For which Service (without which most probably the Criminals would have escaped) Your Petitioner receives no Remuneration" (Petition of Morris Goldsmith, 1820; MS., RG 59, General Records, Department of State, National Archives).

67. William Johnson (1771–1834) of Charleston, was appointed by Thomas Jefferson, in 1804, to the position of Associate Justice of the Supreme Court of the United States. Despite the Republican auspices under which Johnson reached the highest bench, his record as a judge reveals mildly Federalist leanings. Johnson sat on many cases in the United States Circuit Court for South Carolina. See *DAB*, X, 128.

68. Charles Pinckney to James Monroe, without place, March 16, 1820; MS., National Archives.

69. Petition of Morris Goldsmith to the Secretary of the Treasury, 1834; MS., RG 217, Records of General Accounting Office, National Archives.

70. Morton A. Waring, of Charleston, nominated in 1811 to be Commissioner of Loans for the State of South Carolina (*Executive Journal*, II, 194); in 1813, named as Marshal of the same State (*Ibid.*, II, 347, 348); reappointed 1817 (*Ibid.*, III, 96, 98); in 1821 (*Ibid.*, III, 258, 264); in 1825 (*Ibid.*, III, 448, 457); in 1829 (*Ibid.*, IV, 29); his long term ended in 1832.

71. Thomas Parker of South Carolina was named by George Washington, in 1792, to be Attorney for the United States in the South Carolina District (*Executive Journal*, I, 126); in 1812, made Judge of the District of South Carolina (*Ibid.*, II, 235, 237). Yet in 1816 his name appears (in *Official Register*) as Attorney in South Carolina District.

72. John Cadsden of South Carolina was nominated by James Monroe in 1821 to be Attorney of the United States for the District of South Carolina, "vice Thomas Parker deceased"; he was renamed in 1825 and 1829, and died in 1831. *Executive Journal*, III, 236, 240, 401, 405, 624, 629

73. T. P. Devereaux of Raleigh, N.C., was nominated by James Monroe in 1821 to be Attorney of the United States for the District of North Carolina; he was reappointed at four-year intervals until after the period covered in this volume. *Executive Journal*, III, 257, 270; IV, 67, 69, 77, 343; V, 87, 90.

74. Thomas D. Condy of Charleston was nominated as Marshal of the United States for the District of South Carolina by Andrew Jackson in 1832 and reappointed at four-year intervals until after the period covered in this work. *Executive Journal*, IV, 288, 289, 580, 596; V, 316, 317, 326; VI, 363, 380.

75. James R. Pringle of South Carolina was named Collector of the Port for the District of Charleston in 1820; he was consistently re-nominated to that office until, in 1840, he was appointed to the newly-created post of "receiver-general of public money" for Charleston district. *Executive Journal*, III, 186, 188; V, 299.

76. Thomas Hall Jervey of South Carolina was named by James Madison in 1813 to the post of Surveyor and Inspector of the Revenue for the Port of Charleston, remaining in that position until his death in 1846. *Executive Journal*, II, 464, 466; VII, 53.

77. A bill was reported to Congress compensating Goldsmith and others for services rendered to the United States in arresting certain pirates. This does not seem to be related to the incidents in the document above, nor does it appear connected with the incident reported in the petition in note 66 above. See "Report on the Petition of Morris Goldsmith and Others," March 22, 1824; *Reports of Committees*, no. 91, 18th Congress, First Session, vol. II.

78. See Part One, Documents 43–47.

79. Henry H. Myers (1801–22) was born at Norfolk; he was the son of Moses and Elizah (Judah) Myers. "The place of my nativity is Norfolk in Virginia born on the 5th December 1801," he wrote in a letter to Smith Thompson, dated at Richmond, Sept. 19, 1821 (MS., RG 45, Records of the Department of Navy, National Archives), enclosing his sworn oath of allegiance. This letter acknowledged Myers's receipt of his warrant as midshipman in the U.S. Navy, dated more than two years earlier, April 1, 1819! Myers had been assigned to a ship in 1819, and he had been on a cruise for the intervening two-year period. It must have been very soon after his return that he wrote the letter printed as Document 135 to Smith Thompson. Unfortunately, young Myers did not live long to enjoy his naval career. Less than a year after the receipt of his warrant, Myers died. The Master of the U.S.S. *Hornet* (signature

illegible; Robert Henley was Master Commandant of the *Hornet* in
1822) wrote to Smith Thompson from Hampton Roads, Va., on Aug.
11, 1822, reporting on the voyage of his ship from the Caribbean, a
voyage on which a number of members of the crew came down with
yellow fever. The only fatal case, after a five-day illness, was Henry H.
Myers, midshipman, for whose character and devotion his commanding
officer had words of high praise (MS., RG 45, Records of the Department of Navy, National Archives).

80. Smith Thompson (1768–1843) was appointed Secretary of the
Navy by President James Monroe, Nov., 1819, and served in that position
until August, 1823. See *DAB*, XVIII, 471.

81. Henry H. Myers to Smith Thompson, Norfolk, Aug. 20, 1821;
MS., RG 45, Records of Department of Navy, National Archives.

82. Abraham B. Nones (1794–1835) was one of fourteen children
of that remarkable Philadelphia patriot, Benjamin Nones (1757–1826)
and his wife Miriam Marks (1764–1822). On Benjamin Nones, and to a
lesser extent on his sons, see W. & W., *passim*. David B. Nones (1783–
1837), the oldest son, apparently followed his father in business and
in Pennsylvania politics. Three of the sons served in the consular agencies
of the United States: Solomon B. Nones (1787–1819) was appointed
by Thomas Jefferson as consul-general of the United States in Portugal;
Aaron B. Nones (born 1798) was United States consul at Aux Cayes,
Haiti, from 1820 to 1822; and Abraham B. (1794–1835), who had
served in the First Pennsylvania Volunteer Infantry during the War of
1812, later was United States consul-general to the province of Zulia
in Venezuela, with headquarters in Maracaibo. Two other sons served
in the naval forces of the United States: Joseph B. Nones (1797–1887)
was appointed Midshipman at the age of 17; he resigned his commission in 1821 in order to devote himself to studying methods of food
concentration and preservation, primarily for naval use; on his work,
see Abram Kanof and David Markowitz, "Joseph B. Nones: the Affable
Midshipman," *PAJHS*, XLVI (1956), 1–19, and the documents there
presented. Henry B. Nones (1804–68) also served in the United States
Navy, beginning in 1831, and rising to the rank of captain. There is
scattered information on the family in the *Jewish Encyclopedia*, with an
incomplete genealogical tree, and in the *Universal Jewish Encyclopedia*.
See also Schappes, pp. 92 ff., 581, 583, and Stern, p. 168.

83. See this Part, Document 131.

84. Simon Bolivar (1783–1830) led the revolutionary armies of
South America against the forces of Spain. See Lippincott's *Universal
Pronouncing Dictionary of Biography*, pp. 413–14.

85. Abraham B. Nones to Henry Clay, Maracaibo, Venezuela, June
24, 1825; MS., RG 59, General Records, Department of State, National
Archives.

86. Abraham B. Nones to Henry Clay, Maracaibo, Venezuela, Dec.

31, 1827; MS., RG 59, General Records, Department of State, National Archives.

87. Simon Bolivar.

88. For Noah, see this Part, Documents 141 and 142.

89. For Harby, see this Part, Document 124.

90. Wilson Lumpkin (1783–1870) was Governor of Georgia for two consecutive terms, 1831–35. *DAB*, XI, 503.

91. Benjamin Sheftall to Wilson Lumpkin, Feb., 1833; MS., State Department of Archives and History, Atlanta, Ga.; typescript copy from A.J.A.

92. James B. Lewis was a delegate from Hancock, Ga., at the Great Anti-Tariff Convention in Baldwin, Nov. 12, 1832; see Knight, *Georgia's Landmarks*, II, 559.

93. Bancroft's *Census of Savannah*, 1848, p. 42, lists "Elisha Wylly, Tax Collector" as one of the "County officers residing in Savannah."

94. In 1848, according to Bancroft's *Census of Savannah*, p. 41, William W. Oates was sheriff of the Superior Court of Chatham County.

95. William Davies, who with T. U. P. Charlton and Charles Harris, was appointed in 1823 to examine William Schley's Digest of the State laws and who was commissioned as Judge of the Superior Court in Georgia, Nov. 7, 1828. See Stephen F. Miller, *The Bench and Bar of Georgia* (Philadelphia, 1858), I, 46; II, 369.

96. De Witt Clinton (1769–1828), statesman and politician, as mayor of New York City and Governor of New York State was one of the more farseeing leaders of the first quarter of the nineteenth century. He ran into many partisan conflicts, many over the distribution of patronage. In spite of these conflicts, he was the major proponent of the Erie canal ("Clinton's ditch") and one of the chief advocates of public education in the history of New York. *DAB*, IV, 221.

97. William Harris Crawford (1772–1834), was, after 1820, one of the foremost aspirants to the presidency of the United States. His candidacy was warmly supported by the radical Democratic press, including such papers as the New York *Post* and the Albany *Argus*. See *DAB*, IV, 527.

98. Silvanus Miller was Surrogate of New York County for many years, beginning in 1801 when he succeeded David Gelston in that office. He was a member of the Clinton faction in the party squabbles of the period. See A. C. Flick and others, *History of the State of New York* (New York, 1934), VI, 44.

99. Henry Eckford (1775–1832) was a marine architect by profession; in the 1820s, he was keenly interested and deeply involved in New York Democratic politics. He invested in the *National Advocate,* so that, in Crawford's 1824 campaign for the presidency, Eckford controlled that paper. In 1826, when several major Tammany leaders were indicted for large scale swindles, Eckford was one of the accused. He was con-

victed but fled to the Orient and died in Syria. See *DAB*, VI, 4; also this Part, Document 142.

100. See note 99, and below, notes 138 and 139.

101. L. H. Clarke, *Report of the Trial of an Action on the Case brought by Silvanus Miller . . . against Mordecai M. Noah . . . for an Alleged Libel . . .* (New York, 1823), pp. 3–5; this is the text of Noah's letter as it was read in court.

102. See Part Five, note 23.

103. Charles Gilfert (1787–1829) was himself a musician and conductor. He ventured as a theatrical manager in Charleston and in New York. See Pinckney and Moise, *Selections from the Writings of Isaac Harby*, pp. 8, 251, 252; *National Cyclopedia of American Biography*, IX, 374; II, 441.

104. "Equal in nobility of the brothers."

105. Clarke, *Report of the Trial . . . brought by Silvanus Miller . . . against Mordecai M. Noah. . . . . ,* pp. 5–6; "Extract of a letter from the Editor of the National Advocate, dated Albany, Feb. 1, 1823," as read in the proceedings of the trial.

106. Clarke, *Report of the Trial . . . brought by Silvanus Miller . . . against Mordecai M. Noah . . . ,* pp. 20–22; Silvanus Miller's letter to the editor of the New York *Evening Post,* Jan. 29, 1821, as read into evidence at the trial.

107. Joseph George Holman, father of Agnes Holman, wife of Charles Gilfert; see this Part, note 103.

108. M. M. Noah, *A Statement of Facts Relative to the Conduct of Henry Eckford, Esq., as connected with the National Advocate* (New York, 1824), pp. 9–12.

109. That is, to swing far to the right in its political principles and support of Henry Clay for the presidency.

110. Churchill C. Cambreleng (1786–1862), member of Congress from New York, 1821–39. See *DAB*, III, 432.

111. Naphtali Phillips, Noah's uncle, and Noah's partner in the *National Advocate,* whose financial difficulties led to the whole search for new capital as a result of which the situation related in these documents developed.

112. Jonathan Thompson, in 1841, was president of the Manhattan Company, 23 Wall Street. *New York Business Directory,* 1841, p. 127.

113. There was a gold and silversmith of this name recorded by Longworth's *New York City Directory for 1797,* p. 307. It is conceivable that he or an heir of the same name had money to invest in a newspaper in the 1820s.

114. Matthew Livingston Davis (1773–1850), New York politician and journalist, was Aaron Burr's second in the duel against Hamilton. Davis was both then and later prominent in the Tammany Society, of which he was Grand Sachem in 1814 and 1815. He was acquitted (after

3 trials) when indicted, with others, in 1826, for swindles aggregating several million dollars. *DAB*, V, 138.

115. Jacob Barker (1779–1871) was, like Matthew Davis, a friend of Aaron Burr. He was "a leader of great influence in the political organization [Tammany Hall], and such a power in financial and business circles that at one time he defied the United States Bank." Gustavus Myers, *The History of Tammany Hall* (New York, 1901), p. 58. When a bill prohibiting private banking was passed in New York State, in 1818, Barker's power was so great that he gained an exemption for his bank, The Exchange Bank. This grant of special privilege was one of the elements that led to the sensational trials of 1826 (see this Part, note 114). Barker was convicted, but never went to prison; he went South and lived to be over 90. *National Cyclopedia of American Biography*, XI, 41; Lamb, *Biographical Dictionary of the United States*, I, 188 (which accounts for Barker's move to New Orleans as "owing to financial vicissitudes"); and *DAB*, I, 602.

116. Isaac Harby, "The Presidency, no. XI," reprinted from the Charleston *City Gazette*, 1824, in Pinckney and Moise, *A Selection from the Miscellaneous Writings of the Late Isaac Harby, Esq.* (Charleston, 1829), pp. 156–64.

117. That is, feudal estate.

118. General Jackson's letter dated, Hermitage, Nov. 4, 1823 (Harby's note).

119. "Divide and rule."

120. Niccolo Machiavelli (1469–1527), Italian political thinker and writer who raised certain characteristically modern questions in political theory. See John H. Whitfield, *Machiavelli* (Oxford, 1947).

121. The Boston *Palladium* (Harby's note).

122. The Boston *Daily Advertiser* (Harby's note).

123. Tacitus (54–119 A.D.), *Agricola*, 42. "It belongs to human nature to hate him whom you have injured."

124. Jean-Jacques Rousseau (1712–78), distinguished French philosopher of politics and education. See Ernst Cassirer, *The Question of Jean-Jacques Rousseau* (New York, 1954).

125. Fisher Ames (1758–1808) was one of the outstanding leaders of New England Federalism, a supporter of Alexander Hamilton, and an opponent of the democratic policies of Jefferson and Madison. In 1796, Ames retired from active life because of failing health; one of the fruits of this retirement was his essay on "The Dangers of American Liberty," 1805, giving expression to a theory that democracy is bound to lead to anarchy. *DAB*, I, 246.

126. The full passage from Fisher Ames's "Dangers of American Liberty," reads thus: "The most ferocious of animals when his passions are roused to fury and uncontrolled, is man: and of all governments, the worst is that which never fails to excite, but was never found to restrain

those passions, that is, democracy. It is an illuminated hell . . ." *Works of Fisher Ames,* compiled by a number of his friends (Boston, 1809), p. 432.

127. John Sheffield, Duke of Buckingham (1648–1721), English statesman and poet, patron of arts and literature. See *Encyclopaedia Britannica* (1951), IV, 318.

128. "By legal or illegal means."

129. Shakespeare, *King Henry IV,* Part I, Act I, scene iii, line 256.

130. Hotspur was the nickname of the younger Henry Percy, son of the Earl of Northumberland.

131. Jesse Benton, brother of Senator Thomas Hart Benton. In a tavern brawl, one of the Bentons fired a bullet that Andrew Jackson long carried within him.

132. From a pamphlet by Jesse Benton; see his *Address to the People of the United States on the Presidential Election* (Nashville, Tenn., 1824). In a footnote, Harby reports that a "Letter from Tennessee, published in the 'Constitutional Whig,' (a Richmond paper) states that Mr. Benton once attempted the life of Gen. Jackson; and that he is generally regarded as a *maniac.* Whether before, or since the publication of his pamphlet, is immaterial." Pinckney and Moise, *Selections from Harby,* p. 161.

133. That is, Secretary of the Treasury, the post held by Crawford in the Monroe administration.

134. The "American System" was originally a term used by Henry Clay to describe the protectionist policies that he advocated, especially in his tariff speech of March 30–31, 1824; essentially it was a continuation of the Hamiltonian program of encouragement of home industry. Other collateral measures involved in Clay's program were the building of roads and canals and the distribution to the states of the proceeds from the sale of public lands. See *Dictionary of American History,* I, 65.

135. Shakespeare, *Julius Caesar,* Act III, scene ii, lines 60–62.

136. Shakespeare, *Coriolanus,* Act III, scene ii, lines 257–258.

137. William Lowndes (1782–1822) was the son, by a third wife, of Rawlins Lowndes (1721–1800), prominent South Carolina Anti-Federalist. *DAB,* XI, 473.

138. Shakespeare, *Julius Caesar,* Act III, scene i.

139. An approximately literal quotation of Virgil, *Aeneid,* Book I, line 604; "Justice, and a mind conscious of its own rightness."

140. Martin Van Buren (1782–1862), *DAB,* XIX, 152.

141. William L. Marcy (1786–1857), prominent lawyer and statesman, was thrice elected governor of New York State. Later Marcy served as Secretary of War under President James K. Polk, and Secretary of State under President Franklin Pierce. *DAB,* XII, 274.

142. Azariah C. Flagg (1790–1873), the editor of the Plattsburg (N.Y.) *Republican;* in 1823, as representative of Clinton County to the

New York State Legislature, he became a close associate of the members of the "Albany regency." *DAB*, VI, 447.

143. Silas Wright (1795–1847) led his constituents in northern New York State from Clintonian views through to extremely radical Jacksonianism. He served in the New York State Senate, 1824–27 and during this period was a member of the "Albany regency." Later, he became governor of New York State, serving until 1846, but failing in his bid for reelection. *DAB*, XX, 565.

144. Edwin Crosswell (1797–1871), editor and owner of the Catskill (N.Y.) *Recorder*, in 1824 was chosen state printer and, at the same time, editor of the official organ of the Democratic Party in the state, the Albany *Argus;* he was thus the mouthpiece of the "Albany regency." *DAB*, IV, 571.

145. There is good brief discussion of the "Albany regency" in Dixon Ryan Fox, *The Decline of Aristocracy in the Politics of New York* (New York, 1919), Chapter IX, especially pp. 281–85.

146. Duff Green (1791–1875) was printer to Congress, 1829–33; and a member of Jackson's "kitchen cabinet." From 1826, he was editor of the *U.S. Telegraph*, a Washington newspaper that was founded as an organ of Jackson and his partisans. In 1831, Green and the newspaper turned against Jackson, as a result of Calhoun's break with the president. The newspaper ceased publication in 1837. However, especially in the years from 1826 to 1831, Green's status as editor of the *U.S. Telegraph* made him one of the most influential leaders of the Democratic party. See *DAB*, VII, 540.

147. The New York *Morning Courier*, which merged in 1829 with the *Enquirer* under the new name of the New York *Courier and Enquirer,* was edited by James Watson Webb (1802–84). Webb was a political supporter of Henry Clay; see *DAB*, XIX, 574.

148. Duff Green to Mordecai M. Noah, Washington, April 21, 1829; MS., Duff Green Papers, Library of Congress. See also Green's letter to Noah dated at Washington, Aug. 20, 1829, in the same collection.

149. Samuel Swartwout (1783–1856), soldier, merchant, speculator, and politician, was appointed Collector of the Port of New York by President Jackson. At the same time, Noah was named as Surveyor of the Port. See *DAB*, XVIII, 238; see also Goldberg, *Major Noah*, pp. 228–31.

150. Duff Green to Mordecai M. Noah, Washington, March 24, 1830; MS., Duff Green Papers, Library of Congress.

151. This letter, a very rough draft, is endorsed on the margin "not sent." Duff Green apparently thought better of his impulse to reprove Noah for his too-ready acceptance of Webb.

152. M. M. Noah and Thomas Gill, *Prospectus of "The Evening Star"* (New York, 1833), pp. 7–14.

153. Chapman Levy (1787–1849) was a lawyer, admitted to the bar

in 1806; in 1812, he represented Kershaw in the South Carolina legislature, and, in 1818, served as State Senator; during the War of 1812, he served as a captain in the South Carolina militia; he was again elected to represent Kershaw in the state legislature from 1829 to 1833 and from 1836 to 1838. He was a member of the Nullification convention of 1832 where he took a strong Unionist position. Later, he removed to Mississippi, where he died in 1849. Elzas, *JSC*, p. 193 and *passim*. See also Schappes, p. 613, n. 2, and the literature there cited.

154. Joel Poinsett (1779–1851), diplomat and statesman, was leader of the Union Party in South Carolina from 1828. He retired in 1833, but in 1837 returned to public service when President Van Buren called him to become Secretary of War. *DAB*, XV, 30.

155. Chapman Levy wrote to Andrew Jackson, from Camden, South Carolina, [Dec. 3?], 1832, enclosing "the Resolutions pass'd by a portion of the Citizens of this District," and expressing his own gratification "in being the organ of this Communication, as it affords me the opportunity of expressing my personal respect and admiration for the high and important services you have rendered our Common Country in War and Peace." Levy's letter is clearly intended as a congratulatory message on Jackson's reelection; the reiterated emphasis on the patriotism of the people of the district is a mild hint that if the controversy over nullification arises, there will be a group of loyalists available (Letter in National Archives, Washington, D.C.).

156. In a letter, dated at Washington, Jan. 16, 1833, President Andrew Jackson wrote to Joel R. Poinsett about matters relating to the then-virulent Nullification movement in South Carolina. One paragraph refers to Chapman Levy: "I have recd several letters from Gentlemen in So Carolina, requesting to be furnished with the means of defence. Mr. I. Graham, an old revolutionary patriot, a Mr Harrison and Col Levy, I have requested Genl Blair to inform Col Levy to apply to you & I request that you will make it known confidentially that when necessary, you are authorised, & will furnish the necessary means of defence" (MS., Poinsett Papers, Historical Society of Pennsylvania).

157. Chapman Levy to Joel Poinsett, Camden, S.C., Dec. 22, 1832; MS., Poinsett Papers, Historical Society of Pennsylvania; from typescript copy in A.J.A.

158. The capital of South Carolina.

159. Samuel Maverick lived outside of the town of Pendleton. He was a lawyer who later moved his office to Texas, where his ignorance of range customs led to his name's being applied to unbranded cattle. See W.P.A., *Guide to South Carolina*, p. 444.

160. Chapman Levy to Joel Poinsett, Camden, S.C., Feb. 25, 1833; MS., Poinsett Papers, Historical Society of Pennsylvania; from typescript copy in A.J.A.

161. Francis Preston Blair (1791–1876), journalist and politician. An

ardent Jacksonian, his articles in the *Argus of Western America* after the election of 1828, attacking the Second Bank of the United States and the Nullification principle served as editorial answers to Langdon Cheves and George McDuffie on tariff and nullification questions. Jackson called Blair to Washington in 1831, after the President had broken with Calhoun and Duff Green. Blair now replaced Green in the "kitchen cabinet," and the Washington *Globe*, which Blair established in 1830, replaced Green's *U.S. Telegraph* as the foremost national Jacksonian newspaper. "Few men exerted a political power more potent than Blair through the *Globe* during 1832–41." *DAB*, II, 330.

162. George McDuffie (1790–1851) was a member of the House of Representatives, 1821–34; he became governor of South Carolina, and later one of its senators. He was a leading supporter of Calhoun, a nullifier, and an advocate of the rechartering of the Second Bank of the United States. *DAB*, XII, 34.

163. The beginning of Van Buren's administration coincided with the onset of the Panic of 1837; banks all over the country were closing their doors and their paper money issues were valueless. As the heir of Jackson's anti-bank policies, Van Buren advocated a hard money policy and an independent treasury system. Van Buren's Message of Sept. 4, 1837 (Richardson, *Messages and Papers of the Presidents*, III, 324) dealt courageously with the fiscal and financial problems of the times, but there was little improvement in general conditions and the Act of June 23, 1836, which forbade the government to use those banks that failed to redeem their notes in specie tied the hands of the administration. See Channing, *History of the U.S.*, VI, 460–63.

164. See this Part, Document 144.

165. Benjamin F. Hart may have been Secretary of the New York Stock Exchange in mid-nineteenth century. See Pool, *Old Faith*, p. 483.

166. Benjamin F. Hart to Martin Van Buren, New York, Sept. 6, 1837; MS., National Archives.

167. See, this Part, Document 150.

168. Chapman Levy to Martin Van Buren, Pickensville, Ala., Jan. 6, 1836; MS., National Archives.

169. Richard Irvine Manning (1789–1836) was governor of South Carolina, 1824–26. Later, he was elected by the Union Party to the U.S. House of Representatives, where he served from 1834 to 1836. *DAB*, XII, 251.

170. John F. H. Claiborne (1807–84), in 1835 was nominated for Congress by the first Democratic convention held in Mississippi and was elected by a large majority. *DAB*, IV, 112.

171. Chapman Levy to Joel Poinsett, Columbia, Miss., Nov. 8, 1838; MS., Poinsett Papers, Historical Society of Pennsylvania; from typescript copy in A.J.A.

172. Alexander G. McNutt (1802–48), after moving to Mississippi

from Virginia in his early twenties, practised law in Jackson and Vicksburg. In 1835 and 1837, he was a member of the State Senate; in 1837, its Speaker. From 1838 to 1842, he was Governor of Mississippi; in 1841, in part because of his activity, the University of Mississippi was established. See Mississippi Department of Archives and History, *Biographical Guide to the Mississippi Hall of Fame* (1935), p. 31. See also *William Johnson's Natchez. The Ante-Bellum Diary of a Free Negro.* W. R. Hogan and E. A. Davis, eds. (Baton Rouge, La., 1951), p. 239, n. 23.

173. Probably Joseph Holt (born 1807), originally of Kentucky, a protégé of Amos Kendall. Holt was a lawyer who gained national fame by his speech in favor of the nomination of Richard M. Johnson in the Democratic convention of 1836. Soon thereafter he removed to Mississippi, where he practised law and engaged in political activity for about 10 years before returning to Louisville, Ky. His later career on the national scene, carried him to high prominence. Dunbar Rowland, *Encyclopedia of Mississippi History* (Madison, Wis., 1907), I, 887–88.

174. Roger Barton (1802–55), lawyer originally of Tennessee, became a resident of Mississippi in 1836. In 1838, he was elected to the lower house of the state legislature, an honor repeated in 1849. See the sketch in Rowland, *Encyclopedia of Mississippi History*, I, 216–17.

175. James F. Trotter (1802–66) had represented Lowndes County, Miss. in the constitutional convention of 1832 and served as chairman of the general provisions committee. In Jan., 1838, he was appointed to fill out Judge Black's unexpired term in the U. S. Senate but resigned before taking his seat. Later in that same year, he accepted a judicial post in the Mississippi High Court of Errors and Appeals. Rowland, *Encyclopedia of Mississippi History*, II, 822.

176. A series of letters from Chapman Levy to Joel R. Poinsett, between 1837 and 1840, dated from Camden, S.C., Washington, D.C., and Columbus, Miss., tell the story of Levy's activity as an advance guard of the Democratic Party in Mississippi. In particular, there runs through the earlier of these letters Levy's effort to supply facts upon which a just settlement of a land case involving the Indians of the Mississippi area may be based. Later, as the election of 1840 approached, Levy became active in more directly political ways: "On Tuesday next the election comes on here for Senator of this County and if we loose it, the decided probability is that we will loose the Senator in Congress. There is an election also in Munroe for Representative & Golson is a candidate & I regret to Learn there is every probability of his loosing the election. The Whig which opposes him is an apostate from our party and an intimate acquaintance & I have some hopes that I may possibly bring him back to the fold—if he is elected. . . . If we loose this County and Munroe (which adjoins it) at this election we will recover it before the November elections. I have pledged myself to our friends

here to give them a week in the Spring for this county and Munroe. Do not then loose heart for Mississippi, for we will carry it at the next general election. . . . I shall proceed from there to Jackson to meet the Democratic Convention. It will be numerously attended. I propose to deliver a set speech there by Vote of the Convention, and as it will be listened to by both Parties I have great hopes to bring over several Whig members" (Letter of Dec. 30, 1838). The whole series of letters is to be found in the Poinsett Papers, Historical Society of Pennsylvania, typescript copies in the A.J.A.

177. No case exactly like the one described can be found either in the *Reports* of the Circuit Court or in those of the Supreme Court; there is, however, a similar case, hinging on the applicability of the Maryland law of 1796 in the District of Columbia, which may readily have been distorted by word of mouth transmission into the pattern Levy describes. The similar case, Fenwick *v.* Chapman, was decided in the January term, 1835, Justice Marshall's last term on the Supreme Court bench before his death; see 34 US (9 Peters) 461, affirming the decision of the Circuit Court, District of Columbia, 1834, 4 Cranch C C (f DC) 431, Fed Cas No 2, 604.

178. David Levy (1810–86), son of Moses Elias Levy, pioneer in territorial Florida, was later to convert to Christianity and to have his name legally changed (by the Florida legislature) to David L. Yulee, possibly an anagram of Levy, and to become Florida's first senator in a contested election. For discussion of his career, see L. Hühner, "David L. Yulee, Florida's First Senator," *PAJHS*, XXV (1917); Mills M. Lord, Jr., "David Levy Yulee: Statesman and Railroad Builder" (unpublished Master's Thesis, University of Florida); Arthur W. Thompson, "David Yulee: A Study of Nineteenth Century American Thought and Enterprise" (unpublished Doctoral Dissertation, Columbia University); and Samuel Proctor, "Pioneer Jewish Settlement in Florida, 1765–1900," *Proceedings* of the Conference on the Writing of Regional History in the South, with special emphasis on religious and cultural groups, convened by University of Miami, Historical Association of Southern Florida, and the American Jewish History Center of the Jewish Theological Seminary of America, Miami Beach, Feb. 15, 1956 (offset printing, 1956), pp. 85–97.

179. In spite of the fact that, e.g., St. Augustine was one of the earliest settlements in the New World.

180. Indeed, Moses Elias Levy, father of the writer of this memorandum, did his share of land speculation; see Part Two, Document 91.

181. D. Levy, "Remarks Concerning the Democratic Cause in Florida, Submitted to President Martin Van Buren," no place, no date; marked "[1839?]" by a later hand; MS., National Archives.

182. Yazoo claims, in Western Florida, Alabama and Mississippi, were to lands transferred fraudulently from public to private ownership. See Thomas Donaldson, *The Public Domain.* . . . (U.S. Government Print-

ing Office, Washington, 1884), especially pp. 83–85; Charles H. Haskins, "The Yazoo Land Companies," *Papers* of the American Historical Association, IV (1891), 395–437; Benjamin Horace Hibbard, *A History of the Public Land Policies* (New York, 1939), pp. 213–14.

183. Robert Hackley was Register of the Tallahassee land office, 1835–38. See Sidney W. Martin, *Florida During the Territorial Days* (Athens, Ga., 1944), p. 87; this may be the reference intended by Levy's comment.

Part Five. Stirrings of Cultural Activity

1. Jacob Newton Cardozo (1786–1873) had a distinguished career as journalist, political partisan of Unionism during the critical Nullification controversy in South Carolina, and finally as one of the most able of the early American economists of the classical liberal tradition. Interesting correspondence between Cardozo and Joel Poinsett, South Carolina Unionist, and Secretary of War in Van Buren's Cabinet may be found in The Historical Society of Pennsylvania. For a careful study of Cardozo's economic views, see Joseph Dorfman, *The Economic Mind in American Civilization* (New York, 1946), II, 852–62. See also Alexander Brody, "Jacob Newton Cardozo, American Economist," *Historia Judaica,* XV (1953), 135–66; Reznikoff, *passim.*

2. *An Oration on the Literary Character, Delivered on the Anniversary of the Methulogic Society, 1st October, 1811.* Published at their Request. By Jacob N. Cardozo. Charleston: Printed at Franklin-Head, No. 44, Broad-Street [1811].

3. *An Oration on the Literary Character* . . . , pp. 5–12.

4. Isaac Harby (1788–1828), journalist and playwright, was deeply involved in Charleston political life. He was one of the prime movers of the early and abortive reform movement among the Jews of Charleston. See *DAB,* VIII, 239; L. C. Moise, *Biography of Isaac Harby.* . . . (Columbia, S.C., 1931).

5. This essay originally appeared in the New York *Evening Post,* in the last year of Harby's life. It is reproduced in full in Henry L. Pinckney and Abraham Moise, *A Selection from the Miscellaneous Writings of the late Isaac Harby, Esqu.* . . . to which is prefixed a memoir of his life by Abraham Moise (Charleston, 1829), pp. 249–61.

6. See N. B. Fagin, "Isaac Harby and the Early American Theatre," *American Jewish Archives,* VIII (1956); Isaac Harby's published plays include *The Gordian Knot* (Charleston, 1810) and *Alberti, A Play in Five Acts* (Charleston, 1819).

7. Pinckney and Moise, *A Selection* . . . , pp. 253–57, 260–61.

8. Harby refers here to the general depression of the period following the War of 1812. For parallel references in an economic context, see Part Two.

9. The word is here used in its most general etymological sense, as equivalent to "the creative writer."

10. In the gladiatorial combats in the Roman amphitheatres, the victorious gladiator stood over his prostrate foe and looked to the imperial box for a signal. If, though defeated, the loser had shown courage, the emperor turned his thumbs upward, and the loser was granted life; if however, the emperor "turned thumbs down," the victor remorselessly slew the vanquished.

11. Harby may, perhaps, be using the term "Byronic" here as a general term for romantic verse; the fact that at other places he indicates specific disagreement with Byron would tend to suggest that this phrase is also used specifically. See Pinckney and Moise, *A Selection* . . . , p. 240, for Harby's defense of Napoleon against the adverse view presented in Byron's "Ode to Napoleon Buonaparte."

12. Samuel Foote (1720–77), actor and dramatist, particularly known for his satirical mimicry of famous personages of the day and for his dramatic comedies, also satiric, of which "The Minor" (1760), regarded as his best piece, satirized Whitefield and the Methodists. *Dictionary of National Biography*, VII, 370–75.

13. Alain Rene Lesage (1668–1747), French novelist and dramatist, noted as a satirist, whose comedy *Turcaret* ranks as one of the minor masterpieces of the eighteenth-century French stage.

14. William Dunlap (1766–1839), playwright, theatrical manager, painter, and historian. See *DAB*, V, 516.

15. Samuel Benjamin Helbert Judah (1804–76), playwright, grandson of Baruch Judah, and son of Benjamin S. Judah (1760–1831) and Eliza (Israel) Judah (1784–1860), was for a time the only Jewish lawyer practicing in New York City in the early years of the nineteenth century. He became a lawyer in 1825 and practiced law for the rest of his life with some success. His literary works include: *The Mountain Torrent* (1820); *The Rose of Arragon: or the Vigil of St. Mark* (1822); *Odafriede: The Outcast* (1822); *A Tale of Lexington* (1823); *Gotham and Gothamites* (1823), a crude and libelous satire directed against his literary contemporaries; *The Buccaneers: A Romance of Our Own Country* (1827); and *The Maid of Midian* (1833). See Kunitz and Haycraft, *American Authors, 1600–1900* (New York, 1938), p. 426 and the literature there cited; see also *DAB*, X, 228; Stern, p. 101, and G. C. D. Odell, *Annals*, II, 557.

16. For Noah's career as a playwright see Isaac Goldberg, *Major Noah*, pp. 164–88.

17. Jonas B. Phillips (1805–67) was the son of Benjamin I. Phillips of Philadelphia. A series of stories by Phillips that had been published in the *Saturday Evening Post* were collected in 1827 into a volume called *Tales for Leisure Hours*. His plays were moderately successful; see W. & W., *passim*.

18. Samuel B. H. Judah, *The Mountain Torrent, A Grand Melo-Drama, Interspersed with Songs, Choruses* (New York, 1820), Preface, pp. iii–v. The play was presented by Wallack and Cooper, March 1, 1820, as "their first dramatic novelty." Odell, *Annals*, II, 557.

19. Edmund Simpson (1784–1848), actor and theatrical manager. See Odell, *Annals*, II, *passim; DAB*, XVII, 177.

20. Robert Campbell Maywood, actor, created the role of Baron Trevasi in Judah's play. Odell, *Annals*, II, 557.

21. Ellen Johnson, actress, created the role of Viola in Judah's play. Odell, *Annals*, II, 557. She was widely and favorably known for her talents.

22. Mordecai M. Noah, *Marion; or, The Hero of Lake George: a Drama in Three Acts, Founded on Events of the Revolutionary War* (New York, 1822), pp. 3–4, 6. The first performance of what Odell calls "this important native work" took place at the New Theater in New York on Nov. 25, 1821. The New Theater was literally new at the time; it had opened its doors on Sept. 1, 1821. Messrs. Simpson and Maywood, who had played in Judah's *The Mountain Torrent,* were in the cast of Noah's play as Marion and Colonel Conway, respectively. They also appeared in all of Noah's other plays except *The Siege of Yorktown: She Would Be a Soldier* (1819), *The Wandering Boys* (1820), *The Siege of Tripoli* (1820), and *The Grecian Captive* (1822). Miss Ellen Johnson did not play in *Marion;* she did, however, appear in all other Noah plays. For fuller information see Odell, *Annals*, III, *passim;* and Goldberg, *Major Noah*, pp. 175–81, 281–84. Goldberg refers, p. 181, to the fact that "on April 22, 1932 . . . the students of Columbia University presented at the McMillin Academic Theater *Marion or the Hero of Lake George.*" One of the editors of this volume, who served as production manager for this relatively recent revival of Noah's play, recalls with joy the serious treatment given to this and other early American plays by Mrs. Estelle H. Davis (Coit), and her group of Columbia Laboratory Players.

23. William Coleman (1766–1829), physician and litterateur and Noah's journalistic rival, and after 1821, political opponent, had been editor and proprietor of the New York *Evening Post* since 1800. *DAB*, IV, 294. See Goldberg, *Major Noah*, pp. 177–79.

24. Coleman's criticism is reprinted as a footnote, *Marion,* pp. 4–5. "On Monday a new play called Marion was presented at our theatre, written by the renowned editor of The Advocate, (God bless us!) who with his usual modesty, and more than his usual gallentry, recommended that the soldiery should occupy the dress boxes, and drive the ladies up stairs to the second tier. I *was not* present, (I had been once before at the christening of one of his brats,) but *reports* unite in declaring it was the most wretched stuff that ever insulted an audience. [The italics in this sentence were probably introduced by Noah]. He tells us, this morn-

ing, since nobody else will tell it for him, that there were about 2436 persons present. It is probable there may have been that number; for, it would be strange, indeed, if there could not be found as many in this city, soldiers and all, who would *accept* of a ticket on a holiday night. [November 25 was celebrated as a holiday in New York City in memory of the British evacuation of the city; it was known as Evacuation Day. The italics in this sentence were probably introduced by Noah]. The crowd on a first night can be no test, but let him give it out again, and if he does not hear the second part of the same air which was played at the second representation of the Battle of Chippewa, he may bless his stars for his good luck. That's all."

Coleman had expressed himself much more favorably on at least one of Noah's earlier "brats," *The Siege of Tripoli*, in 1820, but that piece was written before the political falling out of the two gentlemen. Coleman's predictions of failure for *Marion* were not borne out; it was one of the most popular box office successes of the early American theater.

25. Sir Gilbert Blane (1749–1834), physician, wrote on many subjects. The essay referred to in the text is "Observations respecting Intermittent Fevers the cause of the sickness of the army in Walcheren . . . ," *Medico-Chirurgical Transactions*, VI (1815), later reprinted in Blane's *Select Dissertations on Medical Science, Collected* (London, 1827). See *Dictionary of National Biography*, II, 664–66.

26. Shakespeare, *Hamlet*, Act II, Scene 2, line 103.

27. Mordecai M. Noah, *The Grecian Captive, or The Fall of Athens* (New York, 1822), pp. iii–iv. The first performance of this play, June 17, 1822, was marked by unusual events, related by Goldberg, *Major Noah*, pp. 182–85; the play was written in blank verse and printed copies were distributed to the audience who tried to follow the lines as delivered by something less than letter-perfect actors. The fluttering of the pages disturbed not only the human actors, but also an elephant and a camel "procured, in a passion for more realism and for local color, from a nearby menagerie." Miss Ellen Johnson it was who, in the role of Zelia, the Grecian captive, rode the camel; Aaron Phillips (1792–1847), Mordecai Noah's uncle, whose career as an actor was long and somewhat distinguished, appeared in the role of Alexander, the Grecian general, and in the final scene came on "wiggling on the back of a real elephant." See *Thirty Years Passed Among the Players in England and America . . . Theatrical Life of Joe Cowell, Comedian. Written by Himself* (New York, 1844), Part II, chap. 3. Cowell appeared in this play as Roberto, a Greek. His report of the performance and especially of "an unexpected hydraulic experiment" performed by the unhousebroken elephant "to the great astonishment and discomfiture of the musicians" is vivid and, though angry, not without its humor.

In 1832, William Dunlap asked Mordecai M. Noah for an account of his career as a playwright. Noah's reply, in the form of an autobiographical letter dated at New York, July 11, 1832, was printed in William Dunlap, A *History of the American Theatre* (New York, 1832), pp. 38–84. Noah's tone in this letter is self-deprecatory—not, it is only fair to say, his most common vein—as the following account of "The Grecian Captive" reveals: "My next piece, I believe, was written for the benefit of a relative and friend, who wanted something to bring a house; and as the struggle for liberty in Greece was at that period the prevailing excitement, I finished the melo-drama of the Grecian Captive, which was brought out with all the advantages of good scenery and music. As a 'good house' was of more consequence to the actor than fame to the author, it was resolved that the hero of the piece should make his appearance on an elephant, and the heroine on a camel, which were procured from a neighbouring *menagerie,* and the *tout ensemble* was sufficiently imposing, only it happened that the huge elephant, in shaking his skin, so rocked the castle on his back, that the Grecian general nearly lost his balance, and was in imminent danger of coming down from his 'high estate,' to the infinite merriment of the audience. On this occasion, to use another significant phrase, a 'gag' was hit upon of a new character altogether. The play was printed, and each auditor was presented with a copy gratis, as he entered the house. Figure to yourself a thousand people in a theatre, each with a book of the play in his hand, imagine the turning over a thousand leaves simultaneously, the buzz and fluttering it produced, and you will readily believe that the actors entirely forgot their parts, and even the equanimity of the elephant and camel were essentially disturbed." The tone of this letter should be borne in mind as evidence that Noah did not lack the ability to laugh at himself, and, if this is so, he may have laughed even more at the many people who insisted upon taking him seriously.

28. The Greek revolution of the 1820s to achieve independence from Turkish rule won great sympathy among Americans of all shades of political opinion. The aid given by Americans was not inconsiderable, and it was deeply appreciated by the Greek people.

29. One of the historical figures in the Greek revolution; also a character in Noah's play, acted at the first performance by Mr. Pritchard. See Odell, *Annals,* III, 28. John Howard Payne (1791–1852), author of "Home Sweet Home," and dramatist-contemporary of Noah, also wrote a play on the Greek revolution with Ali Pacha as the title part, *Ali Pacha, or the Signet Ring.* Payne's mother, Sarah Isaacs, was the daughter of Aaron Isaacs of East Hampton, Long Island; see Part Eight, Document 208. See also Arthur Hobson Quinn, A *History of the American Drama from the Beginning to the Civil War* (New York, 1946), p. 177.

30. Jonas B. Phillips, *Camillus; or the Self-Exiled Patriot;* a tragedy in five acts (Philadelphia, 1833), "Preface," unpaged. Phillips was Mordecai M. Noah's cousin, and dedicated *Camillus* to him in these words:

"The interest you have ever manifested in the cause of the dramatic literature of our country, and the zeal with which your efforts have always been directed to its advancement, embolden me to dedicate to you my first attempt at tragedy.

"A stronger reason, however, exists, to justify the liberty I have taken, in placing, without permission, your name upon this page, and it is found in the recollection of the frequent manifestations of friendly regard I have experienced at your hands, and which I am gratified in having the opportunity, thus sincerely, however feebly, to acknowledge.

"With sentiments of esteem, allow me to subscribe myself, your grateful and attached friend, Jonas B. Phillips."

Noah was the son of Zipporah (Phillips) Noah; Jonas B. Phillips was the son of Zipporah Noah's brother, Benjamin I. Phillips.

31. H. G. Pearson, classic tragedian, was visiting star in Philadelphia at various times. See Arthur H. Wilson, *A History of the Philadelphia Theatre* (Philadelphia, 1935), pp. 100–1.

32. On the favorable reception of *Camillus,* see W. & W., p. 320.

33. William Jones, theatrical manager. See Reese D. James, *Old Drury of Philadelphia. A History of the Philadelphia Stage, 1800–1835* (Philadelphia, 1932), pp. 61–66; Odell, *Annals,* III, *passim.*

34. William Duffy, actor and theatrical manager, in Philadelphia after London and Dublin experience as early as 1811/12, when he acted at the Chestnut Theatre in the first American performance of "The Lady of the Lake." See James, *Old Drury of Philadelphia,* p. 17; Odell, *Annals,* III, 363.

35. William Forrest, actor, see Odell, *Annals,* III, *passim.*

36. The partnership of Jones, Duffy, and Forrest is referred to in James, *Old Drury of Philadelphia,* p. 61, quoting Charles Durang, annalist of the Philadelphia stage, as "the first legitimate American management in the large American cities." James also mentions, p. 64, that they were called "The Three Williamses," and that their management of the Arch Theatre, which they opened on Aug. 29, 1831, continued until the end of the season on June 18, 1832.

37. Miss Riddle, later Mrs. W. H. Smith, was a popular actress of the time; she played for several consecutive months in the autumn of 1825 in Chatham Gardens, New York. See Odell, *Annals,* III, 302.

38. Penina Moise (1797–1880); see *DAB,* XIII, 78.

39. Penina Moise, *Fancy's Sketch Book* (Charleston, S.C., 1833).

40. Thaddeus A. B. Kosciusko (1746–1817), Polish patriot and general who served in the American Revolutionary Army; after his return to Poland, he commanded the Polish army in its revolt, 1794, against Russia and Prussia. Defeated after a heroic stand, he was imprisoned for two years; then freed. He lived out his life in Switzerland. See J. Thomas, *Universal Pronouncing Dictionary of Biography,* pp. 1455–56.

41. Penina Moise, *Fancy's Sketch Book*, pp. 131–32.

42. It is worthy of note that Miss Moise does not speak here as from within the Jewish group.

43. This cryptic reference to American freedom of religion may have been addressed specifically to the Jews of South Germany, who were at this period suffering under many disabilities.

44. Referred to by Schappes, p. 663, n. 4, as Rev. H. A. Henry. See Grinstein, *passim*.

45. J. M. Jackson was the son of Solomon Henry Jackson, who was also a printer in New York and was editor of the first short-lived American-Jewish magazine to be published, *The Jew;* Rebecca Jackson, Solomon H. Jackson's sister, married Mordecai M. Noah in 1827. See Goldberg, *Major Noah*, p. 219; Grinstein, *passim*.

46. Henry A. Henry, *Imrai Shaipher; a Hebrew Vocabulary: containing a complete list of the Hebrew and Chaldee Roots, which occur in the Bible, together with their significations in English*. Designed to lessen the difficulty which students encounter, in searching for the roots of defective verbs. &c. New York, J. M. Jackson, printer, 145½ William Street, 1838. The Preface to this little work is unimportant, except as it notes that the compiler, Henry A. Henry, was not a native of an English-speaking country. There are a number of testimonials collected and printed on pp. 44–46 of the book.

47. Isaac Nordheimer (1809–42). See *DAB*, XIII, 547; and this Part, Document 163.

48. Jacob B. Seixas (1794–1854), tenth child of Benjamin M. and Zipporah (Levy) Seixas, choir leader in Congregation Shearith Israel. See Grinstein, *passim*.

49. Bela Bates Edwards (1802–52) was appointed professor of the Hebrew language and literature in Andover Theological Seminary, 1837; he was also one of the editors of the influential Christian journal of theology, *Bibliotheca Sacra*. *DAB*, VI, 27.

50. See Part Seven.

51. B. B. Edwards, "Reasons for the Study of the Hebrew Language," *American Biblical Repository*, XII (1838), 117–18, 120, 122–23, 125–26, 129–30, 132. This was Edwards's Inaugural Address, Jan. 18, 1838, in his professorship at Andover; it was delivered in the Chapel of that theological seminary and later published.

52. Edwards is here quoting Charles Lamb's essay "On the Genius and Character of Hogarth." Lamb, *Works* (New York, 1838), II, 391.

53. Founded 1810; first annual report published, 1810; centenary meeting held Oct. 11–14, 1910.

54. Cf., [Ilive, Jacob] (1705–1763) *The Book of Jasher; with Testimony and Notes. . . .* Bristol: Printed for the editor, by P. Rose, 1829 (copy in the New York Public Library). This English edition of 1829 is a reprint of an original printed by Jacob Ilive in 1751, which ficti-

tiously claimed to be a translation by Alcuin of the lost book of Jasher.

55. M. M. Noah, ed., *The Book of Jasher (Sepher H'Yashar)*, (New York, 1840), Preface, pp. iii–vii.

56. John Lightfoot (1602–75), English Hebraist of the seventeenth century, author of *Horae Hebraicae et Talmudicae*, bequeathed his Oriental books to the library of Harvard College. *Dictionary of National Biography*, XI, 1108–10.

57. That is, St. Augustine (354–430), Bishop of Hippo, outstanding among the Latin Fathers of the Christian Church.

58. Hugo Grotius (1583–1645), eminent Dutch jurist and theologian, is best known for his treatise *De jure belli et pacis* (On the Law of War and Peace), on international law. It is interesting to note here that one of Grotius's works discussed the origin of the American Indian tribes.

59. Flavius Josephus (37–95?), most celebrated of ancient Jewish historians, author of a *History of the Jewish War; The Antiquities of the Jews;* an apologetic treatise, *Against Apion;* an autobiography; and other works.

60. Thomas Hartwell Horne (1780–1862), British biblical scholar, bibliographer, and polemic writer. *Dictionary of National Biography*, IX, 1257–58.

61. T. H. Horne, *An Introduction to the Critical Study and Knowledge of the Holy Scriptures* (3 vols., London, 1818; 2d ed., London, 1821).

62. Moses Mendelssohn. See Part One, note 154.

63. Rebecca Gratz's response to this edition of the Book of Jasher shows an interesting conflict between her "will to believe" and her critical judgment. See Rebecca Gratz to Miriam Cohen, Philadelphia, July 12, 1840; MS., University of North Carolina Library:

"You ask what I have been reading? the very little time I have recently given to books has been engaged with 'the book of Iasher,' but whether it is instructive or not I am at a loss to determine. I am disappointed, because there are so many incredible and ridiculous things mixed up with interesting matter, that you are obliged to discredit the whole, and there are some beautiful accounts of bible history that seem like supplements of holy Writ you would fain believe. I asked our old friend Mr. Levy if he had seen the work [']Yes said he in my youth but I do not consider it authentic' It then cannot be the book referred to in the bible, as recording the acts of the kings & judges, tho perhaps as much to be depended on as the speculations of sir (?) Robert K. Porter about the tower of babel. What is particularly attractive in the book of Iasher, is the skill with which the characters of the patriarchs are brought out, and their geneologies [sic] traced. Abraham's motive for sending Hagar & her son away, and the [   ] afterwards maintained between him & his son Ishmael, with many other domestic anecdotes of all the fathers of our race, that bring them into more intimate association with beings of the present day." See also, Rebecca Gratz to Maria Gist Gratz, Aug. 27, 1840, in Philipson, *Letters*, pp. 281–82.

64. Isaac Nordheimer, *A Critical Grammar of the Hebrew Language* (New York, 1838).

65. Friedrich Heinrich Wilhelm Gesenius (1786–1842), German Hebraist, compiler of one of the standard scholarly grammatical texts on the Hebrew language.

66. Heinrich Ewald (1803–65), Germany Hebraist.

67. *The American Biblical Repository*, 2d series, II (October, 1839), 2.

68. Nordheimer, *A Critical Grammar . . .* , pp. iii–vi, xviii–xxiii.

69. Dr. Daniel L. Maduro Peixotto (1799–1843), son of Rev. Moses L. M. Peixotto, married Rachel Seixas (1798–1861), niece of Gershom M. Seixas; see Stern, pp. 172, 192. A well-known member of the medical profession, he served as editor of the *New York Medical and Physical Journal*. See Pool, *Old Faith*, p. 474; Pool, *Portraits*, p. 431; Grinstein, *passim*.

70. Founded, according to Schappes, p. 616, n. 5, in 1827.

71. Johann Heinrich Pestalozzi (1746–1827), Swiss teacher and educational reformer, distinguished for his philanthropic activities as well as for his theoretical writings.

72. In 1822, Jacob S. Solis had presented the public a "Plan for Improving the Condition of Jewish Youth of Both Sexes;" see Edwin Wolf, 2d, "Some Unrecorded American Judaica . . . ," *Essays in American Jewish History*, p. 205, no. 61. On Jewish philanthropy during this period, see Part Six, Document 224.

73. D. L. M. Peixotto, *Anniversary Discourse* (New York, 1830), pp. 32–36.

74. At this time, there was vigorous discussion in American educational circles of the values of "practical" education, i.e., education in the sciences and their technological applications. For republication of some of the documents and discussion of some of the issues, see Joseph L. Blau, ed., *American Philosophic Addresses, 1700–1900* (New York, 1946).

75. Gorham Dummer Abbot (1807–74), clergyman, educator, and author, had succeeded in organizing the Society for the Diffusion of Useful Knowledge, which was incorporated in the State of New York, Oct. 17, 1836. *National Cyclopedia of American Biography*, X, 356.

76. Henry Peter Brougham, Baron Brougham and Vaux (1778–1868), Lord Chancellor of England, writer on legal, philosophic and scientific subjects; see *Dictionary of National Biography*, II, 1356–66.

77. *Census*, 1790, New York, p. 117, New York City, East Ward, records Isaac Gomez, Jr., as head of a household consisting of "free white males 16 years and upwards, 1; free white males under 16 years, 1; free white females, 4; slaves, 7." See also Stern, p. 63.

78. Dr. Philip Milledoler (1775–1852), clergyman and educator. *DAB*, XII, 618.

79. See Part Seven.

80. Possibly a misprint for Samuel Augustus Mitchell (1792–1868), one of the early writers of textbooks in geography.

81. J. W. Kellogg, teacher, lived at 20 Cedar Street in New York City.

82. John W. Picket, teacher, lived at 148 Chambers Street in New York City.

83. Eber Wheaton, teacher, lived at 159 Chatham Street in New York City. He was the author of an elementary textbook in arithmetic, *Analytic Arithmetic, being a natural and easy introduction to the elementary rules of the science* (New York, [1828]).

84. Isaac Gomez, Jr., *Selections of a Father for the Use of his Children* (New York, 1820), Preface, unpaged.

85. Isaac Gomez, Jr., to John Adams, New York, March 28, 1820; MS., Adams Papers, Massachusetts Historical Society.

86. John Adams to Isaac Gomez, Jr., Montezello, April 10, 1820; MS., Adams Papers, Massachusetts Historical Society; typescript copy in A.J.A. An abbreviated version of this letter was printed separately and pasted into copies of Gomez's book.

87. All the works of Cicero referred to by John Adams may be found in the Loeb Classical Library.

88. Isaac Gomez, Jr., to John Adams, New York, April 17, 1820; MS., Adams Papers, Massachusetts Historical Society.

89. See Pool, *Old Faith,* Chapter VI, "Diligently unto thy Children," and Grinstein, *passim.*

90. Alexander M. Dushkin, *Jewish Education in New York City* (New York, 1918), p. 44.

91. Myer Polony or Polonies, died in 1801. There are scattered references to his death and bequest, but no information about his life in the literature.

92. *Constitution, Rules and Regulations of the Talmud Torah Established in the City of New York on the First Day of Sivan, in the year 5568, Corresponding with the 27th Day of May, 1808,* "Preamble," as reprinted in Schappes, pp. 114–15, where the more specific rules and regulations also appear, pp. 115–18. This writing of this constitution was authorized at a meeting "of the Subscribers to the Hebrew and English School," May 15, 1808, with Jacob Hart, Sr. (1746–1822), as chairman and Isaac M. Gomez (1768–1831) as secretary. The meeting elected Gomperts S. Gomperts (1768–1831), Judah Zuntz (1783–1829), and Dr. Joel Hart (1784–1842) to represent the subscribers on the constitutional committee; the trustees of Congregation Shearith Israel appointed Israel B. Kursheedt (1766–1852), Moses L. Moses (1773–

1843), and Mordecai Myers (1776–1871) as their representatives to cooperate with the elected committee. For further information, cf. David de Sola Pool, "The Earliest Jewish Religious School in America," *The Jewish Teacher,* I (1917), 162 ff.

93. Reprinted from the Minute Books of Congregation Shearith Israel by Alexander M. Dushkin, *Jewish Education in New York City,* pp. 452–53.

94. Naphtali Judah (1773–1855), son of Samuel Judah (1728–81) and Jessie (Jones) Judah, was active in Congregation Shearith Israel, in the Tammany Society, and as a Mason. Substantial information about these and other activities in Schappes, pp. 530–31.

95. De Witt Clinton (1769–1828), one of the major figures in New York State political life, was Governor of that state, 1817–22. *DAB,* IV, 221.

96. Isaac Leeser (1806–68), became, in the years after 1840, the outstanding national leader of the Jews of America. During the early years of his ministry in Philadelphia, after 1829, when he was invited to succeed Abraham Isaac Keys as Hazzan of Congregation Mikveh Israel, his chief concerns were personal and local. See W. & W., *passim,* and especially, Maxwell Whiteman, "Isaac Leeser and the Jews of Philadelphia," in *PAJHS,* XLVIII (1958–59), pp. 207–44, for appreciative discussion of Leeser's work and his influence on American Judaism.

97. *The Occident* flourished under Leeser's editorship from 1843 to 1868.

98. See, in particular, Leeser's letters to the congregation and officers of Congregation Mikveh Israel, dated March 31, 1833, April 10, 1835, and 19th Elul, 5596 [1836], all in the Mikveh Israel Papers. For the pitiful condition with respect to Jewish education in Philadelphia at and before this time, see W. & W., *passim.*

99. According to Schappes, p. 659, n. 36, this society was founded in November, 1819, but not incorporated until 1837; see also Part Six, Document 224.

100. Isaac Leeser, *Memorial of the Sunday School for Religious Instruction of Israelites in Philadelphia* (Philadelphia, 1840), pp. 5–8.

101. Not, however, as old, at least in the United States, as Leeser suggests, for the American Sunday School Union, the sponsoring association, was founded in 1824.

102. Isaac B. Seixas (1782–1839) was a nephew of the Rev. Gershom Mendes Seixas; his father, Benjamin M. Seixas (1747–1817), and mother, Zipporah (Levy) Seixas, had 16 children, of whom Isaac B. was the third. He served as a reader of Congregation Beth Shalome in Richmond until shortly after Leeser (who had assisted him in his teaching) had gone to Philadelphia; then Seixas became Hazzan at Congregation Shearith Israel. See Ezekiel and Lichtenstein, *passim;* Grinstein, *passim; PAJHS,* XIX (1910), 63.

103. The Franklin Institute was organized at a meeting held in Old Congress Hall in 1824. Its purpose was to stimulate the discovery of physical and natural laws. See Joseph Jackson, *Encyclopedia of Philadelphia*, III, 689.

104. Solomon Jacob Cohen (1772–1845), *Elements of Faith for the Use of Jewish Youth* . . . (London, 5575 [1815]); this may be the original English edition. W. & W., p. 473, n. 4, record: S. I. Cohen, *Elements of Jewish Faith, Translated from the Hebrew* (Richmond, 1817), and (Philadelphia, 1823), referring to A. S. W. Rosenbach, *An American-Jewish Bibliography* (New York, 1926), pp. 172–73, 210–11. A letter of Rebecca Gratz to Mrs. Ogden Hoffman (March 9, 1818; MS., Rosenbach Collection, A.J.H.S., quoted by W. & W., p. 304), refers to her earlier use of this book: "Our teacher is a German and not sufficiently acquainted with the English to conduct a large school with facility. . . . He published in Richmond last year a little tract, which you may perhaps have seen as they were sold at some of the book stores in N.Y. called 'Elements of Jewish faith.'"

105. Isaac Leeser, *Instruction in the Mosaic Religion*, translated from the German of Joseph Johlson. Philadelphia, 1830.

106. Edwin Wolf, 2d, suggests that this "little work" was E. Pyke's *Scriptural Questions for the Use of Sunday Schools for the Instruction of Israelites* (Philadelphia, 1843); see his "Unrecorded Judaica," p. 227, no. 152.

107. John Hall (1806–40) wrote tracts like *The Harvey Boys* (Philadelphia, 1834) for the American Sunday School Union.

108. Neither Pool, *Old Faith*, nor Goldstein, records a Sunday School in New York.

109. The story of the foundation of the Sunday School of Beth Elohim (Charleston) is told in Reznikoff, pp. 149–50; the account is based upon the minute books of the congregation. Miss Sally Lopez (1806–1902) was the first head of the school; after 1842, she was succeeded by Penina Moise. The school "was the second of its kind in the United States and modelled on that established by Rebecca Gratz in Philadelphia (1838). Miss Gratz used to write the lessons in a copy-book and send it on to Charleston every week; copies of the lessons were then made by Miss Lopez and distributed to the teachers." Reznikoff, p. 150. See also Elzas, *JSC*, p. 182; and the obituary notice of Miss Lopez by Elzas in the *American Israelite* for Jan., 1902.

110. See Philipson, *Letters*, p. 275: "We are now preparing for a second examination of our Sunday School." Rebecca Gratz to Miriam Cohen, Philadelphia, Feb. 24, 1839; MS., University of North Carolina Library:

"We did not get home from school until dinner time to day. for the next Sunday we are to have an anniversary examination, and the children are full of anticipations of the credit & rewards they are to receive in presence of their parents & friends, and the teachers staid in with me after they were dismissed to arrange their simple bits. it was determined to give two premiums in each class, and that none might go away unsatisfied, to make a Purim feast and give each some cake and a little present, to encourage them to earn a premium next time, I have had the 10 Commands in verse printed on white satin & colored silk, which will serve for some and other appropriate simple articles for others, and the girls are all going to task their ingenuity to make articles of favor for their classes."

111. Moses N. Nathan (1807–83), after serving the congregation in Jamaica became reader in St. Thomas in the West Indies; then he served in New Orleans. See Schappes, p. 661, n. 61, citing *The Jewish Chronicle* (London, England), May 18, 1883, pp. 9–10. On March 11, 1840, Rebecca Gratz wrote to her sister-in-law, Maria Gist Gratz, about Mr. Nathan's presence:

"We have had a short visit from a very intelligent and agreeable stranger, the Rev Mr. Nathan from Jamiaca [sic] he introduced himself as nephew of an old acquaintance of the same name, whom Dear Ben [Maria's husband] knows at N. Orleans and we induced him to read for us some of his beautiful sermons it is very rarely that we have eloquent preachers, among the Jews, and I confess I have never heard any I liked as well as Mr. N's tho I have heard many as learned—he has kindly promised to return, and witness our Sunday school examination, and preach on that occasion." Rebecca Gratz to Maria (Gist) Gratz, Philadelphia, March 11, 1840; MS., A.J.H.S.

112. The address was printed in *Second Annual Examination of the Sunday School* . . . (Philadelphia, 1840). See Rosenbach, "An American Jewish Bibliography," *PAJHS*, No. 30 (1926), p. 345, no. 458.

113. Isaac Leeser, *Catechism for Younger Children* (Philadelphia, 5599 [1839]), pp. ix–xii. This work was dedicated in glowing terms to "Miss Rebecca Gratz, Superintendent of the Sunday School for Religious Instruction of Israelites in Philadelphia":

"I long since wished to have an opportunity of acknowledging my great indebtedness to you for the approbation you kindly bestowed on my youthful labours, and the frequent marks of friendship I received from you since my lot has been cast in this place. As this little book has been undertaken to assist your efforts, which have so far been crowned with signal success, to form an institution, whence the waters of life might flow alike to the rich and the poor: permit me to inscribe it to you, that your respected name may contribute to its introduction into the houses and schools of our people, who dwell in this land."

Miss Gratz worked devotedly and without sparing herself. See the letter quoted in note 111 above, and Rebecca Gratz to Miriam Cohen, Philadelphia, Jan. 28, [1840]; MS., University of North Carolina Library; copy from A.J.A.:

"Of all the days in the week, My Dear Miriam Sunday has become the most busy one to me, and it is rarely until after dinner that I can command a quiet moment. . . . I have to leave home in the morning at half past nine, to be ready when the School assembles, and it is generally one in the day before I reach home. Then if I can lure my teachers Becky, Miriam E. or our pupil Frank to dinner we find so many things to talk about and arrange that it is late before we separate. we are preparing for an anniversary examination at Purim, and I hope then to prove that this great labour has been as useful as we anticipated People are beginning to understand that their children are really the party to be benefited, and that nothing is expected from them but to send them decently attired and willing to receive instruction. The first requisition is made easy by the sewing society who provide those who cannot provide themselves."

114. Israel Eduard Kley (1789–1867), was Director, 1817–48, of the Jewish Free School of Hamburg and the first minister of the synagogue that was an outgrowth of the school. His *Katechismus der mosaischen Religionslehre* was published in 1814. *Universal Jewish Encyclopedia,* VI, 418.

115. Samuel Johnson (1696–1772), took up his duties as president of King's College (renamed Columbia College after the Revolution) in April, 1754. See Herbert W. Schneider, "The Mind of Samuel Johnson," in Herbert W. and Carol Schneider, *Samuel Johnson, First President of King's College* (New York, 1929), II, 3–22; *DAB*, X, 118.

116. Gershom Seixas to Richard Varick, New York, Nov. 7, 1814; MS., Columbiana Collection, Columbia University.

117. Richard Varick (1753–1831), Revolutionary soldier; recorder of New York City, first codifier of the Laws of New York State; speaker of the New York State Assembly, 1787–88; Attorney-general, 1788–89; Mayor of New York City, 1790–1801; one of the founders of the American Bible Society and its president, 1828–31; president of the New York Society of the Cincinnati, 1806–31. *DAB*, XIX, 226.

118. "Trustees Minutes," Vol. II, Part 2, June 22, 1809 to Dec. 6, 1819. Minutes of the Trustees of Columbia College . . . , p. 500. This typescript in the Columbiana Collection, Columbia University, is copied from the original manuscript minutes; the passage in the text is from pp. 397–98 of the original.

119. Nathan Nathans (1798–1877) was the son of Moses Nathans (1749–1815) and his second wife, a convert to Judaism. See W. & W., *passim.*

120. Probably the elder William Meredith, distinguished lawyer of Philadelphia, who was prominent in financial affairs as well as in politics; see W. & W., *passim,* for relations of Meredith with other Jews.

121. Harvard College was established under primarily religious auspices in the Congregationalist colony of Massachusetts Bay; since the

establishment of the Congregationalist church in Massachusetts was not rescinded until 1833, as of the date of this letter there was still reason for Nathans to be concerned about the matter of religion. The University of Pennsylvania, on the other hand, dates from 1740; it was founded in a state where since Penn's Great Charter religious toleration had been the rule and where the emphasis of men like Benjamin Franklin and Benjamin Rush on scientific advance and a secular concept of benevolence had reinforced the original Quaker tolerance.

122. Nathan Nathans to William Meredith, Brighton, May 21, 1815; MS., in the collection of Edwin Wolf, 2d.

123. Samuel B. How to William Meredith, New Hope, Dec. 14, 1815; MS., in the collection of Edwin Wolf, 2d.

124. Samuel B. How (1790–1868), a graduate of Princeton Theological Seminary, 1813, was ordained to the Presbyterian Church in Salisbury, Pa., in 1815.

125. From 1792, Rush had served as Professor in the University of Pennsylvania medical faculty.

126. On method, see Rush's lecture, "Observations and Reasoning in Medicine," 1791, as printed in D. G. Runes, ed., *The Selected Writings of Benjamin Rush* (New York, 1947), pp. 245–54, and other incidental discussions in the same volume of selections. For Rush's practice during the epidemic of 1793, see Lester S. King, *The Medical World of the Eighteenth Century* (Chicago, 1958), pp. 147–50. King is sharply critical of Rush's theory of fevers.

127. On Nassy, see W. & W. *passim;* Bernard Felsenthal and Richard Gottheil, "Chronological Sketch of the Jews in Surinam," *PAJHS*, IV (1896), 3–6; B. Felsenthal, "The Jewish Congregation in Surinam," *PAJHS*, II (1894), 29–30; Sigmund Seeligmann, "David Nassy of Surinam and his 'Lettre Politico-Theologico-Morale sur les Juifs,'" *PAJHS*, XXII (1914), pp. 25–38.

128. The epidemic of 1793 may have been aggravated by the presence in Philadelphia of many refugees from the West Indies which were then torn by rebellions. W. & W., pp. 192–94, presents a vivid brief description of Philadelphia during the plague. For more detail, see John H. Powell, *Bring Out your Dead; the Great Plague of Yellow Fever in Philadelphia in 1793* (Philadelphia, 1949).

129. W. & W., p. 194, may be correct in stating that Nassy was elected to membership "within a short time after his arrival." The evidence they cite of letters dated 1793 and 1794 certainly show that Nassy was invited to meetings of the Society. The later date given here is based upon the fact that Nassy's letter of June 19, 1795, to the members of the American Philosophic Society (MS., in the Library of the Society; copy from A.J.A.) begins "Extrement flatte de l'honneur que vous m'avez fait de m'admettre en qualite de membre de la Societe philosophique, Je ne

puis me determiner a quiter ce Pais sans venir moi meme, vous en te-
moigner ma reconnoissance et vous assurer de mes sentimens d'attache-
ment et de respect. Le titre de votre Confrere m'en fait un devoir
qui acquiert une nouvelle force par l'amitie que Je vous ai vouee." and
is endorsed "June 1795 acknowledging Certificate & engaging to make
Communications from Surinam." There is no specific mention of a certificate in Nassy's letter, however, and this may be nothing more than a
polite farewell to a group of scientific colleagues with whom his association had been slight, but had continued for more than a year or perhaps
two.

130. David Nassy, M.D., *Observations on the Cause, Nature and Treatment of the Epidemic Disorder Prevalent in Philadelphia* (Philadelphia,
1793), pp. 7–13, 31–41.

131. Nassy is here taking issue with those who believed the West
Indian refugees responsible for the epidemic; on this point he agreed
with Rush; cf. Runes, ed., *Selected Writings of Benjamin Rush*, p. 413,
letter to his wife, Oct. 28, 1793.

132. See W. & W., p. 194, and Part Three, Document 93.

133. Benjamin Rush, *An Account of the Bilious Remitting Yellow
Fever, as it Appeared in the City of Philadelphia, in the Year 1793*
(Philadelphia, 1794).

134. Moses Sheftall to Benjamin Rush, Savannah, Jan. 24, 1795; MS.,
Benjamin Rush Papers, Library Company of Philadelphia.

135. Thomas Sydenham (1642–89) was the most illustrious of the
seventeenth-century English physicians and writers on medical subjects.
See S. A. Alibone, *A Critical Dictionary of English Literature*, II, 2320.

136. George Cleghorn (1716–89), Scottish physician and medical
writer whose *Observations on the Epidemical Diseases in Minorca from
the Year 1744 to 1749* was published in 1751. See *Dictionary of National
Biography*, IV, 482.

137. Adam Kuhn (1741–1817), physician and botanist, was a professor
in the united medical schools of the College of Physicians of Philadelphia
and the University of Pennsylvania, 1792–97. *DAB*, X, 510.

138. Solomon Bush; see Part Three, Document 93.

139. Abraham Baldwin (1754–1807) served in the Georgia House of
Assembly as well as in the House of Representatives and the Senate.
DAB, I, 530.

140. James Mease (1771–1846), physician and botanist, a young man
at the time of this letter, may have been a classmate of Sheftall during
his years of medical study. For his later career, see *DAB*, XII, 486.

141. James Woodhouse (1770–1809) physician and chemist, may also
have been a classmate, since he received his M.D. from the University
of Pennsylvania in 1792; in 1795, Woodhouse was appointed to the
chair of Chemistry in the University of Pennsylvania. See *DAB*, XX, 491.

142. Adam Seybert (1773–1825), physician and scientist, also served in Congress. He received his M.D. from the University of Pennsylvania in 1793. See *DAB*, XVII, 2.

143. This body appears to have taken its start in a meeting of a few prominent Philadelphia physicians in 1786. Its first recorded meeting took place on Jan. 2, 1787. From 1792 to 1797, the College of Physicians was jointly responsible with the University of Pennsylvania for the operation of the medical school. See *Encyclopedia of Philadelphia*, II, 492.

144. See this Part, note 69, and S. R. Kagan, *Jewish Contributions to Medicine in America (1656–1934)* (Boston, 1934), pp. 10–12.

145. See this Part, Document 164, and Part Six, Document 225.

146. According to James G. Wilson, *The Memorial History of New York* (New York, 1892–93), the first New York City Directory, 1786, listed but 25 physicians (*Memorial History of New York*, IV, 394) and the whole membership of the Medical Society in 1789 amounted to 28 (*Memorial History of New York*, III, 100).

147. See Schappes, p. 182.

148. Daniel L. M. Peixotto, *Address Delivered before the Medical Society of the City and County of New York on the 25th Day of July, 1831* (New York, 1831), pp. 18–27.

149. Julius Caesar Scaliger (1484–1558), physician and writer on scientific subjects. See *Encyclopaedia Britannica* (1956), XX, 44.

150. Francis Bacon, Lord Verulam (1561–1626), one of the most celebrated philosophers of modern times, is credited with the first formulation of the methodological principles of positive science.

151. Charles de Secondat, Baron de la Brede et de Montesquieu (1689–1755), jurist, historian and political scientist, is best known for his work *L'Esprit des Lois* (The Spirit of Laws), published in 1748.

152. *Census*, 1790, Rhode Island, p. 20 records, "Isaacks, Jacob: free white males 16 years and upwards . . . 1; free white males under 16 years . . . 2; free white females . . . 6."

153. National Archives. Jefferson's report traces the history of this sort of distillation back to "Sir Richard Hawkins, in the 16th century, . . . Glauber, Hanton and Lister, in the 17th, and . . . Hales, Appleby, Butler, Chapman, Hoffman and Dove in the 18th." Clearly Isaacks was following a well-trodden path. Of more recent methods, the report points to Dr. Lind's experiments of 1762 and 1767, and Dr. Irvin's method of 1771 which had received a premium of 5000 pounds sterling from the British Parliament and had been used by Lord Mulgrave in 1773 on a "voyage towards the North Pole." Also noted is the fact that "M. de Bougainville in his voyage round the world, used, very successfully, a still which had been contrived in 1763, by Poyssonier." Out of this background, the following account of Isaacks's experiments is presented:

"As the merit of this could be ascertained by experiment only, the Secretary of State asked the favor of Mr. Rittenhouse, President of the

American Philosophical Society, of Dr. Wistar, professor of Chemistry in the college of Philadelphia, and Dr. Hutchinson, professor of chemistry in the university of Pennsylvania, to be present at the experiments. Mr. Isaacks fixed the pot of a small cabouse, with a tin cap and strait tube of tin passing obliquely through a cask of cold water; he made use of a mixture, the composition of which he did not explain, and from 25 pints of sea water, taken up about 3 miles out of the capes of Delaware at flood tide, he distilled 22 pints of fresh water in 4 hours, with 20 lb. of seasoned pine, which was a little wetted by having lain in the rain.

"In a 2d experiment of the 21st of March, performed in a furnace and five gallon still at the college, from 32 pints of sea water he drew 31 pints of fresh water in 7 h. 24 min. with 51 lb. of hickory which had been cut about six months. In order to decide whether Mr. Issacks's mixture contributed in any and what degree to the success of the operation, it was thought proper to repeat his experiment under the same circumstances exactly, except the omission of the mixture. Accordingly on the next day the same quantity of sea water was put into the same still, the same furnace was used, and fuel from the same parcel. It yielded, as his had done, 31 pints of fresh water in 11 min. more of time and with 10 lb. less of wood.

"On the 24th of March Mr. Isaacks performed a 3d experiment. For this, a common iron pot of 3½ gallons was fixed in brick work, and the flue from the hearth wound once around the pot spirally, and then passed off up a chimney. The cap was of tin, and a strait tin tube of about two inches diameter, passing obliquely through a barrel of water, served instead of a worm. From 16 pints of sea water he drew off 15 pints of fresh water in 2 h. 55 min. with 3 lb. of hickory and 8 lb. of seasoned pine. This experiment was also repeated the next day, with the same apparatus and fuel from the same parcel, but without the mixture. Sixteen pints of sea water yielded in like manner 15 pints of fresh, in 1 min. more of time and with half a pound less of wood. On the whole, it was evident that Mr. Issacks's mixture produced no advantage, either in the process or result of the distillation."

Jefferson's conclusion was that, instead of supporting and sponsoring Jacob Isaacks's method, the United States should print, on the reverse side of clearance papers for all vessels leaving American ports, an account of all the known methods of distilling fresh water from sea water, "with a recommendation, in all cases where they shall have occasion to resort to this expedient for obtaining water, to publish the result of their trial in some gazette on their return to the United States, or to communicate it for publication to the office of the Secretary of State, in order that others may, by their success, be encouraged to make similar trials, and be benefitted by any improvements or new ideas which may occur to them in practice."

154. Precisely which of the Da Costa family this is cannot be dis-

covered. Stern lists no member of the family named Francis. The family was prominent in Charleston, and spent some time as refugees in Philadelphia during the Revolution. Most of them returned to Charleston, but it is possible that some members of the younger generation remained in Pennsylvania to administer property that was acquired during the Philadelphia "exile." See W. & W., *passim;* Elzas, *JSC, passim;* Reznikoff, *passim.*

155. Abraham Haim Cohen (died 1841) was, according to Stern, p. 127, the son of Jacob Raphael Cohen (1740–1814), hazzan of Mikveh Israel Congregation. The young man served as assistant to his father, and also as Shohet. He caused a minor scandal in 1806 by marrying Jane Pickens, a Christian. To ease the situation, the girl was converted to Judaism, but she later reverted to her original faith. See Mrs. S. J. Cohen, *Henry Luria; or, the little Jewish Convert: being contained in the memoir of Mrs. S. J. Cohen* (New York, 1860); W. & W., pp. 237–38. See also *ibid.*, p. 352, "[Cohen] supplemented the income he received from the congregation by bottling and selling mineral waters at his Hygeian Fountain and Philadelphia Mineral Water Ware House at No. 31 South Second Street." *Census Directory for 1811* (Philadelphia, 1811), p. 65, reports a different address: "Cohen, A. H. manufacturer of artificial mineral waters, 100 S. Second and back of Jews synagogue."

156. Jacob Isaacks to Thomas Jefferson, Newport, Aug. 17, 1790; MS., RG 59, General Records of the Department of State, National Archives.

157. Testimonials, July 22, 1790, and April 8, 1790; MS., copies in the hand of Jacob Isaacks, RG 59, General Records of the Department of State, National Archives.

158. Isaac Senter was a well-known Newport physician and surgeon.

159. *Census,* 1790, Rhode Island, Newport, p. 21, records: "Tillinghast, Nicholas P., free white males 16 and upwards . . . 1; free white females . . . 6; all other persons . . . 1."

160. Caleb Gardner (1739–1806), one of the most prominent citizens of Newport. *DAB,* VII, 140.

161. Moses Seixas, one of the foremost Jews of Newport, signer of the congregational address to George Washington. See Part One, Document 2.

162. William Ellery (1727–1820), a signer of the Declaration of Independence, in 1790 was appointed by President Washington collector of the customs for the district of Newport. *DAB,* VI, 86.

163. *Census,* 1790, Rhode Island, Newport, p. 19, records: "Sears, George, free white males 16 years and upward . . . 2; free white males under 16 . . . 1; free white females . . . 3; all other free persons . . . 1."

164. *Census,* 1790, Rhode Island, Newport, p. 21, records: "Vernon,

Samuel Jun., free white males 16 and upwards . . . 1; free white males under 16 . . . 1; free white females . . . 1; slaves . . . 1."

165. Jacob Isaacks to Thomas Jefferson, Newport, Nov. 4, 1791; MS., RG 59, General Records of the Department of State, National Archives.

166. Probably Benjamin Bourne (1755–1808), distinguished Rhode Island jurist and first representative from his state to the Congress of the U.S. He served in the first four Congresses. *DAB*, II, 483.

167. Jacob Isaacks to Thomas Jefferson, Newport, March 19, 1792; MS., RG 59, General Records of the Department of State, National Archives.

168. "The Secretary of State, to whom was referred, by the House of Representatives of the United States, the petition of Jacob Isaacks, of Newport, in Rhode-Island, has examined into the truth and importance of the allegations therein set forth, and makes thereon the following REPORT. . . .", Philadelphia, Nov. 21, 1791; printed report, one sheet, RG 59, General Records of Department of State, National Archives. For discussion of the context of Jefferson's report, see this Part, note 153.

169. Francis da Costa to Thomas Jefferson, Philadelphia, Nov. 20, 1804; MS., National Archives.

170. Abraham Haim Cohen to Thomas Jefferson, Philadelphia, Dec. 21, 1807; MS., National Archives.

171. Lemuel Sawyer (1777–1852), author and congressman, was first elected to Congress in 1807. *DAB*, XVI, 394.

172. Thomas Jefferson to Abraham Haim Cohen, Washington, Feb. 10, 1808; MS., National Archives.

173. Daniel Schlesinger (1799–1838) was a pupil of Ferdinand Ries (see this Part, note 181) and Moscheles; he came to New York in 1836, taught and gave a few concerts, and was chosen to lead the Concordia. Grove's *Dictionary of Music and Musicians*. American Supplement, ed. by W. S. Pratt and C. N. Boyd (New York, 1920), p. 20. See Odell, *Annals*, IV, *passim.*

174. *Biographical Notices of Daniel Schlesinger, the Pianist, Prepared for the "New York Mirror," September 1, 1839* (New York, 1839), pp. 50–59.

175. Historians of American musical taste do not all agree with this contemporaneous estimate; but support of the view that the 1830s were a "watershed" may be found in Charles Seeger, "Music and Class Structure in the United States," *American Quarterly*, IX (1957), 281–94; and James H. Stone, "Mid-Nineteenth-Century American Beliefs in the Social Value of Music," *Musical Quarterly*, XVIII (1957), 38–49. Neither writer mentions Daniel Schlesinger.

176. The National Theatre was originally known as the Italian Opera House; after being closed in 1835–36, it reopened as primarily a "home

for drama" under the managership of Flynn and Willard for the season 1836–37. See Odell, *Annals,* IV, *passim.*

177. Alexandre (?) Boucher, reputedly a good 'cellist, came to New York in 1833 with Rivafinali's opera troupe. He collaborated with Schlesinger in 1837. In 1824, he was one of the musicians concerned in the establishment of the Philharmonic Society. See Grove's *Dictionary of Music and Musicians,* American Supplement (New York, 1920), p. 16.

178. Andre Ernest Modeste Gretry (1741–1813), one of the most popular French composers of comic operas in the late eighteenth century; about 50 of his operas were played in Paris, and his influence was felt into the nineteenth century. W. S. Pratt, *The History of Music* (Revised ed., New York, 1930), pp. 367–68; 448.

179. Probably Nicola Mori (1796–1839), violinist and music publisher; a child prodigy, he played his first concert at the age of 8. Grove's *Dictionary of Music and Musicians* (5th ed., London, 1954), V, 891.

180. Johann Nepomuk Hummel (1778–1837) was a distinguished composer, pianist, and teacher. Sigismund Thalberg (1812–71), a child prodigy as a bravura pianist, pupil of Hummel, and a minor composer. W. S. Pratt, *The History of Music,* pp. 389–90, 457–58, 537–38.

181. Ferdinand Ries (1784–1838), violinist, pianist, and composer. See Grove's *Dictionary of Music and Musicians* (5th ed., New York, 1955), VII, 165; W. S. Pratt, *The History of Music,* p. 459.

182. Giovanni Paisiello (1741–1816), one of the most famous of the late eighteenth-century Italian operatic composers, a court favorite of Catherine of Russia (1776–84) and of Napoleon (1802–3), as well as in royal service at Naples. W. S. Pratt, *The History of Music,* p. 359.

183. See this Part, Document 171.

184. See Part Six.

185. There is a full discussion in Pool, *Old Faith,* pp. 152–53.

186. "Report of Committee on Choral Singing," MS., Shearith Israel Minutes of Trustees, III (May 10, 1818), 127–30.

187. On Naphtali Phillips (1773–1870), see Grinstein, *passim;* Pool, *Old Faith, passim;* Pool, *Portraits, passim;* and the literature cited in Schappes, p. 616, n. 6.

188. Eleazar S. Lazarus (1788–1844), grandfather of Emma Lazarus (1849–87), was active in Congregation Shearith Israel for many years. With Solomon H. Jackson, he edited the Sephardic Hebrew and English prayer book that was published in New York in 1826. Pool, *Old Faith, passim.*

189. Aaron Levy (1771–1852), an auctioneer and merchant, active in the affairs of Congregation Shearith Israel. In the War of 1812 he served first as Captain and later became Lieutenant Colonel. He became an art dealer and established one of the first art galleries in the United

States. See Pool, *Old Faith, passim*; and Schappes, pp. 215–6, and p. 624, n. 9.

190. The congregation was founded in 1749–50. After many years of worshipping in houses adapted for the purpose, in 1794 a new synagogue building was constructed, in Georgian style; the exterior "looked like a church of the period." The synagogue building was burned to the ground in 1838 in one of the great fires that ravaged Charleston. See the discussion in Reznikoff, pp. 54–61.

191. Cyrus L. Warner, of Geneseo, N.Y., and New York City, is noted in *Wilson's Business Directory of New York City* (New York, 1848), p. 27, as an architect with offices at 2 Wall Street.

192. Contract for Building of K. K. Beth Elohim Synagogue, between Trustees and David Lopez and David C. Levy, Oct. 10, 1839; MS., Thomas J. Tobias Collection; copy from A.J.A.

193. Signers of the contract on behalf of the Congregation were Nathan Hart (1784–1841), Abraham Ottolengui (1790–1850), H[andel] M[oses] Hertz (1778–1840), Isaiah Moses (1772–1857), Joshua Lazarus (1796–1861); for the builders, David Lopez (1809–84), M[oses] Lopez (1796–1849), and David C. Levy (1805–77); witnesses, S[amuel] N. Hart (1808–80) and W. W. Churchill.

Part Six. The Strains of Religious Adjustment

1. Levy Solomons (1771–1823) was the son of Levy and Rebecca (Franks) Solomons. New York, Albany, and Montreal were the cities in which his activities centered.

2. *Census*, 1790, Rhode Island, p. 21. Newport Town, reports Moses Lopez as head of a household consisting of 3 free white males of 16 or more and 1 free white female; see Part Two, note 115.

3. On G. M. Seixas, see Part One, note 160.

4. From copy in the A.J.A.

5. These MS. entries occur on every available space on the fly-leaves of the Solomons copy of the Lopez calendar, now in the American Jewish Archives. The entries are not arranged in chronological order. There are two groups of entries: those written by Catherine Manuel Solomons (1768–1852), from which the 20 entries printed here are taken; and those written by G. M. Seixas, as a formal record of the naming of the children. The numbers in square brackets have been supplied by the editors to facilitate reference to these entries.

6. The presence of the initial "C," for Catherine M. Solomons, at this point suggests the possibility that entries [1]–[6] were inserted shortly after Levy Solomons had acquired it, which was (according to a MS. notation) Sept. 2, 1806, since all these entries refer to events that took place prior to the publication of the Lopez calendar.

7. The correction of the number of years that Seixas served Con-

gregation Shearith Israel is not in Catherine Solomons's handwriting. In either case, the figure is incorrect; Seixas served 1768–76 and 1784–1816; only by adding in the years from 1776 to 1784, can the lower figure be reached. See Pool, *Old Faith,* p. 502.

8. The second wife of G. M. Seixas, whom he married in 1786, was Hannah Manuel (1766–1856), a sister of Catherine (Manuel) Solomons.

9. See Part One, Document 53.

10. Sarah Abigail Seixas (1778–1854), daughter of G. M. Seixas by his first wife Elkalah (Cohen) Seixas, was the wife of I. B. Kursheedt.

11. Moses Levi Maduro Peixotto (1767–1828), who served as Hazzan of Congregation Shearith Israel from 1816 to 1828.

12. Joshua Mendes Seixas (1802–187-?) was a son of G. M. Seixas by his second wife.

13. See entry [8] above.

14. His father was already dead; see entry [18] below.

15. See entry [7] above.

16. Transliteration of "Shema," approximately as pronounced by Sephardic Jews.

17. See entry [5] above.

18. Samuel Seixas (1793–1852), son of Gershom M. and Hannah (Manuel) Seixas.

19. See entry [8] above.

20. Rebecca (Franks) Solomons (died 1812), the mother of Levy Solomons (entry [1] and mother-in-law of the writer of these entries). She was a daughter of Abraham Franks (1721–97), an early Jewish settler in Canada.

21. For *Haggadah,* the ritual for the Passover *seder.*

22. The father of Levy Solomons (entry [1]) and husband of Rebecca (Franks) Solomons (entry [15]).

23. Sarah, youngest child of Lucius Levy and Rebecca (Franks) Solomons, married a non-Jew, John McCord. Stern, p. 199.

24. See entry [1] above.

25. See entry [6] above.

26. For details, see W. & W., pp. 142–45.

27. This was a common method of fund raising; see Part Two, Document 68. "Christ Church steeple and a large proportion of all the churches in Pennsylvania had been erected or improved by funds obtained from the profits of lotteries." W. & W., p. 144. See also Norris S. Barratt, *Outline of the History of Old St. Paul's Church, Philadelphia* (Philadelphia, 1917), pp. 37–41.

28. Permission was requested as early as Feb., 1788; the enabling act was not passed until April 6, 1790. W. & W., p. 144, citing *Minutes of the Second Session of the Twelfth General Assembly of the Commonwealth of Pennsylvania* (Philadelphia, 1788), p. 115, and *Minutes of the*

Second Session of the Fourteenth General Assembly (Philadelphia, 1790), pp. 261–62.

29. See this Part, Document 215.

30. W. & W., pp. 232–33.

31. "Your Committee begs leave to call to your recollection the prosperous and happy condition of the Congregation some few years back; the increase in the value of property in its possesion [sic], and the comparitively [sic] triflng [sic] amount of debts that were at that time due by the Congregation, and contrasting it with its late disastrous condition. An enquiry naturally arises as to the cause of that adversity. It has been said, that the building of the Shool was one of them, your committee is of opinion, that if a proper system of economy had been exercised at that period, it alone could never have had the effect in embarassing [sic] the finances of this Congregation; that is imputed to it by a number of its members. The unparralelled [sic] liberality of almost every individual in the Congregation; evinced by their subscribing largely in aid of the measure, not alone reached far towards paying the then supposed expence [sic] of the building, but manifested their acquiessence [sic] in it. The cost, it was then supposed would be at the highest estimate about eight thousand Dollars, it unfortunately more than doubled it.

"But altho' that may be said to be a leading cause of the late embarrassment; yet as your committee has already observed, if no other had occurred it alone would not have been of sufficient magnitude, to have been an important obstruction to our financial prosperity. But it may be attributed to two other causes, which combined with the first, darkened in a great degree, the prospects of our future welfare. One was the very ill timed election, of Chazan which at once sunk a Capital of Twenty thousand Dollars. The other was the extraordinary assesment [sic] on the property in oliver street: which however, if the anticipations of the trustees, with regard to its future value, should be realized, will no doubt repay this congregation with interest.

"From this state of embarrassment, this congregation has been providentially extricated, by the truly munificent bequest of the late excellent Mr. A. Touro. and the sale of the property in Chatham street, which by being purchased for a Banking institution, a greater price was obtained than could have been procured from an individual."

This excerpt is from the printed *Report* of the Committee of the Congregation, appointed June 16, 5584 (1824) to examine the *Report of M. L. Moses and Judah Zuntz, Esqrs., Committee of Accounts of K. K. Shearith Israel*, presented to the Board of Trustees, June, 5584. The two reports are printed together; the matter quoted is on pp. 9–10. Abraham Touro was the son of Isaac Touro, who served the Congregation briefly as Hazzan in 1780; Abraham Touro donated the sum of $666.43 toward the cost of the new synagogue building in Mill Street in 1817, the largest gift to come from an individual for this purpose, and, at his death in 1822, was found to have willed the sum of $10,000. to the New York Congregation. Pool, *Old Faith,* pp. 49, 299. The property in Chatham Street adjoined the Congregation's Chatham Square cemetery. The reference to the "Capital of Twenty thousand Dollars" sunk by the "ill timed" election of a new Hazzan undoubtedly refers to the election of Moses L. M. Peixotto to succeed G. M. Seixas. On the death of Seixas, Peixotto "offered to serve as hazzan in his place on the generous condition that the salary and emoluments of the office should go to the family of the late Hazzan Seixas." Pool, *Old Faith,* p. 174. However, after four years, during which Peixotto maintained his mercantile business while also serving the Congregation, he decided that the two were incompatible and asked to be elected as Hazzan on a salaried basis; his request was granted. The Congregation was committed to paying a pension to the Seixas family; now they were paying a Hazzan's salary as well.

32. Printed handbill, The Historical Society of Pennsylvania.

33. Manuel Josephson is included as a householder in the first census, 1790, Pennsylvania: "Josephson, Emanuel (mercht), Free white males . . . 1; free white males under 16 years . . . 1; free white females . . . 2." See Department of Commerce and Labor, Bureau of the Census, S. N. D. North, Director, *Heads of Families at the First Census of the United States Taken in the Year 1790* (Washington, Government Printing Office, 1908), Pennsylvania, p. 226; and W. & W., *passim.*

34. Solomon Lyon, see Part Two, note 19.

35. William Wister, W. & W., p. 144.

36. John Duffield appointed the firm of Simon Gratz & Co. as executors of his estate. See W. & W., p. 486.

37. Samuel Hays, see Part Three, note 8.

38. Solomon Etting, see Part One, note 59.

39. For typical expressions of this control by the laity, see *Rules and Regulations of the Congregation K. K. Mikveh Israel. . . .* (Philadelphia, 1813), articles VI, XIII, XIV, XV, and XXIII. Article VI provides for two stated membership meetings a year, with the Parnass and Adjunto empowered to call other meetings if desirable. Article XIII further specifies the privileges of the Parnass and the Gabay (treasurer). Article XV gives to the Parnass and Adjuntos, or when it is impossible to convene the Adjuntos, the Parnass "solely and exclusively" the right to designate the plot in the cemetery that is to be assigned for any interment. Article XIV is worthy of quotation *in extenso,* since it sets up a congregational court: "Any person offending any officer of the Congregation whilst in discharge of his duty, or transgressing the laws of this Congregation, shall be cited to appear before the Adjuntos (within fifteen days after such offence shall have

been committed), who shall appoint a chairman, (the acting Parnass as head of the Congregation in either case being the prosecutor), which said board shall proceed to the trial of the accused, and if found guilty, may impose on such offender or offenders, and each of them, a fine not exceeding twenty-five dollars, and be suspended from all honours and privileges until complied with, with the privilege of an appeal to the congregation." Article XXIII forbade the Hazzan to perform marriages or to conduct funerals without the consent of the lay officials.

40. Benjamin Nones, see Part Four, note 82.

41. The Junto of Mikveh Israel to Benjamin Nones, Philadelphia, Feb. 23, 1793; MS., Mikveh Israel, Box 882.

42. This was probably Jacob Raphael Cohen, second Hazzan of Congregation Mikveh Israel. See W. & W., *passim.*

43. Jonas Phillips (1735–1803). See W. & W., *passim;* Morais, *Jews of Philadelphia, passim;* and the extended biographical notice in Pool, *Portraits,* pp. 290–97. Pool correctly gives the date 1735 for Phillips's birth, despite the evidence of the tombstone for 1736. Although Phillips had difficulty in his earlier business ventures, by 1790 he seems to have overcome them, for in *Census,* 1790, Pennsylvania, p. 221, Philadelphia County, he is listed as Shopkeeper, on North Second Street, and five pages later, p. 226, he appears as a merchant, occupying property on "Market Street, South from River Delaware to Sixth Street." It is in connection with his Market St. establishment that his family is recorded: "free white males 16 years and upwards . . . 1; free white males under 16 years . . . 5; free white females . . . 4; slaves . . . 1." Phillips and his wife, the former Rebecca Machado, had a very large family. One of their daughters, Zipporah, married Manuel Noah and became the mother of Mordecai M. Noah.

44. Levy Phillips, *Census,* 1790, Pennsylvania, p. 228, Philadelphia County, names Levy Phillips as a shopkeeper with premises "Race Street, South, to Ninth Street, free white males 16 years and upward . . . 2; free white females . . . 2," See W. & W., *passim.*

45. Moses Nathans, see Part Three, note 131.

46. The Junto of Mikveh Israel to Benjamin Nones, Philadelphia, March 24, 1793; MS., Mikveh Israel, Box 882.

47. There is an earlier letter, Feb. 7, 1793, in which the three Adjuntos "wait'd with great patiance of being Summons by you as Parnass." MS., Mikveh Israel, Box 882. It is clear that by this time they had lost their patience.

48. Mrs. G. Philips to Congregation Shearith Israel, New York, April 26, 1796; MS., Shearith Israel Letter Books, Bk. I, no. 119; copy from A.J.H.S.

49. See, for example, Article II, sec. 1, where specific mention of the act of the Legislature is made.

50. See Article 3 of the Constitution of 1728 as printed in Pool, *Old*

Faith, p. 499, and Articles 9–11 of the Constitution of 1761, in Pool, *ibid.*, p. 501.

51. See the discussion of this point in Grinstein.

52. *Constitution and Bye-Laws of Congregation Shearith Israel* (New York, 1805), pp. 5–16.

53. It is clear from this article that, in 1805, Congregation Shearith Israel still regarded itself as the Jewish communal organization, and not merely as an incorporated religious society. Similar provisions, not merely for Charleston, but also for the surrounding area, are found in the 1820 Constitution of Congregation Beth Elohim of Charleston; excerpts in Elzas, *JSC*, pp. 152–53, rules VIII and XII.

54. Abraham Eleazar Israel (1773–1852), shammash of Congregation Mikveh Israel, 1824–52, migrated to America from Amsterdam in 1804. See Morais, *Jews of Philadelphia*, p. 53; W. & W., p. 457, n. 78, and *passim*.

55. On Zalegman Phillips, an important figure in the Philadelphia congregation, see W. & W., *passim*.

56. Abraham E. Israel to Zalegman Phillips, Philadelphia, April 11, 1825; MS., Mikveh Israel records, Box 883.

57. The daughters of Joseph H. Andrews (1753–1824) and his wife Sally, daughter of Haym Salomon, were Eve (1798–1884) and Deborah (born 1800), who were already married at the time of this incident, Esther (1807–94), Miriam (1809–80), and Rachel (born 1814). Esther and Miriam, aged 18 and 16 respectively, would seem the most probable sources of the disturbance. See W. & W., pp. 456–57, and Stern, p. 10.

58. Joseph J. Andrews (1801–75), son of Joseph and Sally (Salomon) Andrews, married in 1849, Miriam Nones. The *Philadelphia Directory for 1825* lists the firm of Joseph Andrews & Sons at 259 North 2d Street, S.E. corner of Callowhill. See Morais, *Jews of Philadelphia*, p. 445; W. & W., pp. 456–57, and Stern, p. 10.

59. Aaron Levy (1771–1852), merchant, auctioneer and art dealer, was active in the affairs of Congregation Shearith Israel. See Schappes, pp. 624-25, note 9 to Document 88; Pool, *Old Faith, passim;* and *PAJHS*, XXVII (1920), *passim*. At the time of this letter, Levy was parnass of Shearith Israel.

60. Simon Gratz (1773–1839), see Part Three, and W. & W., *passim*.

61. Aaron Levy to Simon Gratz, New York, Jan. 14, 1805; MS., Records of Congregation Mikveh Israel, Box 882.

62. Isaac Lazarus, see Stern, pp. 107, 129; W. & W., pp. 247, 346. Lazarus was hired as Shohet by Congregation Mikveh Israel, but resigned in a salary dispute the same year (1805). In 1807, he was rehired; he also ran a business for the provision of kosher meat for the export trade. Later, he removed to Mobile, Alabama.

63. Jacob Abrahams (1784–1866) was Shohet of Congregation Shearith Israel from the end of 1803 to 1813. Thereafter he set himself

up in business as a ritual slaughterer independent of synagogue ties; this resulted "in the complete breakdown of the congregation's monopolistic control of the supply of kosher meat for the city." Pool, *Old Faith*, pp. 241–46 for the story and some documents.

64. Jacob Hart (1746–1822), a merchant born in Germany, was active in the patriot cause during the Revolution and was thanked by Congress, May 24, 1781, for his provision of money to feed and clothe the troops of Lafayette. See Pool, *Portraits*, pp. 411–13; Pool, *Old Faith, passim;* and, for his Philadelphia years, W. & W., *passim.* Hart was listed in *Census*, 1790, New York, p. 121 as head of a household consisting of "Free white males 16 and upward . . . 1; free white males under 16 . . . 3; free white females . . . 5."

65. Israel Baer Kursheedt, see Part One, note 151.

66. Probably Isaac Moses (1742–1818), one of the most prosperous members of the Shearith Israel group, who had been active in Philadelphia during the Revolutionary years. See Pool, *Portraits*, pp. 384–92; Pool, *Old Faith, passim;* and W. & W., *passim.*

67. MS., Minutes of Congregation Shearith Israel, IV, pp. 168–70; Committee Report, dated Aug. 16, 1825, incorporated in Minutes of Trustees' Meeting, Aug. 17, 1825.

68. Mark Solomon[s] (1763–1830) was shohet of Congregation Shearith Israel from 1796 to 1803, after which he went to Charleston; in 1814, he was recalled to New York and again served as shohet until 1828. See Pool, *Portraits*, pp. 343–44; and Pool, *Old Faith*, pp. 240, 242, 246, 247.

69. Abraham H. Cohen, son of the Reverend Jacob Raphael Cohen of Congregation Mikveh Israel, assisted his father both as hazzan and as teacher in Philadelphia. In 1806, he married Jane Pickens, causing a minor scandal; this died down when Mrs. Cohen was converted to Judaism. For further detail see above Part Five, note 155. He left Philadelphia to become a functionary of Congregation Shearith Israel, as teacher in the Polonies Talmud Torah; this position he held, 1823–28. Then he left to become hazzan and shohet of congregation Beth Shalome, Richmond. See Pool, *Old Faith*, pp. 221, 432.

70. Marcus van Gelderen (1798–1871) after 1838 became shohet for Congregation Shearith Israel, according to Pool, *Old Faith*, p. 435. However, on p. 247, Pool wrote that "members of the new congregation B'nai Jeshurun preferred dealing [1828–32] with Marcus Van Gelderen, whom they knew from his former service in Congregation Shearith Israel." I. Goldstein, *A Century of Judaism in New York* (New York, 1930), p. 84, writes "Beginning with 1830 . . . a special Shochet fund was raised by private subscription among the [B'nai Jeshurun] Congregants, so that he received a small salary directly from the Congregation. The first Shochet of the Congregation was A. Van Gelder, who had received his certification from the Hakam in Amsterdam." Can these two

similarly named men be the same? Later in the 1830s, Van Gelderen was active as a trustee and as president of Congregation Anshe Chesed, New York. See Grinstein, *passim.*

71. Naphtali Phillips (1773–1870) had served as parnass of Congregation Shearith Israel briefly in 1804 and again from 1815 to 1824. See Part Four, note 34.

72. Moses L. Moses (1773–1843), a produce broker, was elected parnass of Shearith Israel, 1827–29 and 1834–41. He was one of the most active members of the congregation for many years. See Pool, *Old Faith, passim;* Pool, *Portraits, passim;* and Schappes, pp. 596, 616. See also, *New York Business Directory*, 1841, p. 99.

73. Daniel Solis became shohet of Congregation Mikveh Israel in 1830. See W. & W., pp. 252–53; 455–56.

74. Zalegman Phillips (1799–1839). He was parnass of Congregation Mikveh Israel in Philadelphia, paralleling the congregational services of his brother Naphtali to Shearith Israel in New York. See W. & W., *passim.*

75. Daniel Solis to Zalegman Phillips, Philadelphia, July 19, 1832; MS., Records of Congregation Mikveh Israel, Box 884.

76. That is, *terefah* (more popularly, *trefe* or *treife*), not meeting ritual requirements; the antonym of *Kosher.*

77. Naphtali Phillips, see this Part, note 71.

78. Lewis Allen (1793–1841), see this Part, note 172.

79. Naphtali Phillips to Lewis Allen, New York, May 10, 1836; MS., Records of Congregation Mikveh Israel, Box 884.

80. Before Daniel Solis was accepted by the authorities of Congregation Mikveh Israel in 1830, he was examined by a committee in New York, consisting of Isaac B. Seixas, Joseph Samuel, and Naphtali Phillips. The license they issued to Solis, on Dec. 14, 1830, is preserved in the records of Congregation Mikveh Israel. See W. & W., pp. 252–53, 456.

81. Solis's mission was probably that of helping to find a successor for himself as shohet in Philadelphia, since the *Philadelphia Directory for 1835–36*, p. 169, lists him as "quill manuf Coates a. 6 Lawrence," an indication that he had left the profession of shohet.

82. Netlad and Hyatt to the President and managers of the Congregation [Mikveh Israel], Philadelphia, March 22, 1834; MS., Records of Congregation Mikveh Israel, Box 884.

83. MS., Minutes of Trustees of Shearith Israel, March 1, 1825; March 27, 1825.

84. "The preparation of matzoth was an annually recurrent congregational obligation which had to be scrupulously organized. The congregational administration would make an estimate of the total amount of matzoth required in that year for sale to individual families and for free distribution to synagogue officials and the poor." Pool, *Old Faith*, p. 238.

85. Robert Speir and Son are listed as bakers, 96 Pine Street, in the *New York Business Directory for 1841*, p. 122.

86. "In 1825, the matzoth were baked in a patented new type of oven which eliminated the use of the shingle boards that had at times raised a question as to whether or not the matzoth baked in the old ovens were completely free from leaven." Pool, *Old Faith*, p. 238.

87. Moses L. M. Peixotto, see Part Six, note 69.

88. Prayer shawl worn by all adult males.

89. Joseph L. Joseph (1797–1858) was married to Frances Levy (1806–56), a daughter of Jacob Levy, Jr. He was one of the very few men who were permitted to give instruction in the classes of the "Association for the Moral and Religious Instruction of Children of the Jewish Faith," an organization founded by some of the women of Congregation Shearith Israel on the model of Rebecca Gratz's Hebrew Sunday School Society in Philadelphia (see Part Five, note 99).

90. MS., Minutes of Trustees of Shearith Israel, October 26, 1825.

91. David Hart (1785–1854) was for many years a Trustee of Shearith Israel and its Treasurer, 1835–45. A partial record of his congregational services may be found in Pool, *Portraits, passim*.

92. Moses L. Moses, see this Part, note 31.

93. Barrow Cohen (sometimes with A. or E. or I. as a middle initial) was an English-born New York Jew who appears in *Rode's New York City Directory for 1850–51*, p. 103, as a pawnbroker, at 269 Spring St.

94. The 1805 Constitution of Shearith Israel (this Part, Document 196), Article VII, sec. 2, gave to the Board of Trustees "the power to regulate all offerings to be made in Synagogue" not otherwise specifically provided for in the constitution or bye-laws.

95. This Part, Documents 197, 203.

96. This interpretation follows from Pool's brief discussion of the Barrow Cohen affair, *Old Faith*, p. 438. Goldstein, *A Century of Judaism in New York*, nowhere suggests any such interpretation, though the name of Barrow Cohen appears in Goldstein, p. 382, as one of the founders of Congregation B'nai Jeshurun, and p. 384, as treasurer, 1835–36.

97. MS., Minutes of the Trustees of Shearith Israel, IV, pp. 149–55, abridged.

98. Moses L. Moses.

99. Naphtali Phillips.

100. Haym M. Salomon (1785–1858) was a son of the Revolutionary patriot Haym Salomon and had himself served as a captain during the War of 1812. For his active relationship with Congregation B'nai Jeshurun, see this Part, Document 220.

101. This exchange seems conclusively to show that Cohen's defiance was deliberate. The face-saving decision of the Trustees (below) should not be taken as literally as Pool, *Old Faith*, p. 438, does, when he asserts

that Cohen, "ignorant of this requirement, failed to make the required offering."

102. Joseph Samuel became shohet of Congregation Shearith Israel in 1828 and held the post until 1832.

103. John I. Hart was the leader of the group within Congregation Shearith Israel who seceded to form Congregation B'nai Jeshurun. He was an Englishman by birth, the son of the Reverend Judah Hart of Portsmouth, England. He was elected president of B'nai Jeshurun and served in that office, 1825–29 and 1833–34. In 1845, he was one of the leaders in the establishment of Congregation Shaaray Tefilah, a secession from B'nai Jeshurun. See Goldstein, *A Century of Judaism in New York, passim.*

104. *The Constitution and Bye Laws of the [Chevra Chinuch Nearim] instituted June 5585 [1825]* (New York, 1825). This excerpt from the Minutes of the Trustees of Congregation Shearith Israel is printed in an appendix to the Constitution, pp. 14–15.

105. See *Constitution* . . . , Article 5.

106. See *Constitution* . . . , Article 3.

107. See, too, *Constitution* . . . , Article 11, allowing members the right to attend meetings of the officers of the society.

108. *Constitution* . . . , Appendix, pp. 13–14.

109. Sephardic, as is clear from *Constitution* . . . , Article 5.

110. Presumably, the custom of holding separate services at an hour different from that of the body of the Congregation.

111. *Constitution* . . . , pp. 1–12, abridged.

112. "The synagogue building."

113. "The Sephardic manner."

114. "The Tallith, or prayer shawl"; see this Part, Document 203.

115. *Constitution* . . . , Appendix, pp. 16–18.

116. "Scrolls [of the Law]."

117. "Reading desk."

118. "Ark of the Covenant"; literally, "sanctuary."

119. "May he rest in peace!"

120. Defective; unfit for religious use.

121. Joseph J. Andrews (1801–75), was the son of Joseph H. Andrews (1753–1824), on whom see this Part, note 57, and his wife Sarah or Sallie, daughter of Haym Salomon.

122. Haym M. Salomon to the President and Trustees of Congregation Mikveh Israel, New York, June 23, 1825; MS., Records of Congregation Mikveh Israel, Box 883. W. & W., pp. 256–57, discuss the question raised in this letter.

123. The MS. of Salomon's letter of June 23, 1825, bears the following endorsements: "Rec'd 25th June 1825" in one hand; in a different hand, "Sep. 11/25 laid before the Congn. & by them referred to the Board. Oct. 2/25 laid before the Board & they directed the Parnass to

write to Mr. S. & inform him that the Sophor was always considered the Congns. property & needs no restoration."

124. See this Part, Document 206.

125. Indeed, Haym M. Salomon did present a Hebrew Bible—apparently not a scroll but a printed text—to Congregation B'nai Jeshurun in its earliest days. See Goldstein, *A Century of Judaism in New York*, p. 61.

126. Haym M. Salomon to Zalegman Phillips, New York, Nov. 30, 1825; MS., Records of Congregation Mikveh Israel, Box 883.

127. "Hashcabah," i.e., memorial prayer for the dead.

128. Blessing.

129. The Day of Atonement.

130. It was needed, presumably, because of the refusal of the Trustees of Congregation Shearith Israel to grant the use of a scroll to the petitioner-members of Chevra Chinuch Nearim. See this Part, Document 206.

131. This was not the first time that there had been difficulties at Mikveh Israel with regard to religious objects. On September 1, 1793, Benjamin Nones as Parnass of the Philadelphia congregation had written to Manuel Josephson: "You will much oblige the Congregon. of this City, if you will send by the Beare the Sophar [sc., Shofar]. Left in your Care. to be used on such Occassions as our approaching Hollidays, the Congregation is fully Persuaded Mr. Josephson will not be against sending the Same; for after the Hollidays it shall be sent back. . . ." (Benjamin Nones to Manuel Josephson, Philadelphia, Sept. 1, 1793; MS., certified copy of original letter, Records of Congregation Mikveh Israel, Box 896). This MS. bears the following notation, signed by Nones: "The answer of Manl. Josephson 'that the Parnass the Juntas and the whole Congregation might be Damd. & that he would not send the Sophar.['] "

132. Mordecai M. Noah was at this time editor of the *National Advocate* and was also one of the malcontents in Congregation Shearith Israel.

133. Extracts from the Constitution of Congregation Beth Elohim of Charleston, 1820, as printed in Elzas, *JSC*, pp. 151–53.

134. "Cemetery"; literally, "house of life."

135. Voting members of the Congregation.

136. There is an analysis of this Constitution, in terms of the structure of the Congregation, in Reznikoff, pp. 116–19.

137. The list of signatories is not extant. There is a list of 44 names signed to the Constitution of the Reformed Society of Israelites which is probably very similar; see, for this list, L. C. Moise, *A Biography of Isaac Harby with an Account of the Reform Society of Israelites of Charleston, S.C., 1824–33* (Columbia, S.C., 1931), pp. 71–72. Officers of the Reformed Society, as reported in Elzas, *JSC*, p. 163, include such

names as Aaron Phillips (1780–1834), whose name appears first in
Beth Elohim's records in 1809, Isaac Harby (1806), Abraham Moise
(1799–1869) (1823), Michael Lazarus (1786–1862) (1811), Isaac
N. Cardozo (1792–1855) (1818), Morris Goldsmith (1810), Henry
M. Hyams (1806–1875) (1814), Philip Phillips (1807–84) (1818),
Thomas W. Mordecai, D. N. Carvalho (1784–1860) (1811), E. P.
Cohen (died 1856?) (1825), Philip Benjamin (1823), Myer Jacobs
(1791–1861) (1811), David C. Levy (1805–77), and Isaac C. Moses
(1781–1835) (1802).

138. Schappes, p. 171, places more emphasis on the socio-economic
than on the religious factor. "This impulse [to reform] came from the
needs of the rising Jewish middle class. These well-to-do business men
attempted to adapt themselves as far as possible to the forms of life
of the non-Jewish upper class with which they had or sought ever
closer relations." But, as our documents in Part Two show, the American
Jews had been a "rising middle-class" group long before this and in
other cities as well as Charleston, and many were as "well-to-do" as the
Charleston reformers. And, as Reznikoff points out (p. 132), not all the
leaders of the Reformed Society were "well-to-do": "Some of these had
means, but some had only influence."

139. There has been some disagreement in the literature as to the
degree to which the Charleston Reformed Society was influenced by
the German reform movement; there can be no question that they knew
that this movement was in process.

140. As printed in L. C. Moise, *Biography of Isaac Harby*, pp. 52–59.

141. The section of the Pentateuch designated for reading in the
synagogue on any particular Sabbath.

142. The comment of Professor Jacob R. Marcus, reported in Reznikoff, pp. 128 and 292 (n. 157) is worth noting here; this phrase echoes
the Deism of the Enlightenment of the eighteenth century.

143. The text of this petition was drafted by Abraham Moise. See
Schappes, p. 607, n. 2.

144. Isaac Harby, see Part One, note 168.

145. See Part Five, Document 154.

146. The theme of enlightenment expressed by Harby was developed
further by Abraham Moise in the Second Anniversary Address: "We
claim, then, to be the advocates of a system of rational religion; of
substance, not form. For this we hold ourselves responsible to God and
Our Consciences. We look not to the antiquity of rites and ceremonies
as a just criterion for their observance by us, but to their propriety,
their general utility, their peculiar applicability to the age and country
in which we live, to the feelings, sentiments and opinions of Americans.
We regard the free toleration of religion in this country as a bond of
union between Jew and Non Jew. . . ." Abraham Moise, "An Address
delivered before the Reformed Society of Israelites on its Second An-

niversary Nov. 1826," in L. C. Moise, *Biography of Isaac Harby*, pp. 122–27; the extract quoted from p. 126. It is worth while to compare these sentiments with those presented by Isaac N. Cardozo in the Third Anniversary Discourse (Moise, *Biography of Isaac Harby*, pp. 128–40).

147. Notice of dissolution as printed in L. C. Moise, *Biography of Isaac Harby*, p. 75.

148. Abraham Moise (1799–1869) was prominent as a lawyer and politician in Charleston from about 1824 to 1860. He was intimately connected with the Reformed Society from its inception (see this Part, note 209). In 1827, he was its vice president; from 1828 to 1833, its president. In 1827, he married Caroline Moses (1808–80), daughter of Isaac Moses, and had three children: Charles H. Moise (1830–96), Edwin Warren Moise (1832–1902), not to be confused with his second cousin of the same name (see Part One, note 117), and Caroline Agnes (1828–99), who married Harmon H. DeLeon in 1851.

149. J. N. Cardozo, see Part Five, note 1.

150. Isaac Mordecai (1805–64). See B. A. Elzas, *The Old Jewish Cemeteries at Charleston* (Charleston, 1903), p. 39.

151. Michael Lazarus (died 1862) was a wealthy entrepreneur, who "brought steam navigation to the Savannah River." Reznikoff, p. 91 and *passim*. He was active in the literary and social life of Charleston as well as in synagogal affairs. See Elzas, *JSC*, *passim*.

152. Thomas W. Mordecai (died 1861) participated in both the Seminole War in Florida and the Civil War.

153. Gustave Poznanski (1804–79), was elected to the pulpit of Congregation Beth Elohim on Oct. 9, 1836; born in Poland, he had been educated in Hamburg and was profoundly in sympathy with the reform spirit that was expounded in the Hamburg Temple. Despite much controversy (even including aspersions on the legitimacy of his birth) Poznanski remained as spiritual leader of Beth Elohim until 1860. Details may be found in Elzas, *JSC*, *passim*, and Reznikoff, *passim*. See also *The Occident*, I, 12 (March, 1844), p. 603, for a letter of enthusiastic praise for Poznanski, attributed by the editor (Isaac Leeser) to Dr. Jacob de la Motta.

154. Isaac Harby, *Discourse Before the Reformed Society of Israelites for Promoting True Principles of Judaism according to its Purity and Spirit*. Delivered by Appointment, in Charleston, S.C. on the twenty-first day of November, 1825, as reprinted in H. L. Pinckney and A. Moise, *A Selection from the Miscellaneous Writings of the Late Isaac Harby, Esq.* (Charleston, 1829), pp. 57–87. The excerpt used is from pp. 57–61.

155. The Constitution of the Reformed Society of Israelites is reprinted in full in L. C. Moise, *A Biography of Isaac Harby*, pp. 60–72, from a copy preserved in the Moise family. Its general terms, of course, support Harby's contention that the reformers did not contemplate "the

abolition of the ancient language and form of Jewish worship." It does call, however, "for such alterations and improvements in the present mode of Worship as would tend to perpetuate pure Judaism." (Preamble, p. 61), refers in Article II to "blind observance of the ceremonial law" (p. 61), talks in Article IV of "revising and altering such parts of our prevailing system of Worship, as are inconsistent with the present enlightened state of society" (p. 62), all of which might well be regarded as falling only slightly short of advocacy of "abolition."

156. See Part Five, Document 173.

157. For a vivid account of the impact of a yellow fever epidemic on an American community a decade earlier, before the beginning of the nineteenth century, see J. H. Powell, *Bring Out Your Dead* (Philadelphia, 1949). See also above, Part Five, Documents 177, 178.

158. Seixas's sermon, 1803, MS., A.J.H.S.

159. Abraham Mears Isaacs (1765–1814) of New York, brother-in-law of Sampson Simson, was the author of a special prayer recited on the Day of Atonement during the yellow fever epidemic of 1803. See, for the text of this prayer, "A Prayer Composed for the Day of Atonement during the Prevalence of the Yellow Fever in New York in 1803," *PAJHS*, XX (1911), 158.

160. Jacob de la Motta (1789–1845), see Part One, note 32.

161. See Part Seven, Document 233.

162. See this Part, Document 211.

163. See this Part, Document 212.

164. See this Part, Document 214.

165. Compare his comments with those of Seixas and Noah, above, Part One, Documents 55, 56.

166. Jacob de la Motta, *Discourse Delivered at the Consecration of the Synagogue, of the Hebrew Congregation, Mikva Israel, in the City of Savannah, Georgia, on Friday, the 10 of Ab, 5580; Corresponding with the 21st of July, 1820* (Savannah, 1820); excerpts here as they appear in Schappes, pp. 151–55, from De la Motta's *Discourse*, pp. 6–9, 16–17.

167. Another account of "Jews in Savannah" appeared in *The Occident*, I, 5 (Aug., 1843), pp. 247–50, in the form of a letter to Isaac Leeser from one who signed himself "A Southern Jew." The letter concludes: "Such, sir, is . . . an imperfect sketch of the history of the Jews in this city, and I may add with pride and thankfulness to God, that they have always been a respected and useful body of citizens. They defended their country and its liberties in the war of the Revolution, and their names may be seen among the founders of every charitable and literary society in this city, and in return they have received the most marked and undeviating kindness and liberality from their fellow-citizens. At this very time the City Judge and Sheriff are Jews, the Collector of the Port is a Jew, and a Jew occupies a seat in the

Legislature of the State from this city, and is a member of the Board of Aldermen, besides other offices of minor importance, which are filled by Jews" (p. 250). See also Mordecai Sheftall's communication to *The Occident*, I, 8 (Nov., 1843), pp. 380–84, and I, 10 (Jan., 1844), pp. 486–89, incorporating the content of manuscript records kept by Benjamin Sheftall, one of the original settlers, and his son, Levi Sheftall. The Sheftall statement is, according to Leeser's editorial comments, unfair to Dr. Jacob de la Motta; see *The Occident*, I, 8 (Nov., 1843), pp. 379–80, and I, 10 (Jan., 1844), pp. 489–91.

168. See Part One, Documents 10, 11, for acknowledgements of Jefferson and Madison for copies of De la Motta's *Discourse*.

169. Although, as we have seen (this Part, Documents 206, 210), there was an unfulfilled intention of establishing regular preaching in New York's Chevra Chinuch Nearim and in Charleston's Reformed Society of Israelites.

170. Jacques Judah Lyons (1813–77), son of Judah Eleazar and Mary Asser Levy Lyons, who were both born in Philadelphia, was born in Surinam. At the age of 20, he became hazzan of Neve Shalome congregation in his native land, serving for four years, 1833–37. When he returned to the city of his parents' birth, he was called to serve Congregation Beth Shalome in Richmond where he remained until 1839. In that year, he became hazzan of Congregation Shearith Israel, a post he held until his death. See the detailed account in Pool, *Old Faith*, pp. 178–82.

171. The Jewish community of Surinam (Dutch Guiana) is the oldest permanent settlement of Jews in the Western Hemisphere, dating from 1639. By 1643, the little group was already so well established as to need the services of a rabbi. Surinam's Jews survived conquest by England and reconquest by Holland, though, when the Dutch took over, some of its Jews preferred to follow the British to Jamaica. There is an excellent brief account in the *Universal Jewish Encyclopedia*, X, 106–8, with a comprehensive bibliography.

172. Lewis Allen (1793–1841) was born in London, England, and brought by his family to Philadelphia in 1805. His father, who died in 1815, was in the dry goods business; Lewis Allen took over the family business, on Market Street, between 5th and 6th Sts. In 1823 he married Anna Marks (1800–88) daughter of Michael and Johaveth Marks. From 1834 to his death, he was Parnass of Congregation Mikveh Israel. See Morais, *Jews of Philadelphia*, p. 243.

173. Isaac Leeser to Lewis Allen, Philadelphia, Aug. 23, 1837; MS., Mikveh Israel records, Box 884.

174. Isaac Leeser to the Parnass and members of the Congregation Mikveh Israel, Philadelphia, May 15, 1840; MS., Mikveh Israel records, Box 884.

175. "The years of American Jewish history from 1830 until the close

of the Civil War are, in fact, the 'Age of Leeser.' " W. & W., pp. 372–73.

176. Isaac Leeser, *Discourses, Argumentative and Devotional, on the Subject of the Jewish Religion. Delivered at the Synagogue Mikveh Israel, in Philadelphia.* . . . (2 vols., Philadelphia, 5597 [1837]).

177. This impression is reinforced by the comments of Rebecca Gratz, in various letters. See Part Five, note 63, for a typical remark.

178. Leeser, *Discourses*, I, 1–2; 3–4.

179. "Contributions were undoubtedly solicited, according to the general custom, from other congregations. The Hebrew congregation on the island of Barbados in the West Indies, for example, gave twenty-five pounds." Reznikoff, p. 273, n. 109.

180. See this Part, Document 192.

181. W. & W., in their fine account of the construction and dedication of "The Second Synagogue of Mikveh Israel," pp. 360–71, and notes thereto, pp. 495–99, do not record the invitation to Congregation Beth Shalome, although other congregations are listed, p. 366.

182. W. & W., pp. 250–51, report on a long period during which Mikveh Israel, without the services of a permanent hazzan, sent out circular letters. On p. 455, n. 57, these authors give the date of Mordecai's letter as June 15, 1824.

183. See this Part, note 174.

184. See this Part, Documents 193, 194.

185. Benjamin Nones and others to Congregation Beth Elohim (Charleston), Philadelphia, Sept. 9, 1792; MS., Records of Congregation Mikveh Israel, Box 882. Rough copy of letter sent.

186. Benjamin Nones, see Part Four, note 82.

187. Manuel Josephson, see this Part, note 33.

188. Barnard Gratz, see Part Three, note 15.

189. Solomon Lyons, see Part Two, note 7.

190. A further indication of the nature of these synagogal requests for help may be found in the appeal of the Reformed Society of Israelites of Charleston for aid in building a new house of worship. See L. C. Moise, *Biography of Isaac Harby,* pp. 72 ff. In Savannah, too, when the synagogue burned down in Dec., 1829, the Jewish community energetically raised funds for its rebuilding. See Mordecai Sheftall, "The Jews in Savannah," *The Occident,* I, 10 (Jan., 1844), p. 488.

191. Jacob Mordecai (1762–1838), see Ezekiel and Lichtenstein, pp. 23–25.

192. Jacob Mordecai to B. Phillips, Simon Gratz and Isaac Hays, Richmond, June 15, 1824; MS., Records of Congregation Mikveh Israel, Box 882.

193. Presumably Benjamin I. Phillips, although W. & W., pp. 455–56, read the initial as "Z." and refer to Zalegman Phillips, who was an officer of the congregation.

194. Simon Gratz, see Part Three, note 22.

195. Dr. Isaac Hays (1796–1879), was a distinguished ophthalmologist and medical editor. He was the son of Samuel and Richea (Gratz) Hays. There is a brief biographical notice in Morais, *The Jews of Philadelphia,* pp. 424–25. See also W. & W., *passim.*

196. Isaac B. Seixas (1782–1839), son of Benjamin and Zipporah (Levy) Seixas. He had long served as hazzan and teacher in the Richmond congregation. In 1817, after serving Congregation Mikveh Israel for the High Holy Days, Seixas was offered a permanent position there, which he declined. See Ezekiel and Lichtenstein, *passim;* and W. & W., *passim.*

197. Jacob Mordecai to Zalegman Phillips, Richmond, Jan. 11, 1825; MS., Records of Congregation Mikveh Israel, Box 883.

198. Circular, New York, Jan. 7, 1839; printed letter with MS. insertion, Records of Congregation Mikveh Israel, Box 884.

199. The words "Congn. Mickve Israel Philada" are a handwritten insertion in this otherwise printed circular.

200. Samuel N. Judah (1803–49), a broker, with offices in the Tontine Buildings, was a trustee of Shearith Israel in 1834 and 1835. He was especially interested in promoting the education of poor children, and was active in the Society for the Education of Poor Children and the Relief of Indigent Persons of the Jewish Persuasion (1827). He was elected an honorary member of the Association for the Moral and Religious Instruction of Children in the Jewish Faith. See Grinstein, p. 552; Pool, *Old Faith,* p. 364; Schappes, p. 616; and *New York Business Directory for 1841,* p. 81.

201. Tobias I. Tobias (1785/86–1861), a liquor merchant, located at 20 Broad Street, was active in Congregation Shearith Israel, Hebra Hased Vaamet, and various educational societies. See Grinstein, pp. 547, 552, 566; Pool, *Old Faith,* p. 355; Schappes, p. 616; and *New York Business Directory for 1841,* p. 129.

202. Aaron Lopez Gomez (died 1860) was descended from the Gomez and Lopez families of Newport and was related by marriage to the prominent Hendricks family of New York. Very little is known of his activities. See Pool, *Portraits,* pp. 328, 425, 435, and Pool, *Old Faith,* p. 143.

203. Giving rise to a vast and intricate literature of *responsa.* For the American scene both before and after (but not during) the period 1790–1840, see J. D. Eisenstein, "The Development of Jewish Casuistic Literature in America," *PAJHS,* XII (1904), 139–47.

204. See the discussion of this in Grinstein, pp. 81–84.

205. "In the early 1840's, the first ministers with rabbinical ordination, all German rabbis, began to arrive." Grinstein, p. 89. "The very first rabbi to settle in the United States was Rabbi Abraham Rice of Baltimore. He arrived in New York in 1840 and tarried here for a while to address the Anshe Chesed Congregation. But soon he left for Balti-

more where he assumed a rabbinical position." *Ibid.*, p. 543, n. 14. "Pique, teacher at Shearith Israel in the 1820s, may have had rabbinical ordination but . . . he was . . . elected . . . only as teacher." *Ibid.*, p. 542, n. 4. Pool, *Old Faith*, pp. 129, 187, 219, refers to Dob Pique with the title "Rabbi," and describes him as "learned but in other ways an unfit teacher." No mention of ordination is made by Pool. Pique served Congregation Shearith Israel from 1818 to 1821 as teacher in the reopened Polonies Talmud Torah, but was discharged in the latter year. Pool, *Old Faith*, pp. 219–20.

206. Literally, "wise man," the title given to the Rabbi of a Sephardic community.

207. Rabbinical court.

208. Israel Baer Kursheedt, see Part One, note 145.

209. Solomon Hirschell, or Herschell (1762–1842), English-born but educated in Germany and Poland, became chief rabbi of the Great Synagogue in London in 1802. Gradually, his jurisdiction was extended over the rest of the Ashkenazic Congregations in England, a change that was the manifestation of a growing unity of English Jewry. *JE*, VI, 363.

210. Benjamin Nones was Parnass of Congregation Mikveh Israel 1791–99, and again for a few months in 1820, and finally in 1821–22. He had at least one other term of office in the years 1799 to 1810, but records for this period are inadequate. See Morais, *The Jews of Philadelphia*, p. 45 and n. 61.

211. The letter was addressed to the Sephardic *Beth Din*.

212. Benjamin Nones to the London *Beth Din*, Philadelphia, Aug. 7, 1793; MS., Records of Mikveh Israel. Reproduced here from a typescript copy in the American Jewish Archives, marked No. 51.

213. An attempt at a phonetic spelling of the Sephardic pronunciation of the name of the London Sephardic synagogue, Sha'arey Shamayim (Gates of Heaven).

214. The "yehid," or member, was Moses Nathans (Notation on back of letter in the Mikveh Israel records), on whom see Part Three, note 131.

215. Non-Jewish.

216. Circumcised.

217. Convert.

218. Literally, "canopy and marriage rites."

219. From its foundation, B'nai Jeshurun, as an Ashkenazic congregation, presented its ritual and legal questions to the Chief Rabbi of the Ashkenazic community in England. A selection of questions and answers (unfortunately with names deleted) is presented in Goldstein, *A Century of Judaism in New York*, Appendix A, pp. 323–30.

220. Solomon Hirschell to Congregation B'nai Jeshurun, London, May 12, 1839; as printed in Goldstein, *A Century of Judaism in New York*, pp. 327–28.

221. Technically illegitimate according to Jewish law.

The Strains of Religious Adjustment

665

222. "According to the law of Moses and Israel."

223. Because a "mamzer" could not properly be married in the Jewish fold.

224. When the city of Charleston projected a plan for the establishment of an orphan asylum in 1791, the Jewish Congregation held a meeting to advance the project. A letter and resolution of thanks on behalf of the commissioners of the Orphan Society was sent to the Congregation by A. Vanderhost. For the text of the letter, see *The Occident*, I, 8 (Nov., 1843), pp. 385–86.

225. In a dramatic instance, Congregation Anshe Chesed of New York exerted strong efforts on behalf of a widow and her children to prevent their being defrauded by an impostor. The following account is transcribed from the MS. minutes of the congregation, Oct. 25, 1836:
"Mr Friend Reported that he waited upon the Russian Consul in Company with Mr Samelson at the request of the Committee of Enquiry Apointed [sic] to Examine into the Papers of Abraham Belcaskis

"Reported the above person call'd himself at the Russia [sic] Consul Jacob Eleazar and on other of his papers Abraham Marcus thro' which Impostor he Procured the Opinion of the Consul that he was entitled to the Money left by David Berush he also got Two Men to Swear to the Translation and to the Truth before the Consul of a Paper which was proved before your Committee to be a Forgery.

"Mr Friend further Reported to your Committee that the Consul would have given the said Abraham Belacaskis Alias Jacob Eleazer Alias Abraham Marcus such Documents on that day as would have entitled the above Impostor to Receive the above money where by the Widow and Orphans of the Deceased David Berush would have been cheated out of the Money or the Consul have to pay it out of his own Pocket.

"Mr Friend further Reported that the Consul was thankfull for attention in protecting the Property of the Widow and Orphans and Keeping himself from Claim and offer'd to take the Necessary steps so that the Widow and Orphans should get their Rights "Resolved. that such Letters be wrote to Europe and sent thro' the Consul to obtain the above object."

226. MS., Minutes of the Trustees of Congregation Shearith Israel, March 9, 1800.

227. Isaac Abrahams, a trustee of the congregation and its parnass, 1801–2, may, according to Pool, *Portraits*, pp. 288–89, 335–36, 485, be one of two—possibly three—of that name who were active in congregational affairs.

228. Naphtali Judah, see Part Two, note 97.

229. Michael S. Hays, who acted as sexton of Congregation Shearith Israel during the British occupation of New York in the Revolution (Pool, *Old Faith*, p. 287) is reported as a householder in *Census*, 1790, New York, p. 118, New York City, East Ward. The household consisted of Hays and three females.

230. Literally, "righteousness" used with the meaning of "charitable assistance."

231. Bernard Hart (1764–1855) was long active in the service of Congregation Shearith Israel in various official capacities, including that of Parnass, 1806–9. From 1831 to 1853, he was secretary of the New York Stock Exchange. See Schappes, p. 596, n. 6; Pool, *Portraits Etched in Stone, passim;* and Pool, *Old Faith, passim.*

232. Benjamin M. Seixas (1747–1817), younger brother of Gershom M. Seixas, was one of the most active members of Congregation Shearith Israel from its post-Revolutionary reorganization in 1784 until his last years. He was one of the organizers of the New York Stock Exchange. See Pool, *Portraits,* pp. 378–82, and Pool, *Old Faith, passim.*

233. Pool, *Old Faith,* p. 471, refers to Rachel Hays as a mantilla maker. She should not be identified as the Rachel Hays mentioned in Pool, *Portraits Etched in Stone,* p. 474, who was virtually disinherited by her father, Judah Hays (1703–64). In Pool, *Portraits,* p. 405, Rachel Hays is noted as boarding and caring for invalids "around the end of the eighteenth century," and *ibid.,* p. 388, as boarding old Isaac Moses for the community. If this is the lady referred to, she was born Rachel da Costa and married Baruch S. Hays in 1783 (*ibid.,* p. 308). Longworth's *American Almanack, New York Register and City Directory* (New York, 1797), p. 199, reports "Hays, Rachel, Mantuamaker, 1 Dutch-street."

234. It is impossible to tell which "Mr. Solomons" is referred to here. Conceivably, it is Mark Solomons (1763–1830), who was shohet for the New York Jewish community, 1796–1803. See this Part, note 68.

235. Aaron Levy, Jr. (1774–1852), called "Junior" to distinguish him from his uncle Aaron Levy, the founder of Aaronsburg, was one of the founders of Congregation Rodeph Shalom of Philadelphia, but soon left it and returned to membership in Congregation Mikveh Israel. He was active in philanthropy. See W. & W., *passim.*

236. Benjamin I. Phillips, Parnass of Congregation Mikveh Israel, 1811–15. See W. & W., *passim.*

237. Aaron Levy Jr., to Benjamin Phillips, Philadelphia, March 30, 1814; MS., Records of Congregation Mikveh Israel, Box 883.

238. See W. & W., p. 274.

239. "The basis of the religious structure which our ancestors had established, was charity; that godlike virtue, which blesses the bestower as well as the recipient; and the sums yearly expended for charitable purposes in relieving the sick and indigent, frequently exceeded £400. To extend the sphere of their charity and usefulness, the members of the congregation formed the [Hevra Gemiluth Hasadim] (which still exists), a society for relieving the sick and destitute strangers who might visit our shores. The members of this excellent institution visited and nursed the sick, clothed the naked, and buried the dead. . . ." "The Jewish

Congregation of Charleston," *The Occident,* I, 7 (Oct., 1843), p. 338. See also Grinstein, pp. 103–6, for mutual aid societies in New York Jewish life before 1840.

240. Mrs. Rebecca J. Phillips, First Directress; Mrs. Bell Cohen, Second Directress; Mrs. S. Bravo, Treasurer; Miss Rebecca Gratz, Secretary; Mrs. Rebecca J. Phillips, Mrs. Bell Cohen, Mrs. S. Bravo, Mrs. Richea Hays, Mrs. Phila Pesoa, Mrs. Miriam Nones, Mrs. Esther Hart, Mrs. Fanny Levy, Mrs. Arabella Phillips, Mrs. Rebecca Moss, Miss Sarah M. Cohen, Miss Hannah Levy, Miss Rebecca Gratz, Managers.

241. Preamble to the Constitution of the Hebrew Orphan Society of Charleston, 1801; as printed in Elzas, *JSC,* p. 285.

242. An act of incorporation for the "Abi Yetomim Ubne Ebyonim, or Society for the Relief of Orphans and Children of Indigent Parents" was passed by the General Assembly of the State of South Carolina in 1802. Elzas, *JSC,* pp. 285–87, gives a brief sketch of the history of this, the second oldest Jewish philanthropic society in Charleston.

243. *The Constitution of the Female Benevolent Society of Philadelphia* (Philadelphia, 1825), excerpts. A copy of this rare print is in the library of the Dropsie College for Hebrew and Cognate Learning in Philadelphia.

244. Membership requirements in this Society were quite light, requiring only an annual contribution of $2. (Article II). In some other aid societies, there were far more rigid requirements. The Philadelphia Hebrew Society for the Visitation of the Sick and Mutual Assistance, for example, excluded those who married outside the faith or neglected to circumcise their children. See *Constitution and By Laws of the Hebrew Society for the Visitation of the Sick and Mutual Assistance* (Philadelphia, 1835), Article 2, secs. 2 and 3; see also *Constitution and By-Laws of the "United Hebrew Beneficent Society of Philadelphia"* (Philadelphia, 1837), Article 8, sec. 2, "no person who shall be married otherwise than according to the Jewish rites, can apply for, or be admitted to membership in this Society."

245. Some societies required those seeking their aid to bind their children as apprentices, the Society acting as supervisor to make sure that the children so apprenticed would be able to observe Jewish law. "In every instance where a child of a poor person may be bound an apprentice by this Society, it shall be the duty of the Board to see that he is bound out in such a manner as to keep his Sabbaths and Holy-days, and in all other respects to adhere as nearly as possible to his religion, agreeably to the Jewish laws. . . . And no person shall have any claim to the charity of this Society, unless when applied to by the Board, he will agree to their binding his child or children apprentices to learn mechanical trades, unless he shall give a satisfactory reason why he will not comply with their wishes." *Constitution and By-Laws of the "United Hebrew Beneficent Society of Philadelphia,"* pp. 9–10.

246. In some of the constitutions of benevolent societies, a wise provision absolved members from the obligation of making personal visits to those with contagious diseases: "If a physician shall declare the disease with which a patient may be afflicted, malignant or contagious, no member shall be compelled to attend him; but the board shall supply a nurse or nurses at the expense of the [Hebra]." *Constitution and By-Laws of the Hebrew Society for the Visitation of the Sick and Mutual Assistance* (Philadelphia, 1824), p. 6.

247. Manuel Phillips, a son of Jonas Phillips, after attending the Medical School of the University of Pennsylvania (but apparently not graduating) served as an Assistant Surgeon in the U.S. Navy, and later practiced in Philadelphia—in 1820, at 41 north Fourth Street, according to the *Philadelphia Directory* for that year; see W. & W., *passim*.

248. Isaac Hays, see this Part, note 195.

249. Daniel L. M. Peixotto, see Part Five, note 69.

250. Founded in 1827; see Grinstein, pp. 148–49.

251. He was one of the organizers of a meeting in honor of the French July Revolution of 1830. Schappes, p. 182.

252. See Joseph L. Blau, *Social Theories of Jacksonian Democracy* (New York, 1947), for further definition of these demands.

253. Daniel L. M. Peixotto, *Anniversary Discourse Pronounced before the Society for the Education of Orphan Children and the Relief of Indigent Persons of the Jewish Persuasion* (New York, 1830), pp. 10–17.